MATT PRESTON'S

WORLD OF FLAVOUR

MATT PRESTON'S

WORLD OF FLAVOUR

The recipes, myths and surprising stories behind the world's best-loved food

Photography by William Meppem

PENGUIN
LANTERN

CONTENTS

INTRODUCTION

The world is a wonderland of flavour, and I for one downright love it! For flavour, to me, is pleasure: mouth-watering, tap-the-table pleasure.

It is also the visceral experience of a place; the smoke-trails of a thousand different stories, the whispered memories of moments snatched and the joy of those pleasures shared.

The pursuit of flavour has drawn me across seas and up mountains, to quaint medieval villages and down dark, dodgy alleys past bottle-filled dumpsters, to find *that dish*. The endless search for flavour can lead to the most unlikely places. The quest also comes with a need to broaden my understanding. I always want to know more – not just the *hows* but the *whys* and the *whens* of every great dish I've ever tasted.

The cookbook in your hands is simply a way of putting all of that down on paper – the pleasure, the stories and the fervent hope that you'll discover dishes here that you'll come to love as much as I do. If this book brings pleasure to you, and to the people for whom you cook, then I am happy.

And while I think that's a noble quest in itself, that's not all! This book isn't just about bringing you the tastiest recipes for more than one hundred of our favourite dishes from across Australia and around the world. It also aims to be a snapshot of the truth.

Whoa, slow down there, tiger! you might be thinking, but I'm wild eyed, fired up and on a bit of a mission here. There are wrongs to be righted.

With misinformation everywhere on the internet, I've set out to bust the most prominent food myths and, in the process, give credit where credit's due, by celebrating these beloved dishes and their evolution throughout history.

You'll see that each recipe starts with a myth about the dish, which I'll try to dispel and replace with something closer to the truth. In taking this approach, the hard part for me has been the realisation that, over the years, I've been guilty of perpetuating some of these myths myself. So, please see this book partly as my redemption story.

Picking the dishes to feature was also a thorny challenge, but we ended up with a selection that I hope you'll want to cook as well as eat. You'll find Australia's most searched-for dishes prioritised here, because it is often more interesting to learn new facts about something you already care about.

We've favoured dishes with resonance for the modern Australian kitchen, because I want as many of these recipes as possible to become beloved regulars on your table and, more importantly, for you to subsequently identify them as 'your' recipes. That's the holy grail for any recipe writer: to pass on the amazing flavours we've tasted and loved ourselves.

In choosing the recipes to feature, I've also leant towards dishes with big myths to rip into, despite the ire I'm sure this will arouse. We live in a time in which hard evidence is too easily dismissed if it challenges someone's deeply held point of view. That challenge is just too uncomfortable for many. It might be foolish on my part, but I think sometimes cages have to be rattled in spite of the consequences. We need to remain open to updating our beliefs and changing our minds when presented with shiny new information.

Like unpeeling an onion, once you start digging into the history of a dish, there is always another layer underneath, and then another. The more layers you uncover, the more you can strip away the lies and the closer you get to that elusive truth – even if sometimes those returns eventually diminish.

The process of writing this book was like following threads back through time, whether in the yellowing pages of old newspapers or by delving into my collection of antiquarian cookbooks; through unravelling digitised ancient texts written in forgotten dialects, or luxuriating in the research of other, highly qualified, food historians, be they enthusiastic amateurs or measured academics.

It helped that I have a rather nerdy, almost photographic memory for food, as often the dead end for one dish became a valuable new avenue of enquiry for another. And, while the newspaper food columns of yesteryear are rich hunting grounds for myth-busting facts, it was just as often a throwaway line in the news pages that shed new light on age-old but previously unanswered questions, such as whether shepherd's pie was a dish created in the north of England or Scotland (see p. 240). For example, unpicking the lie-laced story of lemon meringue pie started with nineteenth-century news reports on the infamous New York City lemon meringue pie poisonings of 1878!

All this meant I happily lost days – even weeks – down culinary rabbit holes. Eventually, I would emerge like a happy terrier, with my tail furiously wagging and with what I felt was some nugget of truth tightly clamped between my teeth.

It was discovering gems such as the extremely controversial provenance of the pavlova (p. 299), or the amazing truth that the first recipe for spaghetti bolognese wasn't published in Italy or the United Kingdom, but in Adelaide, years before it appeared anywhere else (see p. 195), that made this book so much fun to write.

It also left me with the very clear understanding that history, rather than being fixed, is a fluid, ever-changing thing. The truth about a dish is written not on tablets of stone but on shifting sands, and I am sure that, years from now, new evidence will come to light that will further evolve or even pivot away from some of the stories I've told here. I relish and encourage that prospect, as it will move us all closer to the truth. (The recipes themselves, however, I'm sure will stand the test of time.)

It is worth saying that any work that looks at a global phenomenon such as food must acknowledge that where you are writing or reading from – both geographically and intellectually – will give you a specific perspective on any story. So, where possible, I've tried to look at many sides of the story – for example, by consulting primary and secondary Spanish and Portuguese sources to see what insights they could offer about the English and Italian history of the sponge cake or the trifle.

At times these sources could be tricky to work with, since much medieval writing on food comes in the form of household accounts or shopping lists, and ancient recipes frequently take a certain amount of knowledge about cooking times and quantities as understood. Food was often seen as a prosaic, functional thing, in contrast to the evocative food writing we are used to today, so it required some imagination, a little linguistic detective work and much cross-referencing to hydrate some of this drier prose. Further frustrating my efforts was the fact that names and spellings vary and change, and a recipe that's in a second edition of an old book may not have been there in the first edition published ten years earlier.

Now, it's time for one further admission. I have tried to be as dispassionate as possible about the data, but there were times when the research didn't point to one definitive answer. In those cases, I've felt compelled to tell you what my gut is feeling – and occasionally my gut might be a wee bit biased towards an Australian interpretation of the facts. I can't help but barrack for my home side!

If you are reading this outside of Australia and you feel that your country's contribution to a dish has been under-represented by my lionising Australian developments, or if you have access to evidence that I did not uncover, please blog or post your findings. I'd love to see them, and for you to join me in my mission to get the truth trending.

As this is a book written by a home cook for home cooks, you might find that some legendary dishes are missing because they require specialist equipment or are too tricky or too time-consuming to prepare at home – and, between you and me, we're better off getting them from a good takeaway joint. That's why there's no pad thai here. However, I've broken my own rule, because while I think it is nigh on impossible to make perfect pizza in a conventional home oven, I couldn't imagine a book called *Matt Preston's World of Flavour* that didn't feature my favourite ever dish. It would be like Delta Goodrem without her piano, or Ash Barty without her Head racquet.

Besides focusing on simple techniques and everyday kitchen equipment – I promise I won't force you to buy a $180 poppy-seed grinder or cavatelli press, although I might nag you about investing in a $20 rice cooker – the usual rules of my recipes apply. Supermarket-available ingredients dominate, unless there's a good reason to send you on an adventure to seek out something unique from a specialty grocer or online (such as the *kasuri methi* that has been controversially included in more recent versions of butter chicken, or the yellow soybean paste for the Singaporean chilli crab).

Here, the point is simple: easy, achievable recipes that never, ever, compromise on flavour or miss an opportunity to boost it to the next level. Flavour, after all, is all.

Seafood

Slow-cooked kingfish 'salad'

SERVES 4 **PREP** 30 minutes **COOK** 20 minutes

Myth

This dish has no history.

My Truth

It is true that this dish did not exist nine months ago. It wasn't based on anything other than a bit of noodling after I bought a side of kingfish that I couldn't be bothered slicing up for sashimi. While this is thus a totally new dish, it's pretty clear to me from whence the inspiration came. There is no doubt that the flavour profile of Thai green curry was in my mind when I came up with the idea, but it would be understandable if that was unrecognisable to Thai cooks in this form.

Green curry is the youngest of Thailand's traffic light of curries. It dates back to the reign of King Rama VI, or perhaps even Rama VII, early in the twentieth century. Unlike the older red curry, the recipe does not appear in any of the seminal Thai cookbooks of the eighteenth and nineteenth centuries.

The earliest evolutionary stage of Thai braises and curries was sauces made with water, garlic, shallots and fermented shrimp or fish paste, with the heat coming from pepper, *grachai* and galangal or ginger – not chilli, as this was yet to leave the Americas.

According to the reputable Thaifoodmaster website, the first published recipes for Thai green curry both feature fried duck. These were in Lor. Phaehtraarat's cookbooks *Khuu meuu maae kruaa* ('Cook's Guide', 1926) and *Dtam raa khaan waan* ('Sweet and Savory Cookbook', 1934).

As the name suggests, and just like this recipe, a green curry is flavoured only by green veg, green herbs and green chillies. While the dish we present here is in no way Thai, other than in its core flavour inspiration, Thai food expert David Thompson explains in his comprehensive bible *Thai Food* that green curry is a hot, salty and never artificially sweet gravy from the central plains of Thailand that is most often eaten with grilled, salted or deep-fried proteins. It should be garnished with threads of lime leaf, green chilli and fresh Thai basil.

Like Prince Harry, there's no denying the parentage of this dish. While the flavours are originally Thai, they have travelled a long way. Fish sauce has replaced the more traditional addition of *kapi* (shrimp paste), and I've added a little palm sugar because I think you may find that more comfortable given the sweetness of green curries usually served in Oz. The ingredients are proudly local and this is, above all, a dish of the best Australian seafood, solidly but sensitively cooked with flavours that, through migration, travel and other forms of culinary cross-pollination, have also become an important part of Australia's culinary landscape.

Slow-cooked kingfish 'salad' *(CONTINUED)*

1 side kingfish

1 bunch coriander, leaves and stems separated, stems finely chopped

2 cm piece galangal (or ginger), peeled and roughly chopped

3 long green chillies, deseeded, 2 roughly chopped, 1 thinly sliced

1 lemongrass stalk, tender white centre only

1 tablespoon coarsely grated palm sugar

2 × 15 g packets (or 1 bunch) Thai basil, leaves picked

4 limes; 2 juiced and 2 cut into quarters

2 tablespoons fish sauce

270 ml can coconut cream

½ iceberg lettuce, shredded

1 continental (telegraph) cucumber, cut into thin slices (see Tips)

1 bunch spring onions, trimmed and sliced

steamed white rice, to serve

Dressing

1 tablespoon fish sauce

1 heaped tablespoon grated palm sugar

1 tablespoon lime juice

2 long green chillies, deseeded and finely chopped

Preheat the oven to 120°C (100°C fan-forced) and line a baking tray with baking paper.

Trim the kingfish fillet, removing the thin belly flap so you are left with a neat rectangle of fish. Cut the bony centre strip out of the centre of the kingfish. If you're getting your fish from a fishmonger, you could ask them to do this for you. Keep the flap and bony strip to barbecue later (see Tips).

Cut the rest of the kingfish lengthways into long rectangular batons of equal girth – these will be about 4 cm thick.

Blitz the coriander stems, galangal, chopped green chillies, lemongrass, palm sugar, half the Thai basil leaves, the lime juice and 1 tablespoon of fish sauce in a small food processor until a paste forms. Taste and add more fish sauce if necessary – it needs to be there but not dominant. (If it's a good fish sauce I reckon you'll need at least another tablespoon.) Add half the coconut cream and pulse until smooth and a pretty pale green. Strain through a fine sieve. Reserve the liquid for the dressing, and use the coarse paste for the fish.

Place the batons of kingfish onto the prepared tray and top with the paste. Mound it on, and don't worry if liquid drips off. Bake for 18–20 minutes, until the fish is just cooked through.

To make the dressing, start with the reserved drained liquid, then mix in the fish sauce and palm sugar. Add the lime juice, taste and add more if you need to get a nicely balanced flavour. When you are happy with it, stir in the chilli. Set aside.

Line a serving platter with the lettuce. Nestle the cooked batons of fish in the lettuce. Throw the cucumber, coriander leaves, spring onion, sliced green chilli and remaining Thai basil leaves around it. Dot the top of the fish with tiny dollops of the remaining coconut cream, or drizzle it on, for contrast.

Serve with steamed white rice, and the dressing on the side.

TIPS

I like to peel half the cucumber, 'cos I like the texture and bitterness of the skin. You can peel it on one side only, or peel it so it looks like a green-striped football jumper. Let your artistic temperament decide. If you want to peel it all, that's fine too. No one will judge you.

Tomorrow night, barbecue the bony middle section of the kingfish on a hot grill plate for 10 minutes with the fatty belly flap. Shred the cooked flesh and pick out the bones. Stir the flesh through steamed brown rice with crumbled toasted nori and salmon roe, gently warmed in soy sauce. Sprinkle *furikake* seasoning over the top. Serve with a salad of diced, deseeded cucumber tossed with Japanese mayo and a few drops of Maggi seasoning liquid, if you have it; soy sauce if not.

Easy paella

SERVES 6 **PREP** 30 minutes **COOK** 45 minutes

Myth
The original paellas were made with seafood.

My Truth
Like Italian osso buco, or chowder, the first paellas were peasant dishes born out of poverty and necessity, made using whatever was available. The dish is named after the shallow frying pan in which it is cooked, and first arose in the rice fields of Spain.

After the capture of Valencia around 714 AD by invading Moors (Arabs and Amazigh people from Morocco), the land around the Albufera lake south of the city was irrigated and turned into rice paddies – rice being one of the bounties, along with oranges, almonds and sugar, that the Arab conquerors introduced or popularised on the Iberian Peninsula.

It was in these paddies that the first paellas originated, as the workers' lunch. The work was wet, but this was undeniably a dish of the land. It was cooked over flaring orange prunings, and the rice was loaded with proteins easily found around the lake: ducks, rabbits, snails (sometimes disgorged by feeding on rosemary) and even local water voles.

While both dried beans and green beans would be added to paella when in season, or artichokes when beans were not, seafood was never a traditional inclusion. The closest thing might be the addition of local eel that thrived in the paddies.

It isn't until the eighteenth century that we find the first recipe for *Arroz à la Valenciana*, published in Josep Orri's *Avisos y instruccions per lo principiant cuyner* ('Notices and Instructions for the Beginner Cook'), and it is another one hundred years until a Valencian newspaper refers to this dish as paella, in 1840.

The version of paella we have given here takes a few shortcuts, like adding chorizo to boost the flavour, and the heretical omission of making the *sofrito* to start the dish, which saves time. My favourite Spanish food expert, Emma 'Guapa' Warren, author of *The Catalan Kitchen* and *Islas: Food of the Spanish Islands*, who is a valued long-term collaborator, was scandalised by this when we were cooking the dish to take the photo in this book. She implores you to start this dish by making a proper *sofrito* (see Tips), because this, she says, is the foundation of a great true paella.

Easy paella *(CONTINUED)*

4 cups (1 litre) chicken or fish stock
½ teaspoon saffron threads
2 tablespoons (40 ml) olive oil
1 chorizo sausage, thinly sliced
1 red capsicum (pepper), deseeded and
    coarsely chopped (see Tips)
1 brown onion, finely chopped
2 garlic cloves, crushed
2 cups (400 g) short- to medium-grain rice
    (see Tips)
2 teaspoons smoked paprika
2 large tomatoes, quartered, coarsely
    chopped
2 rosemary sprigs
400 g can cannellini beans or butter beans,
    rinsed and drained
12 large uncooked prawns, peeled (centre
    only, leaving heads and tails intact),
    deveined
12 small black mussels, scrubbed,
    debearded and with shells all intact
1 squid tube, thinly sliced crossways
chopped flat-leaf parsley, to serve
lemon wedges, to serve

Combine the stock and saffron in a saucepan. Cover and bring almost to the boil over high heat. Remove from the heat and set aside to infuse while you start the paella.

Heat 1 tablespoon of oil in a 38 cm (top measurement) paella pan over medium–high heat. Add the chorizo and cook, stirring, for 2–3 minutes or until golden. Transfer to a bowl, leaving any oil behind.

Reduce the heat to medium and add the remaining 1 tablespoon of oil to the pan. Add the capsicum, onion and garlic and cook, stirring, for 5 minutes or until soft and lightly caramelised. Add the rice and paprika and cook, stirring, for 2 minutes to lightly toast.

Add the tomato and saffron-infused stock, reserving ¼ cup (60 ml) for later. Place the rosemary on top. From this point on, do not stir the paella during cooking. Bring to the boil. Reduce the heat to very low and simmer, uncovered, for 20 minutes.

Scatter the beans and chorizo over the top of the rice. Top with the prawns, mussels and squid. Ladle the reserved stock over the top of the rice. You will be tempted, but still *do not stir*.

Cover and cook for a further 8–10 minutes or until the seafood is just cooked. If your pan doesn't have a lid, you can cover with foil. You'll know when your paella is done and when the rice has had time to form that essential crust, as the rice will start to sing. Listen closely and you will hear it.

Remove the pan from the heat and cover with a clean tea towel. Set aside for 5 minutes. Discard any unopened mussels. Sprinkle with the parsley and top with the lemon wedges to serve.

TIPS

Choose a good-sized capsicum (pepper). If it is too small it will get lost, and we want it to add a slippery burst of sweetness against the salty seafood.

For the rice, look for Valencian *senia*, Murcian *calasparra* or any Spanish *bomba* rice, or arborio rice – in that order!

Pay no heed to the paella purists – feel free to make this dish your own. You could tweak this recipe by adding chicken thighs fried with the chorizo to the top of the rice, or chunks of fish, or slabs of lobster, or rabbit, or green beans . . . or even water rat, snails or Valencian *garrofo* butter beans, if you can find them. We should acknowledge that some Spanish commentators decry the use of chorizo. Not sure where they stand on water vole or calamari.

To make a proper *sofrito*, you'll need the following: olive oil, 1 diced onion, 3 cloves of garlic, 1 finely diced green capsicum, 2 tsp of sweet *pimentón* (aka Spanish paprika), ½ cup of red wine and a can of tomatoes. You'll also need about another hour of cooking time! First, slowly fry the onion in lots of olive oil over low heat for 10 minutes, until soft and translucent. Now, add the garlic and capsicum and cook slowly until soft – about 5 minutes. Stir in the paprika and cook for 2 minutes. Deglaze with a good glug of cheap red wine and reduce. Add the tomatoes and a good pinch of salt, then cook for 45 minutes. Keep the heat low and stir regularly as the *sofrito* thickens and darkens. Add the thick, paste-like *sofrito* to your pan after you've toasted the rice.

Crispy fried mussel salad with toum

SERVES 4 **PREP** 30 minutes (plus 15 minutes pickling) **COOK** 15 minutes

Twist

Myth

The Spanish have their *tigres*, the Belgians their *moules frites* and the French their *moules marinière*, but no mussel dish is as ancient as Istanbul's sticks of crispy fried mussels called *midye tava*.

My Truth

I love the Eurocentricity of this myth, even if those mussel-sellers of Beyoğlu and Galata are only a short ferry ride across the Bosporus from the Asian side of the city. The oldest mussel dish in the world for which there is proof, however, is the ember-cooked mussels enjoyed by Australian First Nations people for many thousands of years prior to colonisation.

We know this from the scorched mussel shells found in coastal middens (see p. 30), and from the reports of early European settlers who wrote of seeing Aboriginal people foraging for and eating mussels along the coast and in the waterways where wild mussels grew plentifully. It was possible for one person to gather two hundred mussels in an hour, making them an excellent food source, although the uniformity in the size of mussel shells found in middens indicates that only mature mussels were selected.

While we cannot know for how long these *dalgal*, as the Dharawal people around Sydney call them, were traditionally cooked, I would wager that eating them as soon as the shell opened while the mussel was at its most tender must have been the way to go.

You can try using this approach to cooking mussels on your barbecue, but take care to avoid singed fingers from the hot shell and bubbling juices. In fact, you could dispense with the whole salad pretence of this recipe and just serve mussels with slabs of white bread slathered with the toum instead. I do, however, think that the mussels get a little something extra from being floured and fried.

This is, needless to say, a new dish that combines influences from many mussel dishes I've eaten around the world, but it was initially inspired by a conversation about the joys of 'mussel nuggets' when buying mussels from my local fishing boat! A garlicky white cloud of Lebanese-inspired toum is the perfect creamy foil for their chewy meatiness.

Crispy fried mussel salad *(CONTINUED)*

1 red onion, thinly sliced into rings
1 teaspoon sea salt
1 teaspoon caster sugar
¼ cup (60 ml) lemon juice
½ iceberg lettuce, finely shredded
¼ cup coarsely chopped coriander
¼ cup coarsely chopped mint
¼ cup coarsely chopped dill
2 kg mussels, scrubbed and debearded
½ cup (100 g) rice flour
¼ cup (35 g) plain flour
½ teaspoon smoked paprika
½ teaspoon baking powder
½ teaspoon sea salt
⅔ cup (160 ml) iced water
1 continental (telegraph) cucumber, halved
lengthways, deseeded and cut into thick
matchsticks
2 tablespoons olive oil
sumac, for sprinkling

Toum
1 head of garlic
1 teaspoon sea salt
¼ cup (60 ml) lemon juice
200 ml vegetable oil
1 tablespoon iced water
1 egg white (optional)

TIPS

In the Netherlands, they would serve their fried mussels, or *gebakken mosselen*, with fresh toast or potato salad. Why not serve these with steamed chat potatoes dressed in the toum, like a potato salad gone all Lebanese?

My excitement about fried mussels comes from spending long summers next to the mussel beds of Portarlington on Victoria's Bellarine Peninsula, and thanks to the owner of the local fishboat in Queenscliff's tiny harbour nearby, who told me that floured, fried mussels reminded him of little chicken nuggets. We added rice flour for a crispier finish, but feel free and go all the way and tempura them if you want! They are a revelation.

To make the toum, bring a small saucepan of water to the boil over high heat. Place the garlic upside down on a chopping board, put the palm of your hand on top and press down firmly to separate out the cloves. Add the garlic to the boiling water and cook for 2 minutes to blanch. Drain, and once cool enough to handle, peel.

Place the garlic cloves, salt and lemon juice in the canister of a stick blender. Blitz, scraping down the side occasionally, with the stick blender until smooth. Very gradually add the oil a little at a time, while you blend, bouncing the stick blender up and down to slowly emulsify. It should start looking like a mayonnaise – a little yellow from the oil. This is a very particular art, so don't get stressed if it doesn't work for you first time.

Now here comes the alchemy. Add the iced water while the blender is turning, and if you have the finely honed skills of a Lebanese *teta*, or grandmother, the mixture will magically turn white and fluffy, like a heavily garlic-scented cloud. (If not, add the egg white and blend to bring the mixture together, which will achieve the desired result, but through artifice rather than skill.) Cover with plastic wrap and place in the fridge until serving.

Place the onion in a glass or ceramic bowl. Sprinkle with the salt and sugar. Drizzle with the lemon juice and set aside for 15 minutes to pickle.

Combine the lettuce, coriander, mint and dill in a large bowl. Cover and place in the fridge.

Place the mussels in a steamer over a saucepan of simmering water. Cover and steam for 3–5 minutes or until the mussels open. Discard any unopened mussels and carefully reserve 1 tablespoon of the hot cooking liquid from the mussel shells.

Once cool enough to handle, open the mussels, remove the meat and place on a tray lined with paper towel. Discard the shells.

Combine the rice flour, plain flour, smoked paprika, baking powder and salt in a large bowl. Make a well in the centre. Add the iced water and use a balloon whisk or fork to whisk until well combined.

Spread a ring of toum around a large serving platter. Fill the centre of the toum ring with the lettuce mixture and cucumber. Drain the onion and reserve the liquid. Place the onion on top of the salad. Add the oil and 1 tablespoon of the cooled mussel liquid to the reserved pickling mixture and use a fork to whisk until well combined.

Add enough oil to a saucepan to come halfway up the side. Heat over medium–high heat until the oil reaches 200°C on a cook's thermometer (or, when a cube of bread turns golden in 5 seconds after being added to the oil).

Working in small batches, dip the mussels into the flour mixture and then deep-fry (be careful – the oil can spit) for 30 seconds or until they are golden brown. Lift out with a slotted spoon and transfer to a tray lined with paper towel to drain.

Drizzle the dressing over the salad. Top with the fried mussels and sprinkle with the sumac to serve.

TIP

In Japan, larger *temakizushi* like this are one of the few occasions sushi is made at home. Get some extra rolling mats, put out all the makings on the table and encourage your family or guests to roll their own. Double or triple the ingredients listed here so you have enough to serve a crowd.

California rolls

Twist

Myth
The California roll was invented in Canada.

My Truth
Vancouver chef Hidekazu Tojo tells a compelling story of how he invented an inside-out roll in 1974 at a restaurant called Jinja. Three years earlier, when he had arrived in Canada after training under a sushi master in Osaka, he struggled in his first job to persuade customers who weren't Japanese to eat raw fish. A visit to a fancy French restaurant inspired him to put popular cooked crab into a *maki* (sushi roll) at the next place he worked, and to hide the seaweed by rolling the *maki* 'inside out' – that is, with the rice on the outside. He called this a Tojo roll, which also has spinach and egg omelette in it.

Tojo is undoubtedly a passionate and creative cook – he's also responsible for the BC roll, rainbow roll, golden roll and spider roll – but his explanations of how the Tojo roll came to be known as a California roll are sketchy at best. It seems more likely that Tojo came up with the same idea that chefs in Los Angeles' Little Tokyo did when faced with the challenge of encouraging non-Japanese customers to eat seaweed and raw fish.

Even in California they jostle for bragging rights to creating the first California roll. In a 1979 newspaper article, the manager of Kin Jo in Los Angeles claimed the invention was by their venerable chef Ken Seusa. Others point to a small sushi restaurant called Kawafuku, opened by Noritoshi Kanai in Little Tokyo in 1965. Kanai worked for the importers of the first frozen edamame beans to the US, and he says the California roll was invented at his place.

Ichiro Mashita was the chef at Kawafuku before moving to Tokyo Kaikan, another Little Tokyo restaurant opened by local Japanese food wholesalers. It is here he claims to have invented the *uramaki*, or inside-out roll, after watching customers peel off the nori sheet from around his rolls, thinking it was inedible. His solution was to put the seaweed sheet inside the rice so they knew it was part of the dish. Mashita had also struggled to get consistently good-quality fatty raw tuna for his *maki*, so he decided to use cooked crab instead, for its flavour and ease of supply, and added creamy avocado to replicate the mouthfeel of the fatty *toro*.

As the popularity of the roll grew outside of Little Tokyo, this unique combination of crab and avocado in a roll with the rice on the outside became known for its point of origin, California. And, now nori was accepted, the seaweed could return to the outside of the roll for convenience.

While there is no doubt that the same problem often prompts the same solution independently from more than one person, as seems to be the case here, if I had to bet on the inventor of the first true California roll, my money would be on Mashita – not least because of the clue found in the name.

1½ cups (300 g) sushi rice, rinsed well
2 tablespoons sushi seasoning
4 nori sheets
120 g sashimi-grade salmon, cut into 5 mm batons
1 small Lebanese cucumber, cut into matchsticks
½ firm ripe avocado, cut into 5 mm thick batons
20 g perilla leaves
2 tablespoons Kewpie mayonnaise, plus extra to serve
pickled ginger, to serve
wasabi, to serve

Orange ponzu dipping sauce
½ cup (125 ml) light soy sauce
¼ cup (60 ml) mirin
¼ cup (60 ml) orange juice
1 tablespoon lime juice

Place the rice and 2 cups (500 ml) water in a saucepan over medium–high heat. Bring to the boil, then reduce the heat to low, cover and simmer for 10 minutes or until the liquid is absorbed. Remove from the heat. Set aside for 10 minutes. Use a fork to stir the sushi seasoning into the warm rice, fluffing the rice as you go. Set aside to cool.

To make the ponzu dipping sauce, combine all the ingredients in a bowl.

Wrap a sushi mat in plastic wrap. Place in front of you with the slats running horizontally. Place a nori sheet, shiny-side down, on the mat. Use wet hands to spread one-quarter of the rice over the nori sheet, leaving a 3 cm wide border along the edge furthest away from you.

Place a quarter of the salmon, cucumber, avocado and perilla along the centre of the rice. Use the fine nozzle on the Kewpie bottle to pipe a small amount of mayo beside the filling. Hold the filling in place while rolling the mat over to enclose the rice and filling. Repeat with the remaining nori, rice, salmon, cucumber, avocado and perilla.

Use a sharp knife to slice the sushi into thick slices. Place on serving dishes with the ponzu dipping sauce, pickled ginger, wasabi and extra Kewpie.

Poke buffet

(THAT'S 'POKAY BUFFAY', NOT 'POKE BUFF-IT')

SERVES 6 **PREP** 40 minutes **COOK** 25 minutes

Myth

The poke bowl is Hawaiian.

My Truth

So much of Hawaii's notable street food is a triumph of culinary fusion, whether it's *musubi*, the spam-topped nigiri sushi, or *loco moco*, which is a burger served on rice with nori and brown gravy. There's nothing wrong with that, but it's also easy to sympathise with Hawaiians who feel perturbed that their poke has been turned into a worldwide cafe standard that bears little resemblance to the original.

Traditional poke is a proud dish, one of a suite of cured Polynesian and Melanesian acid-cooked fish dishes that we'll learn more about later in this chapter (see p. 52). After filleting their catch of reef fish, Hawaiian fisherman would cure the trimmings with seaweed and salt.

It's likely that poke predates the similar dish of *lomi-lomi*, which enamoured nineteenth-century European whalers who visited Hawaii. Here, lightly salt-cured salmon chunks were rinsed and massaged with diced tomatoes, onions, chilli flakes and cucumber. Again, fusion is at play: onion seeds were a gift to Hawaii from Captain James Cook in 1778, and salted salmon was introduced to the islands by traders, who swapped barrels of the fish for local salt.

Fusion is also responsible for the evolution of poke to be served on a bowl of rice, and the presence of soy sauce and sesame oil in the fish's dressing. Migrants from Japan moved to the Kingdom of Hawaii in large numbers from 1885 onwards, to work on the island's pineapple and sugarcane plantations, and became a major influence on what Hawaii eats. The Japanese-influenced version of the 'poke bowl' started to pop up in Hawaii in the 1960s and 1970s, using soy-sauce-dressed *ahi* (tuna) rather than traditional reef fish. It is clearly influenced by *chirashizushi*, where sushi fish is scattered over a bowl of rice.

As the concept of poke spread like wildfire across the globe in the 2010s (20teens?), more and more options for toppings were added, further morphing away from the traditional dish and taking on characteristics from the cuisines of the places it spread.

This poke buffet is my way of letting each diner decide exactly what they want in their bowl. The heavily titivated seasoned rice could be a meal by itself. Use this recipe as your staring point and feel free to adapt and substitute.

Poke buffet *(CONTINUED)*

2 cups (400 g) sushi rice

1 side ocean trout or salmon (around 1.2 kg), pin-boned

sesame oil, for rubbing

1 tablespoon sesame seeds, toasted

2 avocados, finely chopped

1 lime, juiced

1 bunch spring onions, whites sliced into coins, greens finely sliced

400 g packet frozen podded edamame, blanched

1 continental (telegraph) cucumber, peeled, halved, deseeded and cut into crescents

2 carrots, peeled and cut into batons, crisped in iced water

1 fennel bulb, trimmed and thinly shaved

200 g jar pickled ginger, drained

3 sheets nori, toasted and torn (see Tips)

50 g salmon pearl roe

¼ cup (60 ml) soy sauce, plus extra to drizzle

2 tablespoons sushi seasoning (see Tips)

½ cup (100 g) golden flying fish roe (see Tips)

1 bunch dill, sprigs picked

25 g *furikake* (see Tips)

Kewpie mayonnaise, to serve

sriracha, to serve

Preheat the oven to 100°C (80°C fan-forced). Put the rice on to cook following packet instructions (preferably in your rice cooker).

Meanwhile, cut the flatter, fattier sides off the fish, leaving you with two unequal flaps and a plump central barrel of flesh. Remove the skin from the plump central part of the fish, using a sharp knife and the technique of pulling the skin rather than pushing the knife away from you. Reserve the skin and flaps.

Line a baking tray with baking paper. Place the skinned fish on the tray and bake for 25 minutes. You don't want to completely cook it through, just enough to lightly set the fish so it flakes into moist petals.

While the fish is in the oven, heat a barbecue grill on high. Oil the flaps and skin with sesame oil and place, skin-side down, on the hot grill. Cook for 5 minutes or until the skin is crispy and the edges of the fish are a little burnt and gnarly. Splash over a little soy sauce and sprinkle lightly with some of the sesame seeds. That's plate #1.

Gently toss the avocado in the lime juice and place in a bowl. Place the spring onion coins, edamame, cucumber, iced carrot batons, shaved fennel, pickled ginger and nori rectangles in separate bowls. That's plates #2 to #8.

Place the salmon pearl roe in the soy sauce and leave to stand.

Place the cooked sushi rice on a large serving plate. Sprinkle over the sushi seasoning and turn the rice to incorporate. Top with the flying fish roe, spring onion greens, drained salmon pearl roe, sprigs of dill and a good sprinkling of *furikake*. Crosshatch with fine lines of Japanese mayo. That's plate #9.

Put all the plates on the table and let people make up their own combo bowls, with the rest of the toasted sesame seeds and *furikake*, Kewpie mayo and sriracha on the side.

TIPS

If you like, just serve the rice on its own with prawns tossed in Kewpie mayo and chopped dill, and forget the fillet of orange fish altogether. Add or subtract other garnishes as you like.

Instead of toasting and cutting nori sheets I sometimes use a packet of Korean crispy snack nori, broken up.

You can use 1 tablespoon each of mirin and rice wine vinegar instead of sushi seasoning if you like.

Flying fish roe is also known as *tobiko*. I like the golden one, but it comes in other colours. You could also use the black seaweed pearls from IKEA.

Furikake is a Japanese seasoning that can be sprinkled on rice, vegetables, fish, soups or even popcorn. You can find it in Asian supermarkets.

THE TOP TEN RULES OF MODERN POKE-ING AT HOME

1. **Only the freshest fish will do –** but poke isn't just about seafood these days. Take your lead from other cultures and play with everything from tofu or just about any veg to grilled chicken or seared beef.

2. **Warm rice and cold fish;** the temperature contrast can be much of the joy of a great poke bowl. Or, try room temperature rice, cold adornments and hot fillets of teriyaki-marinated and pan-fried salmon or ocean trout.

3. **Life is far easier if you make the rice in your rice cooker.** They are cheap (like $20), hassle-free and give you perfect rice every time. Overly wet or starchy rice has ruined many a good poke bowl. I will never get tired of saying it – buy a rice cooker!

4. **Never put dressed sushi rice in the fridge; it goes ooky.**

5. **Don't 'overcook' things,** whether with heat or contact with acid.

6. **Don't forget the crunch –** traditionally crushed candlenuts were used in Hawaiian poke, but feel free to use other nuts like crushed macadamias (which they love and grow in Hawaii) or cashews, or seeds such as sesame, or even wasabi peas.

7. **Don't forget the dressing –** so much of the flavour comes from what you drizzle or squirt over the top of your poke bowl, whether it's soy, citrus or mayonnaise based.

8. **A great poke bowl is about contrasting textures,** and balancing contrasting flavours – a little sweet, a little sour, a little fresh, a little salty, a little creamy, a little crunchy.

9. **When plating, either distribute the ingredients evenly,** for maximum flavour in each bite, or arrange them by colour in wedges around the bowl so it looks like a colourful pie-chart from above, for eye-catching appeal.

10. **Modern poke doesn't need to be served on sushi rice –** consider using brown rice, jasmine rice, quinoa, farro, large-grain couscous or pulses instead. Or you could even serve your poke in lettuce cups or taco shells, or atop seaweed crisps or good old puffed prawn crackers.

AND, FINALLY, REMEMBER IT IS PO-KE AS IN OKAY RATHER THAN POKE AS IN OAK!

Tomato tonnato with bacon pangrattato

SERVES 4 **PREP** 10 minutes **COOK** 15 minutes

Myth
I didn't steal this idea.

My Truth
I can never understand why cooks and chefs don't give credit when they steal a recipe. Even if you don't have a detailed and nearly photographic memory for food, like me, you usually know where your recipe ideas have come from. This is partly what leads me to try to trace the history of dishes, so credit can be given to the true creators where possible. Even if, invariably, there are other influences on the final recipe.

Vitello tonnato, the dish on which this recipe is based, originated in nineteenth-century Piedmont, Italy. The tuna would be landed and marinated on the Ligurian coast, then pounded with capers, herbs and anchovy to make a creamy sauce. Mayonnaise only became a popular addition in the mid-twentieth century, but anchovy had been used in veal recipes in Piedmont since the second half of the eighteenth century, such as in remoulades, or partnered with capers in a sauce for veal brisket.

I've always enjoyed *vitello tonnato* – although the veal makes me feel a little guilty. So the first time I ate *vitello tonnato* with slices of sashimi-grade tuna in the sauce as well, it sparked an idea to do away with the meat and make this a seafood-focused recipe. In fact, precursor recipes to *vitello tonnato* talk of giving veal 'the taste and appearance of tuna' through brining with salt and anchovies, even if dishes containing both fish and meat were uncommon in Europe until the nineteenth century.

According to *Gambero Rosso*, a respected Italian culinary magazine, it was a Milanese doctor who first added tuna to the sauce, in a recipe book for the infirm published in 1862. Take a bow, Angelo Dubini! (Could someone please add 'invented *vitello tonnato*' to Angelo's Wikipedia page, which at the moment just talks about an intestinal parasite he discovered and a rather nasty disease named after him?)

These Italians are not the ones I stole this recipe from, though, even if they undoubtedly influenced all the dishes that came after them. No, it was on the wisteria-shaded balcony of a pop-up gallery in Queenscliff that I tried a delicious plate of peeled, fat, extremely local yellow tomato slices served on a tuna mayo. When I found my first teeny Tomberry tomatoes, which are grown just up the Bellarine Highway, south of Geelong, I thought they'd be perfect in a tomato *tonnato* with *pangrattato* – paddling in a sauce of pounded tuna and anchovies, mixed with mayo and lemon juice, all served under crunchy croutons that soak up the dressing and any rendered tomato juice.

So, chef Louis, thanks for the inspiration! And nice work too to Eminent Seeds, who invented those teeny pearl tomatoes in the Netherlands.

---

425 g can tuna in spring water, drained
3 anchovy fillets, the pinkest/best you can
find (optional, but highly recommended)
½ cup (150 g) whole-egg mayonnaise
1 teaspoon worcestershire sauce
2 lemons, zest finely grated, juiced
500 g smallest tomatoes, quartered if larger
snipped chives, to serve

Caper pangrattato
8 rashers streaky bacon or prosciutto, finely
chopped (the same size as the capers)
2 tablespoons olive oil
2–3 slices stale bread, crusts removed, torn
into bite-sized pieces
¼ cup (50 g) baby capers, drained and
patted dry with paper towel

Place the drained tuna and the anchovy fillets, if using, in a mortar and pound with a pestle until quite smooth. Fold in the mayonnaise and worcestershire sauce, and keep mashing until smoother. Add lemon juice to taste. You can mash the tuna with the back of a spoon if you don't have a mortar and pestle. This is your *tonnato* – set it aside.

To make the *pangrattato*, heat a frying pan over medium–high heat. Add the bacon and cook, tossing, for 5–8 minutes or until the bacon is crispy. Use a slotted spoon to transfer the bacon to a bowl, leaving the rendered fat in the pan. Add the olive oil and heat until sizzling. Add the bread, and cook, tossing, for 5 minutes or until golden and toasted. Toss to ensure all sides of the bread get kissed by the heat.

When the bread is crispy and golden in places, add the capers. Cook for 2–3 minutes, until crisp, then add the bacon. Toss and remove from the heat while you plate.

Spread the *tonnato* on the base of a serving plate. Top with the tomatoes, and spoon over a generous smattering of caper *pangrattato*. Serve with the rest on the side. Sprinkle with the chives and lemon zest to serve.

Oysters with finger lime

SERVES 4 as an appetiser, or 1 as lunch   **PREP** 5 minutes

Myth

Like brambles and rabbits, oysters are a noxious species that were introduced to Australia after colonisation.

My Truth

While some species of oyster, such as the Pacific oyster, were introduced – as recently as 1947 – First Nations people have been eating native oysters like Sydney rock oysters and Angasi or mud oysters since human habitation began on this continent tens of thousands of years ago.

We know this from the analysis of shell middens around Australia. These ancient rubbish dumps provide a fascinating insight into the traditional diet of coastal First Nations peoples, with oyster shells found at these sites being dated back to some 9000 years ago. (It's also likely that even older middens containing older shells have been washed away by rising sea levels.)

A 3000-year-old midden used by the Dharawal people, south of Sydney Harbour, revealed that both Sydney rock oysters (*badangi* in Dharawal) and native mud oysters (*dainya*) were commonly consumed along with local cockles (*gadyan*) and hairy mussels (*dalgal*).

This story is repeated in Gadigal middens around Sydney Harbour and in Botany Bay and Broken Bay. Captain James Cook reported that the area around Sydney was thick with oyster reefs, some of which extended up to ten hectares in size.

Oyster shells are also a common find in middens around the country. Near Hinchinbrook in North Queensland, oysters supplemented a diet that contained crabs and other shellfish, as well as the fish that are likely to have been caught in fish traps found around there.

Huge oyster beds were once common all around the Australian coast, and a few can still be seen in out-of-the-way coastal locations, like outside Coral Bay in Western Australia. European colonists also ate the native oysters, but, more damagingly, they harvested the oysters in order to burn the shells to make lime for the cement used in their buildings. This practice decimated oyster reefs like the ones around Sydney, with the practice eventually banned – too late – in 1868. Dr Dominic Mcafee, a marine ecologist and researcher from the University of Adelaide, suggests that oyster reefs rivalling the size of the Great Barrier Reef were lost after colonisation in South Australia alone.

When people ask me for a truly Australian dish, this is what I now suggest, knowing that *badangi* and *dainya* have been consumed by First Nations people for as long as they have lived here. I have paired the oysters with a dusting of native pepper and a few carpels of acidic finger lime or blood lime, which will make any Sydney rock or Angasi oyster sing, and also speak proudly of the uniqueness of this land.

12 local Sydney rock oysters or Angasi oysters
2 blood limes or finger limes (any colour will do)
1 teaspoon native pepper, crushed

Open the oysters. Turn them to free the flesh, but keep as much of the juice as possible in the shell. Lay on top of crushed ice, if you like, in an edged plate or platter.

Cut the blood or finger limes in half and squeeze out the pearls.

Top each oyster with ¼ teaspoon of lime pearls and a pinch of crushed native pepper.

Serve immediately.

Any leftover finger lime can be used on bright, clean fish dishes or desserts that need a little added pep. Try a finger lime and mango pavlova. They are also great in your gin and tonic – try adding a sprig of lemon myrtle for a fresh, native Aussie twist on the classic drink.

Authentic puttanesca

SERVES 4 **PREP** 15 minutes **COOK** 30 minutes

CLASSIC

Myth
Which myth do you want: that this is the whore's pasta, or the cuckold's dinner, perhaps?

My Truth
Puttanesca is one of the great Italian pasta sauces, but its history is mired in myth. We do know that it originated in the south of Italy, most likely from Naples or the islands off the coast.

The most 'romantic' origin story is that this combination of tomatoes, olives, capers and anchovies was a quick meal favoured by working girls in this rambunctious port when they were between clients. Some even go so far as to credit its invention to a nineteenth-century French courtesan named Yvette who was homesick for the flavours of Provence. This might also explain the name – the Italian word *puttana* can be used to describe someone in this trade. The main problem with this theory is that no recipes called *puttanesca* appear in any of the great Italian cookbooks of the nineteenth or early twentieth centuries. It is not until the 1960s that *puttanesca* shows up in print.

In *Mediterranean Cooking* (1977), the great US food writer Paula Wolfert recounts a tale that the sauce was popular with women who were having affairs, as they could be in the sack with their lovers while the sauce slowly cooked itself, ensuring they still had something to serve their husbands when they came home from work! But again, few if any primary sources exist to support this story.

Another thing that points to *puttanesca* being a creation of the mid-twentieth century is that, in the 1960s and 1970s, the traditional 'red sauces' of southern Italy became fashionable among the country's middle class, and a number of similar tomato sauces for pasta appeared in cookbooks, such as a Neapolitan sauce of anchovies and oregano, or a Sicilian version with the telltale addition of olives and sweet raisins to the tomato, garlic and anchovy sauce.

The most credible point of origin for *puttanesca* appears to be on the holiday island of Ischia, 30 kilometres off the coast of Naples, sometime in the 1950s. On this volcanic island, famed for its rabbits (introduced by Phoenician traders), seafood (including anchovies) and tomatoes, lived the two men to whom the creation of *puttanesca* is most credibly assigned.

First up is Eduardo Maria Colucci, a sporadic local artist who claimed that the dish was a play on marinara, the popular sailor's red sauce found in fishing ports all around the Tyrrhenian Sea. It was that time on the island after World War II where food was scarce and the future uncertain – especially for a 45-year-old artist. Colucci himself was better known on the island as a host than an artist. His brother, Vincenzo, had the real talent and celebrity as a painter. The story goes that late one night, Eduardo was entertaining in his study in his house in Ischia Porto, as was his habit. His friends were hungry so he threw together the first *sugo puttanesca* from what he had on hand in the kitchen, and tossed the sauce through fine Neapolitan vermicelli.

When he was asked what was in the dish, he replied 'any old rubbish', from whence the name came. You see, that Italian word *puttana* or *puttanata* is a multipurpose swear word that can also be translated as 'rubbish'.

The sudden explosion of sauces named *puttanesca* in the 1960s and 1970s does somewhat support Colucci's claim of inventing the dish in the 1950s, even if his supposed creation does bear a passing resemblance to Ippolito Cavalcanti's recipe for vermicelli with capers, olives and anchovies in the fourth edition of *Cucina teorico–pratica* ('Theoretical–Practical Kitchen', 1844). Interestingly, this recipe wasn't included in the Neapolitan author's first edition of the book, published in 1837, which only had vermicelli baked with tomatoes.

However, the plot thickened in 2005 when Colucci's nephew, Sandro Petti, tried to claim that *he* was the one who invented the sauce, in an article written for the local Ischian paper. It was a familiar-sounding tale of late-night guests and a bare pantry at Petti's nightclub cum restaurant, Rancio Fellone (which, perhaps tellingly, translates as 'The Messy Thief'). These hungry guests asked Petti to 'throw together any old rubbish' (*facci una puttanata qualsiasi*). So, he made them a hastily thrown-together sauce of tomatoes, olives and capers. Their enthusiastic reaction meant he put it on the menu as *spaghetti alla puttanata*, but latter changed it to the better known, but grammatically incorrect, *alla puttanesca*. I have to say, I am more drawn to Colucci's story.

Success often has many fathers, and that certainly seems to be the case with *puttanesca*. Part of that success is thanks to the sauce's flexibility. It is quite possible to leave out ingredients with no impact upon the sauce – anchovies, tomatoes and garlic alone make a classic and very tasty version. Just top with crisp fried capers instead of parmesan. My usual *puttanesca*, however, takes a 'more is more' approach, with lots of garlic, capers, anchovies, deseeded long red chillies, black olives and a little tomato sauce, with plenty of parsley or basil stirred through at the end. This sauce isn't just for spaghetti, either; it also goes wonderfully with seafood – try baking fillets of white fish in it. Also try braising chickpeas and kale in it, or letting mussels open in it and then tossing through some orecchiette. You could try it as a sauce for rabbit or lamb, too – if you can get the rabbits from Ischia, even better.

Authentic puttanesca *(CONTINUED)*

¼ cup (60 ml) olive oil
110 g jar baby capers, rinsed and drained well, dried on paper towel
1 brown onion, finely chopped
50 g tin anchovy fillets (the pinkest you can find)
5 garlic cloves, crushed
1 bunch oregano, basil or flat-leaf parsley
½ cup (125 ml) red wine
400 g can cherry tomatoes
150 g black olives, pitted
2 long red chillies, deseeded, finely chopped
1 lemon, zest finely grated, juiced
400 g spaghetti
sea salt and white sugar, to season

Heat the oil in a large, heavy-based frying pan over medium–high heat. Add half the capers and fry for 2–3 minutes or until crispy. Use a slotted spoon to transfer the capers to a plate lined with paper towel to drain.

Add the onion to the oil left in the pan. Cook, stirring, for 8 minutes or until it starts to colour. Mash in the anchovies and stir in the garlic. If using oregano, chop the larger leaves (save the little ones for serving) and add now. If using parsley, finely chop the stems and add now. Cook, stirring, for 3 minutes or until the garlic is coloured but not brown.

Put a large saucepan of water on high heat and bring to the boil. Add enough salt so it tastes as salty as the sea around Ischia (which is quite salty, don'tcha know).

Add the red wine to the onion mixture and cook, stirring, for 3–5 minutes to deglaze the pan and until it has reduced by half. Add the tomatoes, olives, half the chilli, the remaining capers and half the lemon juice. Cook, stirring absent-mindedly, for 10 minutes. Warm your bowls. You can do this by popping them in the sink under the colander when you drain the pasta.

When the sauce is getting close to ready, add the pasta to the boiling water, stir in a cup of cold water and return to the boil. Simmer for 2 minutes less than the packet instructions, until it is cooked but still has a little bite. Drain, reserving ½ cup (125 ml) of the pasta water. This will be caught by the top bowl if you have put the bowls in the sink in a pile and then put the colander on top before draining the pasta.

Splash some of the reserved pasta water into the sauce and toss the pan with a rolling motion to help the pasta water emulsify with the sauce. Taste and adjust seasoning with salt, a little sugar or more lemon juice. Lay in the pasta in nice swooshes with a little more of the reserved pasta water. Toss to combine.

Serve topped with the smaller oregano leaves or chopped parsley or basil leaves, crispy capers, the lemon zest and the rest of the chilli.

Food nerd fact

Pasta has a long history in Italy. Etruscan tomb paintings from between the tenth and the first centuries BC provide proof that Italian people were making pasta in the countryside near where Rome would be founded thousands of years before Marco Polo was even a twinkle in his father's eye. The Romans, they say, continued this tradition with sheets of dough. The poet Horace called these sheets *lagana* in the first century BC, which may well have been a play on the local vernacular for 'chamber pot'. The cooking method seems blurred, however, and these sheets may have been baked or fried in the manner of the Ancient Egyptians, who made pasta with flour and the 'milky' juice from lettuces.

The history here is long, but can't erase the 2002 discovery of 4000-year-old millet-flour noodles on an archaeological dig in north-west China. The pasta dough had even been laminated by hand-pulling. This is the oldest pasta ever discovered, so, at least in regional provenance, Marco Polo's claims might have some substance.

Most ancient recipes are somewhat oblique in their instructions, but there are records of early AD Greek or Palestinian people eating what sounds just like boiled, string-like pasta. Meanwhile, Arab writings from the ninth century talk extensively about *itriyya*, or dried pasta shapes, and the Norman adventurers who conquered Sicily built a thriving Mediterranean trade in this dried Arab pasta in the eleventh and twelfth centuries from a manufacturing base in and around Palermo.

The reason for sharing this enlightening history lesson is to show that Italians have never had the monopoly on pasta. For thousands of years, many other cultures have called pastas their own, from the people of Japan and Nepal to the plains tribes of the Russian steppes and the people of Greece.

The Greeks controlled much of the south of Italy for years and have loads of pastas of their own, whether it's the risoni-like *orzo* grain pasta, *hilopites*, which are like short, flat egg noodles that go into chicken noodle soup, or their own version of a pasta bake, which is called *pasticcio*.

Layered prawn cocktail

SERVES 4 **PREP** 30 minutes

Myth

The prawn cocktail was invented in a chichi New York restaurant in 1956, as the popularity of cocktail culture saw Americans installing home bars and making their own Manhattans before dinner.

My Truth

It was the flagship dish of 1960s and 1970s dinner parties, but the prawn cocktail is actually much older, with roots in three distinct eras: the notorious oyster dives run by vicious New York City street gangs; the '*Laissez les bons temps rouler*' looseness of old New Orleans; and Prohibition.

First, New York. In his book *The Big Oyster*, Mark Kurlansky reports that between 1820 and 1910, oysters were the food of the poor in the city. The waters around Manhattan held some 350 square miles of oyster beds, and the docks were lined with oyster boats shucking 'em and selling them to street stalls, restaurants and the infamous 'oyster cellars' run by the organised criminal gangs from New York's slums, particularly the Five Points neighbourhood.

Charles Dickens loved the dive-like oyster cellars of the Five Points but was mortified by the poverty of the area, which must have been quite something to shock the man who luxuriated in writing about the horrors of England's stews, workhouse and prison hulks.

(I should note also that not all oyster cellars were dives run by criminals like the Five Points Gang, whose members would later include Al Capone, Lucky Luciano and Meyer Lansky. For a diverting hour or so, check out the story of Thomas Downing (1791–1866), the son of freed Virginian slaves from Chesapeake Bay. He took the New York oyster bar to the height of sophistication, where women and children were welcomed and would not be scandalised by the goings-on. He was also a prominent abolitionist. But I digress . . .)

The oysters at these stalls, restaurants and dives were served many ways, but a study of 248 historical menus stored at the New York Public Library shows that cocktails *d'huîtres* were quite the rage in the 1880s. This was a precursor to the prawn cocktail, where oysters natural were served with either a pot of cocktail sauce or the ingredients for making it yourself: tomato ketchup, horseradish, Louisiana hot sauce, worcestershire sauce and lemon juice.

Now to Louisiana. The first recorded US hot sauce was actually made in Massachusetts in 1807, but it is perhaps telling that Tabasco, the Louisiana hot sauce that became almost synonymous with oysters and cocktail sauce, was first sold in 1868. This places it on the market in New York in time for this seafood and cocktail sauce boom – or maybe even helping to initiate it.

Maryland-born Edmund McIlhenny used chillies from Louisiana's Avery Island and old cologne bottles from New Orleans when creating his Tabasco, but oysters weren't nearly so prevalent down in the Deep South, so there local prawns or crawdads were more likely to have been served with the sauce instead.

The next shift in the fate of the prawn cocktail came with Prohibition in the 1920s. Smart restaurateurs (perhaps even the mobster sons of those original oyster cellar owners) put their now under-utilised martini glasses to work by offering iced seafood 'cocktails' to their guests. Beside clam, oyster, lobster and mixed seafood cocktails, all served with cocktail sauce, the prawn cocktail made its first appearance north of the Mason-Dixon line, and first appeared in print in a restaurant ad in a 1926 edition of the *New York Times*.

Perhaps ironically, Prohibition-era recipes for cocktail sauce talk about adding celery salt to the worcestershire sauce, horseradish, lemon and tomato, in a manner that neatly echoes the makings of a Bloody Mary, which would be invented in New York in the 1930s, after Prohibition was repealed. Therefore, the prawn cocktail could be said to have inspired arguably the greatest cocktail ever made. (Remember, in the US a classic bloody Mary includes clam juice in the tomato mix, further hinting at its possible seafood roots.)

In Australia, we also fell in love with the prawn cocktail, no doubt because our prawns are the envy of the world. Prawn and cucumber cocktails were everywhere in the media in 1932, but in these the mayo was just hit with a little paprika. A 1946 recipe from Queensland's *Courier Mail* has the more familiar dressing of celery salt, tomato katsup [sic] and worcestershire sauce. And so we end up with the prawn cocktail we know and love, blushing orange sauce blanketing blanched prawns reclining in a glass atop sliced iceberg lettuce or dangling out of a halved avocado.

The prawn cocktail fell out of favour as the years passed, until the fascination with reinvigorated retro food that started in the early 2010s. While I still think my 2013 idea of serving a prawn cocktail mix in iceberg lettuce cups like a *san choy bao* might be one of my proudest moments, this version is more timely, as we've slavishly incorporated another hot trend: that of the layered salad. The bright, fresh layers will be sure to impress even the most sceptical guests.

Layered prawn cocktail *(CONTINUED)*

24 large cooked prawns, peeled and
    deveined, leave 4 with tails intact
½ iceberg lettuce, thinly shredded
2 tablespoons finely chopped chives, plus
    extra chopped chives, to serve
2 avocados, one thinly sliced crossways and
    one cut into thin wedges
1 small lemon, cut into thin wedges
thinly sliced baguette, toasted, to serve

Marie Rose sauce

1 egg (see Tips)
350 ml grapeseed oil
1 tablespoon lemon juice
2 tablespoons tomato sauce (ketchup)
1 teaspoon worcestershire sauce
10 drops Tabasco sauce
sea salt and freshly ground black pepper

To make the Marie Rose sauce, carefully crack the egg into the canister of a stick blender, without breaking the yolk. Add the grapeseed oil, lemon juice, tomato and worcestershire sauces. Insert the stick blender into the canister carefully so that the basket of the stick blender is completely covering the yolk. Turn on the blender and, as ribbons appear, slowly pull the stick upwards and continue to blitz until thick and creamy. Add the Tabasco and blitz with the stick blender until well combined. Add more Tabasco if you like it hotter. Season with salt and pepper.

Coarsely chop the completely peeled prawns and place in a bowl. Add ¼ cup (60 ml) of the Marie Rose sauce and toss until well combined. Combine the lettuce and chives in a separate bowl.

Divide the remaining sauce among four 1¾ cup (435 ml) serving glasses, or one large glass bowl. Top with the lettuce mixture. Place the sliced avocado on top of the lettuce, laying flat. Place the avocado wedges standing up in the back of the glass. Fill the glasses with the coated prawns. Hang the prawns with the tails still intact on the edge of the glass, and add a lemon wedge. Grind a little black pepper on top and sprinkle with the extra chives. Serve with the toasted baguette.

TIPS

If you are concerned about using raw eggs, substitute with 3 tablespoons of chickpea water (the liquid from a can of chickpeas, also known as aquafaba) instead.

Try adding a teaspoon of whisky or brandy to the Marie Rose sauce for some extra punch!

Tuna mornay bake
TOPPED WITH GRANNY'S POTATO CHIPS

SERVES 4 **PREP** 20 minutes **COOK** 35 minutes

CLASSIC

Myth
Tuna mornay was invented in the United States.

My Truth
Tuna mornay is a dish born out of the modern age of convenience food. This family favourite of canned tuna in cheese sauce simply did not exist one hundred years ago.

While canning was first successfully trialled in 1806, it wasn't until a Pacific sardine shortage in 1903 that Los Angeles fish canner Albert Halfhill switched to using albacore tuna and marvelled at the way this tunny fish turned a lovely pale colour when steam-cooked in the can. Thus, canned tuna was born.

By 1950 the US was consuming 90,000 tons of the stuff. Sandwiches accounted for much of this, but tuna casserole also contributed. The first recipe for this appeared in 1930, but its popularity was propelled by the arrival of Campbell's canned cream of mushroom soup in 1934. With this invention, you no longer needed to make a bechamel for an easy tuna casserole. A typical recipe combined canned soup, canned vegetables and canned tuna baked over a bed of egg noodles, with a crunchy topping of crushed potato chips and possibly cheese. This tunny fish casserole was the very epitome of space-age dining: quick to prepare, tasty and using solely store cupboard ingredients. It could even be frozen and reheated.

In Australia, we developed a classier tuna mornay, with canned tuna blanketed in cheesy bechamel. We also replaced the canned veg with frozen peas and corn for freshness. It was usually accompanied by a ring of steamed white rice, or occasionally wheat pasta, baked potato or a topping of grilled mash; tuna mornay pasta bake was just another evolution away from the US tuna casseroles.

The first tuna mornay recipe I can find (assuming you don't count the description of topping tinned tuna with peas and a creamy cheese sauce, from the *Sydney Morning Herald* in February 1941, as a recipe) is Australian, from the *Australian Women's Weekly* in 1957. Here, cheesy sauce is mixed with tuna, tinned corn kernels and liquid from the can, then baked under buttered breadcrumbs.

Over the years, Michelle Southan and I have toyed with a number of ways of tweaking classic tuna mornay. Our shared love of nachos, and a family recipe handed down from my New York-born grandmother for tunny fish casserole with a topping of crushed potato chips, saw us finally end up with this beauty. The potato chips can be used as golden, edible scoops to pick up dollops of tuna mornay and pasta, bringing some added tactile joy to the dish, as well as some welcome crunch.

---

300 g dried penne
40 g butter
2 tablespoons olive oil
1 brown onion, finely chopped
2 stalks celery, finely chopped
1 garlic clove, crushed
¼ cup (35 g) plain flour
2 cups (500 ml) milk
1 cup (250 ml) chicken stock
425 g can tuna in olive oil, drained and flaked
1 cup (120 g) frozen peas and corn
1 cup (120 g) coarsely grated cheddar
1 teaspoon mustard powder
2 tablespoons lemon juice
sea salt and freshly ground black pepper
2 × 165 g packets sea salt potato chips

Preheat the oven to 180°C (160°C fan-forced).

Cook the pasta in plenty of salted boiling water for 2 minutes less than it says on the packet or until *properly* al dente. Drain well and return to the pan. Yes, I know pasta isn't always traditional for an Aussie tuna mornay, but it makes this meal budget-friendly and super-filling.

While the pasta cooks, heat the butter and oil in a frying pan over medium heat until foaming. Add the onion and celery and cook, stirring, for 4–5 minutes or until soft. Add the garlic and cook, stirring, for 30 seconds or until aromatic. Add the flour and cook, stirring, for 1 minute or until the mixture bubbles and the flour turns the colour of sand. Remove from the heat.

Gradually stir in the milk and stock until combined. Place over medium–high heat and cook, stirring, for 5–6 minutes or until the mixture boils and thickens.

Remove from the heat. Gently stir in the tuna, peas and corn, cheddar, mustard powder and lemon juice. Season with salt and pepper.

Add half the tuna mixture to the pasta and toss until well combined. Spoon into a 12 cup (3 litre) capacity ovenproof dish. Pour over the remaining tuna mixture. Arrange the potato chips in rows on top. Bake for 20 minutes or until golden.

INAUTHENTIC
Home-style^ laksa

SERVES 4 **PREP** 40 minutes (plus 15 minutes soaking) **COOK** 30 minutes

Twist

Myth

There are only two true laksas: curried laksa, which is creamy and made with coconut milk; and sour *asam* laksa, made with tamarind and no coconut milk.

My Truth

This is one of the myths that I was inclined to believe, at least until Diana Chan pointed out to me that there were at least nineteen traditional regional versions of this Malaysian dish, which is popular across the Malay Archipelago and now all around the world. In fact, the last time I counted there were more than forty distinct laksas made in these two broad styles across Malaysia, Indonesia and Singapore. These vary with local tastes as well as access to ingredients.

Bean curd puffs are common but by no means obligatory, and the use of curry powder is something that is hotly debated. Some may feature bobbing mackerel, chicken or snake beans, while others will have none of these whatsoever. While some may use the familiar thick laksa noodles, others might opt for thread-thin vermicelli. The signature laksa of Johor, which has some of the sourness of a classic Penang or Kuching laksa but a gravy that is thick from coconut cream, even uses spaghetti rather than noodles. Sultan Abu Bakar of Johor developed a penchant for spaghetti on a trip to Italy in 1866, and instructed his chefs to use it in an upmarket seafood laksa on his return.

The fact there is no single strong archetype for laksa hints at the dish's origin story, which is one of the simplest of all – a marriage of two different cultures happening near-simultaneously in many locations.

Malaysia occupied a unique place in the world, on the midway point between the two great early civilisations of India and China, meaning it was served by favourable trade winds to both at different times of the year. Hence, Chinese merchants began settling along the Malaysian coastline under the protection of different local sultanates from around the tenth century onwards.

It wasn't until after the marriage of Ming dynasty princess Hang Li Po to the sultan of Malacca in 1459, however, that the groundwork for the creation of laksa was set. The princess arrived with five hundred noblemen in her entourage, many of whom took local wives, thus giving rise to the Peranakan culture, which combines influences from both sides of the marriage. It was in the kitchens of these Peranakan (or '*nonya*') homes that the noodles of China meshed with the curries and sour fish soups of Malaysia to create all these various laksas.

You'll find that often the different laksas originate from different ports along the trade routes, where Chinese merchants who came after those first nobles settled and also married local women. With this geographic variation, it is perhaps no surprise that laksa has grown to be more a state of mind than one master recipe – although here in Australia, the laksa that was most commonly brought by the first significant wave of Malaysian migrants in the early 1980s was the coconut-cream laksa *lemak*, aka laksa *nonya*.

It is this laksa that serves as the inspiration for the recipe that follows, although ours is unashamedly a bogan Aussie supermarket laksa rather than anything achingly authentic. It will give you comforting laksa feels whenever you need them at short notice, but if you want an authentic laksa, I recommend looking up a recipe by the wonderful Diana Chan.

Home-style inauthentic laksa *(CONTINUED)*

12 large uncooked prawns
⅓ cup (80 ml) vegetable oil
4 cups (1 litre) water
230 g thin rice stick noodles (see Tips)
400 ml can coconut milk
4 makrut lime leaves (see Tips)
400 g skinless salmon fillets, pin-boned and
    cut into 3 cm chunks
1 tablespoon fish sauce
1 tablespoon lime juice
100 g tofu puffs, thickly sliced
80 g bean sprouts, trimmed
2 spring onions, thinly sliced diagonally
1 cup fresh herbs (pick a mix of two:
    Vietnamese mint, Thai basil, coriander or
    curry leaves)
lime wedges, to serve
fried egg noodles, to serve (optional – see
    Tips)

Laksa paste

8 dried red chillies, seeds removed
6 red shallots, peeled and coarsely chopped
6 raw unsalted macadamias (or use
    candlenuts if you can)
3 garlic cloves, peeled
3 cm piece galangal, peeled and finely
    chopped
2 cm knob ginger, peeled and finely grated
2 lemongrass stalks, white part only, finely
    chopped
4 long red chillies, deseeded and finely
    chopped
1 tablespoon ground coriander
1 teaspoon pre-roasted belachan shrimp
    paste (see Tips)
1 teaspoon ground cumin
1 teaspoon ground turmeric
2 tablespoons vegetable oil

Start by making the laksa paste. Place the dried chillies in a heatproof bowl. Cover with boiling water and set aside for 15 minutes to soften. Drain, reserving 1 tablespoon of the chilli water.

Coarsely chop the chillies and place in a food processor. Add the shallot, macadamias, garlic, galangal, ginger, lemongrass, fresh chilli, coriander, shrimp paste, cumin, turmeric and reserved chilli water. Process, scraping down the side frequently, until finely chopped and well combined. With the motor running, gradually add the 2 tablespoons oil in a thin stream and process to form a smooth paste. Set aside.

Peel and devein the prawns, reserving the heads and shells.

Heat 3 tablespoons of the vegetable oil in a large saucepan over medium heat. Add the reserved prawn heads and shells and cook for 5 minutes or until very orange and aromatic. Increase the heat to high. Add the water and bring to the boil. Reduce the heat to medium and simmer for 15 minutes. Strain the liquid into a large jug. Discard the heads and shells.

Cook the rice noodles in a large saucepan of boiling water for 2 minutes, or as per packet instructions. Drain in a colander and set aside.

Heat the remaining 1 tablespoon of oil in a large saucepan or wok over medium–high heat. Add the laksa paste and cook, stirring, for 30 seconds or until aromatic. Stir in the coconut milk, lime leaves and prawn stock, and bring to a gentle simmer. Reduce the heat to medium–low, add the prawn meat and salmon and simmer, very gently, for 3–5 minutes or until the seafood changes colour and is just cooked. It is important to simmer the soup gently at this point – the coconut milk may separate if boiled.

Carefully stir in the fish sauce and lime juice. You can adjust the seasoning with a little extra fish sauce at this point if you like. You'll be serving it with lime wedges for those who like it tangier.

Rinse the rice noodles under hot water to reheat. Drain and divide among four deep, warmed soup bowls. Ladle the coconut laksa over the noodles and top with the tofu, bean sprouts, spring onion and herbs. Serve with the lime wedges and fried noodles, if using.

TIPS

Really any noodles will do for laksa, from *bee hoon* or *mee* to fatter wheat noodles or even spaghetti, as they have a yen to do in Johor. I'm partial to a mix of fine rice *bee hoon* and fatter laksa noodles for the textural difference, but I know it's a pain to do both.

Makrut lime leaves are what we used to call 'kaffir' lime leaves (that word is now widely deemed offensive). They keep really well in the freezer, in an airtight ziplock bag. To cut them into fine threads, cut out the central vein and then roll up a few leaves together tightly like a cigar. Using a small, sharp knife, cut across the width of the cigar as finely as you can.

Fry your own egg noodles for perfect crunch and greater presentation.

You can buy roasted shrimp paste in the Asian section of most supermarkets (I like Jeeny's brand). If you buy unroasted, wrap the teaspoon of shrimp paste in foil and place on a barbecue plate on medium heat for 3–4 minutes to toast. You are best to do this on the barbecue outside, if you have one, rather than in the kitchen, as the smell is very strong.

If you can find *daun kesum* (aka laksa leaf), this can be a great addition too.

Creamy Aussie prawn and fish pie

SERVES 6 **PREP** 20 minutes **COOK** 1 hour 15 minutes

Twist

Myth

US President Thomas Jefferson was a pioneer of packaged instant mash potato.

My Truth

The first recipes for mashed potatoes are widely regarded to be Hannah Glasse's recipe for maſhed potatoes in *The Art of Cookery* (1747) and Mary Randolph's slightly less buttery version in *The Virginia House-Wife* (1824). There's also a mash reference dating back to 1802 in Thomas Jefferson's Monticello papers. The correspondence is about the results of trials for desiccating potatoes to make the earliest incarnation of instant mash, thus proving that the history of Deb is a long and venerable one that even features US presidents.

Finding the first recipes for mash-topped fish pies is far more vexatious. I can find more about the history of potato mashers (metal versions of which began to be mass produced by the mid-nineteenth century, with the potato ricer arriving in the early twentieth century – even if the Scots still preferred their wooden 'potato beetles' for making mash to top their shepherd's pies) than I can about the history of the honest fish pie.

Most references to fish pies are for those topped with 'paste', as they used to call pastry, and these fish pies are royally served with stories of how much reign after reign of English monarchs loved them. Queen Elizabeth II was presented with a lamprey pie by the Royal Air Force upon her coronation, and this luckily wasn't taken the wrong way, despite the fact that one of her royal predecessors, Henry I, died after eating a surfeit of lampreys back in 1135. (A surfeit basically means 'too much to be wise', and that RAF pie was rather large!)

There is nothing about mash-topped fish pies in early English cookbooks by Eliza Acton or Mrs Beeton either, which leads me to believe that the idea of sticking the standard filling for a pastry-topped fish pie filling under a layer of mash was something that popped up around the same time as the emergence of the shepherd's pie and cottage pie (see p. 240). Perplexingly, a fish pie is tangentially mentioned in a reader's letter to London's *Lady's Newspaper* in 1863. The letter-writer dwells on the pleasures of using leftover cooked turbot in an 'ordinary fish pie with mashed potato'. I suppose at least we know it was around at that time, even if I can't pinpoint a definitive first recipe.

Things get even more confusing in Australia. At the end of the nineteenth century, recipes start popping up for a type of fish pie where cooked fish is mixed through mash with an egg, parsley and some anchovy essence, and then the whole lot is crammed into a baking dish and browned in the oven. This sounds like a giant salmon fishcake, but without the redeeming pleasure of frying – which basically leaves it with no redeeming features at all.

Upon deeper research, Mrs Beeton's 1923 *All About Cookery* features this recipe as a 'fish pie'. This confirms that this fish pie with potato is a British invention, but there's still no sign of fish pie with mash on top. This also makes me worry that that 1863 mention of leftovers made into an 'ordinary fish pie' with mash might have been an aberration like this. Until some smart person decides to write their PhD thesis on the origins of the Aussie fish pie, we might never know.

I can tell you with certainty that by 1907 we had started to line the pie dish with mash before adding a cooked fish filling and topping with buttered breadcrumbs or – *ta-da!!!* – topping with more mash before browning. Finally, we have something resembling the modern fish pie. I would have recreated that last, mash-heavy recipe here, but Jamie Oliver did a lot of the mash-lined-baking-tray thing in his last book, so I'd better not. Instead, here is an Aussie take on fish pie that champions barramundi, prawns and the ability of carrots to fool you into thinking that there's salmon in here too.

POSTSCRIPT: It bugged me that I'd not been able to find a historical recipe to point to as the ancestor of today's fish pies, so I worked my way back through Mrs Beeton's books again. Our Isabella was a culinary jackdaw who had an uncanny knack of collecting great recipes that stand the test of time, so if anyone has the recipe for our fish pie, I felt sure it would be her. As I said in the introduction, another layer of the onion unpeeled.

I read many of her fish recipes, searching, hoping . . .

Finally, there is joy in her first published work, Mrs Beeton's Book of Household Management *(1861): a recipe for leftover cod pie. Cold, cooked cod is mixed with a dozen oysters and lots of melted butter, and then Isabella instructs us to 'cover with mashed potatoes'. Bingo!*

Interestingly, on the very next page is her recipe for cod à la bechamel, which for all the world reads like a modern-day fish-pie filling.

Even more interestingly, in the same book is her recipe for 'baked minced mutton', the recipe that would go on, nine years later, to become shepherd's pie. So it turns out that, rather than being inspired by cottage pie and shepherd's pie, fish pie actually preceded them both.

Prawn and fish pie (CONTINUED)

4 eggs
60 g butter
2 leeks, white part only, thickly sliced
2 carrots, peeled and quartered lengthways,
    then cut crossways into 3 cm lengths
⅓ cup (80 ml) vermouth, ouzo or Pernod (see
    Tips)
¼ cup (35 g) plain flour
2 cups (500 ml) milk
⅓ cup finely chopped flat-leaf parsley
2 tablespoons finely chopped dill
1 tablespoon finely grated lemon zest
1 tablespoon lemon juice
450 g skinless barramundi fillets, cut into
    4 cm pieces
18 large uncooked prawns, peeled and
    deveined
20 g butter, extra, melted

Mash topping
1 kg washed sebago or other floury potatoes
1⅔ cups (400 ml) milk
50 g butter, chopped and chilled
sea salt and freshly ground white pepper

Cook the eggs in a small saucepan of boiling water for 8 minutes. Drain and cool under cold running water, then peel and quarter.

To make the mash, peel the potatoes and put the clean peelings in a small saucepan. Cover with milk and bring to a gentle simmer over medium heat. Simmer for 10 minutes to infuse the milk with the skins' flavour and starch. Remove from the heat and set aside to continue to infuse. This is a Heston Blumenthal idea, and it results in a thickened milk that's loaded with extra potato flavour.

Chop the potatoes coarsely and cook in a large saucepan of boiling salted water for 10 minutes or until tender. Drain and use a potato masher to mash until smooth with some of the warm, strained potatoey milk. Add the butter and more milk as required to get a nice smooth consistency, but don't add it all at once. Season with salt and white pepper (or you can use black, if you aren't stressed by the black specks in your mash).

Preheat the oven to 220°C (200°C fan-forced). Melt the butter in a frying pan over medium heat. Add the leek and carrot and cook, stirring often, for 8–10 minutes or until soft but not too brown. Increase the heat to high and add the vermouth (or whatever you are using). Bring to the boil, then cook for 3 minutes or until the vermouth is almost evaporated. Stir in the flour and cook, stirring, for 2 minutes. Remove from the heat and gradually stir in the 2 cups of milk. Place over medium heat. Cook, stirring, for 5 minutes or until the sauce boils and thickens.

Add the parsley, dill, lemon zest and juice to the sauce mixture and stir until well combined. Add the barramundi and prawns. Cook, stirring, for 2–3 minutes or until the seafood begins to change colour. Season with salt and pepper, then add the chopped boiled eggs. Transfer the mixture to a 10 cup (2.5 litre) capacity ovenproof dish.

Top the seafood mixture with the mashed potato and use a fork to rough up the top. Brush with the extra melted butter. Place the dish on a baking tray and bake for 25–30 minutes or until golden.

TIPS

I particularly like the flavour of ouzo with fish, but use what you have on hand – white wine, any pastis, dry sherry.

You could use salmon or blue-eye trevalla instead of barra if you prefer. Or, make like Isabella Beeton and add oysters (or even more hard-boiled eggs).

You can play with the mash topping, too, by adding mashed carrots, celeriac or parsnips.

Arroz de camarão

SERVES 4 **PREP** 30 minutes **COOK** 35 minutes

CLASSIC

Myth

The Italians and the Spanish each eat more rice than any other nation in Europe.

My Truth

Surely you'd think it would be Italy, with all that risotto and arancini, or Spain, with all that paella, black rice and that delicious breakfast bowl of lemon and cinnamon rice pudding – but sorry, you'd be wrong. The Portuguese eat more than 14 kilograms of rice per person each year, far eclipsing their Euro rice rivals. Much of that rice is in fresh, wet rice dishes like this one – and no wonder, as the clean, simple flavours really let the seafood shine, free from overly domineering garlic or deadening, creamy, starchy clagginess.

We know that the Romans imported rice as a luxury to their provinces, some of which were in modern-day Portugal, and the Moors introduced rice to the Iberian Peninsula in 714 AD, but the first written record of rice in Portugal dates back to the reign of King Denis (who ruled from 1279–1325). Denis had the nickname 'the farmer king' and encouraged local agriculture, including the planting of rice, but evidence indicates that rice remained a luxury food until local production took off much later.

While I can find little evidence to support early Portuguese rice production at scale, we do know from contemporary sources such as Pero De Magalhães and Gaspar da Madre de Deus that rice was being grown in the Portuguese Brazilian colony of Bakia in the mid-1500s.

Rice was planted at scale in paddies around the Tagus estuary in the eighteenth and nineteenth centuries, after small initial plantings in the 1500s on the Tagus, the Sado and inland marshes. There is increasing evidence that the knowledge of rice production that African slaves brought with them from Africa (where there is a history of rice domestication dating back three thousand years) greatly helped the establishment of rice production in Portugal and Brazil in the 1500s.

Concerns about malaria-bearing mosquitoes breeding in the paddies stalled production in the eighteenth and nineteenth centuries, and it wasn't until the early twentieth century, when laws governing rice production were introduced in 1909, that rice growing started going crazy in estuaries up and down the central and southern coast.

Today, Portugal is 60 per cent self-sufficient in rice production, even if the more common medium-grain Japonica rice, *carolino*, is being increasingly snubbed by foodie Lisboeta (people from the capital, Lisbon) and Portuense (people from Porto – or should that be Porto-rice-eans?) in favour of another indigenous rice, long-grain *agulha*.

While rice is occasionally served with rabbit, tomato and beans, or just loads of coriander, the growth of rice in those coastal estuaries saw the burgeoning popularity of rice dishes made with seafood. Rice with prawns is only part of the picture, and in fact you could argue that *arroz de tamboril* (rice with monkfish – **drool**) or *arroz de marisco* (rice with shellfish, especially clams) are more highly regarded in some areas of Portugal.

Originally this recipe was going to include blue-eye trevalla, but we decided it just doesn't need it. Neither does it need the prawn head peri-peri, if you can't be bothered and are after a clean, light supper; but I think it's pretty good at bringing some funk to the dish, even though it is perhaps more Chinese or Indian than Portuguese in inspiration. Could I say, in my defence, that the Portuguese introduced chillies to both of these places, and the *arroz de camarão* in Mozambique or prawn rice in Goa will be less soupy than the Portuguese version but will sing with chilli and spices like cloves and cardamom, in the Indian fusion version, or vinho verde, more garlic and paprika, in the Mozambican.

As a final digression, may I point out that the nation of Cameroon got its name from the Portuguese word for prawn, which Portuguese sailors noticed an abundance of when they first landed in that part of the world.

Arroz de camarão (CONTINUED)

5 tomatoes

4 cups (1 litre) fish stock

1¼ cups (250 g) short- or medium-grain rice (ideally Portuguese *carolino*, but Spanish *bomba* or even sushi rice will do)

½ cup (125 ml) olive oil, and then some more

1 large red onion, finely chopped

6 reasonably-sized garlic cloves, finely chopped

1 lemon, zest finely grated, juiced

1 bunch coriander, stems and leaves separated, stems finely chopped

12 large uncooked prawns, shells on

4 long red chillies, deseeded

sea salt

1 birdseye chilli, very thinly sliced (optional – only if you like heat)

Cut a small cross in the base of each tomato.

Heat the fish stock in a large saucepan over medium–high heat until it almost comes to the boil. Remove from the heat. Add the tomatoes and set aside for 2–3 minutes to soften the skins. Use a slotted spoon to transfer the tomatoes to a chopping board, and pour the stock into a jug to be reserved. Don't wash the pan as we are about to use it again.

When cool enough to handle, peel the tomatoes and discard the skin. Coarsely grate the tomatoes and discard the knobbly stalky bit in the top centre. Set aside.

Place the rice in a sieve and rinse under cold running water until the water runs clean.

Heat 1 tablespoon of oil in the saucepan over medium heat. Add the onion and cook, stirring, for 5–8 minutes or until translucent. Stir in two-thirds of the garlic, then the lemon zest and coriander stems. Cook for 1 minute or until aromatic.

Throw in the rice and mix around over the heat for 2–3 minutes to toast the rice. It will smell nutty and colour slightly.

Reserve a handful of coriander leaves, then finely chop the rest and add to the pan. Add the grated tomato and turn the heat up to medium–high. Stir for 3 minutes. Add 2 cups (500 ml) of the reserved fish stock and bring to a gentle simmer. Reduce the heat to medium–low. Cook, uncovered, until the rice is cooked but still just a little nutty-tasting. (You want a little bite, never nursery soft.) That's between 12–20 minutes, depending on random factors like altitude and how hot the fish stock is.

While the rice is cooking, heat ⅓ cup (80 ml) of the oil in a large frying pan over high heat. Add the prawns and cook for 3–5 minutes or until the prawn shells just begin to change colour. Don't worry if the prawns aren't totally cooked through, as the prawn flesh will get more cooking later. Remove and reserve the four best whole prawns. Shell and devein the rest, reserving the shells and heads. Chop the partially cooked prawn flesh into meaty chunks and set aside.

To make the prawn head peri-peri oil, throw the shells and heads back into the frying pan to fry for another 8 minutes or until the heads are translucent and crispy. Crush the heads in the pan to help them crisp up and release any tomalley (the stuff inside the heads). Transfer everything from the frying pan to a blender or small food processor. Add the long red chillies, a good pinch of salt and the remaining garlic. Add some extra oil if the blades have trouble churning. You could do this in a mortar and pestle if you like.

When the mixture is smooth (or as smooth as your blender, food processor or $2000 smoothie maker can make it), heat the frying pan over high heat. Add the prawn paste and cook, stirring, for 2 minutes or until toasted and the oil starts rendering out. Taste and season with more salt if necessary. Scrape the contents into a small serving bowl, top with the very thin slices of birdseye chilli, if you want more heat, and set aside until serving.

Heat the remaining oil in the frying pan over high heat. Add the chopped peeled prawns and whole prawns and cook for 1–2 minutes, until just barely cooked but warm. Throw in a little of the lemon juice and toss to emulsify, then pour into the wet rice. Add more warm stock as the consistency has to be soupy rather than risotto-y. You shouldn't need all of the remaining 2 cups (500 ml).

Divide the rice among serving bowls. Top each bowl with one of the head-on prawns and some of the reserved coriander leaves. Serve the prawn head peri-peri oil on the side. It's a dirty, warm blast of prawn trawler engine against the clean, fresh rice.

Moulesabaisse
– AUSSIE MUSSELS THAT DREAM OF BEING A BOUILLABAISSE

SERVES 4 **PREP** 20 minutes (plus 30 minutes soaking) **COOK** 30 minutes

Twist

Myth

Bouillabaisse gets its name from the way the broth kisses the fish; *bouillon baiser*, if you will.

My Truth

They – meaning amateur and professional food historians – say to thank the Romans for the spread of fish soups and stews around the rim of the Mediterranean, from the Tuscan *cacciucco* to the *caldeirada* of Portugal, but the Ancient Greeks were equally influential. They founded Marseille in 600 BC, where a descendant of their loaded fish soup, *kakavia*, became known as bouillabaisse.

All of the fish soups and stews that pop up in ports and coves of the Med rely on locally caught seafood to give them their uniqueness. In the case of bouillabaisse, this was unpopular bycatch such as bony *rascasse* (scorpion fish), conger eel and sea robin. From its origins as an unpretentious fish stew of the poor, the dish was gentrified in the nineteenth century by chefs in Marseille's grand hotel dining rooms, with the addition of saffron and an orange *rouille*. It is this saffron that is often blamed for the supposed soporific effects of a bouillabaisse lunch, but the dish's association with a post-prandial snooze dates back much further.

Kakavia, the precursor to bouillabaisse, played a key role in Ancient Greek mythology. Aphrodite, the Greek goddess of beauty, fed a bowl of it to her husband, Hephaestus, to put him to sleep so she could sneak off to see her lover, Ares (who was also Hephaestus's brother. Scandalous!). Sweet, ugly Hephaestus had the last laugh when he trapped the lovers in bed together, much to the amusement of the other gods. *MAFS* has nothing on Olympus!

The decision to use mussels as the protein in this dish is my attempt to give bouillabaisse a local spin. Even older than that Greek myth is the fact that Australian First Nations people have been eating local mussels for tens of thousands of years (see p. 30). Scorch marks on the shells show that these mussels were also cooked. If a fish stew like bouillabaisse had been invented here, I can imagine that mussels and their stock might have taken the role of the *rascasse*.

Mussels are vastly underrated and underutilised in Oz. I hope by pairing them with the theory of a bouillabaisse and its essential accompaniment *rouille* – even a quick, easy fake version like the one here – they can become more than just a cheap dinner. Also, the idea of colliding *moules* (the French for mussels) with bouillabaisse was inevitable – 'moules-abaisse' is crying out to be created!

2 tablespoons olive oil
1 brown onion, finely chopped
1 baby fennel bulb, trimmed and finely
   chopped, fronds reserved
3 garlic cloves, crushed
3 bay leaves
½ teaspoon chilli flakes (plus extra if you like
   it hot)
½ cup (125 ml) white wine
400 g can crushed Italian tomatoes
2 cups (500 ml) chicken or fish stock
1 kg mussels, scrubbed and debearded
freshly ground black pepper
finely chopped flat-leaf parsley, to serve
crusty bread, to serve

Fake rouille

¼ cup (60 ml) boiling water
½ teaspoon saffron threads
2 slices stale white bread, crusts removed
2 garlic cloves, crushed
1 tablespoon olive oil
sea salt
2 tablespoons mascarpone

Start by making the fake rouille. Place the boiling water in a large heatproof bowl. Sprinkle over the saffron and set aside for 5 minutes to infuse. Tear the bread into smaller pieces and add to the saffron water. Stir the bread to combine. Set aside for 30 minutes to soak and cool completely.

Place the bread mixture in a small food processor. Add the garlic and process until smooth. With the processor running, gradually add the oil in a thin steady stream until well combined and a thick sauce forms. Season with salt. Add the mascarpone and pulse until just combined (but don't over-process, or it will split).

Heat the oil in a large saucepan over medium heat. Add the onion and fennel and cook, stirring, for 5 minutes or until soft. Add the garlic, bay leaves and chilli. Stir for 30 seconds or until aromatic.

Increase the heat to medium–high. Add the wine and bring to the boil. Simmer rapidly for 3–5 minutes or until the wine reduces by two-thirds.

Add the tomatoes and stock. Cover and bring to the boil. Simmer over medium–low heat, partially covered, for 15 minutes, until the sauce reduces slightly.

Add the mussels to the tomato mixture and stir to combine. Cover and simmer gently for 3–5 minutes, until the mussels have opened. Discard any mussels that haven't opened after this time. Season with pepper.

Divide the mussels among serving bowls. Top with a dollop of fake rouille and sprinkle with the fennel fronds. Serve with the crusty bread.

Ceviche? Sebiche? Kokoda? Tiradito? Kinilaw?

SERVES 6 **PREP** 20 minutes (plus 4 hours chilling)

Myth
The Spanish in Peru invented ceviche after taking power in the sixteenth century.

My Truth
On the surface, the story of *sebiche* – which is what the Peruvian government would prefer you call their national dish, rather than ceviche – is a simple one. The Spanish arrived in Peru with onions, oranges and lemons in the sixteenth century, and promptly started curing raw fish. The idea came from Andalusian cooks and settlers who followed the conquistadors and colonists to new Spain. It is argued that the word *sebiche* or ceviche even comes from the Andalusian Arabic word for 'pickled food'.

By 1820, Peruvian soldiers were singing about '*sebiche*' in their marching songs, and Juana M. Gorriti's 1890 Peruvian cookbook *Cocina Eclectica* ('Eclectic Cookbook') mentions leaving fish to pickle in orange juice for *sebiche*. At the same time, Peruvian writer Carlos Prince wrote of enjoying *sebiche* made with orange juice, chilli and salt. He was also particular about that spelling – as are the experts at the Peruvian Academy of Language. You see, *siwichi* is the indigenous Quechua word for 'fresh fish', and the idea of curing fresh raw fish in an acidic or salty liquid was hardly new in Peru, whatever the Spanish colonisers might have claimed.

Pre-Incan archaeological sites in Peru's north-west show that people were eating raw fish cured with passionfruit more than seven hundred years before the Spanish arrived, and there is further proof that the Inca ate fish cured in their corn beer, *chicha*. (Remember that soldiers' marching song that mentions *sebiche*? Its title is 'La Chicha'.)

In fact, if you cast your eye around the Pacific you'll see raw fish dishes popping up everywhere. The Fijians have *kokoda*, there's *ika mata* in the Cook Islands, and Polynesian islands like Samoa and Tonga have *'ota 'ika*. And, while much has been made of ceviche spreading through the Spanish colonies, we know that in the Philippines, they were already making *kinilaw* – their version of a *sebiche*-style dish – long before the Spanish arrived there. Its status as a pre-existing dish is mentioned in a 1613 Spanish–Tagalog dictionary.

While vinegar is the most commonly used souring agent for *kinilaw* these days, star fruit (or carambola), the sour fruit of the *jocote* trees and the juice of *tabon-tabon* were all traditionally employed in *kinilaw* before the Spanish brought vinegars.

The use of star fruit, or *balimbing*, as it is known in Tagalog, also raises an interesting question. Star fruit was brought to the Philippines by Austronesian traders and travellers. It was also Austronesians (people from the islands of the central and south Pacific) who were the first to push to settle Fiji three thousand years ago. Did they take *kinilaw* with them; or did *kokoda* arise from some deep cultural memory? Or did Fijians, like so many others around the Pacific, simply think this was a great idea for preparing fish?

But here's my real challenge. I'm not sure what this dish is. Is it a *kokoda*? Or does the late addition of coconut cream make it more of a Peruvian *tiradito* – a product of the Nikkei kitchen, from when Japanese migrants arrived in Lima from 1899 onwards and reinterpreted *sebiche* with a sashimi cut of fish, dressed with the curing liquid only just before serving? But the fish here is cubed and cured, which is not the way with *tiradito*. So, is it more a ceviche, employing as it does the citrus that the Spanish took to Peru?

I'm stumped. So, let's just call this dish 'Pacifically Fish', because those are the two things that bind all these many versions of cured raw fish together – the vast Pacific Ocean and the freshest seafood that lives therein.

600 g snapper or blue-eye trevalla, cut into
   1.5 cm cubes
3 long red or green chillies, deseeded and
   finely chopped
½ cup (125 ml) lime juice (see Tip opposite)
250 g cherry tomatoes, halved
1 small red onion, finely chopped
1 small green capsicum (pepper), deseeded
   and finely chopped (we used a thinly
   sliced mini capsicum too, for colour)
1 Lebanese cucumber, deseeded and finely
   chopped
270 ml can coconut cream, chilled and well
   shaken
coriander sprigs, to sprinkle

Place the fish and chilli in a glass or ceramic bowl and add the lime juice. Stir until well combined. Cover with plastic wrap and place in the fridge, stirring every hour for 4 hours or until the fish is opaque in colour – this shows it has been 'cooked' by the acid in the juice. (Feel free to cure for less time if you like your fish that way.) The resulting liquid that the fish is paddling in is the magical liquor known as *leche de tigre*, or tiger's milk. It's great on its own as a shot, so if there is too much to plate up, don't throw it away whatever you do!

Add the tomato, onion, capsicum and cucumber to the fish mixture. Stir until well combined. Drizzle with the coconut cream and sprinkle with the coriander sprigs to serve.

YOU'LL NEED ABOUT 8-10 LIMES, SO MAKE THIS WHEN THEY AREN'T $2 EACH!

Chilli crab

SERVES 4 **PREP** 20 minutes **COOK** 20 minutes

CLASSIC

Myth
Chilli crab is the number one reason to go to Singapore.

My Truth
This myth is pretty close to the truth. It's a sad comment on my food obsession that the next eleven reasons to visit the Merlion state are all food related too.

Chilli crab was invented by Singaporean home cook Cher Yam Tian, who added bottled chilli sauce and tomato sauce to her stir-fried crab. The crabs she cooked were caught by her husband, a police officer, on his nights off. Around 1950 she started selling her sweet chilli crab from a hawker cart near her home. She opened a corrugated-iron, hurricane-lamp-lit beach shack in 1956, and eventually a more substantial bricks-and-mortar outlet on Bedok Beach, called Palm Beach, by 1964.

In the early 1960s, chef Hooi Kok Wah refined the dish at the Dragon Phoenix restaurant, reducing the sweetness by doing away with the bottled sauces and adding lemon juice, chilli sambal and those beaten egg whites that divide Singaporean chilli-crab devotees. I have to admit that food editor Michelle blithely ignored my express instructions not to add the egg here, and I suspect she might have been right – it does add a lovely silkiness to the sauce when not overcooked. You can leave the egg out if you wish, but on no account should you lose the yellow soybean paste, which I think is the essential flavour core of this sauce.

Chilli crab is a dish that we in Australia really ought to make friends with, as we produce arguably the best mud crabs in the world, and they have been eaten on this continent for tens of thousands of years. When I went mud-crabbing in the Kimberley with some local Bardi crab fishers, I must confess to being distracted as we waded through the 'sheltered coastal areas influenced by freshwater run-off', worried that we might run into something much larger and toothier than a crab. Still, knowing that you might be dinner while searching for your dinner does realign one's usual arrogance about where one sits on the food chain.

While these days in Singapore you'll likely be served mantou (Chinese buns) with your chilli crab, the first time I ate it, down on Singapore's East Coast Parkway, it was served with slices of fluffy, white loaf-of-death bread. This paired perfectly with the sweet, bogan, bottle-based sauce slathered on the fat crab claws. I have chosen square white bread here as the convenient option for mopping up the chilli crab sauce – it's much easier than frying mantou, or even steaming them – but do as you wish!

2 mud crabs (ask your fishmonger to
   dispatch them for you)
2 tablespoons vegetable oil
⅓ cup (80 ml) tomato sauce (ketchup)
2 tablespoons chilli sauce
1 tablespoon caster sugar
1 cup (250 ml) fish stock
1 egg, lightly whisked
2 spring onions, thinly sliced
sliced cheap white bread, crusts removed,
   to serve

Chilli paste

6 red shallots, peeled and chopped
6 garlic cloves, chopped
4 long red chillies, deseeded and chopped
5 cm knob ginger, finely grated
2 teaspoons yellow soybean paste or miso
2 tablespoons vegetable oil
sea salt

To make the chilli paste, place the shallot, garlic, chilli, ginger and soybean paste or miso in a small food processor and blitz until finely chopped. With the motor running, slowly drizzle in the oil in a thin stream to form a smooth paste. Season with salt.

Prepare the crab. Lift up the flap under the crab's body with your thumb and remove. While holding the body firmly with the one hand, pull the top part of the shell off the body. Remove and discard the spongy, finger-like white gills on either side of the crab's body. Cut the body into quarters using a heavy knife or cleaver.

Heat the oil in a large wok or frying pan over high heat until just smoking. Add the chilli paste and cook for 5 minutes or until well cooked and aromatic. Add the tomato sauce, chilli sauce and sugar and cook for 2–3 minutes or until it thickens slightly. Add the stock and bring to the boil. Add the crab and toss to coat in the sauce. Cover and cook for 8–10 minutes or until the crab is cooked and changes colour to bright red. Remove from the heat.

Use tongs to transfer the crab to a large serving bowl. Quickly add the egg to the chilli mixture, whisking continuously so it doesn't scramble, and cook for 1 minute or until the sauce thickens slightly.

Pour the sauce over the crab. Sprinkle with the spring onion and serve with the white bread.

TIP

Add a good squeeze of lemon juice if you want to cut through the sweetness.

Gravlax

SERVES 10 **PREP** 20 minutes (plus 2 days curing)

Twist

Myth

Old fish always tastes disgusting.

My Truth

On the surface, yes, fresh fish is king. We are constantly told to eat fish on the day we buy it because 'it won't get any fresher', and that telltale ammonia smell of fish past its best is still one of the biggest no-noes in any restaurant. Yet recently, food luminaries the likes of Sydney's Josh Niland have been experimenting with the dry-ageing of fish in the manner that you might age a steak. So, what gives? History, that's what.

While the meat-free days of the early Christian church in Europe drove massive demand for fish, the appeal of curing a catch for transportation or preservation is far, far older. As long as humans have had kitchens, we've looked for ways to preserve fish, whether that's cans of tuna or those wood-hard sides of salt cod that have been brought back from Newfoundland by Basque fishermen since the 1500s. We've smoked kippers, pickled herrings, and dried white anchovies to make ikan bilis. That *bacalao* (the Basque word for salt cod) could even have been freeze-dried as well as salted, given the climate on Canada's east coast. Even the idea of fish-topped nigiri sushi came from a Burmese hill tribe technique of storing fish on fermenting rice in order to preserve it. And now, it seems that the counterintuitive idea of leaving fish to rot, or, rather, ferment, is perhaps one of the oldest preservation methods, predating salting and smoking.

The Chinese were curing fish with salt and soybeans around 500 BC. A little later, the Greeks started making *garos*, a sort of fish sauce. From these two pioneering ideas respectively came the fish sauces of South-East Asia and the *garum* of Ancient Rome. Try the umami-rich, Italian *colatura di alici* for a sense of how elegant this latter fermented tincture could be. The curing and fermenting of fish has a venerable past around Asia, with dishes like Korean *hongeo-hoe* (fermented skate) and Japanese *kusaya*. The *hongeo-hoe* is particularly notable because, when handled correctly, the skate flesh will cure itself without the addition of any salt.

The earliest known example of curing fish, however, is actually much older. It comes from the excavation of a Mesolithic settlement in Sweden, by those wonderful boat-rockers and history-rewriters at Lund University. (Researchers from the same university have found a chilli in an ancient medieval tomb dating back to a time well before any person in Europe should have seen one, let alone been buried with one.)

The archaeologists uncovered the remains of a 9000-year-old stash of buried fermented fish. The stash was so large that it confirmed that Swedish hunter–gatherers were coming together in settlements well before the establishment of agriculture, the usual driver. It also showed that the Scandinavian tradition of fermenting fish is one of the oldest preserving techniques in the world.

It is from this tradition that we get the buried, fermented and dried shark of Iceland called *hákarl*; those equally stinky fermented herring from Sweden called *surströmming*; and an unusual Greenland delicacy made by cramming duck-like auks, beaks, feathers and all, into a seal skin, closing it with seal fat and burying it weighted under rocks to ferment. This is called *kiviak*, should you be interested in ordering it next time you visit an Inuit restaurant (or avoiding it!).

Also from this tradition comes the Scandinavian delicacy of gravlax. During the Middle Ages, when salt became far easier and cheaper to come by, fishermen would pack salmon with salt, wrap them in sailcloth and bury them to keep them cool while they cured and fermented. The absence of fermentation thanks to a quicker curing time means that the eye-watering ammonia hit that comes with those other local delicacies is absent. Call me a wimp if you will, but I think this is a very good thing.

Making gravlax involves nothing tricker than freeing up some space in your fridge so it can cure in peace. The result from the recipe that follows is wonderfully firm and meaty; once you make it, you'll have a new staple for parties or for whenever someone asks you to 'bring an entree'.

Gravlax (CONTINUED)

1.5 kg skin-on salmon or ocean trout fillet,
    pin-boned
⅓ cup (80 ml) vodka
1 red onion, very thinly sliced (use a
    mandolin if you have one)
toasted rye bread or pumpernickel, to serve
baby capers, drained, to serve
lemon wedges, to serve

Dill and lemon salt

1 tablespoon black peppercorns
1 cup coarsely chopped dill
¾ cup (165 g) caster sugar
½ cup (150 g) rock or coarse cooking salt
1 tablespoon finely grated lemon zest

Dill topping

1 cup finely chopped dill
⅓ cup finely chopped chives
1 tablespoon lemon juice

Horseradish cream

½ cup (120 g) crème fraîche (or to taste)
1 tablespoon finely grated horseradish (see
    Tips)
sea salt and freshly ground black pepper

1 really sharp knife and lots of patience

To make the dill and lemon salt, place the peppercorns in a mortar and use a pestle to coarsely crush. Transfer the pepper to a bowl. Add the dill, sugar, salt and lemon zest. Stir until well combined.

Scatter one-third of the salt mixture over the base of a large, shallow glass or ceramic container. (Make sure you choose a container that will fit your salmon sitting flat.) Place the salmon, skin-side down, on top of the salt mixture, then scatter over the remaining salt mixture. Drizzle with the vodka.

Wrap the dish with plastic wrap to seal. Place a small chopping board or tray directly on top of the salmon and place a few cans (like 400 g cans of beans or tomatoes) on top so the board is evenly weighted. Place in the fridge for 12 hours.

Remove the plastic wrap. Turn the fish over in the salt mixture, then re-cover with the plastic wrap. Replace the chopping board and weights, then place in the fridge for a further 12 hours. Repeat for a total of 48 hours, turning the salmon every 12 hours.

Now the time has flown past and it's time to plate your gravlax. First, make the dill topping by combining the ingredients together in a bowl. Then make the horseradish cream the same way. Easy. Season with salt and pepper.

Place the onion in a heatproof bowl. Cover with boiling water and set aside for 2 minutes to soften slightly. Drain and place in a serving bowl.

Remove the salmon from the dish and drain well. Discard the liquid. Scrape any salt mixture from the flesh and pat the fish dry with paper towel. Place on a serving board and spread the top with the dill topping. Starting at the tail end, using a long, sharp knife held at a 45-degree angle, cut paper-thin slices and detach from the skin.

Serve the gravlax with the horseradish cream, onion, rye bread or pumpernickel, capers and lemon wedges.

TIPS

If you can't find fresh horseradish, look for a jar of preserved horseradish – this will give you a far more fruity result, with a different heat, than creamed horseradish, which can be heavy with mustard. In terms of quantity of crème fraîche, let your tastebuds decide!

This gravlax can alternatively be served with boiled potatoes and a dill mustard sauce like the one they sell at IKEA. You can find my recipe for dill honey mustard sauce online – it's also really good with poached salmon or on smoked salmon sandwiches.

Veg

Falafel plate with hummus, yoghurt and pickled red cabbage

SERVES 4 **PREP** 20 minutes (plus 30 minutes chilling and pickling) **COOK** 25 minutes

Twist

Myth

Falafel were invented in Ancient Egypt as food for the pharaohs.

My Truth

While many have dated the origins of falafel back to the kitchens of the pharaohs (who ruled Egypt from approximately 3100–30 BC), evidence to support this theory is lacking.

Food features heavily in the stonework, carvings and court accounts from the Valley of the Kings. Tombs often featured amazingly intricate funeral models of fully staffed Ancient Egyptian kitchens, with staff performing every culinary skill a pharaoh might need in the afterlife. There are butchers, bakers, brewers and people cutting up fish, but there is no one rolling falafel among models displayed at The Museum of Egyptian Antiquities in Cairo, the British Museum or the Ashmolean in Oxford.

Another challenge to the 'falafel for pharaohs' theory is that deep-frying was not common in Ancient Egypt because oil was so expensive. This one is easily debunked, though, as there is proof the residents of Canaan and Ancient Greece were snacking on sweet fried pastries around that time, and the pharaohs themselves weren't exactly short of a bob or two.

A different oft-cited claim is that Coptic Christians made falafel as a fast-day food in the city of Alexandria as early as the fourth century, but again, evidence to support this is scant. Not to say that these falafel-like Egyptian *ta'amiya*, made with soaked fava beans ground together with leeks, parsley, green coriander and seeds of cumin and coriander, did not exist as a common and therefore unremarked-upon street food. The land around Alexandria did grow lots of fresh fava beans (or broad beans, as they're also called in Australia), and there is evidence from archaeological sites that humans have been cultivating and eating fava beans as far back as 8000 BC.

The word falafel is commonly said to come from the Arabic root word for peppercorns, which translates as 'little balls'. The first mentions in print of the falafel in Egypt don't actually appear until the late nineteenth century, which seems strange given how much Ancient Arab poets and writers love writing about food. If falafel are so ancient, wouldn't these crunchy balls have been worthy of a stanza or two before then?

So that's that for the potentially bogus claims. Where it gets interesting, and a little weird, is that there is evidence the Jewish communities in Kerala and Calcutta in India were making little fried split pea cakes called *filowri* back in the nineteenth century.

In 1882, a few years before those first written mentions of falafel, Egypt was taken over by the British army following the bombardment of Alexandria, to quell an anti-government uprising. As a result of this military activity, the port city was flooded with British army officers who were fresh from serving in India. There's a suggestion that they might have brought with them a hunger for Indian snacks like *filowri* and Indian fried chickpea or lentil snacks like *vada*, *bhalla* or Southern *medu vada* and *paruppu vadai* (some of which are said to date back to the sixth century) to enjoy with their pink gins.

It makes me wonder, could enterprising local cooks – perhaps even with those Egyptian *ta'amiya* in mind – have taken local fava beans to make versions of these Indian snacks? And could the name 'falafel' actually come from the collision of the Arabic word for fava beans, *ful*, and a shortening of those Keralan fried treats to give us *filow-ful*? This would have sounded reassuringly like the Aramaic word for 'little round things', which is *fiffal*. (I can't believe I'm even suggesting the roots of the falafel might actually be Indian! That's heresy, surely.)

From Alexandria, the falafel spread across the Middle East, with falafel stands popping up in Beirut in the 1930s and Palestine in the 1940s. It seems that it is during this migration that the chickpea, which was more popular in this part of the world, replaced or overshadowed the fava bean in the modern falafel.

The crunchiness of good falafel needs some creaminess from a tahini sauce, yoghurt sauce or hummus. I like serving falafel on a slick of warmed hummus – 30 seconds in the microwave should do it, then stir – with pickles and warm flatbread on the side. A chilli sauce or a Syrian *mhammara* (which is a puree of roast red capsicums, walnuts, cumin, oil and breadcrumbs) are other great additions.

Falafel plate *(CONTINUED)*

1 cup (120 g) frozen green peas

400 g can chickpeas, rinsed, drained and spread out on paper towel

½ small white onion, coarsely chopped

⅓ cup flat-leaf parsley leaves

⅓ cup coriander leaves, plus extra sprigs to serve

4 garlic cloves, crushed

⅓ cup (45 g) besan flour (see Tip)

3 teaspoons ground cumin

2 teaspoons ground coriander

¼ teaspoon bicarbonate of soda

1 teaspoon sea salt

1 tablespoon lemon juice

2 tablespoons sesame seeds

vegetable or canola oil, to deep-fry

flatbread, pan-fried slightly or microwaved to warm through, to serve

Greek style yoghurt, to serve

Pickled red cabbage

1 long red chilli, split lengthways, deseeded

2 tablespoons caster sugar

1 teaspoon fennel seeds

½ cup (125 ml) apple cider vinegar

¼ (about 250 g) red cabbage, core removed, finely shredded (on a mandolin if you have one)

1 teaspoon sea salt

Hummus

400 g can chickpeas, rinsed and drained

4 garlic cloves, crushed

2 tablespoons tahini

2 teaspoons ground cumin

2 tablespoons lemon juice (and maybe more to taste)

2 ice cubes

½ cup (125 ml) olive oil

sea salt

Start by pickling the red cabbage. Place the chilli, sugar, fennel seeds and vinegar in a small saucepan. Stir over low heat until the sugar dissolves. Increase the heat to medium–low and bring to a simmer, then cook for 5 minutes or until the liquid reduces slightly. Set aside to cool completely.

Place the cabbage in a glass or ceramic bowl. Pour the cooled vinegar mixture over and add salt. Cover with plastic wrap or a beeswax wrap and give the ingredients a toss. Set aside, tossing occasionally, for 30 minutes to pickle.

Now onto the falafel, my friend. Place the peas in a heatproof bowl. Cover with boiling water and set aside for 5 minutes or until tender. Drain well, then spread out on a plate lined with paper towel to remove any excess water. Remember the falafel mantra, 'moisture is the enemy of a crispy crust'.

Place the peas, chickpeas, onion, parsley, coriander leaves, garlic, besan flour, cumin, coriander, bicarbonate of soda, salt and lemon juice in a food processor. Use the pulse button in short bursts to process until the mixture is well combined and finely chopped but not pureed. Add more besan if the falafel mix is too wet. It needs to be firm enough to scoop and hold its shape. Transfer to a large bowl and stir in the sesame seeds.

Line a tray with baking paper. Mould slightly heaped tablespoons of the chickpea mixture into torpedo-shaped balls. You can hone your 'quenelling' skills for this! Arrange on the lined tray and refrigerate for 30 minutes to firm up a little again, which will prevent them from falling apart when deep-frying.

While things are chilling and pickling, make your hummus. Place the chickpeas in a clean tea towel and rub gently for a few minutes, until you see the outer skins coming off. Place the chickpeas in a deep bowl of cold water. Agitate the water with your hand and watch as the loosened skins float to the surface. Scoop out the floating skins and discard them (unless you want to dehydrate them and make a chickpea salt, you waste warrior, you). Repeat until most of the chickpeas are skin-free.

Place the chickpeas, garlic, tahini, cumin and lemon juice in a food processor with the ice cubes. Blitz, scraping down the side occasionally, until smooth. With the motor running, gradually add the oil and blitz until creamy. Season to taste with salt, and more lemon juice if you like.

Half fill a medium–large saucepan with oil. Heat over medium–high heat until the oil reaches 180°C on a cook's thermometer (or a bread cube turns brown in about 15 seconds after being added). Deep-fry the falafel four at a time, turning occasionally, for 2–3 minutes or until golden brown. Transfer to a tray lined with paper towel to drain.

Serve the falafel with the flatbread, hummus, yoghurt, pickled cabbage and extra coriander sprigs.

Besan flour is chickpea flour. It is available from health food stores or Indian grocers if not in your local supermarket.

FALAFEL VARIATIONS

The breakfast falafel

Falafel make a wonderful breakfast with some hummus and maybe some dukkah-rolled soft-boiled or poached eggs, and your favourite chilli sauce to help open the eyes. Remember dukkah? That's the sesame seed, nut and cumin seed rubble that was almost as big in the late 1990s as the Waugh brothers.

The rebel beetroot falafel

Blitz 400 g raw peeled beetroots with a well-drained can of lentils (remember, moisture is the enemy of that much-prized crispy falafel crust!). Fold in finely chopped spring onions, garlic, mint, a little nutritional yeast, lemon juice, cumin seeds and about 40 g of spelt flour to bind. Shape into 26 balls, chill and then deep-fry in batches at 180°C for a few minutes. Serve with an apple slaw and a whipped yoghurt and feta dressing. Distinctly untraditional!

The pumpkin falafel

Your humble pumpkin doesn't know it's a one-stop falafel shop, but blitz 200 g of roast pumpkin with 100 g of roast pepitas (pumpkin seeds) and you'll just need to add some cooked quinoa and a tablespoon or two of cornflour as required to bind them. I'd include some finely chopped onions, garlic, ground coriander and chopped coriander stems for colour and flavour while blitzing. Shape, fully chill and then fry. Serve with the green tahini sauce opposite.

The parsnip and date falafel

Cooked parsnips (300 g) and dates (150 g) add sweetness to these one-can chickpea falafel, which have a little smoked paprika and cumin, a cup of chopped parsley, sliced spring onions and the crunch of flaked almonds folded in to spark them up. Bind them with 50 g besan and 30 g almond flour. To turn these into a midweek meal, serve them tossed through a salad of warm grilled zucchini (courgette), shredded parsley, mint and toasted sunflower seeds with a lemony tzatziki dressing.

SAUCE VARIATIONS

Greek yoghurt sauce

Instead of hummus, try serving your falafel with a little bowl of Greek yoghurt mixed with an 8 to 1 ratio of good tahini (or to taste). I dress that with a couple of tablespoons of brown butter, made with a sprinkling of milk powder, as this seems to make the yoghurt into something altogether more delicious.

Green tahini sauce

Another ripper is a green tahini sauce made with 2 parts coriander, 2 parts parsley and 1 part mint, blitzed together with olive oil and tahini. Add salt, pepper, cumin and lemon juice to taste. Keep the mix cool while processing by adding a couple of ice cubes while the blades are whirring.

White tahini sauce

Combine tahini, lots of lemon juice, olive oil and ground coriander seed. Blitz together and season to taste.

Zhoug

As a spicy addition to falafel served on pita with hummus or the yoghurt sauce, try a good hit of Yemeni *zhoug* – a chilli sauce made by grinding, pounding or blitzing deseeded red or green chillies with garlic, olive oil, salt and a little cardamom. Flavour this with either a bunch of coriander, or black cumin seeds and caraway seeds. I think the all-green version looks prettiest, but you can substitute some, or all, of the coriander with parsley or baby spinach if you prefer.

Red hummus

Mix some tomato ketchup and a squeeze of lemon juice into store-bought hummus for a tangy upgrade.

The other red hummus

Mix 1 tablespoon of tomato paste and 1 teaspoon of harissa into your hummus with salt and a little lemon juice.

Chilli pumpkin hummus

Mix 1½ cups of roast pumpkin with 1 tablespoon of crispy Chinese chilli oil and 2 tablespoons of cream cheese until smooth. Add more cream cheese and crispy chilli to taste. Season with salt and lemon or orange juice.

Bogan nachos

SERVES 4–6 **PREP** 30 minutes **COOK** 1 hour

Myth
'Nacho' is Mexican slang for 'good'.

My Truth
People seem to accept most of my guilty secrets – whether it's a penchant for Cheetos or topping ice cream with a sauce made from melted Mars Bars – but somehow my love for nachos always draws dead eyes and dirty looks. Screw 'em, I think nachos are a great snack, especially when made the way they were first whipped up in 1943 by Ignacio Anaya García, the maître d' of Club Victoria in Piedras Negras, Mexico.

With no one in the kitchen and a table full of hungry military wives from the US army air corps training base at Eagle Pass, just over the border in Texas, he had to improvise. He lard-fried tortillas into *totopos* (chips), covered them with grated cheese (probably Colby or Monterey Jack) and popped the plates under the salamander grill. After the cheese had begun to bubble he topped each with jalapeño and proudly carried them out. So simple, so perfect, so good – so no wonder Club Victoria regular Mamie Finan, who was leading the group of Texas wives, decided they should be called '*Nachos Especiales*' or the 'Nacho Special' ('Nacho' being a shortened form of Ignacio).

Sadly, Ignacio died in 1975, before the fame of his nachos had spread too far from the coal-mining border town where they were invented. It was two things, and two men, that would take nachos to US-wide adoration. In 1976, Frank Liberto decided to sell trays of nachos from a refreshments stand at Texas Rangers baseball games. His crucial innovation was finding a way to keep melted cheese warm without splitting, so it could be pumped over hot corn chips to order. Two years later, Liberto got his nachos stands into the Dallas Cowboys' stadium, and the dish found true national fame when TV commentator Howard Cosell tried some at a Monday Night Football game in 1978. He raved about them on air and started using the word 'nacho' during broadcasts as slang for 'good'.

There have been many attempts at fancifying the dish over the years, but here we want to celebrate nachos' working-class roots. It's basically melted cheese on chips, but with our improved version of a jar salsa, and with a cool dollop of avocado hiding some savage jalapeño heat – the bogan nachos we know and love with just a little polish.

1 bunch coriander, well washed, leaves picked and coarsely chopped, stems finely chopped
1½ cups (180 g) coarsely grated cheddar (or tasty cheese)
1½ cups (150 g) coarsely grated mozzarella
500 g corn chips
1 red onion, finely chopped
sour cream, to serve

Roasted tomato salsa
6 ripe roma tomatoes, halved
1 red onion, cut into thin wedges
2 green jalapeño chillies, halved lengthways and deseeded
1 tablespoon olive oil
sea salt and freshly ground black pepper
2 garlic cloves, crushed
1 tablespoon lime juice

Savage guacamole
2 ripe avocados, flesh coarsely chopped
2 green jalapeño chillies (or more, if this is too tame for your taste), deseeded, finely chopped
¼ white onion, coarsely grated
1 teaspoon lime juice

Preheat oven to 220°C (200°C fan-forced). Line a large baking dish with baking paper.

Start by making the salsa. Place the tomatoes, onion and jalapeño in the lined dish. Drizzle with the oil and season with salt and pepper. Roast for 40 minutes or until the tomatoes start to burn slightly on the edges. Set aside to cool completely, and reduce the oven to 180°C (160°C fan-forced).

To make the guacamole, place the avocado in a bowl. Use a fork to roughly mash, leaving it a little chunky. Add the jalapeño, onion, lime juice and 2 tablespoons of the chopped coriander leaves. Mix together and season with salt and pepper.

Time to finish the salsa. Place the roasted tomato, onion and jalapeño in a food processor. Process until well combined. Add the garlic, lime juice and 2 tablespoons of the remaining chopped coriander leaves. Process until nice and saucy. Season well.

Add the cheddar and mozzarella to a bowl with the coriander stems and combine.

Get out two baking trays (about 30 cm × 20 cm × 3 cm deep). Spread a quarter of the corn chips over the base of one of the trays. Sprinkle a quarter of the cheese mixture and a quarter of the onion over the chips. Continue with a second layer of corn chips, cheese mixture and onion. Bake for 10 minutes or until the cheese has melted and the chips are toasted. While the first batch cooks, make a second batch of nachos in the same way.

Remove the first batch from the oven and put the second batch in. Top the first batch with dollops of half of the salsa, guacamole, coriander leaves and sour cream. Eat, and repeat with the second batch when ready.

Sweet potato, lentil and ancient grain salad with grilled broccolini

SERVES 4–6 **PREP** 30 minutes (plus cooling) **COOK** 45 minutes

Myth

Ancient grain salads made with freekeh are ancient.

My Truth

The popularity of freekeh is very much a twenty-first century success story, but this grain has been harvested for more than four thousand years. My first contact with freekeh was reading about it in Jenni Muir's *A Cook's Guide to Grains* in 2002, where she tells the creation story of the residents of a walled city in northern Syria harvesting their wheat crop early to stop it falling into the hands of an advancing army. Stored inside the walls, the sheaves dried out and eventually spontaneously combusted. This burnt off the husks while the green wheat berries toasted slightly but, due to their moisture content, didn't burn. The besieged residents rubbed off the remnants of the husks – the name freekeh comes from the word 'to rub' – and a culinary delicacy was born.

The grain subsequently pops up in recipes from fourteenth century Baghdad as *farikiyya*, and it may well also get a biblical shout-out in Leviticus, which says, 'If you bring a grain offering of first fruits to the Lord, offer crushed heads of new grain roasted in the fire.'

Twenty years ago in Australia, freekeh was most frequently eaten by Jordanian and Armenian families in pilafs and stuffings, or used like burghul wheat, but seldom in salads. (Burghul, however, would pop up in salads like Middle Eastern tabouleh, Cypriot *tambuli* and Turkish *kisir*.) The Australian obsession with ancient grain salads began in 2007, when Andrew McConnell put his freekeh salad on the opening menu at Cumulus Inc. He'd been playing with it as a pilaf, but he enjoyed the cooked green wheat much more when he ate leftovers cold the next day, so he paired it with herbs, preserved lemon and labneh for a salad.

In 2009 at Hellenic Republic in Brunswick, George Calombaris reimagined his mother's Cypriot grain salad with freekeh. The dish, which he called an ancient grain salad, sold by the truckload and became one of the most downloaded recipes ever at *The Age*. It was loaded with coriander, parsley, lentils, pumpkin seeds, almonds, pine nuts, capers and currants.

Since then, McConnell and Calombaris's idea has spread to the US and the UK. Ironically, one place that seems immune to freekeh salad's charms is Cyprus, where recipes for freekeh salad remain a rarity in online search results compared to burghul salads.

¼ cup (80 g) redcurrant jelly
1 orange, zest finely grated, juiced
1 kg sweet potatoes, peeled and cut into
    2 cm cubes
1 large red onion, cut into thick wedges
2 tablespoons olive oil
sea salt and freshly ground black pepper
1 cup (180 g) freekeh (or pearl barley)
⅓ cup (55 g) pepita (pumpkin seed) and
    sunflower seed mix
1 bunch broccolini, halved lengthways
400 g can brown lentils, rinsed and drained
1 cup firmly packed flat-leaf parsley leaves,
    torn slightly
½ cup firmly packed mint leaves, torn slightly
100 g feta, crumbled

Orange and harissa dressing

⅓ cup (80 ml) orange juice (from orange
    above)
¼ cup (60 ml) extra virgin olive oil
2 tablespoons honey
1 teaspoon harissa paste

Preheat the oven to 220°C (200°C fan-forced). Line two large baking trays with baking paper and spray the paper with olive oil.

Combine the redcurrant jelly and 1 tablespoon of the orange juice in a bowl (keep the rest of the juice for the dressing). Add the sweet potato and toss until well coated. Use a slotted spoon to transfer the sweet potato to one of the trays. Add the onion to the remaining tray and drizzle with 1 tablespoon of oil. Season with salt and pepper. Roast for 45 minutes or until golden and tender. Cool to room temperature.

Meanwhile, place the freekeh and 3 cups (750 ml) water in a saucepan over medium–high heat. Bring to the boil, then reduce the heat to low and simmer, covered, for 20 minutes or until tender. Drain and set aside to cool.

While your salad bits cool, place the seed mix in a non-stick frying pan over medium–high heat. Cook, tossing occasionally, for 5 minutes or until lightly toasted. Watch them – they're easy to burn. Transfer to a large bowl.

Heat the remaining oil in the pan and add the sliced broccolini. Cook, tossing, for 3 minutes or until bright green and tender crisp. Set aside on a plate.

To make the dressing, whisk all the ingredients together in a jug.

Add the freekeh, lentils, parsley, mint and orange zest to the bowl with the seed mixture. Add half the dressing and toss until well combined. Place in a shallow serving bowl. Top with the sweet potato, onion and broccolini. Sprinkle with the feta and drizzle with the remaining dressing.

Pumpkin soup

SERVES 4 **PREP** 20 minutes (plus cooling) **COOK** 1 hour 55 minutes

Myth
Pumpkin soup is always made with pumpkin.

My Truth
When European settlers landed on Plymouth Rock, it was the gift of local pumpkins from Native Americans that helped keep them alive, as this Pilgrim Fathers' verse from 1633 attests: '*For pottage and puddings and custards and pies/Our pumpkins and parsnips are common supplies/We have pumpkins at morning and pumpkins at noon/If it were not for pumpkins we should be undoon.*'

In all those encounters, however, no one talks about pumpkins being used for soup. Fried, dried, baked, roasted and stewed, yes, but never as the warming bowl of goodness we know and love today. It wasn't until the middle of the nineteenth century that recipes for pumpkin soup started to appear in recipe books across the US, including *The Encyclopaedia of Practical Cookery* (1891).

What is seen as the very first pumpkin soup is recorded as being served on 1 January 1804, when the Caribbean island of Haiti celebrated its independence from France – and an end to slavery – with a feast featuring '*soup joumou*'. Described as a hearty pumpkin soup with stewed beef, vegetables and spices, it was actually made with winter squash rather than those round orange Halloween pumpkins the Pilgrims knew. During the colonial years, soup was a luxury denied to enslaved Haitians, so what better dish to serve to celebrate their freedom? Even today, *soup joumou* remains a potent symbol of liberty in Haiti.

Here in Australia, it is also largely winter squashes like butternut, or pumpkins like the Queensland Blue, that feature in our pumpkin soups. The Blue was first grown in Queensland, after World War I, but the modern butternut wasn't developed until 1944, in the United States.

Butternut wasn't the first winter squash used for soup in Australia – *tromboncino* or *zucchetta* (a summer squash left to grow huge and three feet long into winter) and other heritage breeds have that honour. The flavour of the *tromboncino* has been described as like a watery butternut. These and other pumpkins (which were really winter squashes) rapidly established themselves as the favourite veg of the new colony. Australian writer Alexander Harris recalled in 1830 that these 'pumpkins' were the major garden veg of homes along the Hawkesbury river. Ludwig Leichhardt even described them as 'the potato of the colony' in a letter to his brother back in potato-obsessed Prussia in 1844.

The first Australian recipe for soup I can find comes from Philip E. Muskett's *The Art of Living in Australia* (1893), where 'pumpkin' is cubed, fried in butter, then boiled, sieved and mixed with milk. It is finished with a squeeze of lemon juice, which is an excellent idea.

Pumpkin soup (CONTINUED)

1.5 kg butternut pumpkin (squash), deseeded, cut into 2.5 cm slices crossways
2 tablespoons olive oil
sea salt and freshly ground black pepper
1 large red onion, coarsely chopped
4 garlic cloves, crushed
1 tablespoon ground cumin
2 teaspoons coriander seeds
1.5 litres (6 cups) vegetable stock
1 teaspoon lemon juice
thickened cream, to serve
2 tablespoons each pepitas (pumpkin seeds), sunflower seeds and pistachios, toasted

Preheat the oven to 200°C (180°C fan-forced). Line a large baking tray with baking paper.

Place the pumpkin on the lined tray and drizzle with 1 tablespoon of the oil. Season with salt and pepper. Roast for 1 hour or until tender but slightly burnt around the edges. Set aside until cool enough to handle, then peel the pumpkin skin away from the flesh. Discard the skin (or, toss it with butter and parmesan and serve with buttered spaghetti for lunch).

Heat the remaining oil in a large saucepan or stockpot over medium heat. Add the onion and cook, stirring, for 5 minutes or until soft. Add the garlic, cumin and coriander seeds and cook, stirring, for 30 seconds or until aromatic. Add the stock and pumpkin flesh. Place over medium–high heat and bring to the boil. Reduce the heat to medium and simmer, uncovered, for 20 minutes or until the soup thickens. Stir in the lemon juice.

Use a stick blender to blend the pumpkin mixture until smooth (there will be a few flecks of coriander seed). Season with pepper. Ladle into serving bowls. Top with a drizzle of cream and sprinkle with the nuts and seeds.

VARIATIONS

Pumpkin soup is Aussies' favourite winter soup, judging by the hits on taste.com.au, and we are the proven experts at customising this simplest of dishes.

I particularly love roast pumpkin soup made with the addition of a couple of roasted Granny Smith apples for freshness and bite. Around the cafes and restaurants of this wide brown land I've seen it flavoured deliciously with everything from Thai spices, nutmeg, sage or ginger, to dukkah, chorizo or bacon.

Pumpkin soup also loves a little creaminess, whether it comes from coconut milk, yoghurt, cream, crème fraîche, tofu (!) or a touch of brown butter.

That's the great joy about pumpkin soup: it's just so versatile. At home I like it with maple syrup for extra sweetness, toasted pumpkin seeds for crunch, and some vinegar, lemon zest or even plums for sourness.

When it comes to an added salty hit, pumpkin marries perfectly with something porky, so rather than just some crispy bacon as a garnish, try using the broth and meat from a smoked ham hock as the base for a properly meaty pumpkin soup.

Mushroom vol-au-vent

SERVES 4 **PREP** 30 minutes (plus 20 minutes chilling) **COOK** 25 minutes

Twist

Myth

It was the most potent symbol of 1970s entertaining, but it fell out of favour along with loon pants and burnt-orange kitchen cabinets.

My Truth

Of course, the vol-au-vent has an illustrious history that extends much further than the 1970s. Recipes for puff pastry appeared from the sixteenth century onwards, in *The Good Huswifes Jewell* by Thomas Dawson (1596), Domingo Hernández de Maceras's Spanish cookbook *Libro del arte de cozina* ('Book of the Art of Cooking', 1607) and in Gervase Markham's *The English Huswife* (1660). It seems obvious that, in an age so in love with this delicacy, making a puff pastry case so light that it could be blown away by the wind – hence the name *vol au vent*, which means 'windblown' in French – was inevitable.

The first recipe for a vol-au-vent – as a large, single-serve dish – appears in 1739, in François Marin's *Les dons de Comus*. It was the excesses of the years at the end of the French aristocracy that saw the vol-au-vent become tiny.

The story goes that Madame de Pompadour, Louis XV's influential mistress from 1745 to 1764, recruited celebrity chef Vincent La Chapelle to bake dainty puff-pastry bites filled with jam to sweeten her time in the sack with the king. These crispy balls were called 'wells of love'.

Not to be outdone, Louis XV's wife, Marie Leczinska, asked pâtissier Nicolas Stohrer (who had previously created the rhum baba for Marie's father, the exiled King of Poland) to dedicate a bite-sized savoury treat to her. Thus the *bouchées à la reine* ('bites of the queen') were born, the direct ancestor of the vol-au-vent as we know it. Rather than a competition for the sexual attentions of the king, it seems more likely that this pastry rivalry was about status – the Queen was largely dismissed by the court, while Madame de Pompadour was everybody's darling.

These delicious bites started people thinking small, and by the end of the eighteenth century it had become quite the trendy thing to serve pre-dinner drinks with canapés. This name comes from the Old French for 'sofa', as spicy or salty toppings were served reclining on tiles or sofas of toasted or stale bread, or puff pastry. Both Marie's and Madame de Pompadour's dishes survived the French Revolution, spreading around the world with fleeing aristocrats and their cooks.

Marie-Antoine Carême championed and popularised bite-sized *bouchées à la reine* and vol-au-vents as chic canapés in the nineteenth century. By 1901, the vol-au-vent was so established as a classic dish that it was served at an official dinner to celebrate Australian Federation at Sydney Town Hall. In 1903, it was described by Auguste Escoffier as the 'queen of hors d'oeuvres' in his *Le guide culinaire*.

Now, the vol-au-vent is back, gaining traction with a cameo in *The Great British Bake Off*, support from the likes of three-star Parisian chefs Alain Passard and Alain Ducasse, and appearing on cool menus across Australia. So get ready to puff, as we take the vol-au-vent back to its original large size.

Mushroom vol-au-vent (CONTINUED)

6 sheets frozen butter puff pastry, just thawed (see Tip)

2 egg yolks, beaten

Filling

1 tablespoon olive oil

80 g butter

4 small thyme sprigs, plus extra thyme leaves to serve

200 g button mushrooms, thinly sliced

200 g Swiss brown mushrooms, thinly sliced

1 small leek, white part only, thinly sliced

2 garlic cloves, crushed

1½ tablespoons plain flour

¼ cup (60 ml) white wine

¾ cup (185 ml) vegetable stock

2 tablespoons pouring cream

1 teaspoon dijon mustard

sea salt and freshly ground black pepper

½ cup (60 g) coarsely grated Gruyere

TIP

To get max rise in the puff pastry, use a thicker piece of store-bought puff. We used two packets of Carême brand pastry.

Line two large baking trays with baking paper. Using a small plate or bowl as a guide, cut two 14 cm discs from each pastry sheet. That's 12 circles in total. Use an 8 cm cutter to remove the centre of 8 circles. Place the 4 whole discs on the baking trays and brush each very lightly with the egg yolk, making sure to go just short of the edge and not over it – doing so would prevent the pastry from rising evenly. Place a round with the centre cut out neatly on top of each and brush with the egg yolk. Top with the final rounds and brush again (so you should have 4 stacks with 3 discs on each stack). Repeat the process with the egg yolk and the 8 cm smaller circles so you have 4 lids of 2 layers each. Place in the fridge for 20 minutes to chill.

Preheat the oven to 200°C (180°C fan-forced). Bake the pastry cases and lids for 20 minutes or until risen and golden. Keep an eye on the lids, as they may bake more quickly than the cases. Set aside to cool slightly.

Meanwhile, make the filling. Heat half the oil and 20 g of the butter in a large frying pan over medium–high heat until foaming. Add 2 thyme sprigs and half the mushroom and cook, stirring occasionally, for 5 minutes or until soft and golden. Transfer to a bowl. Repeat with the remaining oil, another 20 g of butter, the remaining thyme sprigs and mushrooms. Transfer to a bowl and discard the thyme sprigs.

Melt the remaining butter in the pan and reduce the heat to medium. Add the leek and cook, stirring, for 3–4 minutes or until soft but not browned. Stir in the garlic and cook for 30 seconds. Add the flour and cook, stirring, for 1 minute or until bubbling. Remove from the heat.

Gradually add the wine, whisking constantly until smooth. Return to the heat. Add the stock a little at a time, stirring constantly, until evenly combined. Cook, stirring, for a further 2–3 minutes or until the sauce starts to thicken. Stir in the cream and mustard. Simmer for 2–3 minutes or until thickened. Season with salt and pepper.

Set aside about 12 of the best looking golden mushroom slices. Add the remaining mushroom to the sauce mixture. Stir in the Gruyere and cook for 1–2 minutes or until the cheese melts.

Spoon filling into vol-au-vent cases. Top with reserved mushrooms and sprinkle with extra thyme leaves. Serve with pastry lids on the side.

VARIATIONS

Bacon and mushroom filling
Cook 2 coarsely chopped rindless bacon rashers with the leek mixture.

Prawn and leek filling
Replace the mushrooms with 100 g of chopped green prawn meat and take out the thyme. Add a tablespoon of chopped dill and a little finely grated lemon zest to the sauce just before spooning into the cases.

Chicken and mushroom filling
Add 2 tablespoons of finely chopped cooked chicken to the filling when you add the cream and mustard, and heat through as the sauce thickens.

Potato salad

SERVES 6 **PREP** 20 minutes (plus 15 minutes cooling) **COOK** 40 minutes

Myth

Germans invented potato salad when they served cooked potatoes with a warm dressing of vinegar mixed with bacon and its rendered fat.

My Truth

It's certainly true that Germany was one of the earliest adopters of potatoes. While other countries worried about them being poisonous or causing leprosy, Frederick the Great, the frugal ruler of Prussia, saw potatoes as a fantastic, cheap way of keeping his people fed. He made potatoes part of his army's rations from 1744 onwards, and during a famine in 1774 he distributed potato plants to peasants and ordered them to be planted. From this visionary base, the potato became a central part of Germany's culinary life.

Frederick's vision was also important in bringing France around to the potato. French scientist and agronomist Antoine-Augustin Parmentier was a prisoner of war in Prussia during the Seven Years' War (1756–1763), and credited his survival to the potato diet he was fed. Subsequently, he not only championed the planting of potatoes in France but fed them to influential members of the court at Versailles and other dignitaries, such as Benjamin Franklin.

The American state of Virginia was already closely associated with potatoes. In the extensive botanical work of the sixteenth century, John Gerard's *The Herball, or Generall Historie of Plantes* (1597), the author talks of eating cooked '*batata virginiana*' tossed with red wine or roasted and then dressed in a vinaigrette. You might think this sounds rather like a potato salad – so is the dish truly English?

Quite probably, it seems! Even though Gerard is regarded as a bit of a shonk and his book was largely a translation of Flemish botanist Rembert Dodoens's seminal work *Cruydeboeck* ('Herb Book'), Gerard did add some of his own colourful commentary. For example, he's particularly keen on discussing the 'windie' properties of broad beans, as well as how he'd once seen the (mythical) barnacle tree.

As I can find no reference to *batatas*, *patatten*, *aardappels* or even potatoes in Dodoens's original Flemish text, or in Henry Lyte's earlier Elizabethan translation of his work, it looks like the potato was another of Gerard's inclusions. A woodcut illustration of a potato plant that was commissioned for Gerard's book appears to confirm this. Admittedly, Gerard stayed true to shonky form by classifying the potato as being native to North America – in spite of conquistadors having written extensively about it originating in the Andes – because that's where his potato plants had come from.

While the Germans stood by their warm potato salads, mayo-dressed potato salads were a later development. In 1891 *The Encyclopaedia of Practical Cookery* listed several potato salads, including one with a prototype mayonnaise dressing made by pounding anchovy fillets with hard-boiled eggs and 'salad oil'.

The potato salad here offers the best of all worlds. It is cold, but the dressing was taught to me by a German, and it also includes eggs.

4 large eggs, at room temperature
1.5 kg baby coliban (chat) potatoes
2 tablespoons olive oil
2 brown onions, thinly sliced into rings
3 whole star anise
sea salt and freshly ground black pepper
¾ cup (225 g) good-quality whole egg
    mayonnaise
¾ cup (210 g) Greek-style yoghurt
1 teaspoon caster sugar
4 spring onions, thinly sliced
100 g cornichons, finely chopped
¼ cup (50 g) drained capers
½ cup coarsely chopped dill

For perfectly jammy eggs, bring a saucepan of water to the boil, add the room-temperature eggs and cook for 6 minutes 45 seconds. Drain under cold water, then peel and cut in half. This timing works for large (59 g) eggs.

Place the potatoes in a large saucepan and cover with plenty of cold water. Bring to the boil over medium–high heat. Reduce the heat to medium and cook for 15 minutes or until just tender. Drain. Set aside for 15 minutes to cool. When cool enough to handle but still warm, peel the potatoes. Cut into quarters and transfer to a large bowl.

While the potatoes cool, heat the oil in a frying pan over medium–high heat. Add the onion and star anise, and season well with salt. The star anise will make the onion taste meatier – it's science, go figure. Cook for 20–25 minutes, but only stir very occasionally so the onion has time to catch on the bottom of the pan a little, to get crisp and golden brown. Remove the star anise and set the onion aside to cool.

Combine the mayonnaise, yoghurt and sugar in a large bowl. Season with salt and pepper. Add the spring onion, cornichon, capers and ⅓ cup of the dill and mix until well combined.

Add the yoghurt mixture to the potatoes and toss until well combined. Spoon half the potatoes into a serving bowl and top with half the egg. Layer again with the remaining potato and egg. Scatter with the fried onion and the remaining dill.

Ricotta gnocchi with creamy spinach sauce

SERVES 4 **PREP** 30 minutes **COOK** 20 minutes

Myth

Potato gnocchi is the greatest version of gnocchi because it came first.

My Truth

Whether the name comes from the Lombardy word for a knot in wood (*nocchio*) or the Latin for knucklebone (*nocca*), there is no doubt that gnocchi was nourishing the people for hundreds of years before the potato was commonly grown in Italy. My sense is that the origin of the word is the former, because there are just so many stories about gnocchi from the Lombardy region over the centuries.

To all intents and purposes, those early gnocchi were pasta by another name. Many versions were no more than flour and water, whether that be chestnut flour, plain wheat flour or semolina. Sardinian *gnocchetti Sardi*, golden with saffron, is an example of the last type, although the earliest recipe that sounds like gnocchi is in *De re coquinaria*, aka *Apicius*, from the first century. Here, a dough of flour and milk is boiled, fried and served with honey and black pepper. Yum!

No less luxurious was the *zanzarelli* eaten at the fifteenth-century court of the powerful Sforza family in Milan. These gnocchi were made with ground almonds, bread, milk and grated Granone Lodigiano cheese, and are part of the long connection between gnocchi and the Lombardy region of northern Italy.

We find a far more down-to-earth recipe for gnocchi in the first great Italian cookbook, *Opera dell'arte del cucinare* by Bartolomeo Scappi, published in 1570. Scappi had been chef to two popes, and among the approximately 1000 recipes in the book, his gnocchi is made with equal weights grated bread and flour, turned into a dough with the addition of olive oil, boiling water and saffron. This was then cooked and served with a sauce made from pounded walnuts, soaked breadcrumbs and garlic. He advises using a grater, but it's unclear whether this is to coarsely grate the dough (as one might do for *spätzle*) or use it to texture the surface of the gnocchi, as suggested by the king of Italian cuisine, Pellegrino Artusi, in his 1891 potato gnocchi recipe.

Gnocchi was so central to the Italian diet that in Verona during the famine of 1531, braziers and large cauldrons of gnocchi and cheese were set up by a local philanthropist to feed residents in the poorest suburb of San Zeno. This act is commemorated in Verona (and other cities in Italy's north) with the Gnoccolaro Friday festival and the crowning of a Gnocco King.

As common as pasta at the time, the simplicity of this hand-rolled gnocchi meant there were versions all over the Italian peninsula, using everything from flour and eggs to breadcrumbs and mashed winter squash, making pumpkin gnocchi effectively a precursor to the potato version. In Rome they cooked semolina flour into a porridge with eggs and Asiago and pecorino cheeses, and let it set like polenta. They then cut it into circles to be baked, a technique that is still used today, thus ensuring the Roman gnocchi also predates potato gnocchi. In Venice they did something similar with flour, eggs and milk, while the Tuscans made their gnocchi-like *gnudi* with ricotta, eggs, breadcrumbs and sheep's cheese. These lighter pillows undoubtedly inspired the seventeenth-century Lombardian gnocchi of ricotta and spinach that in turn inspires my recipe here. It's not hard to imagine their name, *malfatti*, as a snipe at Tuscany. (It means 'poorly made'.) Milan and Florence were great rivals.

The potato finally made its way to Italy in the late sixteenth century, but took time to establish itself. It was helped by chefs like Antonio Nebbia, who wanted to shake off French, Spanish and Austrian culinary influence in favour of a truly local Italian cuisine. In his *Il cuoco maceratese* ('The Chef from Macerata', 1779), Nebbia argued that this new cuisine should be built around three things – vegetables, pasta and gnocchi. What better way to do this than by embracing vegetables from the new world that had no connection with Italy's three colonial overlords, many of which (like tomatoes, potatoes and capsicums) had been largely overlooked by them?

The arrival of potato gnocchi comes a little later, from the north of the country. While I'm sure there are many cooks who could claim to have created the first potato gnocchi, one of the most delightful origin stories also comes from Lombardy.

Born and bred at Lake Como, Alessandro Volta was the genius who invented the battery. In 1801 he was summoned to Paris to present his invention to Napoleon Bonaparte. Here he met Antoine-Augustin Parmentier (the potato pioneer we met in the previous recipe). Napoleon had appointed Parmentier as the army's first pharmacist. Parmentier did what he did and cooked Volta a series of potato dishes for dinner, just as he had done previously for Benjamin Franklin and King Louis XV. This would have intrigued Volta greatly, because he was a huge fan of Franklin. It was reading Franklin's paper on 'flammable air' that drove him to discover the existence of methane. Following his return home to Lombardy, Volta substituted potato for the usual ricotta with his eggs and flour to make the first potato gnocchi. If anyone has access to Volta's papers confirming this story, I'd love to see a copy!

I've picked ricotta gnocchi as the recipe here because it is far quicker and easier to make than the potato version – and it came first. So there!

Ricotta gnocchi with creamy spinach sauce *(CONTINUED)*

60g butter
1 small brown onion, finely chopped
2 garlic cloves, crushed
125 g cream cheese, cut into cubes
½ cup (125 ml) thickened cream
250 g packet frozen spinach portions
1 teaspoon finely grated lemon zest
good pinch of ground nutmeg
sea salt and freshly ground black pepper
finely grated parmesan, to serve

Ricotta gnocchi

500 g fresh but firm ricotta, cut from the
    wheel at the deli
⅓ cup (50 g) plain flour, plus extra for dusting

Preheat the oven to 120°C (100°C fan-forced).

To make the gnocchi, line a tray with paper towel. Cut the ricotta into slices and place on the lined tray to drain. Place more paper towel on top of the slices and press down slightly to help draw out excess moisture. The more moisture you can remove, the less flour you will need to use and the lighter the gnocchi will be.

Crumble the dry ricotta into a large bowl and sprinkle with ¼ cup (40 g) of the flour. Use your fingers to gently mix the flour into the ricotta, carefully pulling it together as a dough. Use your fingertips to minimise the pressure, to ensure the gluten in the flour doesn't develop, as that will give you bullet-like gnocchi. If the mixture is wet, add the last bit of flour.

Flour your work surface. Split the dough into four even portions. Knead the dough very gently for just a minute until almost smooth, then shape each portion into a fat sausage about 3 cm thick. Don't overwork the dough, knead just enough so that it holds together well.

Bring a large saucepan of salted water to the boil. While the water heats up, melt half the butter in a large, deep frying pan over medium heat. Add the onion and garlic and cook, stirring, for 3–4 minutes or until soft. Add the cream cheese and cream and cook, stirring, for 2–3 minutes or until smooth. Add the spinach and cover the pan with a lid. Heat for a few minutes for the spinach to thaw (the liquid helps thin down your sauce), then stir to combine. Stir in the lemon zest and nutmeg. Cook, uncovered, stirring often, for 3 minutes or until heated through. Season with salt and pepper.

Place the remaining butter in an ovenproof dish and place in the oven to melt.

Tear off a sheet of baking paper around 30 cm long. Take one of the fat dough sausages and gently place it in the centre of the paper. Then, pick up the two edges of the paper and roll the dough, acting as if you are 'towelling dry' the sausage. This will help it lengthen and thin without direct pressure – another example of minimising the pressure and therefore the development of gluten. Yes, it really works! Repeat for each of the fat dough sausages.

Cut the lengthened dough sausage into 1 cm slices. Use the baking paper to gently lift the gnocchi into the boiling water. Cook for about 1½ minutes or until the gnocchi rises to the surface. Use a slotted spoon to transfer the gnocchi to the ovenproof dish, making sure you drain well and toss in the butter. Return to the oven to keep warm while you cook the remaining batches of gnocchi.

Reheat the spinach sauce over low heat and loosen with a tiny splash of water if it seems too thick. Spoon the sauce among serving plates and create a little well in the centre. Pile your gnocchi into the well, sprinkle with the parmesan and season with pepper.

A Neapolitan-style pizza - ALMOST

MAKES 4 pizzas **PREP** 20 minutes (plus 1 hour proving) **COOK** 50 minutes

Myth

Great pizza can be made in the home oven.

My Truth

Great pizza needs heat, and, regardless of the quality or selection of the toppings, without a proper woodfired or commercial oven that surpasses 400 *gradi* (i.e. 400°C), you won't get the blister and the puff that sets Neapolitan pizza apart – and for me (I say this after chasing down the famous *pizze* of Buenos Aires, Chicago, Rome, Spain and New York), the *pizze* of Naples are the best.

Some say that pizza is as old as the pyramids; that Ancient Greeks ate topped round flatbreads called *plankuntos* 2500 years ago; that Persian soldiers baked pizza-like bread topped with cheese and dates on their shields over the fire back in the sixth century BC; and that there's even what looks like an early pizzeria among the ruins of Pompeii (which probably served a sort of topped focaccia). But in my book it's not a pizza if the toppings are just put on already-cooked bread, or if it's not baked in a very, very hot oven.

It should also be noted that all these ancient ancestors of pizza were sans tomato, because tomatoes didn't arrive in Europe from Central America until about 500 years ago, making them 2000 years late by some counts. That is important, as to my mind the tomato sauce is as defining of a great pizza as the oven and the dough.

Now, there are mentions of 'pizza' before the Columbian exchange and the acceptance of the tomato in Europe, but the exact meaning of the word is obscure until the mid-sixteenth century when the Neapolitan poet Velardiniello talks of 'pizza the size of a carriage wheel'. This continued pizza's reputation as a street food from the poorer parts of town.

Spanish troops occupying Naples when Sicily and the south were under Spanish rule raved about the thin pizza 'folded like a book' at the seventeenth-century Taverna del Cerriglio, a dodgy dive near Naples' docks that was as famous for its food as for the roughness of its clientele. The great Renaissance painter Caravaggio was even beaten up here in 1609 by the local toughs (or *lazzaroni*)!

Even though tomatoes were found in the kitchens of Naples' Spanish ruling class by then – there are tomato recipes, including one for an 'extravagant Spanish sauce', in *Lo scalco alla moderna* ('The modern steward'), published in Naples in 1692, for example – a survey of produce for sale in Naples in 1727 found no tomatoes on offer at all, so we can be fairly sure the *'libretto'*, or little folded book pizza, those Spanish troops were eating was free of tomato.

The Spanish connection did seem to hasten the arrival of the tomato in Naples, however. *Il cuoco galante* ('The Gallant Cook', 1773), published fifty years later by Neapolitan Vincenzo Corrado, features no fewer than thirteen recipes featuring tomatoes, including a soup and a tomato-based sauce for lamb, implying that the tomato was now common fare.

With that, we can comfortably say that it was at the end of the eighteenth century that pizza became pizza as we know it, with a tomato sauce. The impact was dramatic: by 1807 there were 68 pizza shops in Naples; by 1861 there were 100, and the city was now world-famous for its pizza. Alexandre Dumas visited in 1835 and wrote that the poor of Naples lived on 'pizza in the winter and watermelon in the summer', while an English visitor reported in the London *Morning Post*, 'the pizza is a favourite Neapolitan delicacy, which is only made and eaten between sunset and two and three in the morning, and it must be baked in five minutes in the oven . . . and served up piping hot, otherwise it is not worth a grano'.

By 1889, the tomato sauce was central enough to Neapolitan pizza to play a role in the tale of a pizza-maker named Raffaele Esposito, who made a patriotic pizza topped with tomato, mozzarella and basil, mirroring the colours of *il Tricolore* – Italy's flag – for Margherita of Savoy, the Queen consort of King Umberto I of Italy. Her pleasure at enjoying this food of the city's poor meant her name would be forever attached to one of the world's most popular pizzas.

It's a romantic story, if somewhat fanciful. Far more interesting in my opinion is how Naples' classic marinara pizza was taken to New York with the wave of *lazzaroni* (the poorest Neapolitan citizens) who left Naples' dirty alleyways for a new life, and thus ensured that a 'marinara' sauce in the US is a tomato sauce, as it is in Italy, and not one with seafood, as it would be if you ordered a dish by that name in Australia or New Zealand. I also think it's telling of the importance of tomato sauce to Naples that a cheap tomato or red sauce came to be called a 'Napoli' outside Italy.

Over my visits to Naples I have grown to understand that while everyone talks about the dough, it is the tomato sauce that really makes a pizza special here. It seems brighter than anywhere else; somehow both sweeter and more acidic. At Pizzeria Mattozzi, which was slinging pizza to toffs and their coachmen heading home from palace balls 170 years ago, patriarch Lello Surace told me their secret was tomatoes grown in the volcanic soil of Vesuvius, which glowers across the bay from Naples. These are hung in string bags after harvesting so their flavour can intensify. We won't be doing that here! This recipe will, however, make you a good pizza even if you don't have a woodfired oven.

1⅓ cups (330 ml) lukewarm water
2 teaspoons (7 g sachet) dried yeast
½ teaspoon caster sugar
3 cups (450 g) bread and pizza flour, plus
    extra to dust
½ teaspoon sea salt
1 tablespoon olive oil, plus extra for greasing
2 × 200 g balls fresh mozzarella (see Tips)
polenta or semolina, to dust
basil leaves, to serve

Marinara sauce
¼ cup (60 ml) olive oil
3 large garlic cloves, sliced
400 g can diced Italian tomatoes
1 lemon, juiced
1 teaspoon brown sugar
1 teaspoon sea salt

Combine the water, yeast and sugar in a jug. Set aside for 5 minutes or until slightly frothy on top. Combine the flour and salt in a large bowl and make a well in the centre. Add the yeast mixture and oil. Mix with a wooden spoon until a dough starts to form, then use your hands to make a rough dough.

Turn the dough onto a lightly floured surface. Knead for 10 minutes, until smooth and elastic. Brush a bowl with oil. Place the dough in the bowl and turn to coat. Cover with a damp tea towel. Set aside in a warm place for 30 minutes or until the dough doubles in size.

Punch the air out of the dough with your fist. Divide into four equal portions and knead each portion briefly, then shape into balls. Place on a tray and cover loosely with plastic wrap. Set aside for another 30 minutes to rise.

Meanwhile, make the sauce. Heat the oil in a saucepan over medium–low heat. Add the garlic and cook, stirring, for 1 minute or until the edges of the garlic start to brown. (Don't overbrown the garlic, or it will add a bitter flavour to your sauce.) Use a slotted spoon to remove the garlic slices from the oil and discard. Add the tomatoes to the pan and increase the heat to medium. Simmer rapidly, stirring often, for 15 minutes or until the sauce thickens. Use a potato masher to crush any large lumps of tomato. Stir in the lemon juice, sugar and salt to taste. Keep going until the sauce is very in your face! It should be sour, sweet and salty, in that order. Set aside to cool slightly.

Place an oven shelf in the lowest position and another shelf two positions higher. Preheat the oven to 230°C (210°C fan-forced). If your oven can go hotter, turn it up as far as it can go! Alternatively – and better – use a good tabletop pizza oven or build a woodfired oven in your back garden. Pizza stones would help too (see Tips).

Cut the mozzarella into slices (about 1 cm thick) and lay out on paper towel to drain, patting the top of the mozzarella with another sheet of paper towel.

Sprinkle two baking trays with the polenta or semolina. Roll out a portion of dough on a lightly floured surface to about 27 cm round, leaving the edge slightly thicker than the centre. Ideally use your hands for this, pressing the dough outward so you don't remove all the air from the crust section. Carefully lift this base onto a tray. Repeat with another portion of the dough. Use the back of a spoon to spread about ⅓ cup (80 ml) of the pizza sauce over each pizza base, avoiding the edge. Top the bases with half the sliced mozzarella (put the remaining mozzarella in the fridge while you cook the first two pizzas).

Bake for 15 minutes or until the cheese has melted and the base is crisp. Top with the basil leaves to serve. Eat, and only then repeat to make two more pizzas.

TIPS

Use the milkiest and freshest mozzarella you can find – buffalo milk mozzarella is preferable, but fior di latte will do. Avoid mozzarella that's yellow, as this often congeals too quickly.

Pizza stones are kind of like tiles which retain a lot of heat and emulate the floor of a pizza oven, which ensures a crispy crust. If you get a pizza stone, make sure you follow the instructions that come with it on how to use it correctly.

MATT'S RULES FOR PERFECT PIZZA

During the space race, I think I could have saved NASA the millions of dollars they spent developing those handy meals in cubes or tubes that provided everything you need for living in one mouthful; for I believe in our midst is one food that already combines that life-sustaining mix of carbs, proteins and vitamin-loaded veg in one tasty package. Better yet, it only requires one hand to eat it. It's *pizza*!

Pizza has other magical qualities. First, it can accommodate sweet or savoury flavours. Second, it is suitable to be adapted to any number of cuisines, thanks to the flexibility and universality of the dough. (Please don't tell my mates in Napoli I said that, though!)

However, pizza is also one of those foods that degrades quickly after the cooking process, making it something that should always be eaten straight from the oven and never exposed to extended periods sitting on the dining room table or restaurant pass, or in the hot box on the back of the delivery moped. As the minutes pass, that stringy, melty cheese hardens into indigestible rubbery globs and that crisp base is slowly destroyed by the steam of the risen dough – especially if it's held inside a cardboard box – the very steam that gave the dough its delicious puffy lightness in the first place. So, with that in mind, here are my rules for perfect pizza.

1. The first rule for pizza is to serve it quickly. When eating pizza, whether at home or in a restaurant, think about staggering when they arrive at the table. This means you are always eating pizza in primo condition. Myriad other factors come into play when it comes to getting the best result – the dough, the choice of cheese, the toppings and cooking approach – but this is the golden rule that should never be broken.

2. The next rule is that the dough is king. Making fresh dough yourself is easy and will deliver a far lighter, crisper result than buying a ready-made base.

3. The third rule is that the perfect pizza, once sliced, should be crisp enough and not so laden with toppings that the middle should stay firm and not droop flaccidly when held by the crust edge. This is often a problem caused by too much moisture in the chosen toppings. We all love perky pizza! To help with this I've employed everything from a syringe, a turkey baster and paper towel to remove excess oil or rendered liquid from my toppings. However, while they are high in moisture, I don't suggest removing the seeds from your tomatoes, because they hold so much of the flavour.

4. The fourth rule is the sauce. San Marzano tomatoes deliver an intense tart but sweet sauce for a true Neapolitan pizza. Make your sauce as bright as possible!

5. The final secret to cooking pizza is heat: massive, cheese-browning, crust-puffing heat. Getting the cooking environment hot enough is very hard to achieve in a conventional oven, and at the very least you'll need a heat-retaining tile like a pizza stone to ensure something close to what you're looking for. Far better – assuming you can't afford the thousands of bucks to buy a woodfired oven for the backyard – is to save up for an electric pizza oven. These launched in Australia a decade or so ago priced at over $250, but now you can find them for about $80 on sale, and their fat electric elements deliver the high heat needed to perfectly puff dough and tan toppings. Because these usually fit only one pizza at a time, they also help with the golden rule number 1, because you can eat the first pizza fresh from the oven while the next one is cooking.

Zucca zucchini frittata

SERVES 4 **PREP** 20 minutes **COOK** 50 minutes

Myth

It is illegal for an Aussie cookbook to not include a recipe for frittata.

My Truth

Frittata – the name comes from the Latin for 'to fry' – is one of several famous open-faced omelettes from around the world, like Spain's potato tortilla and Japan's okonomiyaki. Frittata is the one that has found the most resonance here in Australia, however. I joked in my first cookbook that every Australian cookbook was required by law to include a recipe for frittata. I've followed this advice ever since, and yes, correspondingly, I've stayed out of jail. Now I'm too scared to test whether this is a myth or not.

Basically, a frittata is a thicker, usually un-flipped, omelette, and even though use of the word 'omelette' only pops up in 1611, they date right back to our prehistoric ancestors cooking pilfered eggs on hot rocks by an open fire.

The Ancient Romans made thin, plate-sized *lamella*, while in Persia they had the traditional dish of *kookoo*, in which beaten eggs and ham were combined and baked in a pan to form a cake that would be eaten in wedges. This, it seems, is the first frittata.

It seems likely that this inspired idea from the Arab world spread across the Mediterranean with the Muslim conquest of Spain, Sicily and Southern Italy in the eighth, ninth and tenth centuries, along with ingredients like eggplants, mint and sugar, and techniques like woodfired ovens and clay pot cookery, which had made their own way across from China in the preceding centuries.

And while I can't find the actual statute about frittata in the law library at Monash University, I still can't assure any aspiring cookbook authors out there that this is not a myth. Nor can I be sure that making a frittata with pumpkin added to the zucchini won't draw the ire of the court. Gee, it tastes good though.

1 kg butternut pumpkin (squash), peeled, deseeded and cut into roughly 2 cm pieces
2½ tablespoons olive oil
sea salt and freshly ground black pepper
6 eggs, lightly whisked
2 tablespoons pouring cream
12 sage leaves
2 large (about 360 g total) zucchini (courgette), cut into 2 cm thick slices
3 spring onions, thinly sliced
2 garlic cloves, crushed
125 g fresh ricotta

Preheat the oven to 200°C (180°C fan-forced). Line a large baking tray with baking paper.

Place the pumpkin on the lined tray. Drizzle with 1 tablespoon of the oil and season with salt and pepper. Toss to combine. Roast, turning once during cooking, for 30 minutes or until tender and golden. Set aside. Preheat the grill on high.

Whisk the eggs and cream in a jug and season with salt and pepper.

Heat the remaining oil in a 5 cm deep, 22 cm (base measurement) ovenproof non-stick frying pan over medium–high heat. Add the sage leaves and cook for 1–2 minutes or until crisp. Use a slotted spoon to remove from the pan and drain on a plate lined with paper towel.

Add the zucchini to the pan and cook, turning occasionally, for 5 minutes or until soft and lightly golden.

Add the spring onion and garlic and cook, stirring, for 1–2 minutes or until slightly softened. Add the pumpkin and gently stir so the mixture is evenly combined. Reduce the heat to medium.

Pour the egg mixture over the vegetables. Gently shake the pan to allow the egg mixture to spread evenly. Top with dollops of ricotta. Cook, without stirring, for 7–8 minutes or until the frittata is set around the edge but still runny in the centre.

Place under the preheated grill and cook for a further 5 minutes or until golden brown and just set. Remove from the grill. Cut into wedges and sprinkle with the fried sage.

Vegan coleslaw

SERVES 6 **PREP** 30 minutes **COOK** 20 minutes

Myth

Coleslaw was originally called 'kool slaw' because it is served cold.

My Truth

Given the fact that there was a trend for 'hot slaws' in the late 1800s, you could be forgiven for thinking that coleslaw should be spelt 'cold slaw', as it was in some cookbooks of that time. Certainly the Dutch, who created the dish, called it *koolsla*. The '*sla*' was slang for salad, but rather than meaning 'cold', the '*kool*' was Dutch for cabbage.

While today we know coleslaw best as a creamy bowl of mayo-dressed crisp veg like cabbage and carrot, it wasn't always so decadent. The original Dutch salads were dressed with oil and vinegar, and this is the way they still like their coleslaw in Germany, and in Sweden, where coleslaw is a traditional side dish for pizza and commonly known as *pizzasallad*.

In fact, cabbage salads have a long history in Europe. First century Roman cookbook *De re coquinaria* ('On the Subject of Cooking', also known as *Apicius*) contains the first recipe for raw cabbage dressed in oil and vinegar among a long list of cabbage recipes, showing that the vegetable was almost as popular in Ancient Rome as orgies, togas and conquering barbarians.

Mayonnaise, on the other hand, wasn't invented until the latter half of the eighteenth century, and so *koolsla* recipes before this time are always simple, sour affairs, almost verging on pickles, such as the one in the seventeenth century Dutch recipe book *De verstandige kock* ('The Sensible Cook', c. 1667).

The first mentions of mayonnaise appeared in the 1760s, and some might assume that coleslaw suddenly became creamy at that point, but this is not the case. Mayo-dressed coleslaw as we know it is likely less than one hundred years old.

This is because the first mayonnaises were very different beasts. One theory states that the first mayonnaise was made by the chef to the Third Duke of Richelieu to celebrate the French duke's capture of the port of Mahon during the Seven Years' War. It's likely, however, that this sauce used hard-boiled egg yolks, and close study of primary sources reveals that early mayonnaises were thickened through the addition of aspic or gelatine rather than emulsification. Indeed, this was the style of '*magnonnaise*' championed by Marie-Antoine Carême in his groundbreaking 1825 recipe book *Le cuisinier parisien* ('The Parisian chef').

It wasn't until the end of the nineteenth century (c. 1891) that the first emulsified mayonnaises using just egg yolk, oil and a souring agent became popular. Emulsified mayonnaise might have been championed by Auguste Escoffier, but it was in the United States, where they were desperate to seem fashionable and au fait with Parisian style, that dressing food in mayo became a massive craze. A Moscow dish known as 'Olivier salad' was reborn as the 'Russian salad' in 1894 with asparagus, beans and beetroot tossed in mayo. Celery and apple got the same treatment from Oscar Tschirky, maître d' of the Waldorf-Astoria Hotel, two years later when he created the 'Waldorf salad', and by the first decades of the twentieth century, mayo-dressed chicken, tuna and potato salads all graced US cookbooks. There was even a backlash against the growing trend of mayo-dressed fruit salads.

Mayonnaise went commercial around this time, with the launch in 1912 of Richard Hellman's eponymous bottled mayo that had been such a hit on salads and sandwiches at the New York deli owned by his parents-in-law.

This is also when coleslaw finally starts to get creamy, but the dressings tend to be buttermilk based, or sour cream cut with vinegar, as in Fannie Farmer's recipe for 'cole slaw' in her 1904 book *Food and Cookery for the Sick and Convalescent*. We have to wait thirty years or so for mayonnaise-dressed coleslaw to arrive in the US, alongside other American examples of 'culinary creativity' such as adding marshmallows to salads or setting them in jello. Leave it up to Australia, however, to offer three mayonnaises – one egg-free, one cooked and one mixed with piccalilli (aka mustard pickle) – as dressings for coleslaw in a 1918 edition of *The Queenslander* periodical. Even if none of these are just oil emulsified with raw egg.

Here, we've given coleslaw another makeover, adding the creaminess of chickpeas to the cabbage and dressing it with a mayonnaise made out of the liquid from the chickpeas can, known as aquafaba. There's no carrot, but the pickle flavour of the first slaws plays out in the presence of gherkins, and capers that are fried to give some toasty crispiness.

Vegan coleslaw *(CONTINUED)*

150 g raw macadamias

400 g can chickpeas (don't drain yet)

½ (about 500 g) drumhead white cabbage

1 small red onion

2 tablespoons olive oil

110 g jar capers, drained and patted dry with paper towel

1 bunch oregano (or marjoram), leaves finely chopped

350 g jar cornichons, drained and sliced lengthways

Fauxmesan

1 cup (145 g) roasted salted cashews, ground

1 teaspoon garlic powder

1½ teaspoons nutritional yeast

Vegan mayonnaise

¼ cup (60 ml) reserved chickpea water

2 garlic cloves, crushed into a paste with salt

1 tablespoon dijon mustard (vegan if necessary)

1 tablespoon apple cider vinegar

350 ml grapeseed oil (NOT olive oil)

Preheat the oven to 180°C (160°C fan-forced). Scatter the macadamias on a baking tray. Roast, jiggling the tray a couple of times, for 10–15 minutes or until roasted. It's worth it!

Place a sieve over a bowl and drain the chickpeas, reserving ¼ cup (60 ml) of the liquid from the can for the mayonnaise. Rinse the chickpeas and place in a clean tea towel. Fold over to cover and rub to help persuade the chickpeas to part with their papery skins. Throw the chickpeas into a bowl of water and watch the skins float off as you run your fingers through them. Skim off the skins and discard. Drain and reserve the chickpeas. (This isn't essential but it's classy.)

Slice the cabbage as thinly as you can. A mandolin on a fine setting is best for this. Then do the same for the red onion. Place the red onion in a heatproof bowl and cover with boiling water. Set aside for 1 minute to soak. Drain and pat dry with paper towel.

Heat the oil in a small frying pan over medium–high heat. Add the capers and cook for 4–5 minutes or until they are crispy, but watch that they don't burn. Drain on paper towel.

To make the fauxmesan, mix all the ingredients together in a small airtight container. Seal and set aside.

To make the vegan mayonnaise, place the chickpea water in the canister of your stick blender with all the other ingredients and give them a stir. Then place the stick blender at the bottom of the canister and blend. As the mayo forms in ribbons, gently bounce the stick blender through the oily mixture to incorporate.

Arrange the cabbage on a platter and sprinkle with the oregano. Give a little toss until well combined.

Strew over the red onion, chickpeas and cornichons. Dollop on globs of the vegan mayonnaise, throw on the roasted macadamias and sprinkle over the fauxmesan like a dusting of vegan snow. Eat!

TIPS

The fauxmesan is great anywhere you might be tempted to use parmesan.

The vegan mayo can be used as a base for countless variations. For starters, try adding a spoonful of miso, chopped dill or a big blob of gochujang chilli paste for three different versions.

For a thinner mayo, use 100 ml less oil.

Any excess chickpea water can be frozen in an ice-cube tray for later use.

This dish is also really great topped with four halved soft-boiled eggs, assuming there aren't any vegans around.

Caramelised onion, Gruyere and feta quiche

SERVES 6–8 **PREP** 20 minutes (plus chilling) **COOK** 1 hour 40 minutes

Myth
'Real men' don't eat quiche to enhance their reputation.

My Truth
If you were a knight in the buffer state of Lotharingia, as the French region of Lorraine was originally known, you'd be a trifle miffed by Bruce Feirstein's proposition, advanced in the May 1981 edition of *Playboy*, that real mean don't eat quiche. (Or you would be, after your scandalised shock at the other content of the magazine had subsided.)

You needed to be tough and canny to survive in Lotharingia. After all, this is the state (in its previous guise as Austrasia) that had produced the great Carolingian line of kings, which included Charlemagne. The region also survived centuries of invasions from the deeply competitive kingdoms of East Francia and West Francia (modern-day Germany and France), both of whom sought to claim ownership of the homeland of the Carolingian kings.

This history is important because it is the Lothringian pronunciation of the German word *kuchen*, meaning cake, which is '*kuche*', that gives us the French word 'quiche'. This rather confirms that quiche Lorraine, or, more accurately *kuche Lothringian*, is a German dish that predates the French takeover. Lorraine finally became a province of France in 1766.

The earliest French recipe I can find for the dish is Auguste Escoffier's *quiche à la Lorraine* in his *Le guide culinaire* (1903), although there are earlier nineteenth-century references to the dish. Escoffier includes rashers of butter-fried bacon in his quiche and suggests adding Gruyere, but he does say that cheese is not a traditional ingredient in Lorraine. Escoffier's masterwork was translated into English as *A Guide to Modern Cookery* in 1907, which appears to be the first time quiche passes into the English-speaking world.

The French food bible *Larousse Gastronomique* specifies that the original quiche Lorraine was eggs and crème fraîche only, with the region's famous smoked bacon a later addition, when it was called the far less appealing *quiche au lard*. Adding the sweetness of caramelised onions, which I think is a wee bit essential, was something they only did over the border in Alsace, apparently. Interestingly, the fourteenth-century recipe for an egg pie called '*Tart de Bry*' in *The Forme of Cury* was made with soft cheese like a ricotta or feta rather than Gruyere or Emmental. This pushed us towards using feta in this recipe.

50 g butter
1 tablespoon olive oil
3 brown onions, thinly sliced (use a mandolin if you have one)
2 whole star anise
2 teaspoons thyme leaves
4 eggs
200 g crème fraîche
sea salt and freshly ground black pepper
¾ cup (90 g) coarsely grated Gruyere
80 g feta, crumbled into large chunks

Sour cream pastry
2 cups (300 g) plain flour
150 g butter, chilled and chopped
½ cup (120 g) sour cream

TIP

If you are feeling the need for some porky goodness, replace the feta with 100 g smoked bacon or *kaiserfleisch* cut into batons and lightly pan-fried in butter.

Start by caramelising the onion. Melt the butter and oil in a large frying pan over low heat. Add the onion and star anise and cook, stirring occasionally, for 40 minutes or until the onion starts to caramelise and turn golden. It should be sticky, with any liquid evaporated away. Stir in the thyme and cook for 1 more minute. Remove the star anise and set aside to cool.

In between stirring the onion, prepare the pastry. Process the flour and butter in a food processor until the mixture resembles fine breadcrumbs. Add the sour cream and pulse until the pastry just starts to come together. Turn onto a lightly floured surface and shape into a disc. Wrap in plastic wrap and refrigerate for 30 minutes.

Roll out the pastry on a lightly floured surface until 4 mm thick. Ease into a 3.5 cm deep, 23 cm (base measurement) fluted tart tin with a removeable base. Gently push in the pastry. Trim the excess and place in the fridge for a further 30 minutes to chill.

Preheat the oven to 200°C (180°C fan-forced). Line the pastry with a large sheet of baking paper and fill with pastry weights or rice. Place the tin on a baking tray and bake for 15 minutes. Remove the paper and weights or rice. Bake for a further 10 minutes or until lightly golden and crisp. Set aside to cool slightly.

Reduce the oven to 180°C (160°C fan-forced). Whisk the eggs and crème fraîche in a jug and season with pepper.

Scatter the onion over the base of the pastry case. Sprinkle with the Gruyere. Pour over the egg mixture and scatter with the feta. Bake for 35 minutes or until just set. Cut into wedges to serve.

Avocado smash on corn fritters

SERVES 4 **PREP** 20 minutes **COOK** 25 minutes

Twist

Myth
Smashed avocado is a Melbourne creation.

My Truth
Surely avocado toast is as Melbournian as the final siren at the G and South Melbourne Market dim sims? Not so, says the *Washington Post*, who crowned the sliced avocado on toast with coriander, a squeeze of lime juice and salt and pepper that has been on the menu at bills in the Sydney suburb of Darlinghurst since 1993 as the first. Stand by for a wave of outrage.

Now, much as I love the charming Mr Granger (and I *could* argue that he is a Melbourne boy who moved to Sydney to open the cafe and, hence, avocado on toast is by default a Melbourne dish), there are just too many versions that precede it. It pops up in a 1986 edition of the *Canberra Times*, for example.

Sadly for our national pride, Mexico's avocado on warm flatbread predates this by hundreds of years. My patriotic ego could dismiss this, as well as venerable breakfast dishes like Peru's *pan con palta* and Chile's crusty *marraqueta* roll smeared with mashed avocado, as being merely on bread, not *toast*, but more difficult to dispute is the hard evidence that smashed avo toast was a thing in San Francisco first.

In November 1885, a recipe for avocado, pulp removed 'with a silver knife' and spread on bread for breakfast, appeared in the *Daily Alta California*. Then, in 1915, the California Avocado Association recommended small squares of hot toast spread thickly with mashed avo as an hors d'oeuvre. There were more recipes in Los Angeles's *Covina Argus* in 1920 and the *San Francisco Chronicle* in 1927.

Providing a final nail in the coffin of both Melbourne's and Sydney's claims is chef Chloe Osborne, who is credited with bringing avocado on toast to Manhattan at Cafe Gitane around 2005. She said she had first eaten it on a trip to Queensland in the 1970s. This is not surprising, because in 1929 a Brisbane newspaper called *The Telegraph* published a piece by Margaret Curran, who wrote that 'Spread on toast or water biscuits and lightly peppered and salted [avocados] make a delicious "savoury".' It might not be smashed avo with lime for breakfast, but it was most certainly a pioneering start, undoubtedly inspired by the fact that avocados have been grown in South East Queensland since at least 1857.

Having the mantle of 'creators of smashed avo' snatched away from my hometown smarts, so I've vowed to redress the balance. What could be greater than smashed avo on toast? How about smashed avo on corn fritters with granola – three breakfast greats combined into one!

---

2 large (about 300 g each) avocados
2 tablespoons lemon juice
sea salt and freshly ground black pepper
100 g good-quality feta
coriander leaves, to serve
2 limes, quartered

Chilli granola
½ cup (80 g) pepita (pumpkin seed) and
    sunflower seed mix
¼ cup (20 g) flaked almonds
2 tablespoons maple syrup
2 tablespoons brown sugar
1 teaspoon sea salt
2 teaspoons chilli flakes

The corniest corn fritters
2 × 420 g cans corn kernels, drained, or
    1½ cups (240 g) frozen corn kernels,
    thawed
1 red onion, finely chopped
½ cup (75 g) plain flour
¼ cup finely chopped flat-leaf parsley
2 teaspoons finely grated lemon zest
2 eggs, lightly whisked
olive oil, for shallow frying

To make the granola, line a tray with baking paper. Heat a non-stick frying pan over medium heat. Add the seed mix and almonds and cook, tossing, for 5 minutes or until toasted. Add the maple syrup and brown sugar and cook, stirring, for 2–3 minutes or until reduced slightly and thick and sticky. Transfer to the tray and sprinkle over the salt and chilli flakes. Set aside to cool. Clean the pan – it will be easier now than later, when the syrup has set into toffee!

To make the fritters, preheat the oven to 140°C (120°C fan-forced). Combine the corn, onion, flour, parsley and lemon zest in a large bowl. Mix until well combined, and season. Make a well in the centre and add the eggs. Stir with a spatula until well combined.

Add enough oil to the clean frying pan so it is 5 mm deep and heat over medium heat. Spoon ¼ cupfuls of the batter into the pan. Cook for 3 minutes each side or until golden brown and crisp. Transfer to a baking tray lined with paper towel to drain. Place in the oven to keep warm while you cook the next batch. Repeat with the remaining batter, adding extra oil to the pan when necessary (it may be a few batches, depending on the size of your pan).

Halve the avocados and remove the stones. Scoop the flesh into a bowl and add the lemon juice. Season with salt and pepper. Use a fork to roughly mash or smash, leaving it a little chunky.

To serve, top the fritters with the smashed avocado and sprinkle with the granola, crumbled feta and some torn coriander leaves, and have wedges of lime on the side.

Roast mushroom bibimbap

SERVES 4 **PREP** 20 minutes (plus cooling) **COOK** 25 minutes

Myth

Rice is just an ingredient in Korean food.

My Truth

Rice isn't just rice, or *ssal*, in Korea. Cook it and it becomes *bap*, which means so much more than just 'cooked rice'. It has value akin to that of bread in some cultures – like the Korean equivalent of the staff of life – and *bap* has become synonymous not just with a whole meal but also the feeling of wellbeing and hospitality that comes with it. Rice *is* Korean food. There is no 'just' about it.

Bibimbap – literally 'mixed rice' in Hangul script – has been mentioned in print since the late sixteenth century. It was initially known by a number of Chinese names, one of which rather charmingly translates as 'dizzy rice'. The first recording of the name *bibimbap* was not until the first half of the nineteenth century, in a collection of writing on various cultural topics by Minister Yi Gyu-bo of Korea that lists over a dozen different *bibimbap*s, including salted shrimp, marinated crab and soybean sprout. The first recipe for the dish appeared later in that century.

It's basically a farmer's leftovers meal that uses up cooked rice, veg, meat and *banchan*, those copious Korean side dishes (such as, most famously, kimchi), with other traditional flavours like gochujang chilli paste mixed in. Served cold, warm or in a searing-hot stone bowl, the 'mixed' element can be as much about combining the ingredients and dressing the rice as it is about mixing the deliciously crunchy toasted rice at the bottom of a hot bowl with the rest of the dish.

Bearing in mind Minister Yi Gyu-bo's nineteenth-century soybean-sprout *bibimbap*, it seemed perfectly logical to add mung beans and other sprouts to ours, positioning it less as a crunchy hot bowl (which is hard to do well at home) and more as a predecessor to the modern trend of 'bowl food' alongside the Hawaiian poke bowl.

There are only two rules to remember with this *bibimbap* – first, it must be served piping hot, and second, the egg yolk must be runny enough to mix through the bowl. If you want, you can just add an egg yolk instead of cooking a runny fried egg.

¼ cup (60 ml) rice wine vinegar
½ teaspoon caster sugar
½ teaspoon sea salt, plus extra to season
4 dutch (baby) carrots, thinly sliced lengthways or shaved with a vegetable peeler
1 cup (200 g) sushi rice (or arborio in a pinch)
2 tablespoons barbecue sauce
1 tablespoon gochujang chilli paste
2 teaspoons sesame oil
100 ml vegetable oil
300 g shiitake mushrooms
2 garlic cloves, sliced
4 eggs
250 g mixed sprouts (I used mung, chickpea, onion and lentil)
100 g bean sprouts
1 tablespoon sesame seeds, toasted
150 g sugar snap peas, blanched
¼ cup (60 ml) soy sauce
gochugaru or Japanese *togarashi* chilli flakes, to serve (see Tip)

Preheat the oven to 200°C (180°C fan-forced) and line a baking tray with baking paper.

Combine the vinegar, sugar and salt in a bowl. Add the carrot and toss to combine. Set aside to pickle while you prep the rest.

Place the rice and 1½ cups (375 ml) water in a saucepan and place over medium heat. Bring to a simmer, cover, then reduce the heat to low and cook for 10 minutes or until the rice is tender and the water has been absorbed. Uncover and set aside to cool.

Combine the barbecue sauce, gochujang, sesame oil and 1 tablespoon of the vegetable oil in a bowl. Season with salt. Add the mushrooms and toss to coat, then arrange on the lined tray. Roast for 15 minutes or until tender and slightly charred.

While the mushrooms are roasting, heat the remaining ⅓ cup (80 ml) vegetable oil in a non-stick frying pan over medium–low heat. Add the garlic and cook for 1–2 minutes or until golden and the oil is perfumed. Crack in the eggs and cook until the whites are just set but yolks are runny.

Combine the rice with the sprouts and sesame seeds, and divide among serving bowls. Top with the fried eggs, mushrooms, pickled carrot and sugar snaps. Drizzle with the soy sauce and sprinkle with the *gochugaru* or chilli flakes.

TIP

You'll find *gochugaru* or *togarashi* chilli flakes in Asian grocery shops. The Koreans are justifiably very proud of their *gochugaru*, as the heat and flavour in it is much more mellow than everyday supermarket chilli powder.

Sri Lankan cashew curry

SERVES 4 **PREP** 2 hours 20 minutes (relax, it's 95% soaking time) **COOK** 30 minutes

CLASSIC

Myth

I know an awful lot about the history of the cashew nut curry.

My Truth

Like a batsman who's wandered out of his crease, bamboozled by Muralitharan and claimed by Jayawardene, I'm stumped. I can tell you that the cashew arrived in Sri Lanka with the Portuguese in the middle of the sixteenth century, from Brazil via Goa. I can also tell you that the Sri Lanka Cashew Corporation was set up on 25 May 1972. Thanks to an excellent paper by G. B. B. Surendra from the corporation's research division, I can tell you there are 77,809 cashew holdings across the country, producing almost 5000 tonnes of nuts per year, and that cashew exports contribute about 431 million rupees (around 2.8 million Australian dollars) to the Sri Lankan economy each year – although these figures do date back to when Sanath Jayasuriya, or even Aravinda de Silva, was at the crease.

While all this is fascinating, I'm afraid I can't deliver any facts on the history of the cashew *curry*. Even my go-to book on Sri Lankan cookery, Chandra Dissanayake's definitive *Ceylon Cookery*, is quite quiet on the subject, with the curry not getting a look-in among the 516 recipes. If you know anything about the origins of the dish, do DM me at @mattscravat.

What I do know is that, with 40 per cent of Sri Lanka's annual cashew production eaten on the island, the nut has a vital role in the local diet and is far more than just a snack to nibble on with your passionfruit and coconut arrack cocktail.

Travelling around the south and centre of the county, I rather fell in love with the Sri Lankan idea of making cashews the meat in a curry rather than just a garnish. While I've played with recipes for cashew nut curries with beetroot and with chicken before, this one is the pure original – and I think it's the best.

Sri Lankan cashew curry *(CONTINUED)*

500 g raw cashews

¼ cup (60 ml) vegetable, grapeseed oil or ghee

4 brown onions, sliced

4 long green chillies, split in half lengthways, deveined and deseeded

40 curry leaves (buy 1 packet or a couple of sprigs)

5 green cardamom pods, crushed

1 small cinnamon stick

1 teaspoon ground cumin

4 cm knob fresh turmeric (or 1 teaspoon ground turmeric)

400 ml can coconut milk

270 ml can coconut cream

sea salt

2 teaspoons curry powder (or garam masala, but ideally a real roasted Sri Lankan curry powder – see Tips)

steamed rice, to serve

Place the cashews in a large bowl and cover with plenty of water. Set aside for 2 hours to soak (soaking them any longer will affect their texture, and we want them to bring at least some crunch to the curry). Drain well.

Heat 2 tablespoons of the oil or ghee in a large, deep frying pan over medium heat. When hot and sizzly, throw in the onion, green chilli and half the curry leaves. Cook, stirring occasionally, for 10 minutes or until the onion softens and is lightly golden.

Stir in the cardamom, cinnamon and cumin, then grate in the turmeric. Cook, stirring, for 2 minutes or until you smell the cumin. Add the drained cashews and stir until well combined. Cook, stirring occasionally, for 3 minutes so the cashews suck up some of the spicy flavours.

Stir in the coconut milk and half the coconut cream to the cashews. Simmer for 10–15 minutes or until the mixture thickens (or cook a little longer if you want a drier curry). Season with salt to taste and transfer to a large serving bowl.

Just before serving, heat the remaining oil in another frying pan over medium–high heat. Once the oil is nice and hot, throw in the curry powder and the remaining curry leaves. Stir for 1 minute or so, then pour over the cashew curry, with a swirl of coconut cream from the remaining half can. Serve the curry with the rice.

Authentic Sri Lankan roasted curry powder

To make an authentic Sri Lankan roasted curry powder, start by toasting 2 tablespoons of basmati rice in a dry frying pan over medium heat for 3 minutes or until golden and toasty.

Add ¼ cup (20 g) coriander seeds, 2 tablespoons cumin seeds, 2 tablespoons black peppercorns, 1 tablespoon roasted cashews, crushed, 1 tablespoon desiccated coconut, 1 tablespoon mustard seeds, 6 whole cloves, the seeds from 12 green cardamom pods and 2 teaspoons ground cinnamon or fennel seeds. Continue to cook, moving the spices around constantly, for 1–2 minutes or until aromatic and golden. Do not let them catch or burn. Set aside to cool. Grind in a spice grinder or a mortar and pestle to a fine texture.

Use this recipe as your base for the cashew curry. You can also play around by customising the curry with additions like 1–2 cups of green peas, diced beetroot or roasted pumpkin near the end of cooking. A few finely chopped cloves of garlic are good, and a teaspoon of crushed fennel seeds, fenugreek or a little ginger are a nice spice change up. Six crushed cardamom pods added when you are tempering the curry leaves and green chillies at the beginning will also do the trick.

Feel free to add dried red chillies, chilli powder or those wild yoghurt-dried chillies instead of the boring green ones if you want more heat.

You can also buy roasted Sri Lankan curry powder in specialist groceries.

Spinach and ricotta filo toasties
– THE NEW SPANAKOPITA

SERVES 6 for a snack, or 3 for a light lunch with a side salad **PREP** 20 minutes **COOK** 35 minutes

Myth
Cookbooks are full of new recipes.

My Truth
Originality is a rare thing. Show me a cookbook and I can usually point to someone who has written that recipe or something similar earlier. It's the nature of the beast that small differences are, however, enough to make something new and exciting. So it is with my spanakopita toastie, which really is the usual cheese and greens filling wrapped in filo, but it's different and new because I use a toastie maker to cook them more quickly and easily. Personally, I think that is quite radical.

Similarly, the first person to fill filo with spinach and greens couldn't have known that wags and historians would try to claim that this pie was just the same as the pie Philoxenos of Cythera was referring to in the fifth century BC. Sure, that was also a cheese pie, but it was baked with honey, as were so many in Ancient Greece and Rome. There were many of these cheesy pies, like the *en tyritas plakountas* of Anatolia and the layered placenta cake of Ancient Rome, but they still weren't spanakopita (and in fact they might have had more in common with baklava, as we'll see later on p. 278).

Closer ancestors to spanakopita were the pies of Epirus. Up here in Greece's north-west they were famous for three things: a merciless pursuit of war – it was their leader Pyrrhus who gave his name to a 'pyrrhic victory'; baking pies, or *pide*; and foraging for wild greens. These greens went into the pies, as did the spinach they started growing in the Byzantine era.

These still weren't spanakopita, however, and wouldn't be until one hundred years after the Ottomans had conquered Constantinople and the kitchens of the Topkapi Palace introduced the world to filo pastry. Only now could the cooks of Epirus give us spanakopita.

There are other pies that are similar, but I'd argue that meat-filled *börek* or the *iflaghun* made by Armenians in the Cilician region are delicious but only distant relations, while Turkish *ispanaki* would be more like a brother, thanks to its crispy thin layers of *yufka* pastry giving way to a filling of white cheese and greens flavoured with that very Turkish ingredient, dried mint. None of them ever used a toastie maker to cook them, though.

60 g butter
180 g baby spinach leaves
300 g fresh ricotta
150 g feta, crumbled
3 spring onions, thinly sliced
¼ cup coarsely chopped dill
1 teaspoon finely grated lemon zest
freshly ground black pepper
12 sheets filo pastry
100 g ghee (or butter, if you don't have ghee), melted
1 egg, lightly whisked
lemon wedges, to serve

Leftover curry or even bolognese can also be the filling for an ultimate filo toastie.

Melt the butter in a large frying pan over medium heat. Add the spinach and cook, stirring, for 2–3 minutes or until wilted. Transfer to a colander and use the back of a spoon to press out excess moisture. Coarsely chop the spinach and place in a large bowl. Add the ricotta, feta, spring onion, dill and lemon zest. Season with pepper.

Measure your toastie (jaffle) maker to see what size filo sheet will fit neatly in there. You'll need six sheets of layered greased filo for the top and for the bottom of each of your spanakopita toasties. Push the filo into the wells of the toastie maker to gauge the size. If you don't, your pastry may be crucially short where it should seal.

Place a sheet of filo pastry on a work surface and brush with the ghee. Place another filo sheet on top. Continue layering with ghee and filo until you have six layers. Repeat with the remaining filo and ghee to make another stack of six layers. Cut each stack into thirds crossways (if, like us, you are cutting down filo for a standard double toastie maker).

Preheat the toastie maker. Brush the base with ghee. Place one cut filo stack over the base of the toastie maker to cover. Push the filo down into the wells so you can maximise how much filling you can get in there.

Brush over the edges and down the centre of the pastry in the toastie maker with the whisked egg. This will help to seal the edges together. Spoon about 3 tablespoons of ricotta mixture into each well. You'll want it to be full but not *over*full, as too much filling may prevent the toastie from sealing properly while cooking. Lay another cut filo stack over the filling, and brush with ghee. Close the lid and cook for 8–10 minutes or until golden and crisp.

Repeat to make 4 more toasties. Cut into triangles and serve with lemon wedges.

Risotto

SERVES 4 **PREP** 10 minutes **COOK** 30 minutes

CLASSIC

Myth

The best rice for risotto is arborio.

My Truth

Rice has been grown in northern Italy since the fifteenth century, and while risotto was based on gruels and porridges that date back to Palaeolithic times, the first recipe for what we'd actually recognise as a risotto was only published in 1809. Rice was sautéed in butter, sausage, onions and bone marrow before broth and saffron were added. This is very similar to an older technique from Tuscany that turned stale bread into a polenta-like *pearà*.

It is a mark of how fast risotto spread that, by 1854, regional variations of risotto were set. In the *Trattato di cucina* ('Treatise on Cuisine'), written by Giovanni Vialardi, head chef to the royal house of Savoy in Turin, there were recipes for '*Risotto alla Piedmontese*' made with white truffle, nutmeg, fresh butter and cheese, and a version '*alla Milanese*', with the signature saffron joining nutmeg and of course butter and cheese. The rice was started by frying with onions and brains, although it is unclear from the Italian text whether these are real brains or the coiled beef, pork and fennel sausage from Bari called '*cervella*' or '*cervellata*', which also translates as 'brains'. By 1901, Pellegrino Artusi included thirteen different variations for risotto in his seminal cookbook.

Neither of these early recipes specifies what rice to use, but personally I find the higher starch content of Vialone Nano or Carnaroli makes for a creamier risotto than arborio, meaning less butter and cheese are required for the perfect taste and texture.

6 cups (1.5 litres) salt-reduced vegetable stock
½ teaspoon saffron threads
1 tablespoon olive oil
50 g butter
1 brown onion, finely chopped
2 garlic cloves, crushed
1½ cups (300 g) Vialone Nano, Carnaroli or arborio rice
½ cup (125 ml) dry white wine
1 cup (80 g) finely grated parmesan
sea salt and freshly ground black pepper
gold leaf, to serve (optional)

Food nerd fact

Galeazzo Maria Sforza, the Duke of Milan, was one of the biggest champions of Italian rice cultivation, first planting it in 1475 and sharing sacks of the grains with the neighbouring nobility to encourage them to plant it. This is how rice cultivation became central to agriculture along the Po River, and, alongside gnocchi, another feather in the cap of the foodie dukes of Milan.

Bring the stock and saffron just to the boil in a saucepan over high heat. Reduce the heat to low and hold at a very gentle simmer.

Heat the oil and half the butter in a large saucepan over medium heat. Cook the onion and garlic, stirring, for 5 minutes or until soft and translucent, but don't let them brown. Add the rice and cook, stirring, for 2–3 minutes or until the grains appear slightly glassy. Toasting the grains like this ensures the rice cooks evenly.

Add the wine and cook, stirring, until the liquid is almost all absorbed. The rice should move in the pan like wet sand. Now add a ladleful – about ½ cup (125 ml) – of hot stock and stir until the liquid is absorbed.

Keep adding stock one ladleful at a time, stirring until absorbed before adding the next. Continue for 20 minutes or until rice is tender yet firm to the bite. A rice grain should still have a small star of starch at its centre when pressed with your thumb onto the back of a wooden spoon. It may be ready earlier, so keep checking.

When you have used almost all the stock and are down to about the last cup, check the rice again; when pressed that single star should have split into three tiny white dots. This is perfect. If your risotto is a good-but-not-too-stiff consistency, then you are definitely done; if it's a little stiff and you need to loosen it up, add the remaining stock. It should be a little oozy, so that it is loose enough to settle out on a plate when the plate is tapped firmly a couple of times on the bench.

Remove the risotto from the heat. Stir in the parmesan and remaining butter with gusto. Season and serve topped with a little gold leaf, if you like. This is great eaten alone or as an accompaniment to any stewed meats, such as osso buco.

TIP

This risotto is perfect for customising. Lose the saffron and customise the stock accordingly to make everything from prawn to wild mushroom risotto.

Chicken

Roast chicken with chicken-fat rice, *MANDI STYLE*

SERVES 4 **PREP** 30 minutes (plus marinating and overnight chilling) **COOK** 2 hours

Myth
The inspiration for this dish, Hainanese chicken rice, comes from Hainan Island off the coast of Southern China.

My Truth
The *mandi* technique of roasting a chicken over a pot of rice that I'm using here is originally Yemeni (but also very popular on the Arabian peninsula). I've transferred it 6259 kilometres east, to that vortex of deliciousness that exists between Malaysia and Singapore, for a new version of the much-loved dish that has become known worldwide as Hainanese chicken rice.

I am being careful with my words here, because while the dish was invented by Hainanese migrants in Singapore and Malaysia, it is not a traditional dish on the island of Hainan. Hainanese traders visited Singapore from 1821 onwards to trade wax, umbrellas and medicinal herbs, but migration only became possible once the island was opened up to foreign trade fifty years later.

Later, many Hainanese moved to Malaysia to work in tin mines and rubber plantations between the 1880s and 1940s. This was lucrative work. However, those who arrived in Singapore found it harder to find employment and many began working in hospitality or domestic service. The first Singapore Sling was mixed by a barman of Hainanese background, Ngiam Tong Boon, in 1915.

The Hainanese cooks who moved to Singapore and Malaysia at the end of the nineteenth century reinterpreted a chicken dish from the Wenchang region of their home island using local chooks. This evolved into the chicken rice we know and love today.

Back on the island, they'd poach the particularly tasty free-range chooks that came from Wenchang to make white cut chicken. In Singapore or Malaysia, they attempted to boost the flavour of less delicious birds by poaching them with stock or aromats, or even dousing them with a mix of shaoxing wine, sesame or fried shallot oil and soy sauce before serving.

The Hainanese cooks drew on techniques from other parts of China to improve the dish, like the Cantonese technique of poaching the bird at a lower temperature and then dunking it in iced water to set the fat under the skin into a jelly. This gave the skin prized, extra-gelatinous properties and made the meat ridiculously tender. It is a technique used when making Cantonese *see yao gai* (see p. 119).

It wasn't until the Great Depression that some of these Hainanese cooks were able to open their own restaurants and coffee houses and, after World War II, their pioneering kopitiams. It was at this time that Hainanese chicken rice came out of home kitchens and started on its journey to being recognised as one of the world's greatest recipes.

Other cooks like Wong Yi Guan turned to the streets to sell their chicken rice. His success as a travelling street vendor saw him open one of the first chicken rice stalls in Singapore in 1940. Wong's apprentices, such as Moh Lee Twee, struck out to open their own chicken rice places, including Swee Kee and Yet Con, later in the 1940s.

For me, this dish isn't made special by the chook so much as the chicken fat rice that comes with it, and I'm not alone. In Thailand, the dish is evocatively called *khao man gai*, or 'fatty rice chicken'. The rendering of fat from the chook not only gives you that fatty rice, but is also used to sear spring onion or chillies to make the dish's all-important dipping sauces.

While Malaysia and Singapore have both tried to claim chicken rice as uniquely theirs, the broad spread of the dish across South-East Asia refutes this almost as much as the name, which gives an immediate geographical provenance and affirms that it belongs to Hainanese migrants wherever they settled and cooked it. (It's also worth remembering that Singapore and Malaysia were part of the same country through the years of the development of Hainanese chicken rice, and that the Hainanese community in Singapore today stands at 220,000 people, and 140,000 people in Malaysia.)

Chicken rice is most commonly seen with poached chicken, but it can be served with roast chicken if you are willing to part with the gelatinous skin of the poached and quick-chilled bird that makes Singaporean and Malaysian food lovers go weak at the knees.

What I hope is that this recipe gives you the familiarity of roast chicken but with all the delicious joy of rice that's rich from the chicken fat and fragrant with aromats, thanks to using this Yemeni method of roasting the whole bird so all the juices and fatty drippings drop into your rice cooking beneath.

So, please ignore the tutting of your *nai nai*, *lao lao*, *amah* or *nenek* – I understand that this is probably not the way they did it, but, honestly, it's quick, clever and super tasty. You can even slice the chicken and lay it on the rice if that is pleasing to you. Just keep the slices nice and thick so they stay juicy.

Roast chicken with chicken-fat rice *(CONTINUED)*

1.5 kg whole chicken (ask your butcher for a nice fat bird)
¼ cup (60 ml) rice malt syrup
2 tablespoons shaoxing rice wine (or dry sherry)
2 tablespoons dark soy sauce
4 red shallots, peeled, finely chopped
6 cm knob ginger, peeled and thinly sliced
3 garlic cloves, thinly sliced
3 whole star anise
2½ cups (500 g) long-grain rice
4 cups (1 litre) chicken stock
sesame oil, to drizzle
2 Lebanese cucumbers, halved lengthways then sliced diagonally, to serve
coriander sprigs, to serve

Chinese-style red chilli sauce

20 long red chillies, deseeded
3 cm knob ginger, peeled and finely grated
1 head of garlic, cloves separated and peeled
¼ cup (60 ml) white vinegar
1 tablespoon white sugar
sea salt, to season

Spring onion oil

¼ cup (60 ml) peanut or vegetable oil
5 cm knob ginger, peeled and finely grated
1 bunch spring onions, thinly sliced
1 teaspoon soy sauce
¼ teaspoon white vinegar
½ teaspoon sea salt

TIP

If you want to make a classic poached Hainanese chicken rice, I can recommend Tony Tan's or Adam Liaw's beautiful and thoughtful recipes. You'll find them online.

Remove any fatty pieces of chicken just inside the cavity and place them in a small bowl. Cover with plastic wrap and place in the fridge until needed.

Combine the malt syrup, rice wine and soy sauce in a large glass or ceramic bowl. Add the chicken and turn to coat. Cover and place in the fridge, turning once, for 3 hours or longer if time permits.

Drain the chicken well from the marinade. Place on a plate in the fridge, uncovered, for at least 6 hours, or overnight if you like. (This dries the skin out, making it crispy.) Discard the marinade.

Before you start cooking the chicken, make the red chilli sauce. Blend all the ingredients in a blender until well combined. Adjust the seasoning with a bit more vinegar, sugar and ginger if you like. Season with salt. Set aside.

Preheat the oven to 220°C (200°C fan-forced). Remove all but the bottom rack from the oven. Remove the chook from the fridge and set aside for 30 minutes to come to room temperature.

Heat the reserved chicken fat in a large, heavy-based flameproof casserole dish (that is larger than the chicken across the top) over medium–low heat, stirring occasionally, for 5 minutes or until the fat renders down to an oil. Remove any leftover fat that hasn't dissolved. If you don't have much oil in the base of your pan, add a touch of vegetable oil.

Add the shallot, ginger, garlic and star anise to the pan. Cook, stirring, for 5 minutes or until soft and translucent. Add the rice and cook, stirring constantly, for 1–2 minutes to toast the rice and until things start smelling rather aromatic. Add the stock and stir to combine. Bring just to the boil.

Place the casserole dish in the oven and place an oiled oven rack over the top of the dish. Lay the chicken, breast-side down, on the rack, so any juices will drip into the pot as it cooks. Roast for 15 minutes. Reduce the oven temperature to 160°C (140°C fan-forced). Roast for a further 30 minutes, until the rice has absorbed the liquid and it has a dry crust on top.

Transfer the chicken and the rack to a baking tray and turn the chicken over. Use foil to cover any of the wing tips or leg ends that are already golden. Remove the rice from the oven, cover with a lid and set aside to keep warm. Return the chicken to the oven and roast for a further 45–55 minutes or until cooked through and golden. When cooked, transfer the chicken to a plate and cover loosely with foil for 5 minutes to rest. Reserve any fat and juices from the baking tray.

Meanwhile, make the spring onion oil. Heat the oil in a small saucepan until just smoking. Add the ginger and spring onion, then remove from the heat. Stir through the soy, vinegar and salt.

Pour any fat juices and drippings from the chicken resting plate or reserved from the baking tray over the rice and use a fork to fluff the grains. Cut the chicken into portions and place on top of the rice. Drizzle over the sesame oil and top with the cucumber and coriander. Serve with the chilli sauce and spring onion oil.

Buffalo wings with ranch dressing

SERVES 4 **PREP** 30 minutes (plus chilling and pickling) **COOK** 1 hour

Myth
Buffalo wings were created at the Anchor Bar in the upstate New York city of Buffalo in 1964.

My Truth
So, first the orthodoxy. Late one night, bar owner Teressa Bellissimo used what she had at hand – leftover chicken wings destined to become stock – to feed either a) her son, and his college mates who had turned up unexpectedly, or b) Catholic patrons who wanted something meaty when a Friday of abstinence and drinking turned into 12.01 am Saturday. She fried the wings and doused them with an improvised sauce of butter, apple cider vinegar and hot sauce. The cooling celery and blue cheese on the side were an afterthought.

Not so, say a number of African American restaurateurs whose families ran barbecue joints on the South Side of Chicago, especially around Bronzeville. They argue that fried wings with sauce originated in the Windy City in the 1950s. Here it was called 'mumbo sauce' or 'mild sauce', and was a mix of tomato ketchup, vinegar, sugar and chilli.

Argia B. Collins, whose family came from Mississippi, ran rib joints in Bronzeville with his brothers and trademarked his mumbo sauce in 1958. Royal Chicken was opened by another Mississippian migrant in Chicago selling barbecue with 'mild sauce' in 1964. There is also a long history of wings and an Alabama-inspired mumbo sauce in Washington, DC. Alabama-born John Young claims he was selling fried wings in mumbo sauce in Buffalo as early as 1961.

While wings and sauce weren't invented by Teressa Bellissimo, and these earlier recipes may even have served as inspiration, her wing sauce was a hot and spicy creation that also contained cayenne, worcestershire and garlic powder. This is a long way from the mild sauce and mumbo sauce of Alabama and Mississippi. I reckon this difference is enough to let her retain the title of inventor of buffalo wings. Either way, the dish that became world famous was named after her home town.

The fame of the dish was accelerated when whole bird sales in supermarkets started to be replaced with cuts of thigh and breast sold separately. This created a glut of wings that were sold off at rock-bottom prices, making buffalo wings a wonderfully profitable item to have on any bar menu – especially at the emerging sports bars of the 1980s, where buffalo wings became as ubiquitous as the recently invented large-screen, rear-projection TVs playing the night's big game.

1.5 kg chicken wings
2 teaspoons sweet paprika
2 teaspoons sea salt
freshly ground black pepper
148 ml bottle Frank's hot sauce
¼ cup (55 g) brown sugar
80 g butter
1 butter lettuce, leaves separated
120 g blue cheese, crumbled

Pickled celery

½ cup (125 ml) apple cider vinegar
½ cup (125 ml) water
2 tablespoons caster sugar
2 fresh or dried bay leaves
1 teaspoon whole black peppercorns
½ teaspoon sea salt
300 g celery stalks, de-stringed, cut into
   8 cm lengths, halved lengthways

Ranch dressing

½ cup (120 g) sour cream
½ cup (150 g) whole-egg mayonnaise
½ cup (125 ml) buttermilk
2 garlic cloves, crushed
1 tablespoon finely chopped chives
1 tablespoon finely chopped dill
1 tablespoon finely chopped flat-leaf parsley

Place the wings on a tray in a single layer. Place, uncovered, in the fridge for 6 hours or overnight. If you are really short on time you can just pat dry with paper towel.

To pickle the celery, place the vinegar, water, sugar, bay leaves, peppercorns and salt in a small saucepan. Stir over low heat for 2–3 minutes or until the sugar dissolves. Place the celery in a glass or ceramic container. While warm, pour over the vinegar mixture and set aside, stirring occasionally, for at least 1 hour.

Preheat the oven to 200°C (180°C fan-forced). Line a large baking tray with baking paper. Place a wire rack on top and spray the rack well with oil.

Use paper towel to pat the wings dry and place in a large bowl. Sprinkle over the paprika, salt and pepper. Toss until the chicken is well coated. Place the wings in a single layer on the rack. Bake for 1 hour or until golden and cooked.

Meanwhile, place the hot sauce, sugar and butter in a small saucepan. Stir over low heat for 2–3 minutes or until the sugar dissolves. Set aside.

To make the ranch dressing, combine all the ingredients in a jug and whisk to combine. Season well with salt and pepper. Stir in 1 tablespoon of the celery pickling liquid.

Place the butter lettuce leaves in a large bowl. Add ½ cup (125 ml) of the ranch dressing and toss until the leaves are lightly coated. Place in a serving bowl and sprinkle with the blue cheese. Coarsely chop half of the pickled celery and add to the salad.

Place the wings in a large bowl again and toss through the hot sauce. Place on a serving plate. Drain the remaining celery and add to the platter. Serve with the salad and extra ranch dressing on the side.

Soy-poached chicken salad with bacon miso mayonnaise

SERVES 4 **PREP** 30 minutes **COOK** 50 minutes

Twist

Myth
In the debate about which came first, the chicken or the egg, the answer is the chicken.

My Truth
This is a new dish, but one that is 4500 years in the making. That's how far back we can trace both the domestication of the bird that would become the modern chicken and the advent of pickling cucumbers as a way of preserving excess produce for the meaner seasons.

It was believed by the likes of Charles Darwin that the chicken was descended from the red jungle fowl of Thailand. However, genome analysis published in scientific journal *Nature* in 2020 suggests that the chicken was domesticated in five separate locations, from China to South-East Asia, with each subspecies interbreeding over the years to give us the range of chickens we know and love today. This knowledge of selective interbreeding to give us the first chicken is incontrovertible proof that the egg containing that chicken came first, because the bird that laid the egg wasn't a chicken as we now know it!

While poaching is a common cooking technique around the world, in China it is an art form, whether you are poaching in a lightly aromatic pot of water to make superbly tender *bai qie ji* ('white cut chicken') or being more generous with the spices, Chinese wine and soy sauces to make the Cantonese delicacy of *see yao gai* ('soy sauce chicken'). Both of these dishes have countless variations, passed down from family cook to family cook over the generations, each recipe differing slightly in the composition or aromas, the favoured chook or the nuances of the technique. Do you leave the chicken in the cooling pot of boiling stock to cook through, or do you remove it four times to re-boil the cooking stock and then add the bird again to let it cook in the reheated liquid?

The only rule all recipes seem to agree on is that you should always poach a whole chook. We've broken that rule here, as I just want the satiny-smooth chicken breast in this salad. Such is the luxury of modern days.

We've also broken the rules with the mayonnaise, which should be a slow liaison of egg yolks and olive oil. The instant mayo that I've made my own over the past ten years was originally sent to me by New Zealand-born UK *MasterChef* winner Mat Follas. Over the years I have experimented with turning his base recipe into a number of different flavoured mayos. The miso and bacon combination used here is a particular favourite, and so perfect with chicken. The miso–bacon pairing is very much a reflection of the dude-food movement of around eight years ago, but I think I actually first had that combo at David Chang's Momofuku Noodle Bar in New York in 2004 when he was serving bowls of summer corn with miso butter and smoky bacon while playing the Ramones really, really loud.

The home-pickling of cucumber and ginger is another fave trick of mine, using my patented 'quickling' technique. Pickling is a preserving process that first reared its sour, salty, crunchy head in Mesopotamia about the same time jungle fowl were being domesticated in South-East Asia and China. This quick-pickle process, however, comes from more like ten years ago and is an early example of an internet 'hack'.

Salads themselves were originally just 'salted things', back in the days when togas were all the rage. Yup, the '*sal*' in salad comes from the same Latin root word as salt and salary. The meaning of the word evolved to become the pretty olde English *sallets* of tender leaves, herbs and flowers in the fourteenth century, then morphed into 'grand sallets' in the seventeenth century, which were over-the-top salads with everything thrown in them – potatoes, pickled oysters, capon meat, tarragon, lettuce, broom buds, orange, raisins, etc., etc., etc.

By then, *oyl* and vinegar whisked together had become the default dressing for a salade, sallet or salad. The Chevalier d'Albignac, an entrepreneurial Frenchman living in London after the French Revolution, charged the princely sum of a guinea per visit to your dinner table, and could perform the theatrical dressing of salads four times a night. Earning the equivalent of $1500 a night, he soon had his own liveried coach-and-pair, and a special swing-lid walnut case with all the oil, vinegars and other tinctures he might apply to one's meal for that fine price.

On that note, let's say that this isn't just a salad 4500 years in the making; I've also saved you $375 in the dressing!

Soy-poached chicken salad *(CONTINUED)*

2 teaspoons caster sugar

½ teaspoon salt

2 Lebanese cucumbers, thinly sliced into rounds (on a mandolin if you have one)

4 cm knob ginger, peeled and very thinly sliced

¼ cup (60 ml) rice wine vinegar

150 g snow peas, trimmed and de-stringed

¾ cup (80 g) frozen podded edamame (or green peas)

½ iceberg lettuce, cut into wedges

½ bunch coriander, leaves picked

1 large avocado, cut into thick wedges

¼ cup (40 g) smoked almonds, coarsely chopped

Soy and ginger poached chicken

1 tablespoon grapeseed oil

6 cm knob ginger, thinly sliced

1 cup (250 ml) Chinese cooking wine (shaoxing)

4 cups (1 litre) water

¼ cup (60 ml) soy sauce

¼ cup (60 ml) dark soy sauce

2 teaspoons sichuan peppercorns

2 spring onions, white parts and green parts separated, both parts thinly sliced

2 chicken breast fillets

Bacon miso mayonnaise

2 rashers rindless bacon, finely chopped

1½ tablespoons white miso paste

2 teaspoons mirin

2 teaspoons rice wine vinegar

2 teaspoons soy sauce

1 egg

350 ml grapeseed oil

Begin with poaching the chicken. Pick the smallest lidded saucepan you have that will hold the breasts easily and efficiently. Heat the oil in the saucepan over medium heat. Add the ginger and cook for 2–3 minutes or until it starts to colour slightly. Add the wine and boil for a minute or so until reduced slightly.

Add the water, soy sauces, peppercorns and white parts of the spring onion to the pan. Add the chicken breasts, making sure there is enough liquid to cover them. Return the saucepan to medium heat. As soon as the liquid comes to the boil, remove from the heat immediately and cover with a tight-fitting lid. Set aside for 45 minutes to poach in the liquid.

Meanwhile, to make the mayonnaise, heat a small frying pan over medium heat. Add the bacon and cook, stirring, for 4–5 minutes or until golden and crisp. Remove from the pan and set aside.

Place the miso, mirin, vinegar and soy sauce in the canister of a stick blender. Blend briefly to combine. Carefully crack the egg into the canister, without breaking the yolk. Add the grapeseed oil. Insert the stick blender into the canister carefully so that the basket of the stick blender is completely covering the yolk. Turn on the stick blender, and as pale ribbons appear, slowly pull it upwards and continue to blitz to incorporate the oil until thick and creamy. Add the bacon and blitz with the stick blender until the bacon is well combined. Refrigerate until serving time.

Place the sugar and salt in a glass or ceramic bowl. Add the cucumber and ginger and set aside, tossing occasionally, for 10 minutes to cure. Pour over the vinegar and set aside for at least 5 minutes or until needed.

Blanch the snow peas and edamame in a small saucepan of boiling water over medium–high heat for 1–2 minutes, until they just turn bright green and are tender crisp. Drain and plunge into a bowl of ice-cold water to stop the cooking process.

Use tongs to transfer the chicken to a plate. Reserve the poaching liquid (see Tips). Shred the chicken meat.

Arrange the lettuce wedges, coriander, avocado, chicken, snow peas and edamame on a large serving platter. Dollop some of the bacon miso mayonnaise on the salad. Drain the cucumber mixture and discard the liquid. Scatter the cucumber and ginger on top. Sprinkle with the almonds and green parts of the spring onion.

TIPS

Don't waste the poaching liquid. Strain through a fine sieve and place in an airtight container. Freeze or use it to boil potatoes in, or poach chicken or eggs for tomorrow night's dinner.

The bacon miso mayonnaise will keep in an airtight container in the fridge for up to 1 week. As with any recipe that uses raw eggs, care should be taken over the provenance of your eggs and this mayo should be avoided if you are concerned the raw eggs you are using could pose a risk to you. This mayo can also be made with chickpea water (aquafaba) instead of eggs.

Look for rose wine (*mei kwei lu*) at Chinese grocers. Use it to replace the shaoxing wine for a more fragrant outcome.

Chicken kiev

SERVES 4 **PREP** 15 minutes (plus chilling) **COOK** 30 minutes

Myth

Chicken kiev was invented for the grand feasts of the Tsars at the Winter Palace in St Petersburg.

My Truth

Chicken kiev sounds like a recipe that ought to have been smuggled out of St Petersburg in a Fabergé egg by a Romanov princess, but it wasn't. Certainly, the roots of chicken kiev are in the late eighteenth and early nineteenth century kitchens of the Russian aristocracy, who had the roubles to employ France's greatest chefs. It was chefs of this era who decided to stuff the breasts of fowl or gamebirds with something decadent, like a truffle-studded chicken mousse, and then crumb them for cooking. However, this is really only the first stage of the dish's evolution, and certainly not chicken kiev as we know it.

(Even Marie-Antoine Carême was lured to Russia to work for the Tsar in 1819. Carême didn't invent any new dishes in Russia, but he did return to France with a big idea. The founder of haute cuisine decreed that, rather than all dishes being served on the table together, in a manner known as *service à la française*, they should be served one by one in individual courses, in the Russian manner, aka *service à la russe*. That's where we got the idea of separate courses that exists today. But I digress . . .)

After the Russian Revolution, the affluently stuffed fillets were replaced with patty-like cutlets or croquettes of pounded beef or chicken, formed and crumbed in the French or South Indian style. This version was served at the St Petersburg Merchants' Club in 1912.

But the third piece in the chicken kiev story comes from the luxurious Continental Hotel in Kiev, which gave us stuffed chicken breast 'in the style of Kiev' at the start of the twentieth century. It is here that the name emerged. Chicken kiev recipes that followed were either those crumbed cutlets formed around a log of chilled butter, or butterflied chicken breast treated the same way. The latter is a close relation to or perhaps inspiration for crumbed, fried, ham-and-cheese-stuffed dishes like Northern Italian *cotoletta alla Valdostana* or French chicken cordon bleu.

While simple, butter-filled kievs were popular during the Soviet era, in the decadent West we added garlic, herbs or even blue cheese to the butter. The magic of the oozy filling fitted perfectly with the showmanship of 1970s restaurant dining, but I reckon Finnish Russian restaurant the Grey Door went too far in 1979 when it offered a chicken kiev stuffed with vodka-saturated butter and served on curried rice. We are keeping things far simpler here with our recipe!

4 chicken breast fillets
¼ cup (35 g) plain flour
5 eggs
4 cups (300 g) panko breadcrumbs
grapeseed oil, to shallow fry
creamy mashed potatoes and steamed green
beans *or* crusty bread and green salad, to
serve

Garlic butter

80 g butter, at room temperature
2 garlic cloves, crushed
1 tablespoon finely chopped flat-leaf parsley

Start by making the garlic butter. Combine the butter, garlic and parsley in a small bowl. Scoop onto a sheet of plastic wrap and shape to form a log about 8 cm long. Place in the freezer for 2 hours or until firm.

Use a small sharp knife to make a deep cut about 4 cm long in the thicker side of each chicken breast to form a pocket. Take care not to cut all the way through. Cut the garlic butter into slices and press the slices into the pockets. If the butter starts to get soft inside the chicken, place back in the freezer until it firms up again.

Place the flour on a large plate. Whisk the eggs in a large shallow bowl. Place the breadcrumbs on a separate large plate. Coat the chicken in the flour and shake off any excess. Dip in the egg mixture, then in the breadcrumbs, pressing firmly to coat. Repeat the process to give the chicken a second coating of just egg and breadcrumbs (not flour). This makes the chicken coating super crisp, but also helps stop the butter from oozing out during cooking. Transfer to a tray, cover with plastic wrap and refrigerate for 30 minutes to set.

Preheat the oven to 200°C (180°C fan-forced). Add enough oil to a large frying pan to come 1 cm up the side and heat over medium–high heat. Add half the chicken and cook for 1½ minutes each side or until golden. Transfer to a baking tray. Repeat with the remaining chicken. Bake for 20 minutes or until golden and cooked through.

Serve with creamy mashed potatoes and steamed green beans sprinkled with toasted almonds in winter, or with a green salad and crusty bread in summer.

Teriyaki chicken

SERVES 4 **PREP** 20 minutes (plus marinating) **COOK** 1 hour 15 minutes

Myth
Tokyo is brimming with shops selling teriyaki chicken.

My Truth
Teriyaki in Japanese literally translates as 'shiny grilling', and this lacquering of fish, meat or vegetables with a mirin-sweetened soy glaze is one of the great Japanese culinary gifts to the world.

The technique originated in seventeenth century Japan, which was newly unified under the Tokugawa shogunate. At this time of urbanisation, soy sauce became cheaper, more widely available and increasingly mass produced. Mirin also become more widely available as commercial production spread in the late 1600s. Prior to this, it had been largely a rich man's tipple rather than a condiment.

Early uses for teriyaki sauce were with fish and seafood, but after the Meiji Restoration in 1868 (and an associated dramatic increase in meat consumption), teriyaki quickly became associated with beef and chicken. Although cattle had been introduced to Japan in the second century AD (along with rice), cows were used as draught animals because Japan's predominant religions of Shintoism and then Buddhism promoted largely vegetarian culinary principles, which lasted until the end of Japan's period of isolationism in the mid-nineteenth century.

As what it was served on evolved, so did teriyaki sauce itself. There were additions like garlic, ginger, sake, honey and even sesame oil. Spring onions became close to the default garnish, while reducing teriyaki over heat to thicken it resulted in the intense *kabayaki* sauce that is perhaps most often seen glistening on bronzed tiles of eel at your local sushi place.

The arrival of 153 Japanese migrants to Hawaii in that first year of the Meiji Restoration began a long and somewhat fraught relationship between Japan and Hawaii, which saw Japanese migration banned, and then the percentage of people with Japanese heritage rise to 43 per cent of Hawaii's population by 1920, with many working on sugar and pineapple plantations. Japanese settlers gave Hawaii everything from the poke bowl and Spam *musubi* (a sort of Spam nigiri sushi) to, in the 1920s or 1930s, a local take on teriyaki, in which pineapple juice and sugar replaced the mirin and sake. The presence of ginger, garlic and spring onions became commonplace in Hawaiian teriyaki too.

In more recent times, teriyaki became nowhere more popular than in Seattle in the United States. At its peak, there were over five hundred holes-in-the-wall and simple takeaway joints that had the word 'teriyaki' in their name! And all this started from the humble beginnings of a single teriyaki joint, Toshi's Teriyaki Grill, set up in 1976 by Toshihiro Kasahara, who had emigrated from Japan at 18 years of age to wrestle for Portland State University. Seattle's 'teriyaki' is a distinctly low-budget version – a thick and sticky mixture made from reducing soy sauce with no more than sugar.

While Kasahara cooked his chicken thighs slowly and served them over rice, rival teriyaki chef John Chung's teriyaki sandwich was all about fast, hot cooking. Chung, of Korean descent, who had moved to Portland from Los Angeles, claimed that most of the many Korean owners of teriyaki grills in Seattle had stopped by his place looking for either work or advice. So, in Seattle you'll find your teriyaki chicken just as likely served on rice or in a sandwich, or occasionally atop shredded, wilted cabbage.

From those heady days, the number of Seattle teriyaki joints has dropped to only 60 or so, but the internet is still loaded with many more mentions of teriyaki in Seattle than in Osaka or Tokyo. In part this may be a matter of nomenclature; Japanese cooks and chefs see teriyaki as a technique for yakitori skewers or sushi items rather than a dish in itself. Certainly, if you are searching for teriyaki chicken joints in Tokyo you'll walk past a whole lot more ramen, tempura and sushi joints to find one.

Which leads me to the question, has teriyaki chicken become more of an American and Australian dish than a Japanese one? In Japan there is word dating from the Meiji Restoration, *yōshoku*, which refers to Western food given a Japanese twist. I wonder if there's a word that goes the other way? If there is, then this recipe most definitely is one from that canon – a proudly Aussie teriyaki chicken.

Teriyaki chicken (CONTINUED)

¼ cup (90 g) honey
6 chicken thigh fillets, cut crossways into
    3 strips
1 head of garlic
8 long green chillies
3 tablespoons (60 ml) grapeseed oil

Teriyaki sauce

2 garlic cloves, peeled
sea salt
2 tablespoons mirin
¼ cup (60 ml) soy sauce
1 tablespoon rice wine vinegar
1 tablespoon caster sugar
¼ teaspoon sesame oil
2 cm knob ginger, peeled, finely grated

Snow pea and edamame salad

ice cubes
200 g snow peas, trimmed and de-stringed
200 g packet frozen podded edamame
1 tablespoon mirin
2 teaspoons sesame oil
2 teaspoons rice wine vinegar
2 teaspoons lemon juice
½ teaspoon soy sauce
½ teaspoon caster sugar
3 spring onions, thinly sliced, soaked in cold
    water and drained
1 teaspoon sesame seeds, toasted

To make the teriyaki sauce, place the garlic on a chopping board and finely chop. Add a little salt and mash into a paste with the side of the knife. Bring the mirin to the boil in a small saucepan over high heat. Reduce the heat to medium. Add the garlic and all the other ingredients. Simmer for 5 minutes or until thickened slightly. Set aside to cool.

Time to marinate the chicken. Combine the teriyaki sauce and honey in a glass or ceramic dish. Add the chicken and turn to coat. Cover and refrigerate for 30 minutes (or up to 4 hours if you want to get ahead).

Preheat the oven to 200°C (180°C fan-forced). Line two baking trays with baking paper. Place the head of garlic and the whole chillies on one of the baking trays and drizzle with 1 tablespoon of the grapeseed oil. Bake for 45 minutes or until soft. Cool slightly.

Drain the chicken and place on the remaining lined tray. Drizzle with 1 tablespoon of oil. Roast for 20–25 minutes or until cooked through.

Squeeze the soft pulp from each garlic clove, discarding the skins. Cut the chillies in half lengthways, remove any stems and use a teaspoon to scrape out the seeds (or keep in if you want it hotter). Place the garlic and chilli in a small food processor and process until finely chopped. With the motor running, drizzle in the remaining 1 tablespoon of oil, scraping down the side frequently, until a smooth paste forms.

Meanwhile, make your salad. Fill a bowl with water and add a few ice cubes. Bring a deep frying pan of water to the boil. In batches, add the snow peas and cook for 5 seconds or until bright green. Use a slotted spoon to transfer to the bowl of iced water to stop the cooking process. After a minute, transfer to a tray lined with paper towel to drain well.

Add the edamame to the boiling water and cook for 2 minutes or until tender. Drain, then transfer to the iced water to stop cooking. Drain well.

To make the salad dressing, whisk the mirin, sesame oil, vinegar, lemon juice, soy sauce and sugar in a jug until well combined. Set aside.

Place the snow peas and edamame on a serving platter. Scatter over the spring onion. Drizzle with the dressing and sprinkle with the sesame seeds. Add the teriyaki chicken to the platter and serve with the chilli and garlic paste on the side.

Food nerd fact

Chinese monks first introduced the two-thousand-year-old idea of soy sauce to Japan in the seventh century. Over the years, soy evolved away from the original Chinese fermented recipe, which sought to produce a salt alternative by using fish or meat to stretch the salinity of the base brine, to the addition and finally the sole use of soybeans in the fermentation.

Traditionally, much soy sauce production centred on the rural prefectures around the old capital of Kyoto, but the new Tokugawa shogunate relocating the ruling family (and thus the capital) to Edo (which today we know as Tokyo) in 1603 created a massive population boom in this once-sleepy fishing village. During the early years of the shogunate, over 160,000 barrels of soy were transported from Yuasa, an area famed for its traditional, soybean-heavy soy sauce, to Japan's new capital. Inevitably, production eventually shifted nearer to this huge new market and to places like Shōdo Island. Here there was salt production, good fresh water and plenty of discarded sake barrels from nearby breweries. These *kioke* (barrels), soy sauce brewers discovered, were perfect for the larger scale production of soy sauce. An added bonus was that maturing and fermenting in wood helped boost the sauce's umami characteristics.

Noda, north of Edo, and Chōshi also had rivers for water and a cold climate suited to starting fermentation, making them the perfect new centres for miso and soy sauce production. It was here, by playing with adding and increasing amounts of wheat to the fermenting, brined soybeans, and by fermenting for longer, brewers created a richer, darker soy sauce with the flavour that we know today. Within thirty years this new 'Kanto jimawari shoyu' had largely replaced 'kudari shoyu' in the kitchens and on the tables of the capital.

Six-minute chicken satay

SERVES 1 **PREP** 10 minutes **COOK** 6 minutes

Twist

Myth
Satay is a peanut sauce.

My Truth
Sate is one of the five national dishes of Indonesia, and appears to have originated in Java with Tamil traders in the early nineteenth century. While Tamil people had been trading with the Indonesian islands since the eleventh century, there was an influx of Tamils in the 1830s, lured there to work on plantations owned by the Dutch colonialists.

The skewers sold on the streets were mutton or beef, and while their point of origin was India, the presence of coriander and cumin in many recipes points to these kebabs possibly having Middle Eastern heritage too.

In Indonesia, the name 'sate' refers to the skewers rather than the peanut sauce, and there are many regional variations that are not served with peanut sauce. Mutton sate is usually served with kecap manis (sweet soy sauce), and shrimp sate with nothing at all. Where a peanut sauce is used, the flavourings still vary; the peanut paste might be mixed with sweet soybean sauce, kecap manis, palm sugar, garlic, deep fried shallots or shrimp paste.

By the end of the nineteenth century, sate had become a hit in Malaysia, too, and quickly spread across South-East Asia. The Kuala Lumpur suburb of Kacang has become rightfully famous for their world-beating take on it. In Singapore, 'satay' became so popular that a group of satay traders and their waterside park location was one of the biggest tourist attractions prior to that Merlion fountain. Here, peanut sauce was de rigeur and the default sauce for sate.

Satay also took root back in the homeland of Indonesia's colonial rulers. In the Netherlands, you'll find the sauce sold in jars at the supermarket and slathered over 2 am serves of fries. Some snobs might look down on satay sauce from a jar or, even worse, made with peanut butter, but peanut pastes have a proud history predating satay sauces by some three thousand years.

This hack peanut satay sauce was invented in 2021 in Australasia as something to make on the plate as you are reheating last night's chicken skewers or cold sausage in the microwave. Obviously, it is not intended to replace the lovingly crafted original. The goal was a quick, fast recipe that would produce the right amount of sauce for just one serve, with minimal washing up. It also uses only four pantry staples, making it perfect for all your late-night snacking needs.

Serve it with a lime wedge, if you've got limes about, as a little acidity is welcome. If you don't have chilli jam, sweet chilli sauce, kecap manis or Chinese *doubanjiang* chilli bean paste can stand in. A little tamarind paste and grated palm sugar are also nice.

3 chicken tenderloins
2 teaspoons coconut oil
300 g last night's leftover steamed jasmine rice (which is pressed into the takeaway container)
½ Lebanese cucumber, cut into wedges
coriander leaves, to serve
roasted peanuts, roughly chopped, to serve (optional)

Cheat's twenty-second satay sauce
1½ tablespoons crunchy peanut butter
1 tablespoon desiccated coconut
2 teaspoons chilli jam
½ teaspoon ground coriander

Thread each chicken tenderloin onto a metal or soaked bamboo skewer. Heat the oil in a frying pan over medium–high heat. Add the chicken skewers and cook for 2 minutes each side or until cooked through.

While the chicken cooks, get your plate ready. Press last night's leftover rice into the takeaway container, then turn out onto a board and cut into cubes. Place the cubes on a serving plate with the cucumber and coriander leaves.

To make the satay sauce, place all the ingredients in a small microwave-safe bowl. Stir to combine. Microwave on high for 10–20 seconds or until heated through. Add 2 tablespoons boiling water and stir to combine (if you like your sauce runnier, just add a touch more water).

Add the skewers to the plate and drizzle with the satay sauce. Top with a sprinkling of roasted peanuts, if you have some at hand.

TIPS

Can't get tenderloins? Place a breast fillet between two pieces of plastic wrap and use a meat mallet or rolling pin to pound until 1 cm thick. Cut into three strips lengthways. Weave each strip onto a skewer and cook for 3–4 minutes each side.

Korean chimaek

SERVES 4 **PREP** 20 minutes (plus 30 minutes marinating) **COOK** 30 minutes

Myth

In 2017, there were more fried chicken restaurants in Korea than there were McDonald's restaurants in the whole world.

My Truth

Fried chicken first gained popularity in South Korea when American troops were stationed there in the 1950s and 1960s. It took off, however, in the 1970s. This was thanks to the broader availability of cooking oil with a high smoke point and increased local chicken production, which meant far cheaper prices for what had previously been seen as a special occasion food. Chicken had also traditionally been steamed, or eaten in soup, in the previous four hundred years since chicken dishes were first mentioned in the writings of sixteenth-century Korean philosopher and writer Yi I (1536–1584).

The first Korean fried chicken franchise, Lim's Chicken, opened in 1977, and research showed that by 2016, one in four food franchises in South Korea sold fried chicken.

Fried chicken was always viewed as *anju*, or drinking food, in Korea: something to be consumed with alcohol after a long day in the factory or at the office. Drinking food always has a preferred alcoholic partner – like pairing *makgeolli*, sour fermented rice wine, with Korean pancakes. Originally, for fried chicken, this was just as likely to be shots of soju as it was glasses of beer.

The 1985 creation of *yangnyeom* (fried chicken coated in a sweet, spicy sauce) by Yoon Jong-gye helped drive the success of Korea's fried chicken shops, and along the way beer became the natural partner to fried chicken. With the coining of the word *chimaek*, that partnership became set in stone. Koreans are obsessed with coining words for the result of two food trends colliding. *Chimaek* is perhaps the most famous of these, combining the Korean words for 'fried chicken' and 'beer'. The word has been in use for a while, but was massively popularised by its use at the public screening sites erected for the 2002 FIFA World Cup.

South Korea were World Cup co-hosts with Japan, and the public screening sites for watching the matches outside the stadium were a huge hit. The unlikely success of the South Korean national team, who reached the semifinals under the management of future Socceroos manager Guus Hiddink, also helped, anchoring the combination of chicken and beer in the national culinary psyche.

The *chimaek* trend was further popularised in both Korea and China with a throwaway line on a successful Korean fantasy rom-com series *My Love from the Star*. The phrase gained almost instant traction, and the resulting Chinese demand for fried chicken helped single-handedly reinvigorate the nation's poultry industry.

So, before frying up this chicken, chill down some beer. In Korea, you'd be angling for frozen frothy pints of bright Cass or longnecks of effervescent Hite. It's possible to track down both in Australia, but any bright lager will do if you can't. Then enjoy *chimaek* time – the simple pleasure of eating fried chicken and drinking beer. Smart people, those Koreans.

Oh, and the myth about there being more fried chicken restaurants in Korea than there are Maccas in the world? As weird and as unlikely as it sounds, it was actually true, at least in 2013. The *Korea Herald* reported that there were about 36,000 fried chicken places in Korea, compared to 35,429 McDonald's stores globally.

Korean chimaek (CONTINUED)

1¼ cups (310 ml) buttermilk, plus
    extra 2 tablespoons
2 teaspoons sesame oil
2 garlic cloves, crushed
2 teaspoons finely grated ginger
6 large or 8 medium chicken thigh fillets
1½ cups (225 g) plain flour
¼ cup (35 g) cornflour (corn starch)
3 eggs
sea salt and freshly ground black pepper
vegetable oil, for deep-frying
⅓ cup (80 ml) Korean Bulldog barbecue
    sauce, or regular barbecue sauce
sesame seeds, toasted, to serve
Kewpie mayonnaise spiked with *ssamjang*
    (see Tips), to serve

Korean seasoning

1 tablespoon onion powder
1 tablespoon garlic powder
3 teaspoons Korean chilli powder (not flakes)
    or 2 teaspoons regular chilli powder
2 teaspoons ground ginger
2 teaspoons sea salt
1 teaspoon white pepper

Combine the buttermilk, sesame oil, garlic and ginger in a glass or ceramic bowl. Add the chicken and toss to combine. Set aside for 30 minutes to marinate. (If you have more time or want to get ahead you can marinate overnight in the fridge.)

To make the Korean seasoning, combine all the ingredients in a bowl.

Combine the Korean seasoning, flour and cornflour in a bowl. Whisk together the eggs and the extra 2 tablespoons of buttermilk in a separate bowl and season with salt.

Half fill a large saucepan with oil. Heat over medium heat until the oil reaches 160°C on a cook's thermometer (or until a cube of bread turns golden in 30 seconds after being added to the oil).

Working in batches so you don't overcrowd the pan, remove the chicken from the buttermilk marinade, then toss in the flour mixture. Dip into the egg mixture and then the flour mixture again to coat.

Add to the oil and cook, turning occasionally, for 10 minutes or until golden. Reheat the oil as you go to make sure you keep it at 160°C. Transfer the fried chicken to a plate lined with paper towel to drain.

Place on a platter and drizzle over the barbecue sauce. Sprinkle with the sesame seeds and serve with the spiked Kewpie mayo on the side.

TIPS

Ssamjang is a spicy Korean barbecue dipping sauce. Most large supermarkets will have it in their Asian food section. You can also pick up Korean chilli powder (*gochugaru*) while you're there.

If you want to be really Korean, take the chicken out halfway through cooking, give it a good shake, and then let it rest for a couple of minutes before returning it to the oil at 180°C for a final crisp. There is a belief in Seoul that this makes for better cooked and more succulent chicken without the crust getting too brown.

Food nerd fact

This is real KFC (Korean Fried Chicken). Like the American version, it uses a buttermilk marinade base with a hint of sesame, but then the crunch is spiked with Korean flavours. You could cook it straightaway, but the chicken benefits mightily from marinating for a few hours or even overnight. Cornflour gives the batter extra crunch. Sometimes the fried chicken is doused in red *yangnyeom* sauce and scattered with sesame seeds so the crunchy batter gets 'soggily delicious'. (Two words that only go together in a few places around the world – Korea, Mexico and Hong Kong in China come immediately to mind.) I get the appeal, but ! love the awesome crunch too much, so here we are just drizzling on the sweet barbecue sauce in places so we get the best of both worlds.

Jerked chicken

SERVES 4 **PREP** 20 minutes (plus 30 minutes marinating) **COOK** 20 minutes

Myth
Barbecuing originally came from Jamaica.

My Truth
The local legend is that Jamaica's Blue Mountains earnt their name from the barbecue smoke that constantly hung over the range, and it is from here that the famous Jamaican tradition of grilling spicy jerked meats comes.

Jerk itself is a traditional cooking method that originated with the Maroon people of the area. These communities date back to runaway slaves who joined with the indigenous Taino people in Jamaica's inaccessible interior to evade Spanish or English slaveholders.

The Maroons predate the English capture of Jamaica from the Spanish in 1655, but their numbers rocketed immediately following the invasion as slaves took the opportunity to escape once the Spanish left and before they could be put to work by the new colonial government.

The Taino peoples' traditional way of cooking or drying meat to preserve it was on a raised lattice of green wood – normally local pimento wood, from the tree that gives us allspice berries. We know this because when Christopher Columbus first landed in the Caribbean in 1492, he saw Taino people cooking meat on a rack of intertwined green wood sticks raised over a fire. It immediately earned the name *barbacoa* in Spanish, taken from the Taino word for such a grill.

Of course, back when the Maroons were hiding out in the country's mountainous interior, smoke would have been an obvious signal to the colonial militias that sought to eradicate or re-enslave them. Thus the slow-cooking and drying of meat became something that was done in ground ovens, where the smoke would be contained, rather than on green wood grills. It was a similar approach to a Maori hāngī or Fijian *lovo*. The meat was usually wrapped in agave-like *maguey* leaves before being covered in earth to keep in both the heat and the smoke. The pimento wood used for the fires in these pit ovens, and indigenous Scotch bonnet chillies, gave jerk its signature flavour, while the roasted *maguey* leaves would impart a caramelly sweetness.

When the Maroons no longer needed to fear capture, they returned to slow-cooking meat over the fire with grills made from green pimento wood. When the technique was exported, the absence of the signature pimento wood meant homesick Jamaicans improvised by using the tree's dried allspice berries in a spice rub to bring in some of that flavour.

The history of jerk is so intertwined with the history of barbecuing that it is practically an ancestor of everything we cook over coals or gas in our backyards today. Thus, the Taino peoples of Caribbean islands like Jamaica can claim to be the creators of the barbecue. However, if we trace the history of jerk, we can see that this technique is much older, and the first barbecues may have been born further south.

Most scholars believe that the Taino arrived in the Caribbean from South America. The Arawakan language group, of which Taino is considered to have been a part, stretched from the Colombian Andes to the northern Brazilian coast and included some of the Amazon basin. The circum-Caribbean theory espoused by American anthropologist Julian Haynes Steward posits that the Taino came to the Caribbean from the Andes.

Here in Latin America, Europeans also saw indigenous peoples cooking on a grill made of green sticks, and called it *boucan*, after the Tupi term for the technique (*buccan*). The Tupi are another major language group from northern South America. This shows us that the technique of drying, smoking and cooking meat on a grill was a common practice in the region from where the Taino are thought to have originally come.

The most plausible explanation for the origin of the words 'jerk' and 'jerky' is that they come from the Andes and the local Quechuan word for the smoky, slow drying process, *charqi*.

All of this seems to point to the fact that the Taino brought the grilling techniques of South America with them when they migrated to the Caribbean. Interestingly, the process of underground cooking of ingredients wrapped in leaves like *maguey* is still common in Mexico under the name *barbacoa*. It is not certain whether that technique originated locally, or spread up from Central America or across from the Caribbean.

With all this evidence, linguistic and otherwise, it seems the origins of barbecue and jerk were in South America and not the Caribbean, so I don't feel at all guilty putting a local spin on it by amping up the spices!

Jerked chicken (CONTINUED)

1 kg chicken wingettes (or wing nibbles)
2 tablespoons olive oil
coriander sprigs, to serve
lime wedges, to serve

Jerk marinade

1 small brown onion, coarsely chopped
3 spring onions, coarsely chopped
2 long red chillies, deseeded but the ribs left
   in for heat, coarsely chopped (see Tips)
¼ cup coarsely chopped coriander
3 garlic cloves, crushed
3 cm knob ginger, peeled, finely grated
2 tablespoons brown sugar
1 tablespoon ground allspice
1 tablespoon thyme leaves
2 teaspoons sea salt
1 teaspoon freshly ground black pepper
1 teaspoon ground cinnamon
½ teaspoon ground nutmeg
1 tablespoon lime juice

Blitz all the jerk marinade ingredients in a food processor until a smooth paste forms (the mixture is a wet paste).

Place the chicken in a glass or ceramic bowl. Add the marinade and toss to coat. Cover and place in the fridge for at least 30 minutes, or overnight, to marinate.

Preheat a barbecue grill on medium heat. Drizzle the chicken with the oil. Add to the barbecue grill. Cook, turning regularly, for 3–4 minutes each side over direct heat, then move and cook over indirect heat for 15 minutes or until cooked through. Alternatively, once you have given the wings some colour on the grill, transfer to a roasting pan and cook in the oven at 180°C (160°C fan-forced) for 10 minutes or until cooked through. (Keep an eye on the little wingette pieces, as they will take less time than the larger pieces. When these are cooked, move them to the side of the grill to keep warm while the larger pieces cook through.)

Pile up your chicken on a serving platter and sprinkle with the coriander. Serve with the lime wedges.

TIPS

For a more authentic and far hotter burn, use Scotch bonnet or habanero chillies instead of long red chillies.

If you have a bit of time, try deboning your wingettes before marinating. Just cut off the cartilage and bone tips at the shoulder (or drumette) end of the wingette. Then ease the flesh down the bone, cutting away or peeling back any cartilage still attached to the bone. Now pull out the bones while easing down the meat. When the bones have been removed, roll back the flesh so the skin side faces out.

You can also serve these with buttered soft bread rolls and some sour cream, which will tame any savage heat and allow the spices to shine.

Food nerd fact

The Tupi word *boucan* was used by both the Spanish and French to refer to the lawless hunters who set up camps on Tortuga and Hispaniola to hunt wild pigs. They cured the pig meat and rendered the lard to sell to passing ships that needed to resupply their stores.

Given that the area was a hotbed of both piracy and state-licensed *corsaires* from France and privateers from Holland and England all preying on the Spanish gold galleons, and that many *boucan* traders signed up to work for privateers like Sir Francis Drake, the name *boucaneer* or buccaneer became synonymous with being something of a pirate.

Kung pao chicken

SERVES 4 **PREP** 20 minutes **COOK** 15 minutes

Myth

Ding Gong Pao, who invented kung pao chicken, is so revered that his mausoleum and former home attract millions of tourists every year.

My Truth

Ding Baozhen (1820–1886) was governor of Shandong and then Sichuan province during the Qing dynasty. He was known as a tough but honest administrator who also had a penchant for flood prevention to improve the life of the citizenry.

Ding helped finance levees on the Yellow River in Shandong, and oversaw the rebuilding of the second-century Dujiangyan irrigation and flood control system, which tempers the Min River when the springtime melt threatens to break its banks. He also played a role in the arrest and execution of An Dehai, a eunuch at the imperial court who was much hated by court officials and common people for his arrogance and for flouting his power.

As well as his achievements in public service, Ding created kung pao chicken, one of China's most famous dishes. Later in life, Ding was given the honorary title of *gong pao*, or 'crown prince teacher', by the emperor. Ding Gong Pao became his commonly used nickname, and this is where the name of the dish comes from.

The first iteration of kung pao chicken was made during Ding's time as head of Shandong province. He employed two local cooks who specialised in what was locally called 'explosive' stir-frying, which perfectly suited the small cubes of chicken breast that Ding liked to serve his guests. There is an in-joke here, as the family name 'Ding' is very close to the Chinese character for 'small cubes'.

He took the dish with him when he became governor general of Sichuan in 1876. Sichuan is famous for chillies, so these were a natural addition to those succulent cubes. Peanuts, vinegar and a little sugar were also added to make the dish we know today. What is lesser known is that in China you can 'kung pao' just about anything. In the first Sichuan cuisine cookbook, published in 1960, you'll find a recipe for kung pao pig's kidneys.

In recent years, Chinese astronauts have taken kung pao chicken to space, and it was served to President Trump on his visit to China in 2017. While there is one statue of Ding that remains near the Dujiangyan dam, there are no other physical monuments celebrating his life and achievements. No old stately home or grand tomb. His testament is the world-famous dish he created, which proves that food is much harder to erase than any physical reminder of our lives.

8 spring onions
2 teaspoons cornflour (corn starch)
⅓ cup (80 ml) chicken stock
¼ cup (60 ml) light soy sauce
2 tablespoons Chinese cooking wine (shaoxing)
2 tablespoons black vinegar
2 teaspoons caster sugar
¼ cup (60 ml) peanut oil
½ cup (70 g) unsalted raw peanuts
500 g chicken tenderloins
1 red capsicum (pepper), deseeded and cut into strips
1 green capsicum (pepper), deseeded and cut into strips
8 dried red chillies, tops cut off and seeds tapped out
4 cm knob ginger, peeled and finely grated
2 garlic cloves, crushed
1 teaspoon sichuan peppercorns, crushed using a mortar and pestle
steamed rice, to serve

Trim the spring onions and cut the white parts of six of them into 3–4 cm lengths. Thinly slice the remaining two spring onions diagonally.

Place the cornflour in a bowl. Add a little of the stock and stir until smooth and evenly combined. Gradually add the remaining stock, stirring continuously as you go. Add the soy sauce, wine, vinegar and sugar and stir to combine. Set aside.

Heat 1 tablespoon of the oil in a wok over medium–high heat, then add the peanuts and cook for 2 minutes or until lightly golden. Remove with a slotted spoon and drain on a tray lined with paper towel.

Turn the heat up nice and high – remember, we can use 'explosive' heat here, albeit not literally. Heat 1 tablespoon of the remaining oil in the wok. Cook the chicken in two batches for 90 seconds each side or until just golden brown, adding more oil for the second batch if required. Transfer to a bowl and set aside.

Add the remaining oil to the wok. Add the capsicum and dried chillies and stir-fry for 3–4 minutes or until slightly charred and starting to soften. Add the spring onion lengths, the ginger, garlic and peppercorns and stir-fry for 1 minute or until aromatic.

Add the chicken, soy sauce mixture and peanuts to the wok. Cook, tossing, for 2 minutes or until the sauce boils and thickens and the chicken is cooked through. Sprinkle with the thinly sliced spring onion. Serve with the steamed rice.

YOU CAN CUBE THE CHICKEN FOR AUTHENTICITY, IF YOU LIKE. CUBES AROUND 2 CM ARE GOOD, BUT REMEMBER THE CHICKEN WILL COOK QUICKER, SO ADJUST YOUR COOKING TIME ACCORDINGLY.

Chow mein

SERVES 4   **PREP** 20 minutes (plus 30 minutes marinating)   **COOK** 35 minutes

Myth

The year 2018 was the 'chow mein resurgence', with Australian households clamouring for a suitably updated version of this once-daggy takeaway favourite.

My Truth

Well, it wasn't, obviously – much as I might have written about how it would be – as there are not now booming chow mein restaurant chains forcing Burger Kings and KFCs out of their leases. But I am still hopeful, because chow mein really is one of the world's greatest dishes, with a story to match.

Chow mein, like *tsap seui*, originated in southern China, and both dishes spread out from the region with migrants from Guangdong province who chanced their arms in the goldfields of California and Australia. These migrants came mainly to dig and pan for gold, but many also set up cook shops offering cheap, simple dishes like chow mein and what had come to be known as 'chop suey'. The name *tsap seui* means 'miscellaneous leftovers or scraps', while *chau mein* roughly, and equally prosaically, translates as 'fried noodles'. Other than that chow mein here has soft noodles, the two dishes are fairly similar.

A small number of Chinese nationals came to work in Australia in the first half of the nineteenth century before gold was discovered, taking jobs as indentured labour as farm hands or cooks at pubs or rural stations. The earliest known Chinese immigrant to arrive in Sydney was twenty-year-old Mak Sai Ying in 1818. He was from Guangzhou, in Guangdong, and he went on to work a variety of jobs, including being the proprietor of a number of pubs in Parramatta.

Prior to 1848, only eighteen Chinese settlers had migrated to Australia. The Gold Rush would dramatically change this. By 1855 there had been 11,493 Chinese arrivals in Melbourne alone, a city that five years earlier had a total population of only 25,000 people. Even with punitive taxation and migration restrictions designed to reduce this flow, six years later the Chinese community made up 7 per cent of the Victorian population. According to historian Barbara Nichol, by 1890, one-third of all cooks in Australia were Chinese, and the two blocks of Melbourne's Chinatown boasted a flurry of Chinese eateries, like Hie Yick's cookshop at 209 Little Bourke Street, serving everything from fried rice and roast duck to chop suey and chow mein.

It is interesting to note that many of the restaurateurs who built Melbourne's reputation for Chinese food came from Taishan – the area of Guangdong where *tsap seui* originated – and this is perhaps why chop suey and chow mein survived on menus long after the gold rush had ended.

While the name chow mein only appears in print for the first time in 1900, by the 1920s visitors to Melbourne were talking about visiting Chinatown to head to places like the Chung Wah Cafe and the Pekin Cafe for both dishes, as well as delicious 'long' (noodle) and 'short' (dumpling) soups.

In fact, over the first two decades of the 1900s Chinese restaurants made up around 10 per cent of Melbourne's restaurant sector. The White Australia policy (anti-immigration legislation that was introduced after Australian Federation) and the subsequent Great Depression slowly reversed this trend. Eighteen Chinese cookshops were listed in trade directories in 1920; by 1930, the Sands and McDougall directory of Melbourne lists just eleven.

There were some migration allowances made in the 1930s to allow Chinese restaurateurs to bring in chefs from China, but the rules were rigorous and favoured more successful and longer running restaurants serving fancier food to Western clientele, something that was likely prejudicial to cheap dishes like chow mein and chop suey.

Elsewhere around the world, chow mein and chop suey were similarly abused. As they are more a combination of whatever ingredients are to hand than hard-and-fast recipes, both were open to egregious reinterpretations by cooks outside the dishes' homelands. The US Army's recipe, for example, was made with beef round or pork shoulder, beef stock, barbecue sauce and salt, but no soy sauce. Seventeen years later, the Navy's cookbook added cabbage and green peppers.

From Pakistan to the Caribbean, you'll find both dishes popping up on restaurant menus and even, god forbid, in cans, or frozen. In Hong Kong, China, your crispy noodle chow mein might be served in a hamburger roll; in the New England region in the US they might flavour it with Italian spices and ingredients like beef mince, tomatoes or macaroni. In Milwaukee there's even a dish known as 'Polish chop suey', which sounds suspiciously like *bigos* trying to steal some of chop suey's limelight!

Today, in Australia, we might just call both dishes 'stir-fry' – which isn't at all bad when it's a tasty family crowd-pleaser like this one, loaded with pretty much everything good we can think of! Because there's so much in there, don't stress if you can't find one of the ingredients; just leave it out. There will still be more than enough deliciousness going on.

Chow mein *(CONTINUED)*

1 egg white
1 tablespoon cornflour (corn starch)
3 tablespoons Chinese cooking wine (shaoxing) (or dry sherry)
3 chicken thigh fillets, excess fat trimmed, cut into 1 cm thick strips
280 g packet fresh chow mein egg noodles
2 tablespoons soy sauce
2 tablespoons hoisin sauce
1 teaspoon sesame oil, plus extra to serve
¼ teaspoon Maggi seasoning liquid
1 corn cob, husks and silk removed
1 tablespoon char siu sauce
3 lap cheong, cut into 3–4 mm slices (see Tips)
¼ cup (60 ml) peanut oil
250 g peeled green prawns
1 carrot, halved crossways, then thinly sliced lengthways into thin strips
4 spring onions, white parts sliced, green parts cut diagonally into 5 cm lengths
100 g Chinese barbecued pork, sliced
100 g bean sprouts, trimmed
2 garlic cloves, crushed
sesame seeds, toasted, to serve

Let's velvet! Whisk together the egg white, cornflour and 1 tablespoon of the wine in a bowl. Add the chicken and toss to coat. Cover and place in the fridge for 30 minutes to marinate.

Place the noodles in a heatproof bowl and cover with boiling water. Set aside for 3 minutes to soften slightly. Drain and dry well on a tray lined with paper towel.

Combine the soy sauce, hoisin, sesame oil, Maggi seasoning and remaining wine in a jug. Set aside.

Place the corn on a microwave-safe plate. Drizzle with a tiny touch of water and cover with plastic wrap. Microwave on high for 4 minutes or until just tender. Set aside to cool slightly. Wipe the corn with paper towel to dry slightly. Use a large knife to cut the cob in half, then brush with the char siu sauce. You are cutting the corn into two shorter pieces so they will fit into the wok, touching the metal base. This is such a delicious thing to do, you'll want to try corn cooked like this on the barbecue as well.

Heat a wok or large, deep frying pan over high heat. Add the lap cheong and cook for 2–3 minutes or until a little crispy. Use a slotted spoon to transfer to a large bowl. Leave any oil that has come out of the lap cheong in the base of the wok.

Add the noodles to the wok and toss for 2–3 minutes to coat in the oil, then spread out to coat the base and side of the wok. Cook for 2 minutes or until the outside is crispy. Transfer the noodles to the bowl with the lap cheong.

Heat 1 tablespoon of peanut oil in the wok, add the corn and cook, turning occasionally, for 4–5 minutes or until slightly charred. Transfer to a chopping board. Cut the kernels off the sides of the corn in slabs, keeping the slabs as intact as possible.

Add another tablespoon of peanut oil to the wok. Add half the chicken and stir-fry for 3–4 minutes or until a golden crust forms. Transfer to the bowl with the noodles. Repeat with the remaining chicken. Add the prawns to the wok and stir-fry for 2 minutes or until just cooked through. Transfer to the same bowl.

Add the remaining peanut oil to the wok. Add the carrot and green spring onion lengths and stir-fry for 2 minutes. Add the barbecued pork, bean sprouts, garlic and all the meat and noodles from the bowl. Toss until well combined. Add the soy mixture and toss for 2 minutes or until well combined and heated through.

Spoon the noodle mixture onto a serving platter and top with the corn slabs. Sprinkle with the sesame seeds and white spring onion slices, and add a few extra drops of sesame oil, if you like.

TIPS

Lap cheong is a dried Chinese sausage. You'll find it in the Asian section of most large supermarkets, or at Asian grocery stores.

If you find tossing the long noodles difficult, snip them in half with scissors to make life easier. Depending on the noodles you're using, you can do this before cooking or after the heat has softened them a little.

The blushing schnitty
AKA THE PARMA, PARMI OR MILANESA

SERVES 4 **PREP** 20 minutes (plus 30 minutes chilling) **COOK** 30 minutes

Twist

Myth
The first schnitty was Italian.

My Truth
There is a stoush going on over the humble schnitty. Italy and Austria cannot seem to agree on who came up with the idea first.

The fact that the name 'schnitzel' comes from the German word for an escalope of meat seems like compelling evidence in Austria's favour. In Germany it usually refers to pork schnitzels, with other meats signified by qualifying words like *'wiener* schnitzel', which is – by law, in Vienna, I might add – a veal schnitzel.

The Italians rely on history: Ancient Romans were known to flatten meat to make it more tender and quicker to cook, but these escalopes were dredged only in flour, not breadcrumbs.

The Turks may also have a claim, thanks to a Byzantine emperor who served schnitzels coated in gold at his feasts, which common folk adapted to use 'golden' breadcrumbs instead. But the evidence mounts quickly for the Italian case.

In Italy they call schnitzel *cotoletta alla Milanese*, and it is traditionally served with a wedge of lemon and finely shredded radicchio. The first record of the dish is on an 1134 menu for a feast at Milan's cathedral. This heritage is relevant to the story of an Austrian general named Joseph Radetzky von Radetz bringing the butter-fried *cotoletta* back to Vienna after visiting Milan in 1862. The dish does not start popping up on Vienna menus until after this date, even if Austrians suggest that they were breading chicken long before von Radetz was born. (A dish of crumbed and fried boneless chicken called *backhendl* was popular in Vienna from the early 1700s.) Perhaps we can agree on a compromise, that the name is Austrian and the original idea northern Italian.

Then we have an even bigger stoush over the birthright of the chicken parma/parmi/parm/parmigiana. This one is between Australia and the US – Italy is not really involved, for this is another one of those 'Italian' dishes that is little known back in the old country, like spag bol, Hawaiian pizza, fettuccine alfredo or spaghetti and meatballs.

In the US, the invention is credited to those red-check-tableclothed places in New York where mobsters got whacked. It was most likely a collision of a northern Italian veal *cotoletta* with the cheese and tomato sauce of a southern Italian eggplant *melanzane alla parmigiana*.

The first written chicken parmigiana recipes appear in the *New York Herald* and the *New York Times* in 1953 and 1962 respectively. Magically, 1953 is also when chicken parmigiana with chicken, melted cheese and ham is first spotted here, in Adelaide, although there are references to eggplant parmigiana on Australian menus dating back to 1898. There is an earlier 1951 mention of chicken parmigiana in the *Weekly Times*, but this is a parma in name only.

The 1953 US recipe was just southern fried chicken topped with mozzarella or Munster cheese and simmered in a tomato sauce, while the 1962 recipe is basically a baked tomato braise of chicken pieces with olives, capsicum and mushrooms – there is no golden crumb, no ham and no melty mozz. In other words, not a parma.

For my money, the migration of the parma to the pub circuit to become a counter meal in the 1980s, and the Australian pub-dining revolution of the 1990s, made the pot and a parma a near-mythical quinella in Australia. I reckon we also added the slice of ham under the cheese, so let's claim the parma as our invention.

PS. Let's ignore the ugly interstate debate about whether it's a parma, parmi or parmy. As far as I am concerned, you can call it what you like . . . it's pretty obvious they are the same thing. Not like the confusing spring onion/eschallot/shallots debate, or the even worse debacle of fritz, bung, devon and strass all being the same thing. Go figure.

PPS. Let's also just ignore the Argentinian claim that their *Milanesa a la Napolitana* predates both the US and Aussie contenders for parma primacy. This is said to have been served at José Napoli's eponymous Buenos Aires restaurant since the 1930s. The *a la Napolitana* comes from his name, and not any spurious link to the old country. It is a breaded cutlet topped with tomato sauce, cheese and ham.

The blushing schnitty (CONTINUED)

4 large chicken breast fillets, excess fat trimmed
1½ cups (110 g) panko breadcrumbs
¾ cup (60 g) coarsely grated parmesan
2 teaspoons sweet paprika
1 teaspoon smoked paprika
1 teaspoon finely grated lemon zest
sea salt and freshly ground black pepper
80 g butter, melted
olive oil spray
120 g double smoked ham slices
420 g jar cherry tomato pasta sauce
150 g fresh mozzarella, sliced
basil leaves, to serve

Preheat the oven to 200°C (180°C fan-forced).

Place one chicken breast between two pieces of plastic wrap or baking paper. Use a rolling pin to pound the thicker part of the chicken breast so it's an even thickness all over. We aren't pounding the breast thin, just evening it out for more even cooking. Repeat with the remaining chicken.

Combine the breadcrumbs, parmesan, sweet and smoked paprika and lemon zest in a large shallow bowl or a rimmed baking tray and toss until well combined. Season with salt and pepper. Place the melted butter in a bowl. Dip a piece of chicken in the butter to coat, allowing the excess to drain off. Place in the breadcrumb mixture, turning and pressing firmly to coat all over. Transfer to a plate or tray. Repeat with the remaining chicken, butter and breadcrumb mixture. Place in the fridge for 30 minutes to chill.

Place the crumbed chicken in a large rimmed baking tray or shallow roasting pan in a single layer. (You want enough room around the chicken so it can get as golden as possible, so don't squash them too close together.) Spray well with olive oil. Bake for 10 minutes, then remove from the oven.

Top the chicken with the ham. Drizzle with the pasta sauce and arrange the mozzarella slices on top. Bake for 20 minutes or until the chicken is cooked through and the cheese is all melty and golden. Sprinkle with the basil leaves to serve.

TIP

If you can't find pre-made cherry tomato pasta sauce, it's easy to make your own. Dice an onion and fry until soft (around 4 minutes). Add 2 sliced garlic cloves and fry for 1 minute. Then, add a tin of cherry tomatoes or 2 × 250 g punnets of cherry tomatoes, diced. Cook over low to medium heat until thick and dollopable (around 30 minutes). Or, you could just use any good-quality tomato sauce for this recipe.

Working-class chicken korma

SERVES 6 **PREP** 30 minutes **COOK** 1 hour

Myth
Korma curries are always mild.

My Truth
Korma is a curry from the great Mughal culinary tradition of India. It is usually mild, but that is not the meaning of the name: it comes from the Persian word *qorma*, meaning 'braise'. The Indian dish that goes by this name uses this technique of braising meat in ghee, and also uses dairy or nuts to thicken the gravy. Traditionally, korma was slow-cooked in an earth oven. This was especially important if yoghurt was being used, as this needs gentler heat to avoid curdling. Flavourings were simple: cardamom, *tejpat* leaves (the slightly clove-flavoured Indian bay leaf), maybe pandanus water, but never any turmeric.

The Mughals reached India from Persia via Uzbekistan, and korma is related to Persian *khoresh* stews, as well as famous Indian dishes that also use the *qorma* technique, like the Mughal *dopiaza* and Kashmiri rogan josh.

Korma became famous when Indian emperor Shah Jahan served a very posh one at a meal celebrating the completion of the Taj Mahal, a mausoleum built for his wife, in 1653. In villages across India, they dumped the silver leaf and fancy poppy seeds used in that version to make korma an everyday curry, with regional variations like an emphasis on dairy in the affluent Punjab, and a much hotter gravy made with tomato in the south, which is the inspiration here – albeit a distant one, as this korma is spicy but not hot.

The Mughal emperors were obsessed foodies. Shah Jahan elevated the court cuisine to new levels, championing the use of turmeric, coriander and cumin for their medicinal benefits. He also rewarded his *khansamahs* (court chefs) for creating new dishes. He could afford it; at this time, India was the most prosperous country in the world, responsible for almost 25 per cent of global GDP.

Shah Jahan had grown up in the palace of his grandfather, Emperor Akbar, who employed four hundred Persian cooks in his kitchens as well as those from India. Ingredients like saffron, nuts like almonds and pistachios, meats like lamb and chicken, and sweet and sour flavours, alongside dishes like *dopiazas*, *dolma*, *halvas*, sherbets, *pasandas*, *jalebis* and *kulfis*, were some of the influences from outside India that were brought together here.

It is often claimed that korma was first written about in the time of Akbar's court; however, I could find no results for korma, *qorma* or *quorma* in a search of Abu'l Fazl's multi-volume account of his sixteenth-century reign, *Ain-i-Akbari*, although both the in-ground oven, or *dum pukht* cookery, as well as a recipe for *dopiaza* are mentioned. This is the closest braise to a korma to be found, leaving the *shahi*, or royal white korma, on Shah Jahan's 1653 menu as the first mention of the dish.

Working-class chicken korma (CONTINUED)

1 tablespoon peanut or vegetable oil
3 red onions, halved and thinly sliced
2 whole star anise
3 garlic cloves, crushed
3 cm knob ginger, peeled and finely grated
2 teaspoons brown sugar, plus extra if
    needed
1 teaspoon ground coriander
½ teaspoon ground cumin
2 teaspoons apple cider vinegar
1½ teaspoons soy sauce
1 teaspoon sea salt
400 g can diced tomatoes
1 lemon, juiced
125 g raw cashews, ground in a food
    processor to a fine meal
750 g chicken thigh fillets, cut into 3 cm
    pieces
3 cardamom pods, crushed
1 teaspoon curry powder (or garam masala)
1 cup (250 ml) chicken stock
thick natural yoghurt, to serve (see Tips)
coriander leaves, to serve

Heat the oil in a large, heavy-based saucepan over low heat. Add the onion and star anise and cook very slowly, stirring occasionally but more frequently towards the end, for 30 minutes or until the onion is nicely browned and caramelised.

Add the garlic and ginger to the onion and cook, stirring, for 4 minutes or until starting to caramelise.

Add the sugar, ground coriander and cumin and cook, stirring, for 2 minutes, then add the vinegar, soy sauce and salt. Cook, stirring, for 1–2 minutes or until reduced and you have deglazed the pan.

Stir in the tomatoes and 1 tablespoon of the lemon juice, adding a little more salt, sugar and lemon juice to taste. Cook, stirring, for 10 minutes or until thick and pulpy. Remove the star anise and stir in the cashew meal. Cook, stirring occasionally, for 5 minutes. Remove from the heat and set aside for 5 minutes to cool slightly.

Transfer the mixture to a food processor and blitz until smooth, scraping down the side occasionally. Return to the pan over medium heat. Stir in the chicken, cardamom pods and curry powder until well combined. Add the stock and bring to a simmer. Cook, stirring occasionally, for 8 minutes or until the chicken is just cooked through.

Serve with the yoghurt and coriander leaves.

Add a couple of Indian bay leaves with the star anise and a teaspoon or two of pandanus water when you add the lemon juice for a smattering of authenticity. Ask for *tejpat* leaves and kewra water at your local Indian store.

Instead of serving with yoghurt, pretend you are in Lucknow and add crème fraîche for an even richer finish.

Apricot chicken tray bake

SERVES 4 **PREP** 20 minutes **COOK** 45 minutes

Myth

This 1970s classic started its life on the back of a soup packet.

My Truth

When it comes to the invention of apricot chicken, no one seems to know nothing for certain. Maybe people are just too embarrassed to talk about it. There are few daggier dishes than chook braised in tinned apricot nectar and a packet of French onion soup mix. It is practically the poster child for naff 1970s cooking. To make matters worse, the recipe most likely originated in a 1952 Lipton advert designed to sell their French onion soup mix in the United States. We are talking about one tawdry past!

Apricot chicken rears its ugly head in Australia in the mid-1970s, probably first on a packet of soup mix, although it was just one in a long line of dreadful-sounding chook-with-fruit dishes, like Marguerite Patten's recipe for chicken baked with potato chips and garnished with a can of peaches dumped on top that appeared in the 1967 edition of *Entertaining at Home*.

Yes, apricot chicken was the food equivalent of the space hopper, the polyester jumpsuit or Steve Austin (either one): huge at one moment in time, vanished (or even laughed at) the next. There is, however, a long and glorious history of fruit served with meat.

North Africa and the Middle East are the epicentre of such pairings. In Morocco, they have been baking pigeons with prunes and cooking tagines of lamb with apricots for hundreds of years. The English only started adding dried fruit to their mincemeat pies and adding mint or redcurrant jelly to their lamb after the Crusades.

In regions famous for their apricots, like Sichuan in China – no less a luminary than Marco Polo remarked on their quality – the local delicacy of roast or tea-smoked duck sometimes came with an apricot and plum sauce, though chicken was never used.

There is a good reason for this. While the humble chook has long been valued for its eggs and was prized by the Ancient Greeks and Romans for its fighting spirit – Pompeii even had its own cockfighting arena – after the fall of Rome, chicken was only occasionally seen as good meat. In fact, chicken didn't even warrant its own section of cookbooks until its value as an industrialised protein source was realised in the late 1800s. Instead, it sat alongside recipes for duck, turkey, pheasant and goose in the 'fowl' section.

This raises the question, why would you waste something as revered as an apricot on it? After all, this is the fruit that was known by Ancient Greeks as 'the golden egg of the sun', and it so enamoured Europe's great and good, from Pompey to Henry VIII, that they all were determined to grow it in their lands after tasting it.

The only dish I can find that has a tradition of pairing chicken with apricot is the *khoresh*, or stews, of Iran, such as *khoresh gheysi*. Anyone with a knowledge of Persian cuisine could tell you that that the love of meat paired with fruit is something that was spread through the Arab world by the Persians!

So, there's our inspiration: to reset apricot chicken by writing the recipe as if it was created by someone who actually loved food, rather than someone who was trying to sell powdered soup.

2 tablespoons extra virgin olive oil
6 chicken marylands
⅓ cup (110 g) apricot jam
1 tablespoon apple cider vinegar
2 teaspoons coriander seeds, crushed
  slightly
1 teaspoon harissa paste
1 teaspoon sea salt
1½ cups (225 g) Turkish dried apricots, or
  any good-quality, plump dried apricots
¾ cup (185 ml) white wine
40 g butter
1 head of garlic, cloves separated, unpeeled
1 large red onion, cut into wedges
1 bunch baby carrots, trimmed leaving some
  stalks attached, peeled
¼ cup (20 g) flaked almonds, toasted
thick natural yoghurt, to serve
ground sumac, to dust

Preheat the oven to 200°C (180°C fan-forced). Heat half the oil in a frying pan over high heat. Add half the chicken and cook for 3 minutes each side or until golden. Transfer to a large shallow roasting pan or rimmed baking tray. Repeat with the remaining chicken.

Combine the jam, vinegar, coriander seeds, harissa and salt in a bowl and stir well.

Add the apricots and wine to the frying pan. Simmer, stirring occasionally, for 3 minutes or until the wine reduces by half. Stir in the butter until it melts and combines. Pour around the chicken in the roasting pan.

Add the garlic, onion and carrots to the roasting pan. Brush the chicken with the jam mixture, scatter the vegetables around the chicken and drizzle with the remaining oil.

Bake for 30 minutes or until the chicken has caramelised and is cooked through. Scatter the almonds over, dollop with the yoghurt and sprinkle with the sumac. Serve with baked potatoes or saffron rice. Persian *chelo* rice would also be good.

A quicker butter chicken WITH KASURI METHI

SERVES 4 **PREP** 30 minutes **COOK** 35 minutes

Twist

Myth

Butter chicken has to have *kasuri methi* (dried fenugreek leaves) in it in order to be authentic.

My Truth

A recent boom in butter chicken sales in India has seen a renewed focus on this delicious dish, as well as a mistaken belief that it needs to be made with fenugreek leaves, as it so often is there.

The thing is, butter chicken is one of those dishes whose creation is so clearly documented and unchallenged, we can be quite certain of the truth. We know it was first made in the Gora Bazar in Peshawar in the early 1940s as a way of jazzing up last night's slightly dried out tandoori chicken, and *kasuri methi* definitely wasn't part of the recipe. Cumin and chilli powder were the only spices used.

Even when presented with the evidence, there's a certain type of mansplaining foodie who'll tell me that, in spite of the facts, I am wrong. It's something you will see anywhere around the world when you bust a food myth.

I feel this is a little disrespectful to chef Kundan Lal Jaggi, and his business partners Kundan Lal Gujral and Thakur Das Mago, who fled Peshawar after the partition of India in 1947 and relocated to Delhi, taking their butter chicken with them. They still only use cumin and chilli at Moti Mahal, the restaurant the three men founded in Delhi. It continues to be a favourite on the menu, alongside other unique creations of the restaurant like *dal makhani* and *burra kebab*.

Still, I tried *kasuri methi* in my next butter chicken. While it might not be authentic to the original recipe, this dried herb really adds a delicious savoury touch to the gravy.

Once I'd surrendered to that, food guru Michelle Southan found ways to shorten the cooking process, and I've taken to marinating the chook, cooking it on the barbecue for more char and giving it a rudimentary smoking at the same time to get closer to the essence of the original tandoori chicken that went into those first butter chickens. It's dead tasty.

⅓ cup (95 g) natural yoghurt
2 tablespoons tomato paste (puree)
¼ teaspoon chilli powder
4 garlic cloves, crushed
1 kg chicken thigh fillets, excess fat trimmed, halved
1 kg very ripe tomatoes, coarsely chopped
1 large red onion, coarsely chopped
2 tablespoons coconut oil
4 cm knob ginger, peeled and finely grated
2 teaspoons ground cumin
1 teaspoon ground coriander
½–1 teaspoon chilli powder (depending how hot you like it)
½ teaspoon ground mace (optional)
80 g butter
100 ml pouring cream
1 tablespoon caster sugar
1 teaspoon garam masala
1½ tablespoons *kasuri methi* (see Tip)
sea salt

TIP

You'll find *kasuri methi* (dried fenugreek leaves) at Indian grocers – buy lots, as it's great sprinkled on any barbecued meats.

Combine the yoghurt, tomato paste, chilli powder and half the garlic in a large glass or ceramic bowl. Add the chicken and toss until well coated. Cover and refrigerate.

Combine the tomato and onion in a large, deep frying pan over medium heat and bring to a simmer. Cook, stirring occasionally, for 20 minutes or until the tomato is thick and the liquid has reduced. Push the tomato mixture to one side of the pan and add the oil to the empty side. Add the ginger, ground cumin and coriander, chilli powder, mace, if using, and the remaining garlic, and cook for 1–2 minutes or until aromatic. Set aside for 5 minutes to cool slightly.

Transfer the mixture to a jug and use a stick blender to blitz until smooth. Wipe out the pan with paper towel to clean. In batches, strain the mixture through a fine sieve into the clean pan, pressing with the back of a spoon or ladle to push through. Discard what's left in the sieve. Cover the mixture in the pan and keep warm while you finish cooking the chook.

Preheat the grill plate and flat plate of a covered barbecue until nice and hot. Add the chicken to the grill – we are looking for fierce sizzle and the promise of bar marks, so commit when you put each piece of chicken down and don't move them around. Throw some wood chips onto the flat plate. Cook the chicken for 3 minutes. Turn the chicken over and turn the grill side of the barbecue off. Enclose the barbecue (put down the lid) and cook for 5 minutes or until cooked through and lightly smoked.

Add the chicken and butter to the tomato mixture and cook for 2–3 minutes or until heated through. Stir in the cream, sugar, garam masala, 1 tablespoon of the *kasuri methi* and season with salt. Sprinkle with the remaining *kasuri methi* to serve, with cardamom rice or naan.

Coq au vin

SERVES 4 **PREP** 20 minutes **COOK** 1 hour 25 minutes

Twist

Myth

Coq au vin was first made by Julius Caesar when he conquered Gaul.

My Truth

Sadly, there is no proof that Julius Caesar took the gift of a fine rooster from a rebellious Arverni chieftain and served it back to him cooked in wine when he was quelling resistance to Roman rule in the Auvergne region in southern France. This purported act is held up as Caesar's elegant way of showing what the future would hold for any plucky Gallic cockerel, and doing it with the luxury of wine, which the Romans gifted to their allies as part of Caesar's divide-and-conquer strategy. Here – a carrot or a stick.

The story is crafty propaganda, because the Arverni chieftain Caesar was facing at the time was Vercingetorix, the great warrior and uniter of Gallic tribes who handed the Roman general several bloody noses on the battlefield. Vercingetorix was a true example of the rooster's fighting spirit, so it was important for Caesar to have the last word.

It was also beautifully deft, because in Latin the word for a rooster and for a Gaul was the same. It's so deft, in fact, that you'd expect Caesar to crow about it in his diary of the campaign, the eight-volume *Commentarii de Bello Gallico* ('Commentaries on the Gallic War'). I have searched every page, and while there are lots of Gauls, there are no roosters in wine.

The stewing of tough old rooster to make it edible is something that peasants must have been doing for generations. After all, it has always been the case that, while hens lay eggs, the majority of male birds are good only for the pot. And the twin rules of proximity and availability mean that roosters, whether young or old, were destined to be stewed with different local wines all over France – say, with riesling in Alsace, or with *vin jaune* and morels in the Jura.

We do know that Georges Danton and his eighteenth-century revolutionary buddies would meet in an out-of-the-way tavern near Montmartre. There, at La Mère Catherine, they would drink, plot glorious futures and eat chicken and wine stew. The first published recipe for chicken and wine, however, is the *poulet au vin blanc* in the 1864 *Cookery for English Households, by a French Lady*. This uses onions and bacon along with some white burgundy (think a chardonnay). There's even a bouquet garni of thyme, parsley and bay. It all sounds very familiar, apart from the wine choice.

The closest we get to any earlier provenance is from the 1913 edition of *L'Art du Bien Manger* ('The Art of Eating Well'). Here, French journalist and critic Adolphe Brisson writes of how he persuaded a cook in the Auvergne to show him the original recipe for the coq au vin he'd had for dinner. The chef at the tavern supposedly produced a handwritten notebook from a long-departed sixteenth-century cook, from which Brisson copied out a magnificently (and suspiciously) contemporary recipe for coq au vin, all the way down to thickening at the end with flour and butter. According to the Merriam-Webster dictionary, the first recorded mention of this *beurre manié* method was only in 1905, so I'd reach for a pinch of salt with this story. That said, by 1938 even the venerable old *Larousse Gastronomique* was referring to coq au vin as '*une recette ancienne*' (an ancient recipe), but it was still white wine that was most commonly recommended across France.

Hit the brakes there – yes, what I am saying is that coq au vin, which has pretty much been known only as a red-wine-based dish in my lifetime, was actually originally made with white wine.

In fact, the stewing of fowl was so prevalent back in sixteenth-century France that King Henry IV declared, 'I want there to be no peasant in my realm so poor that he will not have a chicken in his pot every Sunday'. Perhaps it is because it was such a common, simple peasant's dish that it wasn't worthy of being included in those early cookbooks, which largely featured the fancy food of royalty.

More contentious is the claim that coq au vin was a slow-cooked dish where roosters past their prime would be cooked into stringy submission. While this dish must have existed, the dish popularised as coq au vin does seem to have been one built around the quick-cooking of young, tender hens. Rooster, young or old, is seldom mentioned at all in the earliest recipes.

It seems it is sometime in the postwar years that the closely related recipes of coq au vin and boeuf bourguignon merge. Red wine replaces white wine, and bacon, mushrooms and onions all star. It was red wine coq au vin that Julia Child, bestselling author and America's first TV cook, included in her first cookbook, *Mastering the Art of French Cooking* (1961), and TV show, *The French Chef* (1963). The book, show and recipe were smash-hits, and coq au vin became one of the best known and most cooked French recipes around the world.

Most tellingly, when Michelin 3-star chef Paul Bocuse stepped away from the haute cuisine world to champion France's regional *grand-mère* cuisine in the 1970s, it was a very similar version of coq au vin to Child's that he put in his first book – one where the completed dish was only cooked for half an hour, with *red*, not white, wine. He did at least omit the bacon and the mushrooms, to try to shift it away from a bourguignon. We have elected to keep them, but have omitted any carrots or whole small onions.

The recipe that follows is proudly made with red wine, as that's the way we know and love the dish in Australia.

Coq au vin *(CONTINUED)*

¼ cup (35 g) plain flour
sea salt and freshly ground black pepper
8 (about 1 kg) chicken pieces (we used
    4 drumsticks and 4 thighs)
¼ cup (60 ml) olive oil
200 g piece speck, cut into batons 1.5 cm
    long and 5 mm thick
1 brown onion, coarsely chopped
200 g small cup mushrooms, halved
3 garlic cloves, finely chopped
3 rosemary sprigs
2 cups (500 ml) red wine (such as pinot noir)
1 cup (250 ml) chicken stock
finely chopped flat-leaf parsley, to serve
    (optional)

Preheat the oven to 200°C (180°C fan-forced).

Place the flour in a large bowl and season with salt and pepper. Add the chicken pieces and toss until well coated. Shake off excess flour.

Heat 1 tablespoon of the oil in a large flameproof casserole dish over medium–high heat. Add the speck and cook, tossing, for 3–4 minutes or until lightly browned and crisp. Transfer to a bowl and set aside. Keep any rendered fat and oil.

Add 1 tablespoon of the remaining oil to the dish and heat. Cook the chicken in batches for about 6 minutes each, turning occasionally, until golden. Transfer to a plate.

Reduce the heat to medium. Add the remaining oil to the dish and add the chopped onion and mushrooms. Cook, stirring, for 5 minutes or until the onion is soft. Add the garlic and rosemary and cook for 1 minute or until aromatic. Add the wine and stock and bring to the boil. Season well with salt and pepper. Return the chicken pieces to the dish. Cover and bake for 30 minutes.

Remove the casserole from the oven and stir in half the reserved speck. Leaving uncovered, bake for a further 30 minutes or until the chicken is cooked through and the sauce thickens slightly. Sprinkle with the remaining speck, and parsley if using. I suggest serving with roast root veggies, including roast potatoes or baked potatoes, or mash and butter-cooked silverbeet and spinach, or buttered brown rice and some steamed green veg.

There are a few ways to tweak the flavour. You could use another type of wine, add half a dozen allspice berries, flambé the onion with brandy before adding the wine and stock, or use a whole jointed bird.

You could even get funky and take your *coq* on a holiday to Mexico by adding oregano instead of rosemary, plus allspice, 2 cinnamon sticks, 3 whole cloves and 1 teaspoon of cumin seeds. At the end of cooking, whisk in 25 g of grated good dark chocolate for a rich finish.

Beef

Old-school chilli con carne

SERVES 6 **PREP** 20 minutes **COOK** 2 hours 30 minutes

CLASSIC

Myth

Chilli was a cowboy dish invented to serve from their chuckwagons on long cattle drives. In these horse-drawn kitchens, the beans were an essential ingredient for everything, including chilli.

My Truth

While dried beans were portable and filling, those cowpokes were more likely to have theirs cooked down with salt pork than beef from the herd of *dogies* they were *pushing*. The chuckwagon story is just more *taradiddles*. Yes, I have read a lot of pulp Western novels, hence my impressively shallow knowledge of cowboy slang.

The truth is that the 'chilli queens' – the Hispanic street vendors of San Antonio who took ownership of chilli in the nineteenth century – seldom added beans to the dish, preferring to sell refried beans as a side dish. One commentator of the time reported that a 'big plate of chili and beans, with a tortilla on the side, cost a dime'. Beans have also been banned from use in any chilli competition run by the US Chili Appreciation Society International since 1999.

Even so, San Antonio's chilli queens cannot claim the dish as their own creation. The local First Nations people had stews of game meat and fresh chillies well before that time, and the first chilli con carne as we know it today was actually served by settlers from the Canary Islands who moved to San Antonio in 1731. These 'Isleños' were famous for their cumin-heavy stews, and the use of garlic, which is common in chilli recipes, is also characteristic of Isleño cuisine. These first chillies were served in insalubrious dives – chilli speakeasies, of sorts – around San Antonio's Military Plaza.

So, sadly, that myth is, as us tenderfoots and curly wolves say, 'nailed to the counter'. In swing-door saloon parlance, that means it's a proven lie.

This version of chilli plays back to those two earlier incarnations, with beef in chunks rather than the mince we often see today, and lots of cumin. Losing the beans means this chilli can risk being a little soupy, so we use a nifty old trick of adding polenta to thicken it. It has the same effect the cooking down of those beans would have had. And, yes, I know the sour cream is an inauthentic affectation, but I reckon it's an easier way to cool down the dish than the fire hose recommended by one early visitor to those original dodgy Isleños chilli parlours two hundred years ago!

---

2 tablespoons olive oil
1.8 kg chuck steak or gravy beef, trimmed and cut into 4 cm pieces (you should have about 1.5 kg after trimming)
1 brown onion, finely chopped
3 garlic cloves, crushed
2 tablespoons tomato paste (puree)
2 tablespoons ground cumin
2 teaspoons ground coriander
1 teaspoon chilli flakes (or ground cayenne . . . or both, if you are a daredevil)
1 teaspoon dried oregano leaves
800 g can diced tomatoes
1½ cups (375 ml) beef stock
sea salt and freshly ground black pepper
2 tablespoons polenta (optional)
2 long red chillies, thinly sliced
2 limes, quartered
sour cream, to serve
½ bunch coriander, leaves picked
steamed rice or warm tortillas, to serve

Heat half the oil in a large saucepan or stockpot on medium–high heat. In batches, cook the beef for 3–4 minutes or until well browned. Transfer to a heatproof bowl.

Add the remaining oil to the pan. Add the onion and cook, stirring often, for 8 minutes or until soft and golden. Stir in the garlic and tomato paste and cook for 5 minutes or until the paste starts to darken in colour.

Add the cumin, ground coriander, chilli flakes and oregano and cook, stirring, for 30 seconds or until aromatic. Return the beef to the pan and add the tomatoes and 1¼ cups (310 ml) of the stock. Season well with salt and pepper. Cover and bring to the boil, then reduce the heat to low. Partially cover and cook, stirring occasionally, for 2 hours or until the beef is very tender and the sauce smells like San Antonio heaven.

The finishing touch is to combine the polenta, if using, and remaining stock in a small bowl. This is optional, but will help thicken the sauce. Add to the beef mixture and stir to combine. Cook, uncovered, for 5 minutes or until the mixture thickens slightly. Place the red chilli slices in a bowl. Squeeze over half a lime and season with salt. Set aside for 5 minutes to pickle slightly.

Round up your posse and divide the chilli con carne among serving bowls. Top with the sour cream, pickled chilli slices and coriander leaves. Serve with rice or lots of warm tortillas, and the remaining lime wedges.

TIP

Chilli con carne is even better the next day. You could make it a day ahead and store in the fridge overnight. It also freezes well. Allow it to cool slightly, then place in airtight containers and freeze for up to 3 months. Thaw overnight in the fridge, then it's ready to warm through on the stove over low heat. Remember to label and date your containers.

Barbecue ribs, *KALBI STYLE*

SERVES 4 **PREP** 20 minutes (plus 3 hours marinating) **COOK** 3 hours 25 minutes

Myth
Americans make the best ribs.

My Truth
Nope, it's the Koreans.

The Koreans love beef in a way that is almost religious – whether it's *bulgogi* at home, some prized cut – *chadolbaegi*, *usamgyeop* or *deungsim* – sizzling and smoking on a table grill in a barbecue restaurant, or the exclusive and highly marbled *hanu* beef that requires a senior Samsung salary to acquire. Shopping at Seoul's huge Majang-dong meat market is like worshipping at the shrine of Korean meat – even if the image of a bloke pushing a trolley full of dead-eyed cow's heads, which I witnessed there, will stay with me forever.

And then there's *yangnyeom kalbi* – one of the world's greatest ways to cook ribs. In a Seoul cafe you might have to cook them yourself over a coal grill set into the dining table, but here we've used the oven to pre-cook them because it's less hassle.

You'll sometimes see this recipe called *galbi* instead of *kalbi*. The difference between the G and the K sound is very subtle in Korean, so it gets both versions in English. Hence, Gangnam style is also Kangnam style.

⅓ cup (80 ml) soy sauce
⅓ cup (75 g) brown sugar
4 garlic cloves, chopped
4 pears
2 kg beef short ribs
1 cup (250 ml) chicken stock
2 limes, juiced
steamed brown rice, butter lettuce leaves
  and *ssamjang*, to serve

TIPS

If you have access to perilla leaves, use these too. Wrapping meat or fish in perilla is as Korean as kimchi – add one inside the lettuce wrap. Japanese shiso leaves will also do the job.

Ssamjang is a funky soybean paste available from Asian grocers. It's ace with grilled meats.

Make a marinade by combining the soy sauce, sugar and garlic in a large glass or ceramic bowl.

Peel and grate 2 of the pears, discarding the core, and place in the bowl with the marinade. Add the short ribs and toss to coat. Cover and place in the fridge for at least 3 hours, or overnight is even better, if you have the time.

Preheat the oven to 160°C (140°C fan-forced). Line a roasting pan with baking paper. Add the short ribs and any extra marinade from the bowl. Pour over the stock and cover the pan with foil. Roast for 3 hours or until the meat is tender, but still attached to the bone. Transfer the beef to a plate. Strain the liquid in the pan through a sieve into a saucepan. Place over medium–high heat and bring to a simmer. Cook for 10 minutes or until the sauce is reduced and thickened.

Return the beef to the roasting pan. Brush the sauce over the beef, increase the oven temperature to 200°C (180°C fan-forced), and baste for 15 minutes or until well glossed.

Thinly slice the remaining pears and toss in the lime juice.

Shred the meat and serve in lettuce cups with pear slices, brown rice and *ssamjang*.

Food nerd fact
Traditionally with beef short ribs for *kalbi* the meat is cut crossways, so you get strips of beef. The trouble with this is if it is not cooked for long enough they can be tough. We've avoided this problem by using a more traditional cut of short ribs, which are first slow cooked and then cooked at high heat with a rich sticky glaze for a rib-sticking, finger-licking result.

The ultimate burger with ketsiap
(NOT 'THE LOT')

SERVES 4 **PREP** 15 minutes **COOK** 20 minutes

Twist

Myth
The hamburger was originally made with ham.

My Truth
The burger patty has a long and valiant history. The fifth-century Roman cookbook *De re coquinaria* ('On the Subject of Cooking') features chopped meat combined with spices and bread soaked in wine and pine nuts, all formed into a patty. It could be a recipe for a trendy burger today! Dating the first burger served in a bun is a tricky matter, however, and let's be honest, it just ain't a burger if it's not in a bun.

The 1904 St Louis World's Fair is widely credited with having the first burgers served between bread, but there are actually earlier records of a patty flavoured with spices, brown sugar and coffee being served this way at the Erie County Fair in Hamburg, New York, in 1885. There are even earlier reports of burger sandwiches topped with a fried egg being sold on the docks of Hamburg, Germany, in 1860. In fact, hamburger steaks – and I think we can all agree that the name comes from the city (or cities), not the meat, as burgers seldom contain ham – were already on the menu at Delmonico's restaurant in New York in 1836 – bun-free, of course.

It seems that it was Mr Oscar Bilby of Weber's Root Beer Stand in Tulsa, Oklahoma, who first came up with the bright idea of serving burgers in buns, on Independence Day in 1891, which took the burger from plate food to perfect one-handed grazing fare. The real explosion in burger popularity, however, arrived with the automobile age. People would drive out to pick up dinner from early burger chains like White Castle, which opened in Kansas in 1921, selling 5 cent sliders. Then the McDonald brothers opened their first fast food burger joint in 1948, and the rest, as they say, is history.

For me, the best burgers are about crunch from charry-edged meat and chilled iceberg lettuce, and contrasting creaminess from, say, melted cheese, egg or mayo. It is also good if there is some tang in there, from beetroot, pineapple, kimchi or gherkins, as well as some sweetness, perhaps even in the bun itself (which is why brioche is so popular in modern burgers), and loads of freshness, maybe from ribbons of lightly pickled cucumber or slices of super-ripe tomato. Bacon adds salt, savour and smokiness.

I do think a dollop of tomato ketchup is also essential, and I'm somewhat fearful to admit that I prefer sweeter, thicker ketchup to the more vinegary Australian tomato sauce, which I'd rather squeeze on top of a meat pie at the footy.

Before there was tomato ketchup, there was *ketsiap*. The '*kachiaps*' or '*ketsiaps*' of East Asia got their name from the words in a Chinese dialect for the brine of pickled fish. While fish sauces weren't unknown in Europe – the Ancient Romans of the third and fourth centuries BC loved their *garum* – they became popular again with the 1837 launch of an anchovy and tamarind driven ketchup created by two Worcester pharmacists for the ex-governor of Bengal. The governor missed the umami-driven *ketsiaps* he had tasted while working in Asia for the East India Company.

The idea of using sugar and vinegar to create preserved condiments was already enjoying a renaissance in Europe – especially in Britain – well before Messrs Lea and Perrins got in on the act with their worcestershire sauce. However, as the tomato had yet to become a popular food in Europe, these original highly spiced ketchups or sauces were made with ingredients such as anchovies, oysters or mushrooms, or fruit such as plums.

By 1896, tomatoes had taken over, given their umami richness, and the *New York Tribune* had named tomato ketchup America's national condiment. It quickly grew in acceptance in the late nineteenth century because it was the perfect partner to the newly emerging fast foods such as French fries, the hot dog and the hamburger.

In Victorian-era Melbourne, street-stall saveloys were sold slathered with tomato sauce, earning the name 'cutthroats' after the fact that they looked like the cut throat of some poor unfortunate! Obviously confused over whether they should call this rich sauce a ketchup, *ketsiap* or *catsup*, Australians did what they do best and just stated the obvious. Hence in this country we have tomato sauce.

The no-cook tamarind and chipotle ketchup in this recipe, however, is most definitely a ketchup or *ketsiap*, as it's thicker, sweet from brown sugar and loaded with the sourness of tamarind to bounce against the smoky heat of the chipotle chillies. I think it pairs brilliantly with the classic burger components here – and, let's face it, it would be a blooming messy nightmare to eat were it not for Oscar Bilby's bright idea.

The ultimate burger with ketsiap (CONTINUED)

80 g finely shredded iceberg lettuce leaves
30 g finely shredded plain white cabbage
500 g beef brisket and 150 g speck, minced together (see Tips)
4 rashers rindless middle bacon
1 brown onion, finely chopped
sea salt and freshly ground black pepper
4 cheddar slices (bought pre-sliced)
4 hamburger buns, split
butter, at room temperature, to spread
½ cup (150 g) whole-egg mayonnaise
2 large ripe tomatoes, sliced

Tamarind and chipotle ketchup

100 g tamarind paste from a jar
60 g canned chipotle chilli flesh, rinsed and deseeded (see Tips)
½ cup (110 g) brown sugar, plus extra to season
½–1 teaspoon apple cider vinegar, or to taste

To make the ketchup, blend the tamarind, chipotle, sugar and vinegar together in a blender. Taste and adjust the flavouring with more tamarind or sugar if needed. The balance is right when you go 'Yum!'. Finish with a little salt to season. Set aside.

Combine the lettuce and cabbage in a bowl. Keep in the fridge until needed.

Divide the mince mixture into four portions and shape into 1.5 cm thick patties that are wide enough to cover the base of the buns.

Heat a large non-stick frying pan over high heat. Add the bacon and cook for 3 minutes each side or until starting to crisp up. Transfer the bacon to a bowl and cover with foil to keep warm.

Reduce the heat to medium–high. Add the onion and then quickly place the patties on top of the onion in the pan. Press down slightly to get the onion to stick to the base of the patties. Cook for 3 minutes, then season with salt and pepper just before turning over. Flip and cook for 1 minute, then top each patty with a cheese slice. Cook for 2 minutes or until the cheese starts to melt.

Spread the cut faces of the four buns with the butter and toast in the pan with the burgers (or pop under the grill or on the flat grill of the barbecue). We want them a little golden and toasty – it will help with the structural integrity of the burger.

Spread the ketchup on the bun base, then add a cheese-topped patty, bacon, a couple of tomato slices and lettuce mix (in that order!). Slather the mayo on the bun lid before placing on top.

TIPS

Ask your butcher to coarsely mince the brisket and speck together for patties with perfect flavour and texture.

Chipotle chillies are available in small cans, packed in adobo sauce. Remember that much of a chilli's heat comes from the ribs that the seeds are attached to, not the seeds themselves. Remove or scrape out these ribs for milder chillies.

I believe that this is the perfect burger because it has the right mix of richness, saltiness, freshness and creaminess, but what you put in your burgers is a very personal matter. Feel free to add pickled beetroot, rings of grilled pineapple, sliced gherkins, fried eggs, onion rings or slices of pickled jalapeños, and pretty much any cheese you like. I reckon you'll be well served to use this chipotle and tamarind ketchup with most of these (bar the pineapple rings and the jalapeños. Go for regular ketchup with these instead!).

Don't be scared to play with your mayonnaise, too, given that the flavour of the burger itself is so neutral. Try adding chopped herbs like tarragon or basil, or a few drops of liquid smoke, a dollop of mustard or a splash of Maggi seasoning liquid.

If you find your burger is slipping and sliding, I suggest stacking your tomato slices under the meat patty for some extra grip (as you can see in the background burger in the previous shot). It may not be as pretty, but it works!

Simple pho

SERVES 4 **PREP** 20 minutes (plus 20 minutes marinating and 10 minutes resting) **COOK** 20 minutes

CLASSIC

Myth
Pho is named after *pot-au-feu*, a French beef stew. That's why pho is pronounced 'feu'.

My Truth
There are a handful of villages south-east of Hanoi that claim to have been making pho prior to the French colonial period in Vietnam (that is, pre-1885). It was apparently the soup of the local textile workers, made with water buffalo meat and noodles. There is also some evidence that Chinese traders were selling a clear beef broth to workers at the Hanoi docks, made using offcuts gleaned from the butchers who were producing beef for the French in Hanoi at the end of the nineteenth and start of the twentieth centuries. Either way, both versions sound simple in comparison to the pho we know today, and nowhere is either ever referred to as 'pho'.

Mentions of pho only pop up after 1910, although the soup was likely sold by cooks in the streets of Hanoi before that. Their shortened spruiking cries of '*xao bo*', meaning 'meat and noodles', is what supposedly gave us the soup name that misleadingly sounds like the French word for fire, *feu*. (There is also tell of an 1827 Hán-Nôm dictionary that talks about a Vietnamese noodle soup as '*là bánh phở bò*', but I've not been able to verify this with my own eyes. If you have a copy of Pham Dinh Ho's dictionary, I'd love to see this listing!)

What we know for sure is that it was all the beef bones that were left over from butchering cows for the *steak frites* and boeuf bourguignons of the French colonisers that drove the availability and popularity of Vietnam's signature soup.

It wasn't until pho moved south, away from Hanoi, when Vietnam was partitioned after World War II that pho became the vibrant riot of bean sprouts, lime, fresh coriander and chilli sauce that we know today. Of course, making great pho can be a painstaking, meticulous process, but this version is for the days when you need the nurturing goodness of pho in less time than it takes to drive to your local Vietnamese hub.

2 (about 250 g) beef scotch fillet steaks
1 tablespoon kecap manis
2 tablespoons vegetable oil
200 g rice stick noodles

Pho stock
8 cups (2 litres) beef stock
½ white onion
5 cm knob ginger, peeled and thinly sliced
5 whole cloves
3 whole star anise
1 long red chilli, halved lengthways, deseeded
1 garlic clove, halved
1 tablespoon coarsely grated palm sugar (firmly packed)
1 teaspoon coriander seeds
½ teaspoon black peppercorns
1 tablespoon fish sauce

Onion pickle
1 white onion, sliced
1 teaspoon salt
3 teaspoons caster sugar
¼ cup (60 ml) rice wine vinegar

To serve
150 g bean sprouts, trimmed
1 long red chilli, thinly sliced
2 spring onions, thinly sliced diagonally
1 bunch each coriander, Vietnamese mint and Thai basil, leaves picked
1 lime, cut into wedges

Place the beef steaks in a shallow tray or bowl. Pour over the kecap manis and 1 tablespoon of the oil. Toss until well coated. Set aside for 20 minutes to marinate. Using the kecap manis is going to quickly give us a nice crust on the beef without having to overcook it. It's not traditional but it works.

To make your pho stock, place all the ingredients except the fish sauce into a large saucepan. Heat over medium–high heat, bringing just to the boil. Reduce the heat to low and simmer gently, uncovered, for 15 minutes to infuse. Drain the stock through a fine sieve into a clean saucepan. Discard the solids. Bring the stock back to a gentle simmer. Stir in the fish sauce and keep simmering gently.

Meanwhile, heat the remaining 1 tablespoon of vegetable oil in a frying pan over high heat. When the pan is really hot, add the steaks and cook for 30 seconds each side or until well charred but still rare inside. Transfer to a plate and set aside for 10 minutes to rest.

For the onion pickle, combine all the ingredients in a bowl.

Place the rice noodles in a heatproof bowl. Cover with boiling water and set aside for 10 minutes or until just tender. Drain.

Cut the beef into thin slices. Divide the noodles among serving bowls and ladle over the hot stock. Top with the beef, bean sprouts, chilli, spring onion and herbs. Serve with the lime wedges and onion pickle.

Beef fajitas

SERVES 4 **PREP** 30 minutes (plus 1 hour marinating and 5 minutes resting) **COOK** 15 minutes

Twist

Myth
Fajitas have always been served on a sizzling metal hotplate, and were always called fajitas.

My Truth
Few dishes inspire undeniable 'I need to get me some of those' cravings in a restaurant by sound alone. Sizzling fajitas are one of this rare breed. The roots of this Tex-Mex dish are remarkably humble and date back to the *vaqueros*, Mexican cowboys, who worked along the Rio Grande Valley in Texas at the turn of the nineteenth century. The *vaqueros* would receive part of their pay in the form of less-loved bits from the steers being butchered for the ranch. The boss would get all the steaks while the stockmen would pick up the hooves, head, innards and, best of all, four strips of skirt steak: two from outside the diaphragm and two from the flank by the hindquarters.

From this meaty grab-bag would evolve such dishes as *barbacoa de cabeza* (head barbecue) and *menudo* (tripe stew), while the skirt, known in Spanish as *arrachera*, would be pounded, marinated in lime juice and grilled over the local mesquite wood. This is the cut that would go on to eventually become sizzling fajitas.

In her first cookbook, *Elena's Famous Mexican and Spanish Recipes* (1944), Elena Zelayeta, the famous California-based Mexican cook, included a recipe for *arrachera adobada*. This skirt was marinated in oregano, vinegar, oil, salt and pepper, and then tossed with a tomato sauce and cooked under the grill. In her next book, *Elena's Secrets of Mexican Cooking* (1958), she dumped the tomato sauce and simply grilled the meat over the fire.

The first restaurants serving the dish as we would recognise it also didn't call them fajitas. *Texas Monthly* magazine records that restaurateur Otilia Garza was serving grilled skirt steak on a hot metal plate with warm flour tortillas, guacamole, *pico de gallo* salsa and grated cheese when she opened her Round-Up restaurant in the border town of Pharr in 1969. She called the dish *botanzas* and said she had learned the recipe from her grandmother, who was also a restaurant owner just over the border in Mexico. When Ninfa Rodriguez Laurenzo – who grew up in the Rio Grande Valley – opened her Tex-Mex restaurant in Houston in 1973, the dish was called *tacos al carbon*.

According to the Oxford Dictionary, the word fajitas was first seen in print in 1971, but obviously it was in use prior to that. Texas A&M University professor Homero Recio, who wrote the definitive history of fajitas in 1984, says fajita – which means 'little belt' or 'little band' in Spanish – was used much earlier as a local Texas slang term by butchers like his grandfather. It was a meat processing manager from Austin named Juan Antonio 'Sonny' Falcon who adopted the butchers' slang term for the meat tacos he sold at his pop-up grills, the first of which appeared at a fair in the city of Kyle, Texas, in 1969.

Falcon went on to take his fajita stand to fairs and rodeos across the great state of Texas, earning himself the nickname 'The Fajita King'. He maintained that unseasoned, unmarinated outside skirt steaks were the best for the dish and that they should be butterflied, cooked over a very hot fire and turned regularly so they don't get grill marks. Always a purist, Falcon insisted that true fajitas were served in a warm flour tortilla with a few slices of this meat, cut against the grain, with salt and hot sauce on the table. 'That's the genuine article, a real fajita. Everything else is *tacos al carbon*, chicken girdles and shrimp belts,' said the great man, somewhat archly.

It is the sizzling hotplate and distinctive sound that took fajitas from regional delicacy to worldwide smash. That was the smart idea of German chef George Weidmann, who worked at the Hyatt Regency in Austin, Texas. He had beef tacos on the Tex-Mex menu at the hotel's restaurant when it opened, but when he changed this to 'sizzling fajitas', things took off. By 1982 they were selling 13,000 dishes a month, and as a result skirt steak prices skyrocketed, which meant George soon replaced it with easier-to-find sirloin.

Like George's, this recipe uses sirloin steak, along with smoked paprika and cumin in the rub to give a hint of the old mesquite grill. You can add a little chilli powder, too, if you want. That what's many of the homestyle *arrechera* recipes from the Rio Grande Valley would have called for, but I don't reckon you need it.

Beef fajitas *(CONTINUED)*

2 teaspoons ground cumin

2 teaspoons smoked paprika

1 teaspoon dried oregano leaves (if you can find dried Mexican oregano, use it!)

2 garlic cloves, crushed

1 bunch coriander, well washed, leaves reserved and stems finely chopped

¼ cup (60 ml) olive oil

sea salt and freshly ground black pepper

2 (about 550 g) beef sirloin, porterhouse or rump steaks

1 each red, green and yellow capsicums (peppers), deseeded, cut into strips

2 red onions, sliced into thin wedges

8 flour tortillas

2 avocados, quartered

lime wedges, to serve

Tomato salsa (aka *pico de gallo*)

3 ripe tomatoes, finely chopped

½ white onion, finely chopped

1 jalapeño or long green chilli, deseeded and finely chopped

2 tablespoons lime juice

Place the cumin, paprika, oregano, garlic, coriander stems and 2 tablespoons of the oil in a mortar and use a pestle to pound until well combined. Season well with salt. You can just stir in a bowl, or use a small blender if you don't have a mortar and pestle.

Place the beef in a bowl and cover with the spice mixture. Use clean hands to rub all over the beef. Place in the fridge for 1 hour to marinate.

To make the tomato salsa, combine all the ingredients in a bowl. Season well with salt. This will help draw out the juices of the tomato and the onion. Set aside for about 30 minutes. We'll add coriander leaves just before serving to keep them looking bright green and perky.

Combine the capsicum, onion and remaining oil in a separate bowl. Season with salt and toss until well combined.

Heat the barbecue grill and flat plate on medium–high. Cook the beef for 3 minutes each side on the grill for medium, or until cooked to your liking. (Remember to always take it off a little before you think it's done, as it will continue to cook while resting.) Transfer to a plate and cover loosely with foil. Set aside to rest while you cook the capsicum. Add the capsicum mixture to the flat plate and cook for 5 minutes or until charred and tender.

While the capsicum mixture cooks, throw the tortillas on the grill for 10 seconds each side to warm through.

Finely chop 2 tablespoons of the coriander leaves and add to the tomato salsa. Cut the beef into thin slices. Transfer to a serving plate and add the capsicum mixture. Serve with the warmed tortillas, avocado, tomato salsa, lime wedges and the remaining coriander leaves.

TIPS

This recipe works well with prawns or chicken. Substitute 550 g peeled green prawns for the beef and barbecue for 3–4 minutes on the flat plate. Or try with 550 g chicken thigh fillets and barbecue on the grill for 4 minutes each side or until cooked through.

If you've got an electric tabletop barbecue, or can eat next to your barbecue, you can finish the steak strips on the flat plate (pre-heated very hot) just before serving. Toss them on the hot metal and remember that this will give you a medium to well-done finish to the meat, unless you take them off the grill a little earlier when you first cook them. That's the price for the theatrical smoke and sizzle.

Steak diane

SERVES 4 **PREP** 20 minutes **COOK** 1 hour

Myth
Steak diane is one of Australia's most successful and famous dishes overseas.

My Truth
One great joy of writing this book has been discovering that the first record of steak diane comes not from some stuffy old French restaurant where the waiters still wear white gloves, but from Australia. According to one of my favourite websites, Australian Food Timeline, steak diane appeared in Australia in the 1940s. The first mention of the dish's popularity is found in the 29 February 1940 edition of the *Sydney Morning Herald*. It was already a hit by this time thanks to maître d' Tony Clerici, who had arrived back in Sydney at the end of 1939 to work at Romano's restaurant. Clerici had previously migrated to Australia in 1923 to work with Romano's owner and former head waiter at London's Ritz Hotel, Azzalin Orlando Romano, but had returned to London in the 1930s to open his own restaurant in Mayfair, Tony's Grill. He built a reputation there for his 'woodcock flambé' and other game dishes. You'll even find a caricature of Clerici in society mag *The Bystander* in 1938, such was his celebrity. Tony's Grill closed early in 1939, leaving Clerici free to return to Australia.

This was the era when tableside cooking (aka chafing dish cuisine) was the height of fashion in smart restaurants, and Clerici was a master of the craft. The dish he is credited with inventing was simple: thin steak cooked quickly in butter and a little worcestershire sauce, then tossed in the juices of the pan with garlic and parsley. It was a huge hit, helping to make Romano's the hottest restaurant of the war years, popular with US army officers and visiting American performers, who spread the fame of steak diane back home. It was the Americans who later added the theatre of flambéing the pan with brandy.

Now, admittedly, Clerici's tale is that he came up with the dish back home in London, but it was not to become world famous until it reached Australian shores. The story goes that he freestyled it tableside at Tony's Grill in an effort to cheer up the it girl of the day, actress and famous society beauty Lady Diana Cooper, on 1 October 1938. She was depressed about the annexation of Sudetenland the previous day and Hitler's inexorable rise to power.

There are of course others who lay claim to inventing the dish and, as we've said before, while success always has many fathers, none of the other creation stories have quite so much detail, which I feel gives great weight to Clerici's claim. His is also the version of the story that justifies the name 'steak diane', so while there may well have been other tableside steak dishes, I think we can safety assert Australian ownership of steak diane.

The version here is an evolution of Clerici's simple dish. There's still a good hit of garlic, which was lost when the dish made its way to the United States, downplayed with the addition of cream and brandy. Oh, and you don't need a chafing dish to cook it!

Steak diane (CONTINUED)

4 large (about 300 g each) sebago potatoes, well scrubbed
4 (about 200 g each) thick beef eye fillet steaks or scotch, rump or sirloin steaks
1 tablespoon olive oil
sea salt and freshly ground black pepper
60 g butter
2 golden shallots, finely chopped
3 garlic cloves, crushed
¼ cup (60 ml) brandy or cognac
½ cup (125 ml) double cream
1½ tablespoons worcestershire sauce
1 tablespoon dijon mustard
butter lettuce leaves, to serve

Herb and garlic butter

150 g butter, at room temperature
2 tablespoons finely chopped flat-leaf parsley
1 tablespoon finely chopped chives
1 garlic clove, crushed

Preheat the oven to 200°C (180°C fan-forced). Pierce the potatoes a few times with a fork and wrap each potato in foil. Place in the oven, straight on the shelf, and bake for 1 hour or until tender when skewered.

While your potatoes cook, get the steaks out of the fridge and set aside for about 30 minutes, to come to room temperature.

Use a meat mallet, rolling pin or a heavy wine bottle to pound the steaks until they are evenly about 1 cm thick. This makes sure they cook quickly.

To make the herb and garlic butter, use a fork to combine all the ingredients in a bowl.

Sparingly drizzle the beef with a little of the oil and massage it all over the meat. Season well on one side with salt just before hitting the pan.

Add 10 g of the plain butter to a large frying pan and melt over medium–high heat. Place two of the steaks seasoned-side down in the pan. Cook for 2 minutes, or when the meat changes colour at least halfway up the side. Season the steak a minute before you reach the turnover point. Turn and cook for a further 1 minute (or half the time the steak has been cooked on the first side) for medium–rare. Transfer to a plate and set aside, uncovered, in a warm place. Repeat with another 10 g of butter and remaining steaks.

Once your steaks are resting, heat the remaining butter in the pan. Add the shallot and garlic and cook, stirring, for 2–3 minutes or until softened. Add the brandy and cook for 2 minutes or until reduced slightly. Stir in the cream, worcestershire sauce and mustard and cook for 2 minutes or until the sauce thickens slightly. You could toss the steaks in the sauce in the pan, but remember you'll need to cook them a little less before resting if you do. (I think it's prettier not to and simply drizzle the sauce.)

Cut a cross in the top of the potatoes and squeeze open. Place onto serving plates and top with a dollop of the herb and garlic butter. Add the steaks to the plates and drizzle with the diane sauce. Serve with the lettuce on the side.

VARIATIONS

Switch up the sauce

Mushroom sauce: Sauté 200 g of sliced button mushrooms and 2 thyme sprigs with the shallots.

Peppercorn sauce: Add 2 tablespoons of drained green peppercorns, crushed slightly.

Switch up the butter

Café de Paris: Add 3 finely chopped anchovies and 1 tablespoon of drained baby capers to the butter mixture to make a simple Café de Paris butter.

Smoked chipotle butter: Replace all the herbs with chopped coriander, and mix 1 tablespoon of chopped chipotle chilli in adobe sauce into the butter mixture.

Maple bacon butter: Omit the herbs and garlic from the butter and instead mix in 2 short cut bacon rashers that have been cooked until crispy, then finely chopped, and 1 tablespoon of maple syrup.

Switch down the sauce

If you want to be more like Clerici, leave out any of the ingredients you object to apart from the garlic, butter and worcestershire sauce, and add some chopped parsley. Toss the steaks in the sauce flamboyantly tableside and serve the dish, as he did, with fries and battered green beans.

Beef stroganoff

SERVES 4 **PREP** 15 minutes **COOK** 30 minutes

CLASSIC

Myth

This dish is named after the Stroganovs, one of the richest families in Russian history. They made their wealth by controlling all of the furs, minerals, salt and timber that Siberia and the Urals could offer, thanks to a 'special arrangement' with Ivan the Terrible. This deal was so successful that the Stroganovs matched the Tsars for excess, building palaces in St Petersburg and employing fancy French chefs.

My Truth

While we can be fairly certain that beef stroganoff was named after the family by one of these chefs, the question of which one remains. Pavel Stroganov (1774–1817) was known to have had a French chef before his death from tuberculosis in Siberia. Some say stroganoff was named for him because the only way to prep frozen beef in Siberia was to shave off thin strips as it thawed. Or was it Grigory Stroganov (1770–1857), who had terrible teeth, so his chef designed an easy-to-chew dish of beef morsels in a creamy sauce? Or perhaps it was named after Grigory's son Alexander. His French cook Charles Brière snuck in a paprika-laden recipe for stroganoff as his entry in an 1891 culinary competition, and his recipe was subsequently included in the French food bible *Larousse Gastronomique*. Given France's culinary hegemony at the time, this rather became the default recipe for stroganoff as we know it.

The truth here is incredibly elusive. Especially as there is evidence to suggest that the dish existed in Russia before the Stroganov name was ever attached to it. It also bears a striking similarity to a traditional Hungarian dish called *tokany*.

While the noble branch of the Stroganov family died out in the early 1900s, their name lives on, albeit in the French form, in beef stroganoff. The fact that the dish has that 'ff' ending may be proof that it was a French chef who invented it. Or it could just be that when the ignoble Stroganov descendants fled Russia for Paris and China in 1917 – they'd supported the White Russian side against the Bolsheviks and lost – they took the dish with them and the name became localised with the French spelling.

The strog recipe here is served with crispy *pommes pailles* (aka shoestring fries). They are perfect together. It's a Russian idea.

2 tablespoons plain flour
1 teaspoon ground allspice
1 teaspoon ground nutmeg
sea salt and freshly ground black pepper
3 (about 350 g total) veal rump medallion steaks
¼ cup (60 ml) olive oil
25 g unsalted butter
1 brown onion, cut into 8 wedges
400 g button mushrooms, thickly sliced
¼ cup (70 g) tomato paste (puree)
3 teaspoons English mustard
1½ cups (375 ml) beef stock
⅓ cup (80 g) crème fraîche
1 teaspoon lemon juice
finely chopped flat-leaf parsley, to serve

Potato straws

800 g russet or sebago potatoes, peeled
vegetable oil, for frying
sea salt

Start by making the potato straws. Cut the potatoes into matchsticks, or use a mandolin if you have one. Place in a bowl and cover with cold water. Set aside for 10 minutes to soak. Drain then place on a tray lined with paper towel. Pat with paper towel to dry well.

While the straws soak, combine the flour, allspice and nutmeg in a bowl. Season well with salt and pepper. Add the veal and turn to coat both sides well.

Heat 1 tablespoon of the oil in a large frying pan over high heat. Add half the veal and cook for 1–2 minutes each side or until just golden and a crust has formed. Transfer to a plate. Repeat with the remaining veal and another tablespoon of oil.

Increase the heat to high. Add the remaining oil and the butter to the pan and add the onion and mushrooms. Cook, stirring only occasionally, so the mushrooms have time to catch slightly, for 5 minutes or until golden.

Reduce the heat to medium. Add the tomato paste and mustard to the pan and cook, stirring, for 2–3 minutes or until the tomato paste darkens slightly. Add the beef stock and stir to combine and deglaze the pan. Simmer, stirring occasionally, for 5 minutes or until the sauce reduces slightly.

While the sauce simmers, thinly slice the veal.

Now it is time to cook the potato straws. Add enough oil to a saucepan to come a third of the way up the side (don't overfill, because at this high temperature the oil will rise a lot when the straws are added). Heat over medium–high heat until the oil reaches 190°C on a cook's thermometer (or until a cube of bread turns golden in 10 seconds after being added). In batches, deep-fry the potato straws for 2–3 minutes or until they are golden brown. Transfer to a tray lined with paper towel to drain. Sprinkle with salt.

Reduce the heat to low on the stroganoff and stir in the crème fraîche and lemon juice. Cook for 2 minutes or until heated through and well combined. Return the sliced veal and any pan juices to the pan. Toss for 1 minute or until combined and just heated through. Serve the stroganoff with the potato straws and sprinkle with parsley.

Beef goulash

SERVES 4 **PREP** 20 minutes **COOK** 3 hours 20 minutes

CLASSIC

Myth

In the Australian goldfields they served a thin goulash unappetisingly called 'slumgullion'.

My Truth

Dating back to the ninth century, rich and slightly sour goulash was the pot noodle or two-minute noodles of its day – a go-to dish of the herdsmen (aka *gulyás*) of the Hungarian steppes. Meat would be cooked, flavoured and then sun-dried to be packed into a sheep's stomach so these medieval drovers had something to eat as they walked their herds to market across the plains. During the nineteenth century, the dish spread beyond its homeland to all reaches of the Austro-Hungarian Empire, where it gained regional variations in places such as Albania, Italy and Kosovo.

A dish this warming and soulful could not be contained by an area as small as Europe, and so it spread to gold diggings, first in the United States and then to Australia in the 1800s. Here it was renamed 'slumgullion', as its murky brown depths bobbing with mysterious bits resembled the 'slum' or slime that filled the miners' sluice pits, or 'gullions'. So, there's no myth here.

By the twentieth century, however, goulash had become so closely associated with the Hungarian psyche that in the 1960s that country's more relaxed brand of postwar communism was even called *gulyáskommunizmus*, or 'Goulash Communism'.

Today, goulash is something like a valued old friend who you love just as they are, but who could also probably do with a bit of a makeover. So here's our attempt to refresh it while staying true to the classic. Where sour sauerkraut was once used in the noodles, you'll now find fresh green cabbage; where there was once ugly smoked beef, here there is a faint murmur of delicious smokiness from a little smoked paprika. Yet the beautiful soul of the Hungarian dish – beef, caraway, red wine, tomatoes – remains. This is slumgullion no longer.

2 tablespoons olive oil

1.5 kg chuck steak, gravy beef or brisket, trimmed of excess fat and cut into 3 cm pieces

1 brown onion, coarsely chopped

1 red capsicum (pepper), deseeded, coarsely chopped

8 garlic cloves, crushed

1½ tablespoons sweet paprika

2 teaspoons smoked paprika

1 teaspoon caraway seeds (if you love caraway as much as I do, you can sprinkle a few more over the top after cooking!)

400 g can diced tomatoes

2 tablespoons tomato paste (puree)

2 cups (500 ml) beef stock

1 cup (250 ml) red wine (such as pinot or merlot)

sea salt and freshly ground black pepper

400 g dried thick fettuccine or pappardelle pasta

200 g cabbage (white or drumhead) cut into fettuccine-thick ribbons (8 mm or so across – but don't worry, no one is measuring)

20 g butter

200 g crème fraîche

½ bunch flat-leaf parsley, leaves and stems separated, both finely chopped

Heat 1 tablespoon of the oil in a large saucepan over medium–high heat. In batches, cook the beef for 3–4 minutes or until browned all over. Transfer to a heatproof bowl.

Heat the remaining oil in the pan. Add the onion and capsicum and cook, stirring, for 5 minutes or until softened. Add the garlic, paprika and caraway seeds and cook, stirring, for 1 minute or until aromatic.

Return the beef to the pan and add the tomatoes, tomato paste, stock and wine. Bring to the boil. Reduce the heat to low and cook, covered, stirring occasionally, for 2½ hours, until the beef is tender. Uncover and bring to a rapid simmer. Simmer, stirring occasionally, for 30 minutes or until the sauce thickens slightly. Season well with salt and pepper.

When the beef mixture is close to being ready, cook the pasta in a very large saucepan of salted boiling water, for 2 minutes less than it says on the packet, until just al dente. Throw in the cabbage for the last 4 minutes of cooking. It too should retain some bite.

Drain the pasta and cabbage, reserving ½ cup (125 ml) of the cooking liquid.

Return the pasta and cabbage to the saucepan with the butter. Turn up the heat and fry for a couple of minutes. You want to hear some sizzle. Turn down the heat and add the crème fraîche, parsley stems and reserved cooking liquid. Mix until well combined.

Divide the creamy pasta mixture and the goulash among serving bowls. Sprinkle with the chopped parsley leaves to serve.

Beef rendang with cucumber pickle

SERVES 4 **PREP** 30 minutes (plus 30 minutes pickling) **COOK** 3 hours

CLASSIC

Myth

Beef rendang is just a curry: it doesn't matter whether it is sloppy or dry, whether the meat is dry-fried or pre-poached, or whether it is Malaysian, Indonesian or Singaporean.

My Truth

No recipe I have ever written has required as much consultation and argument as the beef rendang in my third cookbook. This is because rendang is an expression of national pride in each of the countries that claims it as their own. Personally, I've had great rendangs in all three places. What I will be drawn on is that it is a dry curry, which makes the most of showing off the roasted coconut used in its preparation. We know that because the verb *rendang* refers to the slow drying off of the liquid through stirring, coming from *randang*, meaning 'slowly'.

When it comes to the dish's provenance, I'll leave it up to the venerable *Journal of Ethnic Foods* to make the call. In the article 'Rendang: The treasure of Minangkabau', the authors argue that rendang was originally a West Sumatran dish, created by Indian traders but improved upon by the local Minang people by cooking it for longer to thicken and dry out the curry, taking it to a point where the oil splits out and is then reabsorbed into the meat.

As rendang is really a cooking process rather than a singular dish, like stir-fry or a roast, it can be made with anything from chicken or lamb to black glutinous rice or egg, or even soured with starfruit leaves. Here, I have improved on my old beef rendang recipe by boosting the amount of galangal and makrut lime leaves used; my experience of Indonesian food is that they are the masters of fleetingly fragrant dishes. I've also upped the desiccated coconut, because one of the best things about rendang is the squeak of the gravy in the finished dish.

¼ cup (20 g) desiccated coconut
1 tablespoon grapeseed oil
1 kg oyster blade or other braising beef such as chuck or cheek, cut into 4 cm cubes
9 makrut lime leaves, cut into fine threads (see Tips p. 42)
400 ml can coconut cream
1 tablespoon brown sugar
sea salt, to taste
steamed rice, to serve

Spice paste

2 brown onions, coarsely chopped
4 garlic cloves, peeled
6 long red chillies, tops trimmed, coarsely chopped
5 candlenuts (*buah keras*) or 8 raw unsalted macadamias
2 lemongrass stalks, white parts only, smashed or bruised with the back of a knife, then finely chopped
3 cm piece fresh galangal, peeled and finely chopped
2 teaspoons ground turmeric
1 tablespoon grapeseed oil
2 tablespoons fish sauce

Sweet pickled cucumber

2 tablespoons coconut or rice wine vinegar
1 tablespoon caster sugar
1 long continental (telegraph) cucumber, sliced

To make the spice paste, blitz all the ingredients except the fish sauce in a food processor until you have a fine paste. Add the fish sauce last and process until well combined. Set aside.

Heat a frying pan without oil over low heat. Add the desiccated coconut and cook, tossing, for 3–4 minutes or until it is bronzed – that's a bit more than golden. Don't skip this essential step! Transfer to a bowl and set aside to cool.

Heat the oil in a large saucepan or stockpot over medium–high heat. In batches, add the beef and cook for 3–4 minutes to brown all over. Transfer the browned meat to a heatproof bowl.

In the same pan, add the spice paste and cook over medium heat, stirring, for 8–10 minutes or until it smells fragrant and the liquid evaporates. Add the browned beef and toss until coated. Stir in the toasted coconut and two-thirds of the makrut lime leaves. Cook, stirring occasionally, for 1–2 minutes or until well combined.

Add the coconut cream, brown sugar and 2 cups (500 ml) water to the pan. Bring to the boil then reduce the heat to low. Cook, uncovered, stirring occasionally, for 2½ hours or until the meat is soft and the sauce is thick. If you find your meat is catching on the bottom in the last 30 minutes, just add a touch more water from time to time. When the beef is cooked, the meat should be a little sticky and dried out. Season with salt.

While the meat cooks, make the pickle. Combine the vinegar, sugar and 1 teaspoon of salt in a glass or ceramic bowl (not metal). Add the cucumber and cover the bowl securely with plastic wrap, then tumble the cucumber around to coat it. Set aside for 30 minutes to pickle.

Serve with the steamed rice and sweet pickled cucumber, and sprinkle with the remaining makrut lime leaves.

YOU CAN ALSO USE THIS RECIPE TO MAKE
A LAMB RENDANG USING DICED LAMB
SHOULDER, OR A CHICKEN RENDANG
USING CHICKEN THIGHS.

Beef lasagne

SERVES 8 **PREP** 40 minutes **COOK** 3 hours

Myth
The correct way to spell 'lasagna' is 'lasagne'.

My Truth
The original lasagne, called *lasanis* by the Romans, was squares of fermented pasta dough cut into strips as wide as 'three fingers', according to an ancient recipe I uncovered.* The sheets (or 'bed of towels') were layered with *caseum grattatum* between. That's grated cheese, according to my trusty online translator.

You've got to love a good online translator; well, until it throws up the English translation of '*lasanis*' as 'washroom' or 'chamber-pot', which makes our lasagne sound a whole lot less appetising! Maybe it was something to do with all those sheets of pasta. Keen students of Latin will also note from the recipe below that it's advised this *lasanis* should be eaten with a pointed wooden stick. I won't insist you do that here!

The Ancient Greeks saw the creation of lasagne differently, claiming the Romans stole their dish of *laganon* when they invaded and occupied Greece around 146 BC. However, the first recipes weren't written down until fourteenth-century cookbooks such as the *Liber de coquina* ('The Book of Cooking'), written by a cook from the Naples area, and *The Forme of Cury* ('The Method of Cooking'). This is the first documented English cookbook, and the presence of a recipe for *loseyn* caused an international incident in 2003 when some British scamps tried to claim that lasagne was thus originally British. It took the revelation, from the Italian ambassador to the United Kingdom no less, of records of a lasagne producer called Maria Borgogno trading in and around Naples in 1316 (some thirty years before *Forme* was written) to quash that rumour.

In Italy, there are actually many versions of lasagne (and lasagna). What we know as lasagne in Australia, baked with a meat sauce and bechamel, comes from Emilia Romagna in the middle of the country, but in Liguria they make a version of lasagne with pesto and bechamel. In Marche they use sausage meat and chicken livers instead of bolognese sauce and mozzarella instead of bechamel. In Calabria, it's very much a meat-lover's lasagna with ham, mortadella and even hard-boiled eggs joining the party. In Tuscany they make an extra decadent version which dates back to the end of the eighteenth century and is called *vincisgrassi*. It also uses mozzarella, but throws chicken giblets and cockscombs into the mince sauce along with livers and sometimes prosciutto.

The big debate, however, is over the spelling: whether it's 'lasagne' or 'lasagna'. The answer all comes down to where you are from. In Italy's north it's 'lasagne', and in the south it's 'lasagna'. The United States, which enjoyed mass migration from the impoverished south of Italy, has adopted that southern spelling, so Garfield is obsessed with 'lasagna', while the United Kingdom plumped for the northern version of the name. So both are right.

* *De lasanis* (from the *Liber de coquina*):

Ad lasanas, accipe pastam fermentatam et fac tortellum ita tenuem sicut poteris. Deinde, diuide eum per partes quadratas ad quantitatem trium digitorum. Postea, habeas aquam bullientem salsatam, et pone ibi ad coquendum predictas lasanas. Et quando erunt fortiter decocte, accipe caseum grattatum.

Et si uolueris, potes simul ponere bonas species pulverizatas, et pulveriza cum istis super cissorium. Postea, fac desuper unum lectum de lasanis et iterum pulveriza; et desuper, alium lectum, et pulveriza: et sic fac usque cissorium uel scutella sit plena. Postea, comede cum uno punctorio ligneo accipiendo.

Beef lasagne *(CONTINUED)*

1 lemon
40 g butter
2 tablespoons olive oil
2 rashers rindless bacon, finely chopped
2 carrots, peeled and finely chopped
2 large celery stalks, finely chopped
1 brown onion, finely chopped
1 tablespoon brown sugar
4 garlic cloves, crushed
¼ cup (70 g) tomato paste (puree)
1 kg lean beef mince
2 cups (500 ml) red wine (pinot or merlot are good)
2 × 400 g cans chopped tomatoes
3 cups (750 ml) beef stock
2 tablespoons worcestershire sauce
3 bay leaves
sea salt and freshly ground black pepper
375 g packet fresh lasagne sheets
1 cup (120 g) coarsely grated cheddar

Bechamel
600 ml milk
2 bay leaves (fresh, ideally)
70 g butter
½ cup (75 g) plain flour
¾ cup (60 g) coarsely grated parmesan
1 teaspoon salt flakes
2 eggs, lightly whisked

Use a vegetable peeler to peel a piece of zest from the lemon, about 4 cm long and 2 cm wide. Squeeze the lemon and reserve 2 tablespoons of the juice.

Heat the butter and 1 tablespoon of the oil in a large saucepan or stockpot over medium–high heat. Add the bacon, carrot, celery and onion. Cook, stirring, for 5–8 minutes or until the vegetables are soft.

Add the sugar, garlic and tomato paste and cook, stirring, for 5 minutes or until the tomato paste starts to darken slightly. Transfer to a large heatproof bowl.

Heat the remaining oil in the same pan or pot. Cook the mince, breaking it up with a wooden spoon, for 5 minutes or until browned. Transfer to the bowl with the vegetables.

Increase the heat to high. Add the wine and bring to the boil. Simmer for 5 minutes or until reduced by half. Return the mince and veggie mixture to the pot. Add the tomatoes, stock, worcestershire sauce, bay leaves, lemon zest and the reserved lemon juice.

Cover and bring everything to the boil, then reduce the heat to very low. Cook, stirring occasionally, for 2 hours or until the sauce is a glossy dark red and has thickened. Season with salt.

Meanwhile, to make the bechamel, place the milk and bay leaves in a small saucepan. Heat over low heat until it almost comes to the boil. Remove from the heat and set aside for 5 minutes to infuse. Remove the bay leaves and discard.

Melt the butter in a large saucepan over low heat. Add the flour and cook, stirring, for 1 minute, until smooth. Remove from the heat. Gradually add the milk a little at a time, whisking well after each addition, ensuring each bit is incorporated before adding the next. Return to medium heat. Cook, stirring, for 3 minutes or until the mixture comes to a simmer and thickens. Stir in the parmesan and cook, stirring, for 2 minutes or until melted and smooth. Season with the salt. Remove from the heat and whisk in the eggs thoroughly. If your meat is still cooking, place a piece of plastic wrap over the surface of the bechamel to prevent a skin forming.

Preheat the oven to 200°C (180°C fan-forced). Spread 1 cup of mince mixture over the base of a 22 cm × 30 cm × 7 cm deep ovenproof dish or roasting pan. Top with two lasagne sheets. Spoon a third of the remaining mince mixture on top and use the back of a spoon to spread out. Repeat the layers, finishing with a final layer of pasta. Spoon the bechamel over the top and spread out evenly. Sprinkle with the cheddar. Bake for 30–35 minutes or until golden. Check if the pasta is cooked by piercing the lasagne with a wooden skewer or any other thin pointed stick. It should be tender but there should be some resistance. Set aside for 15 minutes to cool slightly before serving.

TIP

Lasagne is the perfect freeze-ahead meal. Cool slightly, then place in the fridge overnight to chill. Either cover the whole dish with a double layer of plastic wrap, or cut the lasagne into portions and wrap individually. Freeze for up to 3 months. Thaw overnight in the fridge and reheat the whole lasagne in a low oven, or microwave portions until heated through.

VEGETARIAN LASAGNE

Over the years, recipe guru Michelle and I have both played with loads of different types of lasagne, including many vegetarian versions, among them the classic spinach and ricotta. My personal favourite is a green lasagne, where slabs of roast zucchini (courgette) replace the meat sauce and the bechamel is loaded with spinach and nutmeg, turning it as verdant as billiard baize. Oh, and then there's the classic combination of ricotta, mushrooms and spinach.

Slices of thick roast butternut pumpkin (squash) also make a great layer for a vegetarian lasagne, especially if tossed with butter-crisped sage, toasted pine nuts and currants. Try adding a layer of juicy roasted fennel slices tossed in parmesan (or, more controversially, goat's cheese) to this one. Do, however, always put a sheet of pasta down before you layer in the bechamel or Napoli (tomato) sauce.

You could even try my lentil bolognese in this queen of pasta bakes. Stick with the usual bechamel though. (You might find my recipe for this online if you don't want to pay for the book that it's in!)

You want more ideas? How about using a ratatouille or caponata instead of the bolognese and including slabs of creamy fried or grilled eggplant (aubergine) for meatiness, and mozzarella for its melty goodness. This is like a collision between a lasagne and *melanzane alla parmigiana*. Top with a final layer of the garlic-heavy sauce and then a mound of oil-tossed chunky breadcrumbs, with lots of grated parmesan and picked oregano or marjoram leaves.

Boeuf bourguignon

SERVES 4 **PREP** 30 minutes **COOK** 3 hours

Myth
It's a signature Burgundian dish that dates back to the Middle Ages.

My Truth
Sure, Southern Burgundy was famous for its Charolais cattle, and Burgundy gave its name to a number of dishes that featured red wine or a garnish of bacon, onions and mushrooms, but there is no record of boeuf bourguignon before the late nineteenth century. The terrible truth may be that the dish owes more to female recipe writers from England and the United States than any medieval French peasant.

You see, no one has been able to find a recipe for the dish from earlier than 1903. There is a disparaging comment in a nineteenth-century guidebook about it being served at a working-class Paris *bouillon* (or dining room) in 1878. It sounds as if a bourguignon sauce was something you poured over yesterday's grey roast to make it vaguely palatable and, better yet, disguised for dinner the next night. Hence the disparaging tone! This, combined with the fact that the first mentions of dishes served *à la bourguignon*, *à la bourguignotte* or *à la bourguignonne* are for a) a boned and trussed leg of lamb; b) carp or pike; and c) rabbit, in a recipe dated 1846, points to boeuf bourguignon being a far more recent invention. The lamb recipe even comes from a British recipe book, *Cookery for English Households, by a French Lady* (1864).

At least the suggestion of serving eel or carp in this fashion came from the legendary French chef and master of fine dining Marie-Antoine Carême, in his masterwork *L'Art de la cuisine française* ('The Art of French Cuisine'). Although he doesn't actually include a recipe for the sauce and garnish, it does suggest that the red wine, onion and mushroom combo was already known. Carême was obviously a fan, because in 1817 he'd put the dish on the menu with fillets of wild duck as one of the thirty-six main courses served at a grand dinner for the Prince Regent (later King George IV) and his fashion-obsessed cronies at the Brighton Pavilion. This makes the first written mention of *à la bourguignon* a menu from the United Kingdom and not from France, although Carême used the words *à la bourguignotte*, an alternative word that is most often used to describe helmets cast in the Burgundian style!

The publication of Alfred Contour's *Le cuisinier Bourguignon* in 1910 makes matters even worse for the myth, as, in this extensive opus on the classic cooking of Burgundy, boeuf bourguignon didn't even cop a mention.

At least the first recipe for beef cooked Burgundian style was French. Auguste Escoffier included it in his *Le guide culinaire* (1903), instructing the use of a whole topside of beef, larded with strips of salt pork and then marinated in red wine. The joint is cooked in the marinade with a tomatoey Espagnole sauce, removed to be glazed in the oven, then reunited with the red wine sauce, mushrooms and onions on the serving plate. This still isn't what I'd recognise as boeuf bourguignon, though – surely that is chunks of beef cooked and served in the sauce (even if Escoffier suggests it is acceptable to slice the topside lengthways, and only lengthways, if a 3 kilogram joint is too big)?

Enter Julia Child and Elizabeth David, two pioneering giants of home cooking. David included a recipe for homestyle boeuf bourguignon in her massively popular *French Provincial Cooking* (1960), where she advised cutting slices of topside into 6 cm squares before marinating in red wine. Child's recipe is even more familiar. In her groundbreaking first book, *Mastering the Art of French Cooking* (1961), she suggested cutting stewing beef into 5 cm chunks, doing away with the marinating and turning the cured pork that larded Escoffier's topside into lardons. So much more approachable, it was a hit and has become the version even the French recognise as the classic boeuf bourguignon. It didn't hurt the fame of the dish that when Julia debuted on US television with her cooking show *The French Chef*, it was the very first recipe she demonstrated.

Imagine that: the dish that was voted by the French public as being the epitome of the nation's cuisine in 2017 was actually made what it is today by cooks from the US and the UK.

Our boeuf bourguignon includes most of the ingredients from Escoffier's original recipe (although we add thyme, bay leaves and a little tomato puree rather than making an Espagnole), but also acknowledges the huge impact of Child's version.

Boeuf bourguignon *(CONTINUED)*

¼ cup (35 g) plain flour
sea salt and freshly ground black pepper
1.5 kg beef brisket, gravy beef or chuck
  steak, trimmed, cut into 4 cm pieces (you
  should have about 1.3 kg after trimming)
¼ cup (60 ml) olive oil
300 g speck, cut into 1 cm thick batons
2 carrots, thickly sliced
1 brown onion, finely chopped
3 garlic cloves, crushed
1 tablespoon tomato paste (puree)
2 cups (500 ml) beef stock
1½ cups (375 ml) red wine (a pinot would be
  perfect)
300 g cup mushrooms, quartered
10 (about 250 g) golden shallots, peeled and
  left whole
finely chopped flat-leaf parsley, to serve
  (optional)

Bouquet garni

4 thyme sprigs
3 bay leaves
2 flat-leaf parsley stems
2 small stalks celery

Preheat the oven to 180°C (160°C fan-forced). To make the bouquet garni, tie the thyme, bay leaves, parsley and celery together with kitchen string.

Place the flour in a large ziplock bag and season well with salt and pepper. Add the beef and gently toss until well coated. Remove the beef and shake off the excess flour.

Heat 1 tablespoon of the oil in a large flameproof casserole dish over medium–high heat. Add the speck to the dish and cook over medium heat for 5–8 minutes or until golden and crisp. Transfer two-thirds to a large heatproof bowl. Place the remaining third in a small bowl. Set aside.

Heat 1 tablespoon of the remaining oil in the dish over medium–high heat. Cook the beef, in batches, for 3–4 minutes or until lightly browned. Transfer to the large bowl with the speck.

Add the carrot and onion to the dish and cook for 3–4 minutes or until the onion is browned. Add the garlic and cook, stirring, for 30 seconds or until aromatic. Stir in the tomato paste.

Return the beef mixture to the dish. Add the stock, wine and bouquet garni. Bring to the boil, then remove from the heat. Cover and bake for 2 hours.

About 10 minutes before the beef is done, heat the remaining oil in a frying pan over medium–high heat.

Add the mushrooms and shallots and cook, tossing occasionally, for 4–5 minutes or until lightly golden.

Uncover the dish and stir in the mushroom mixture. Bake, uncovered, for a further 45 minutes or until the sauce thickens slightly. Season well with salt and pepper. Sprinkle with the reserved speck to serve, and parsley, if you like some greenness.

Massaman curry

SERVES 6 **PREP** 20 minutes **COOK** 3 hours 55 minutes

Twist

Myth
Massaman curry is a creation of the Indo-Malay population of Southern Thailand.

My Truth
Sorry, but that's far too boring an origin story for what is arguably the greatest Thai dish, and one of the best to cook at home. My take is much more romantic.

When pioneering Thai food writer Lady Plean Passakornrawong published her first ever recipe in 1889, it was for massaman curry. Even more fitting is that hers is the first written massaman recipe anyone can find. By the time Lady Plean committed the dish to paper, it was already a favourite of the royal household, described as being like 'a lover . . . that would arouse any man' in a poem written by King Rama II of Siam in the early nineteenth century.

Rama was born in 1767 in the former Thai kingdom of Ayutthaya, where massaman curry had originated 150 or so years earlier in the kitchens of Persian trader and court advisor Sheikh Ahmad Qomi. Ayutthaya was an affluent city on a trade route between India and China, which welcomed trade missions from around Europe and Asia at its port, and massaman curry is just the sort of fusion dish you'd expect to come from such a melting pot.

After the fall of Ayutthaya, Sheikh Ahmad's aristocratic descendants fled with the royal family to Bangkok, where they helped to set up the Thai Muslim community there and also ensured the continued influence of Persian culinary ideas on Thai royal cuisine. The name 'massaman' is itself drawn from the Thai words meaning Muslim, '*moot salim*'. It makes sense then that the dish marries influences from the Persian kitchen with classic Thai flavours and ingredients from across the spice routes.

Our version respects this origin story but has a slightly more modern twist, using tamarind and sweet orange rather than the bitter orange juice that featured in the first written recipes. The cumin and coriander seeds are also gone, replaced by the Indian-influenced flavours of cardamom and cinnamon that are so closely associated with the massamans you'll find across Thailand today.

You won't normally find raisins or sultanas in modern massaman curries, but they are there in Lady Plean's recipe, and as she was married to a direct descendent of Sheikh Ahmad, one feels she might have had the inside word on the dish. Also like her recipe, ours is cooked for a long time over a whisper of heat. We are cheating, however, by using additional spices to soup up a shop-bought massaman paste – the result is still most pleasing.

---

2 tablespoons coconut oil (or ghee)

1.5 kg gravy beef, such as chuck, trimmed and cut into 4 cm chunks (you should have about 1.2 kg after trimming)

2 large red shallots, finely chopped

2 tablespoons massaman curry paste

4 garlic cloves, crushed

4 cm knob ginger, finely grated

4 cardamom pods, bruised

1 cinnamon stick

pinch of ground nutmeg

2 long red chillies, split in half lengthways and deseeded, plus extra thinly sliced chilli to serve

400 ml can coconut milk

270 ml can coconut cream

3 (about 600 g) coliban potatoes, peeled, cut into 4 cm chunks

½ cup (80 g) sultanas (or raisins)

2 tablespoons tamarind puree

1 tablespoon coarsely grated palm sugar (or caster sugar)

½ orange, zest finely grated, juiced

1 tablespoon fish sauce

⅓ cup (45 g) roasted unsalted peanuts or cashews, coarsely chopped

2 tablespoons fried shallots

Melt 1 tablespoon of the coconut oil in a large saucepan over medium–high heat. In batches, fry the beef for 3–4 minutes or until well browned. Transfer to a heatproof bowl.

Reduce the heat to medium. Add the remaining coconut oil to the pan. Add the shallot and cook, stirring, for 2–3 minutes or until it softens slightly. Add the curry paste and cook for 1 minute or until aromatic. You want it to toast up slightly.

Now add the garlic, ginger, cardamom, cinnamon, nutmeg and halved chillies and stir to combine. Cook for a couple of minutes, until the aromas coming from the pan start to overwhelm you.

Return the beef to the pan and toss until well coated in the spice mixture. Add the coconut milk, coconut cream and 2 cups (500 ml) water. Cover and bring to the boil.

Reduce the heat to very low – like I said, barely a whisper. Keep covered and cook, stirring occasionally, for 3 hours or until the beef is tender.

Add the potatoes and sultanas. Uncover and cook for 30–35 minutes or until the potato is tender. Stir in the tamarind, sugar, orange juice and fish sauce. You want the sourness to be noticeable, so add a little extra tamarind if you feel it needs it, or more orange juice for freshness.

Divide the curry among serving bowls and sprinkle with the peanuts or cashews, fried shallots, orange zest and extra sliced chilli.

Pork

Spaghetti bolognese
'CON TRE TIPI DI CARNE'

SERVES 8 **PREP** 20 minutes **COOK** 3 hours 35 minutes

CLASSIC

Myth
Spaghetti bolognese is an Italian dish from the city of Bologna.

My Truth
There are a few recipes in this book that I've struggled to improve, and this is one of them. Sure, we've specced up the mince and have tried to find ways to shorten the cooking process without impacting on the richness of the dish, but it remains very similar to the bolognese that has been one of my most popular recipes since it appeared in my first cookbook ten years ago. I have also not changed my views on bolognese's origin. While the dish has roots in Italy, it was Italian migrants living in the UK, Australia or the US who created the dish as we know it – a combination of tomatoes, mince and spaghetti.

The gastronomic city of Bologna is famed for its tortellini, mortadella, *gelati* and *zuppa inglese*; a city so associated with rich food and good living that its nickname is '*Bologna la grassa*', or 'Bologna the fat'! However, the dish of spaghetti bolognese is largely unknown there. Sure, they serve meat sauce or '*ragù Bolognese*' over wide pasta (ideally a rich, fresh egg tagliatelle, but it can also be fettuccine or pappardelle), but these sauces are made with little, if any, tomato at all.

The first recipes for ragùs to serve on pasta appear in Italy at the end of the eighteenth century. While there had been standalone stews in Italy before, the 'ragout' was a sexy new French idea. It didn't arrive with Napoleon's invading troops in 1796, as is commonly thought, but was adopted by the royal court in Naples. Vincenzo Corrado, a cook at the court, includes recipes both for ragù as well as a tomato sauce for spaghetti in his *Il cuoco galante* ('The Gallant Cook', 1773), but Alberto Alvisi was the first to put a ragù with pasta in his recipe for *ragù per i maccheroni*. Alvisi was the cook to the Cardinal of Imola, Gregorio Chiaramonti, from 1783 to 1799. Alvisi's meat sauce was made with diced beef, pork or chicken giblets flavoured with lard, onions, cinnamon, black pepper and tomatoes. This is then baked with the pasta, or *maccheroni*.

After this point, ragùs to be served atop pasta became commonplace. There are versions from Bari and Sicily. In Naples and Abruzzo they made a tomato sauce with meatballs; and in Genoa they had *il tocco,* a rich ragù made from cooking a slab of beef for an age with tomatoes and onions. Niccolò Paganini, the great violist who also had a prodigious appetite, shared his recipe for this sauce with ravioli in a letter from 1839. Other than his choice of pasta and not mincing the beef, it's pretty much a modern-day bolognese.

While these ragùs have some similarities to our bolognese, the first recipe to actually partner the name 'bolognese' with pasta wasn't published until 1891.

Pellegrino Artusi's groundbreaking Italian cookbook *La scienza in cucina e l'arte di mangiar bene* ('Science in the Kitchen and the Art of Eating Well', 1891) was an attempt to document the culinary unification of Italy, but his recipe for *maccheroni alla Bolognese* is very different from what we would call a bolognese. Artusi doesn't use tomato, and his ragù was made with livers, cream and little cubes of beef. He even recommended adding truffles and mushrooms. The pasta used also wasn't the flat tagliatelle or fettuccine that they demand in Bologna today but *denti di cavallo* (aka horse teeth!), a type of wide, ridged rigatoni.

So, with a tomato-free meat sauce from Bologna and endless instructions to use wide or thick pasta for this ragù, it's clear that Italy was not on board with our spaghetti bolognese. It's worth remembering a few things here. First, before World War II, 80 per cent of Italians ate a plant-based diet, as meat was so expensive. Second, tomato-based sauces like Naples' simple marinara were largely a southern Italian thing – the first recipe for a 'red' or vegetarian tomato sauce with pasta was published in 1770 by Francesco Leonardi. And finally, for many Italians, fresh pasta was a Sunday or feast day meal. Polenta, bread and rice were more common everyday staples.

These factors help underpin the theory that spaghetti bolognese was the creation of Italian migrants in the United States, United Kingdom and/or Australia. Meat was so much cheaper in these nations – food represented just 25 per cent of the weekly household budget, rather than 75 per cent back in the old country – and ingredients like tinned tomatoes, dried spaghetti and cheap cardboard tubes of parmesan were readily available in the early twentieth century. Add in the fact that so many of these migrants from around the turn of the nineteenth century came from Italy's south, home of tomato sauce on vermicelli or spaghetti, and it almost seems inevitable that a meat-based tomato sauce for spaghetti would be created as an everyday meal.

Many point to Elizabeth David as the one who introduced the English-speaking world to 'ragù Bolognese' in her *Italian Food* (1954), but even a cursory study of papers in the British Newspaper Archive shows that bolognese was well established by then. It is there in a fulsome restaurant review in the *Daily Herald* (1936), and the earliest UK recipe I can find for something called spaghetti bolognese pops up in the *Daily Mirror* in 1938 (although it uses kidneys and tomato ketchup?!).

By 1939, cans of spaghetti bolognese were being sold for 9 pence a tin, showing the dish must have achieved some form of mainstream acceptance. The recipe came from Gennaro's, a London restaurant that the Tasmanian *Mercury* reported in 1937 was a 'favourite haunt for Australians with epicurean tastes'. Here in Australia, Cribb & Foote of Ipswich had been selling tinned spaghetti with tomato sauce and cheese since 1925.

Mentions of spag bol in the UK rise dramatically after World War II. However, in 1958, *The People* reported that Londoners were more adventurous eaters than other Brits because they were 'eager to try exotic foreign things like spaghetti Bolognese and yoghourt'. There's also a great story from 1949 about a UK hotel manager seeking to please twenty Italian tourists by serving spaghetti bolognese, only to find when he walked into the dining room that the Italians had refused to eat it as they didn't know what it was. The English guests, on the other hand, had devoured it, confirming that spag bol was still unknown in Italy but already popular in the UK.

While we are getting all anecdotal, the shortening of spaghetti bolognese to 'spag bol' or 'spag bog' was, *The Times* of London opined, because people were nervous about pronouncing or spelling bolognese (or bolognaise, as it is known in the UK, where they adopted the French spelling).

The US history of bolognese is a little more sketchy. Over the almost 18 million digitised newspaper pages held by the Library of Congress, spag bol gets only a handful of mentions, compared to well over 120 hits for spaghetti and meatballs. It seems that spaghetti and meatballs was really the US's spag bol.

And so to Australia. Put the words 'spaghetti' and 'bolognese' into the National Library of Australia's newspaper archive, and you immediately hit gold.

There's a recipe for tomato sauce with cheese on spaghetti in the *Queensland Times* in 1925, and in 1931, in the *Italo-Australian*, there's talk of a department store, Mark Foy's, selling spaghetti with 'juicy' bolognese sauce for Lent. This is the earliest mention of spag bol I can find *anywhere* – not just here in Australia. I'd also argue that the fact it is being used as a selling point in an advertisement implies readers were already happily familiar with the dish.

The tagliatelle bolognese on the menu at Romano's in Sydney in 1938 had morphed into spaghetti bolognese by 1939 (*Daily Telegraph*). Through this we can see that spaghetti bolognese was firmly established as a dish in Australia by the late 1930s. Further evidence comes in May 1939, when *Il Giornale Italiano* reported on the opening of Luigi's Spaghetti Bar in Kings Cross and mentioned chef Chinelli's *tagliatelle alla Bolognese*; in a copy of the *Sydney Morning Herald* from July 1939, where we see four smartly dressed Sydney women seated around a chafing dish of spaghetti bolognese at the fashionable Prince's; and, in the same year, the founder of Sydney menswear institution Lowes is pictured in the *Daily Telegraph*, dressed in white tie and tails, in the process of tossing spag bol for his guests. The only issue is that there is little written about what was in these early spag bols. We have to wait another ten years or so for that.

In 1952, spag bol was on the counter lunch menu at Mario's (*The Sun*, Melbourne), and later that year it popped up as a recipe in the *Australian Women's Weekly*, although the writers of the wonderful Australian Food Timeline website point out that this was for a spag bol pasta bake topped with melted cheese. The sauce, however, is instantly recognisable as the one we know and love today. Even more telling, in an edition of *Farmer and Settler* (1953), writer Lucie Hamilton suggests a recipe presented for spaghetti bolognese is 'still the best I've come across', implying that there's nothing new about spag bol in Oz. Pretty much all the recipes from around this time feature the familiar core of tomatoes, mince and spaghetti.

All these are recipes that appeared *before* Elizabeth David's ragù Bolognese that is so often cited as the first mention of the dish in English.

Ironically, however, it is *The Mail* in Adelaide that published the first proper recipe for a *spaghetti alla Bolognese* that we'd recognise, on 13 May 1950. It came from Joy Campoli, the wife of acclaimed violinist Alfredo Campoli, who played with Dame Nellie Melba. In Joy's recipe, minced steak and onions are fried and then slow cooked with tomato, water and tomato puree for four hours to make a sauce for spaghetti that she advises should never be overcooked. She learnt the recipe from her mother-in-law, the lauded Italian opera singer Elvira Celi, who had toured with Enrico Caruso and played to great acclaim from Buenos Aires to New York.

If I could cut this story right now, I'd suggest we have overwhelming evidence to claim spaghetti bolognese is a proudly Australian creation, but my ethics annoyingly insist that this would be a sin of omission. For, even though the earliest recipe for spaghetti bolognese appears in an Aussie paper, and so many of the earliest mentions of spag bol are Australian, it was at Elvira Celi's urging that the Campolis moved to the UK from Rome in 1911, and not Adelaide. So, sadly but honestly, Joy Campoli's recipe has to be credited as coming from Friern Barnet, north of London. We might have to share a little of the honour.

Spaghetti bolognese *(CONTINUED)*

½ cup (125 ml) olive oil
100 g pancetta or bacon, finely chopped
2 carrots, peeled and finely chopped
2 large celery stalks, finely chopped
2 brown onions, finely chopped
1 tablespoon brown sugar
4 garlic cloves, crushed
¼ cup (70 g) tomato paste (puree)
500 g pork mince
500 g pork and veal mince
500 g beef mince
2 cups (500 ml) red wine
2 × 400 g cans diced tomatoes
3 cups (750 ml) chicken stock
2 cups (500 ml) tomato passata
1 tablespoon worcestershire sauce
6 cm piece parmesan rind
4 cm piece pith-free lemon peel
3 bay leaves
sea salt and freshly ground black pepper
cooked spaghetti (or your choice of pasta),
    to serve
grated parmesan, to serve

Heat 2 tablespoons of the oil in a large stockpot over medium–high heat. Add the pancetta or bacon, carrot, celery and onion, and cook, stirring, for 8 minutes or until the vegetables are soft.

Add the sugar, garlic and tomato paste and cook, stirring, for 5 minutes or until the tomato paste starts to darken slightly. Transfer the mixture to a large heatproof bowl.

Heat 1 tablespoon of the remaining oil in the same pot. Cook the pork mince, breaking it up with a wooden spoon, for 5 minutes or until lightly browned. Transfer to the bowl with the vegetables. Repeat in two more batches with the remaining oil and pork and veal mince and beef mince. Set aside.

Increase the heat to high. Add the wine to the pot and bring to the boil. Simmer for 5 minutes or until reduced by half. Deglaze the pot as you stir. Return the mince and veggie mixture to the pot. Add the tomatoes, stock, passata, worcestershire, parmesan rind, lemon peel and bay leaves. Season well with salt and pepper.

Cover and bring to the boil, then reduce the heat to very low. Tilt the lid so the pot is partially covered, and cook, stirring occasionally, for 3 hours or until the sauce has reduced and thickened and is a glossy dark red colour. Serve with the cooked pasta and grated parmesan.

If we truly want to claim spaghetti bolognese as an Australian dish we should start using kangaroo mince rather than pork or beef. Feel free to add extra finely chopped smoked streaky bacon if the mince is very lean. The addition of other indigenous ingredients like lemon myrtle instead of lemon peel or a little ground wattleseed to add a back note of nutty, mild bitterness against all the salty, umami flavours may also be well worth experimenting with. If you do, let me know how you go by DMing me @mattscravat.

I should note that three hours might still seem like a long time for a 'shortened' recipe. In my defence, my original bolognese is a four-hour-plus cook!

Another cheat's ramen

SERVES 4 **PREP** 20 minutes **COOK** 2 hours 10 minutes

Twist

Myth
Ramen is truly Japanese.

My Truth
This history of ramen is tangled. The most repeated myth is that ramen came to Japan via a Confucian scholar called Zhu Zhiyu (1600–1682), who, now resident in Japan, was invited to be the academic mentor of the shogun's cousin, Tokugawa Mitsukuni (1628–1701). Mitsukuni was a budding scholar and gourmet for his age – he had once eaten yoghurt! – who was interested in his teacher's take on udon noodle soup. The advice he received was to add more flavour from onions, garlic and ginger, and to try making the noodles with a mix of wheat and lotus root flour. He recorded this conversation in his journal (*Nichijoshoninnikki*), dating it 1665.

From this we can assume that noodle dishes already existed. A fifteenth-century text, *Inryokennichiroku*, mentions *keitai-men*. The '*men*' there is noodles. In fact, noodles made with acorn flour date back to Neolithic-period Korea, and the earliest archaeological discovery of noodles was an upturned bowl of 4000-year-old long, yellow noodles made from laminated millet-flour found in north-west China. These noodles looked strikingly like the *la mian* noodles of today, from which ramen gets its name.

So, already the Japanese history of ramen intertwines with China, but the reason ramen has an almost spiritual hold over the Japanese psyche is not its noble roots. It is its more humble origins from the last 150 years that have popularised this noodle soup and given it its Japanese uniqueness.

While *la mian* noodles were popular in China, fat udon and then soba noodles dominated in Japan, at least until the late nineteenth century, when the first Chinese ramen hawkers in Japan's open port of Yokohama used these slightly chewy noodles in broth to feed quayside merchants and traders.

In 1870, the first of many Chinese restaurants opened in Nankinmachi, Yokohama. It was around this time that halved hard-boiled eggs and *chashu* (pork) joined the noodles as ramen's signature ingredients. The name for this bashed, browned and soy-braised pork belly differs from roasted Cantonese pork, called *char siu*, but the similarities between the names shows where the inspiration for the braised version came from.

The Meiji era (1868–1912) not only saw the relaxing of Japan's borders but the start of industrialised migration from the country to the cities and the increasing consumption of meat. Both are key in the rising importance of ramen to the people. By 1884, ramen had spread around the country, with a Hokkaido restaurant advertising '*nankin soba*' in a local paper. In 1910, Ozaki Kenichi opened his ramen street stall, Rai Rai Ken, in Tokyo's Asakusa suburb, adding fish cakes and spinach to his '*shina soba*'. Prior to this, soba was something you largely found sold in Chinese restaurants and from handcarts on the street or around the docks.

This is seen as the era when regional variations of ramen began; such as using a 24-hour broth made from chicken backs or pork feet and other cheap ingredients. The arrival of the first readily available mechanised noodle machines in Japan also made much larger production possible for small restaurants.

Losing the racially tinged epithets of '*nankin soba*' or '*shina soba*' and replacing them with a Japanese pronunciation of '*la mian*', cheap bowls of soupy 'ramen' eventually became popular across Japan, but it was the addition of dashi broth to the stock that made ramen uniquely Japanese.

Ramen is also deeply entrenched in the Japanese psyche as a food that can feed and nourish the people in times of war and strife. This was the case after the Great Kanto Earthquake of 1923 and after the devastations of World War II. It was memories of starving postwar Osaka that inspired Momofuku Ando to turn the cakes of dried noodles he'd created into Nissin's instant ramen in 1958, as a cheap and convenient way to feed people who were struggling with money to pay for food as well as for the heat to cook it on.

Ramen remained a cheap workers' food – it fed the construction workers who built much of modern Tokyo and its rail system in the run-up to the 1964 Olympics – until the years of exceptional economic growth from 1955 to 1972 spawned a generation of what were called 'salaryman escapees', who wanted to be their own bosses and set up the fluttering red and white *noren* curtains over the doors of their own ramen shops. Here, ramen started to become the food of the young urbanite rather than the docker or construction worker.

By the 1990s, the ramen cult was at full throttle, with ramen aficionados travelling around the country to sample regional ramen, and some ramen cooks adopting Japanese Buddhist work clothing that accentuated the quasi-religious worship of ramen that had become enshrined in the culture.

The recipe that follows is 22 hours from being a traditional ramen, but it plays to readily available Australian ingredients. Use it as a jumping-off point for your adventures into homemade ramen.

Cheat's ramen *(CONTINUED)*

2 tablespoons dashi miso paste
1 tablespoon light soy sauce
1 tablespoon cooking sake
1–2 teaspoons caster sugar, to taste
½ bunch gai lan, cut in half crossways and
   thick stems thinly sliced lengthways
180 g ramen noodles
sesame oil, to drizzle
chilli flakes, to serve

Ham stock

700 g ham hock
8 dried shiitake mushrooms
3 cm knob ginger, peeled and thinly sliced
3 red shallots, peeled and thinly sliced
2 garlic cloves, halved
2 spring onions, white parts cut into 5 cm
   lengths and green parts thinly sliced
   diagonally
1 teaspoon whole black peppercorns
8 cups (2 litres) chicken stock

Make the ham stock. Place the ham hock, mushrooms, ginger, shallot, garlic, white parts of the spring onion and the peppercorns in a stockpot. Add the stock. Cover and bring to the boil over high heat. Reduce the heat to low and simmer, covered, for 2 hours or until the meat falls away from the bone.

Use tongs to remove the ham hock. Set aside until cool enough to handle and reserve the ham cooking liquid. Remove the ham meat from the bone. Discard the bone and any rind. Shred the ham. Place in a bowl and cover to keep warm.

Strain the stock and reserve the mushrooms. Discard the other solids. Slice the mushrooms and add to the pan of strained stock. Add the miso, soy sauce, sake and sugar to the stock mixture. Bring to a simmer over low heat. Add the gai lan and cook, for 1–2 minutes or until just wilted.

Meanwhile, cook the noodles in a large saucepan of boiling water for 2 minutes or until just tender. Drain.

Divide the noodles among serving bowls. Use tongs to transfer the gai lan to the bowls. Divide the shredded ham among the bowls and ladle over the hot stock. Serve drizzled with sesame oil and sprinkled with chilli and the green parts of the spring onion.

TIP

Some would say it can't be ramen without a sweet, soy-marinated soft-boiled egg. These are crazy easy to make. Carefully peel properly soft-boiled eggs and submerge in a marinade of 3 parts mirin, 1 part light soy sauce and 1 part mushroom soy sauce or sweet soy sauce (such as kecap manis). Ideally, use enough liquid so the eggs float. Cover with folded paper towel and push the eggs down into the marinade – the marinade will soak into the paper towel and help keep the eggs submerged. (Or, for a cheat's version, you could marinate the eggs in a ziplock bag.) For the best result, marinate for 24 hours, but overnight or just while this broth is cooking is okay too. Cut the marinated egg in half lengthways for the most appealing presentation, and drop it in the soup 30 seconds before serving.

Food nerd fact

On the surface, ramen is as simple as broth, noodles and ingredients, but the complexity of those *men* (noodles), the combination of a soup stock with dashi and how the ingredients are treated result in loads of variations. Ramen can be defined by the additions – with salt (*shio*), soy (*shōyu*) or miso; or by how the broth is made. This may be a light chicken broth from Honshu or a 24-hour simmer of pork bones and fat that makes for a milky looking *tonkotsu* of the southern island of Kyushu; it could be a ramen that is heavy with garlic and thick noodles from Sapporo, or *tsukemen* ramen, where the noodles are served in a separate bowl and designed to be dipped into the broth that has been flavoured and reduced into a sauce. All this makes ramen a wonderfully complex and rewarding religion.

Sweet and sour pork and prawn meatballs WITH CARAMELISED PINEAPPLE

SERVES 4 **PREP** 20 minutes (plus 2 minutes soaking and 30 minutes chilling) **COOK** 35 minutes

Twist

Myth

Sweet and sour pork is a 1970s creation of suburban Australian Chinese restaurants.

My Truth

Is it the magical ruby-glass colour of the sauce or the brutal juxtaposition of flavours which demand attention that makes sweet and sour so special; a mesmeric combination of our two favourite flavours of childhood?

The combo of sweet and sour has held sway over humans for as long as we have had the skills and interest to write down records of what we eat. While there is no evidence that Ancient Egyptians melded sweet with sour or salty flavours, the Ancient Romans loved this combo, often cooking meat and fish in a combination of fruit, must (or honey) and vinegar.

The 'uncooked sauce for birds' in Ancient Roman food bible *Apicius* is typical of this. The first-century recipe collection also features slightly more unusual sauces combining honey, vinegar and the Roman version of umami-heavy fish sauce called *garum*. These were kept alive after the fall of Rome in Byzantine kitchens, with their *oxymel*-style sauces of herbs steeped in a mix of honey and vinegar.

This appreciation of the sweet–sour axis carried through early medieval kitchens of the Arab world, with dishes like the Andalusian chicken *zirbaya*, which contains saffron, sugar and vinegar, and is thickened with almonds, or with lamb dishes like *mulahwajah* or *tabaahaja*. And while the use of *garum* died out in Italy and across the old Roman Empire, the love of sweet and sour did not; with game like wild boar or venison being served with a sweet and sour sauce in Tuscany, France creating *gastrique* reductions and *duck à l'orange*, with its sweet and sour sauce, and Venice achieving fame for its fried sardines served dressed with sugar, raisins, candied fruit and vinegar.

The earliest English cookbooks, published in the fourteenth century, also show a love of sweet and sour. *The Forme of Cury* ('The Method of Cooking') talks of rabbits braised in a sauce of vinegar and ground currants flavoured with cinnamon, cloves and ground ginger. *Utilis Coquinario* has a recipe for '*A dauce egre*', in which fried fish is doused in a sweet and sour onion sauce. This sounds eerily like a dish from Hunan that is often singled out as one of the ancestors of modern Chinese sweet and sour, alongside the sweet and sour pork ribs of Shanghai and *guo bao rou*, a dish of a sweet and sour sauce covering swags of battered pork fillet from Harbin in China's north-east, which was created for foreign traders in the early Qing dynasty (i.e. in the mid-seventeenth century).

The strongest claim to the creation of China's famous sweet and sour dish – and it was most definitely Chinese before it made its way to Australia during the gold rush – also has links to foreign traders who already had a predisposition to sweet and sour.

It's said that in the 1600s, when Westerners first started operating out of the area that today is Guangdong Province in southern China, their favourite thing to eat was the local pork in sweet and sour sauce. The original recipe came from the town of Chencun, in the Shunde district. It was traditionally made with pork ribs, but the Westerners preferred boneless chunks of pork shoulder. This new dish was named *gu lou yook*, the name coming from either a) the sound the foreigners made when slurping down the sauce; b) '*wu lou*', a derogatory term for the traders, or c) their exclamations of 'good!' as they ate, which were transcribed as 'gu lou' by non-English-speaking cooks.

The search for gold in the mid-nineteenth century saw many locals move from Guangdong to the US and Australia, taking their sweet and sour with them. The dish was still popular in Melbourne during World War II, where Aussie and US servicemen on leave would flock to eat sweet and sour dishes of pork and 'schnapper'. What's not so sure is who first started adding tomato ketchup to the sauce, but the odds are that it was probably some canny restaurateur in China, as this addition is a long running-feature of the sweet and sour there, at places like the famous and historic Luk Yu Tea House in Hong Kong.

The other thing I'm not sure about is serving the sauce over chewy battered pieces of pork. It's better in my book with lovely, light pork meatballs, but it is rare that a recipe can't be improved upon, and we've added prawn to the meatballs here to make them more luxe. This is a fleeting reference to another Chinese sweet and sour dish, *loong har kow*, where golden lobster balls arrive at the table doused in the sweet, sticky sauce. It's just my way of giving this Aussie suburban classic – with two thousand years of culinary history behind it – some class to match its pedigree.

Sweet and sour pork and prawn meatballs *(CONTINUED)*

2 slices white bread, crusts removed

¼ cup (60 ml) milk

250 g pork mince

150 g peeled green prawns, finely chopped

3 spring onions, white parts finely chopped and green parts sliced diagonally

3 cm knob ginger, peeled and finely grated

2 garlic cloves, crushed

2 teaspoons cornflour (corn starch)

1 tablespoon soy sauce, plus extra 2 tablespoons

1 egg

freshly ground white pepper

227 g can pineapple rings in syrup, drained, syrup reserved

2 tablespoons peanut oil

1 brown onion, coarsely chopped

1 red capsicum (pepper), deseeded and coarsely chopped

1 green capsicum (pepper), deseeded and coarsely chopped

½ cup (125 ml) tomato sauce (ketchup)

¼ cup (60 ml) rice wine vinegar

Place the bread in a bowl and cover with the milk. Set aside for 2 minutes to soak. Squeeze out the milk as much as you can to remove the excess liquid. Place the bread in a large clean bowl.

Add the pork mince, chopped prawn, white parts of the spring onion, ginger, garlic, cornflour, soy sauce and egg in the bowl with the bread. Use clean hands to mix until well combined. Season with white pepper. Place the mixture in the fridge for 30 minutes to chill. (Chilling helps firm the mixture slightly.)

Use wetted hands to roll tablespoonfuls of the mixture into balls. Transfer to a plate.

Heat a large, non-stick frying pan over high heat. Add the pineapple rings and cook for 3 minutes each side or until caramelised and bronzed in spots. Transfer to a chopping board and cut into quarters. Set aside.

Heat half the oil in the pan over medium heat. Add half the meatballs and cook, tossing, for 8 minutes or until golden. Don't overcrowd the pan. Transfer to a plate. Repeat with the remaining meatballs.

Heat the remaining oil in the pan over medium–high heat. Add the onion and capsicums and cook, stirring, for 3–4 minutes or until softened slightly. Reduce the heat to medium. Add the tomato sauce or ketchup, vinegar, extra soy sauce and the reserved pineapple syrup and bring to the boil. Add the meatballs and cook, gently turning occasionally, for 4–5 minutes or until the meatballs are cooked through and are covered in a thick and glossy sauce. Return the pineapple to the pan. Serve sprinkled with the green parts of the spring onion. This is nice with plain white rice or fluffy white steamed bao and lemon-dressed shredded cabbage.

Banh mi

SERVES 8 **PREP** 15 minutes (plus overnight chilling) **COOK** 50 minutes

Myth
Fusion food is Frankenstein food.

My Truth
So many of the dishes in this book are evidence that culinary cross-pollination is a good thing, and banh mi is just another example.

The French introduced the baguette and pâté into Vietnam in the late nineteenth century. Bread suffered in the humid climate, however, which meant baking two or three times a day was common. Initially this bread was often sold as part of a platter of cold cuts, pâté, ham, cheese and butter known as *cat-cut*. This was primarily enjoyed by French expats, both because it was expensive and because the colonisers frowned on Vietnamese people eating French food (and vice versa).

This all changed with the outbreak of World War I. Many of the French were called home to fight, and in August 1914 Saigon police expelled all German and Austrian nationals. By the next morning they had been sent to Java with nothing more than what they could carry.

With the market for European food seriously contracted, closing the warehouses of German importers meant flooding Vietnamese markets with perishables like cold cuts, cheese and pâté as well as coffee, cans of condensed milk and bottles of the Swiss Maggi seasoning liquid that still has a valued place in some banh mi shops today.

As Vietnamese people discovered the European luxuries they had previously been denied, the families of French soldiers who had returned to Europe were left poorly supported and had to supplement their usual diet with local ingredients. European imports also became scarce.

All this meant a very different Vietnam between the wars, and a country with a growing sense of its own identity. Prototype banh mi moguls started using mayonnaise instead of the butter favoured for classic French rolls like *jambon-beurre*. Mayonnaise could handle the heat of Hanoi a whole lot better than butter (or many of the French colonialists, for that matter). Meanwhile, enterprising Vietnamese bakers found ways to make the crumb inside the bread lighter and the crust just as crispy, but thinner and easier to tear into, by adding ascorbic acid.

Simple, stripped-backed prototype banh mi rolls became a popular street snack during World War II. While Saigon bakeries were serving banh mi in the postwar years, these were for the wealthy until 1954. This changed with the partition of Vietnam, which saw one million people move south. Many arrived in Saigon, and some opened sandwich stands to make a living. The banh mi as we know it was officially born here in 1958. Mr and Mrs Le, newly arrived from Hanoi, basically put everything from that *cat-cut* platter into a roll, but kept prices low by using shorter rolls and replacing some of the expensive meats with more veg, giving us the riot of texture, flavour and temperature that we know and love today.

In Vietnam you'll find banh mi stuffed with everything from meatballs, brawn, grilled chicken or pork to shredded pig's skin. This got me thinking about making a banh mi with just the best part of the pig, the crackled skin. And, yes, I know that pickled carrot and daikon (*do chua*) are traditional in banh mi, but when I discovered that *do chua* just means 'pickled stuff', that got me thinking too . . .

---

500 g piece pork rind
olive oil, for brushing
1 tablespoon sea salt
8 long crusty bread rolls
2 × 120 g cartons good-quality pâté
⅔ cup (200 g) Kewpie mayonnaise
4 spring onions, trimmed and cut in half
1 bunch coriander, stems trimmed and sprigs
 well washed
Maggi seasoning liquid, to taste

Radish and beetroot pickles
⅓ cup (80 ml) white vinegar
2 tablespoons caster sugar
1 teaspoon sea salt
1 bunch radishes, thinly sliced (on a
 mandolin if you have one)
125 g cooked small beetroot, thinly sliced
1 long red chilli, thinly sliced

Score the pork skin at 1 cm intervals. Place the rind, skin-side up, on a baking tray lined with baking paper and pat the skin dry with paper towel. Place in the fridge overnight, uncovered, to dry out.

Preheat the oven to 220°C (200°C fan-forced). Place the rind on a rack over a baking tray, then brush with oil and sprinkle with the salt.

Roast for 45–50 minutes or until the skin bubbles and crackles. Set aside for 5 minutes to cool slightly, then use a sharp knife to cut into shards.

While the pork is crackling up, make the radish and beetroot pickles. Combine the vinegar, sugar and salt in a large glass or ceramic bowl. Add the radish, beetroot and chilli and toss to combine. Set aside for 20 minutes to pickle.

Use a large serrated knife to cut the rolls in half lengthways along the top, without cutting all the way through. Spread one side of the inside surface of the cut bread with pâté. Spread the other cut side with mayonnaise. Drain the radish and beetroot from the pickling liquid and divide among the rolls. Add the spring onion, coriander and pork crackling shards. Drizzle with a little Maggi seasoning to serve.

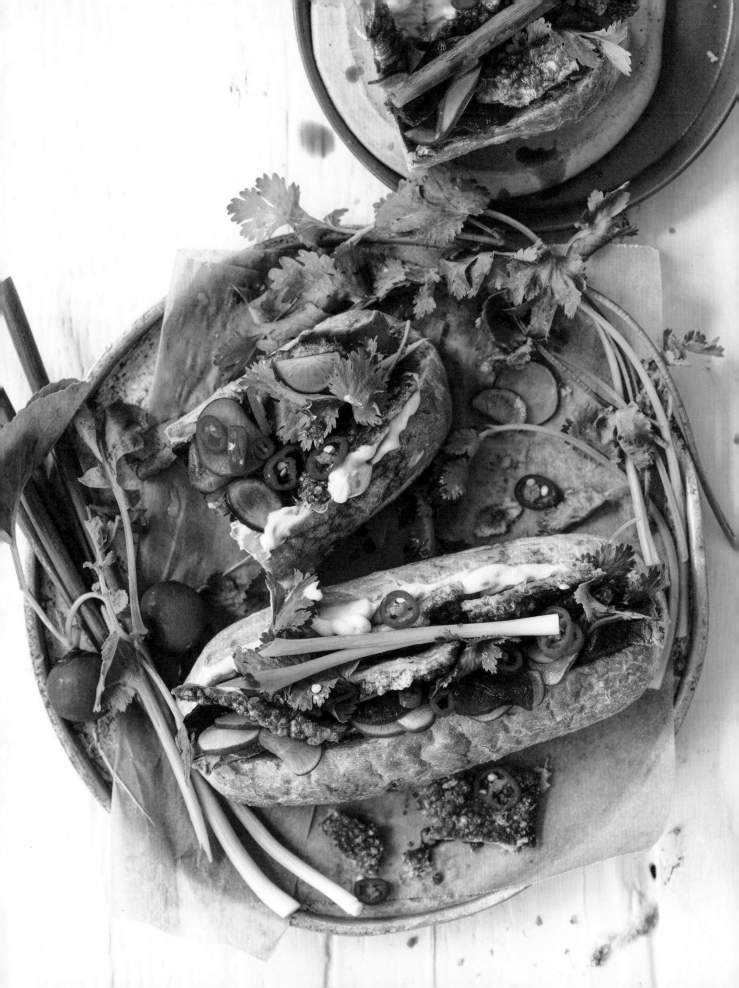

Pork potstickers

MAKES 30 **PREP** 30 minutes (plus soaking) **COOK** 15 minutes

Twist

Myth

Dim sims are Chinese.

My Truth

While the steamed Aussie 'dimmie' might give a nod towards the traditional *siu mai* dumplings of China, the filling of pork (or sometimes even lamb) mixed with cabbage and spices is unique to the Australian dish. It's also larger than Chinese dumplings, and its skin thicker, making it suitable for eating with your fingers over a number of bites and also able to stand up to sloshing about in lashings of industrial-strength soy sauce in a lined paper bag.

While it might be sold in servos, chippies, footy club canteens and on the first tee at Kew Golf Course, the dimmie is seldom seen in Chinese restaurants in Australia these days, confirming its unique cultural standing.

William Chen Wing Young, of the now-shuttered Wing Lee restaurant in Melbourne's Chinatown, is credited with popularising the dim sim and setting the standard for a thicker-skinned Australian dim sim, although he would always modestly insist that his dimmie was inspired by classic Cantonese pork *siu mai*.

William started making his pork dim sims commercially in 1945, and was known to hire older men from the Chinese community for this to give them some work. The dimmies were then sold to footy fans at the Punt Road oval. The MCG had been commandeered by the US Air Force at that time, so Melbourne Football Club was sharing Punt Road with Richmond. This meant there were games every weekend, not just on alternate weekends, and up to 38,000 fans could turn up to see a big game – and eat William's dimmies.

Despite William's role in bringing the dish to the masses, the dim sim was already well known in Melbourne's cook shops and Chinese restaurants. Melbourne paper *The Argus* mentions dim sims by name in articles printed in 1928, 1929 and 1945, usually in quite glowing terms. There are also reports of US service personnel enjoying dim sims at Melbourne's Chinese restaurants, of which there were twenty-three open at the time of World War II.

Even earlier, there are a lot of unsubstantiated claims that the dim sim was first made in the Australian goldfields after the gold rush, which began in 1851. While there is little evidence to back this up, we know that many of the migrants who arrived in Victoria from Southern China, the home of yum cha, started food stalls or cookshops to feed the growing number of men digging for gold.

These goldfield dumplings were said to be filled with mutton – just like some commercially produced dimmies are today. While this is just as likely to be about availability than anything else, the original *siu mai* dumplings from Hohhot in what is now the Inner Mongolia region were filled with mutton, spring onions and ginger rather than pork. History's first recorded dumplings, Northern Chinese *jiaozi*, could also be filled with well-peppered stewed mutton and medicinal herbs. These dumplings inspired the fried version, often filled with pork, the potsticker (*guotie*) and Japanese gyoza.

Jiaozi get a mention in China's first ever dictionary, thus becoming the oldest dumpling on record and a distant ancestor of the dimmie. Three hundred years later, *jiaozi* had taken off and were referred to as 'a common food in the world' by politician and courtier Yan Zhitui, in his writings about sixth-century China. We even have physical proof of this: a well-preserved pork-filled *jiaozi* some 1300 years old was unearthed on an archaeological dig along the Silk Road. (They were found next to a 1000-year-old naan!)

It is interesting to consider how the dim sim might have got its name, because that term is not used in China. William Chen Wing Young's daughter, pioneering TV chef and Australian culinary icon Elizabeth Chong, believes it comes from the way Toisanese people from Southern China – like her father, and like many of those early migrants who worked on the goldfields and in Chinese restaurants back in Melbourne – pronounced the phrase 'dim sum', i.e. the small dishes such as dumplings that might be eaten at yum cha (which literally means 'drink tea' in Cantonese but embodies the meal of tea and small shared dishes).

Elizabeth also credits William with inventing the first chicken roll, which Bendigo boilermaker Frank McEncroe would later re-envision as the even more robust Chiko Roll. This was another unique Victorian snack-food innovation designed to withstand handling by crowds at the footy and other big events. The Chiko Roll debuted at the Wagga Wagga Show in 1951, but Frank always claimed that his inspiration came from those 'chop suey rolls' sold at Punt Road.

While we could have had a dimmie recipe here, I felt it would be out of place to recreate something that was always a commercial product for the home kitchen. And frankly, these fried *guotie* are a wee bit prettier and more dainty, especially with their filigree lace collar. So, before we cook up a plate of these distant ancestors of the dimmie, let us take a moment to thank William Chen Wing Young, Frank McEncroe and Kuen Cheng as well. His round dim sims sold at the South Melbourne Market are another unique Melbourne culinary icon. Together, these men have shaped the way Australia ate, and saved many from the horrors of the morning after.

Pork potstickers *(CONTINUED)*

6 dried shiitake mushrooms
300 g pork mince
4 spring onions, white parts only, finely chopped
4 cm knob ginger, peeled and finely grated
2 garlic cloves, crushed
2 tablespoons finely chopped coriander
1 tablespoon soy sauce
1 teaspoon sesame oil
1 egg white
freshly ground white pepper
30 gow gee wrappers (1 packet)
¼ cup (60 ml) peanut oil
2 teaspoons sesame seeds, toasted

Chilli dipping sauce

2 tablespoons soy sauce
2 tablespoons black vinegar
2 teaspoons *chiu chow* chilli oil

Place the mushrooms in a heatproof bowl. Cover with boiling water and set aside for 15 minutes to soak and soften. Drain and finely chop the mushrooms. Place in a large bowl.

Add the pork, spring onion, ginger, garlic, coriander, soy sauce and sesame oil to the bowl with the mushroom. Use clean hands to mix until evenly combined. Place the egg white in a small bowl and use a fork to whisk until foamy. Add to the mince mixture and mix until well combined. Season with white pepper.

Place one wrapper on a flat surface. Place 1 heaped teaspoon of mince mixture in the centre. Brush the edge with water. Fold in half to enclose the filling. Press the edges to seal. Pleat. Repeat with the remaining wrappers and mixture to make 30 dumplings.

To make the dipping sauce, place all the ingredients in a small bowl and mix together. Set aside.

Heat 1 tablespoon of the oil in a large, non-stick frying pan over medium–high heat. Add a third of the dumplings. Cook on one side for 2 minutes or until golden. Reduce the heat to medium. Add ⅓ cup (80 ml) water to the pan. Cover with a lid. Cook for a further 3 minutes or until the dumplings are cooked through and the liquid has evaporated. Transfer to a plate. Cover with foil to keep warm. Repeat the process in two more batches with the remaining oil, dumplings and another ⅓ cup (80 ml) water for each batch.

Place the potstickers on a serving plate and sprinkle with the sesame seeds. Serve immediately with the dipping sauce.

TIPS

Uncooked dumplings freeze well. Arrange in a single layer on a tray lined with baking paper and place in the freezer until firm. Once frozen, transfer to an airtight container to make storing easier. Freeze for up to 3 months. Cook from frozen – no need to thaw.

To make a frilly crispy skirt (for up to 10 dumplings), use a fork to whisk together ½ cup (125 ml) water, 1 teaspoon cornflour (corn starch), 1 teaspoon plain flour and ½ teaspoon rice wine vinegar in a jug. To cook the dumplings, heat the oil in a small 16 cm (base measurement) non-stick frying pan over medium heat. Place 4–5 dumplings flat-side down in a decorative pattern in the base of the pan. Cook for 1 minute or until lightly golden. Add ¼ cup of the flour mixture to the pan, pouring in between the dumplings. Cover with a lid and cook for a further 5 minutes or until the dumplings are cooked through. Remove the lid and the slurry should be thick, white and bubbly. Uncover and cook for a further 4–5 minutes or until a golden lace is in the base of the pan and the edges of the lace are starting to curl away from the edge of the pan. Place a serving plate on top of the dumplings and invert the dumplings with their skirt onto the plate. Serve with the dipping sauce. Repeat the process with 4–5 more dumplings and the remaining flour mixture. Continue making small batches of the flour mixture every 10 dumplings.

If you want to do a bigger batch of dumplings, place up to 10 dumplings in a larger frying pan and use all the flour mixture per batch. Any more than this and it gets hard to handle.

Pat grapao moo saap

SERVES 4 **PREP** 10 minutes **COOK** 15 minutes

CLASSIC

Myth #1

The delay in the popularity of fried dishes like *pat grapao* – often seen on Thai takeaway menus as *pad krapow* – is thanks to the most food loving of all Thai kings, Rama II (1767–1824). He decreed that there were to be no savoury dishes that were fried.

Myth #2

Frying was banned by the king of Siam, so when Marshall P. (aka Field Marshal Plaek Phibunsongkhram, also known as Phibun in the West) became prime minister during World War II, part of his nationalist and anti-aristocratic agenda was to elevate pad thai and *pat grapao*, fried beef mince with holy basil, to the role of exemplars for new Thai cuisine, rather than some fancy palace food.

My Truth

When it comes to Thai food I tend to defer to David Thompson, the Aussie-born, Bangkok-based chef and Thai food expert. I've been a fan of David's for thirty years, travelling to London, Sydney and Bangkok to eat his food.

After reading his recipe for *neua pat bai grapao* in his book *Thai Street Food*, which uses beef mince, rather than pork, I email him for his take on the history of the dish. He's actually eating *pat bai grapao* when the email arrives.

He tells me that *pat grapao* holds a special place in the hearts of Thai people everywhere. 'It's a simple dish and yet it is one of the dishes that Thais long for the most. It's reassuring Thai comfort food of the most piquant kind. It is also an old dish, much older than the 1940s. How far it stretches back, I cannot be certain,' he explains.

'While there's general agreement about *pat Thai's* origin with the Field Marshal, I have never heard of *pat grapao* coming from Phibun's decrees. Marshall P. released a number of mandates on how a good Thai citizen should behave and one of them, Mandate 5, issued in November 1939, was aimed at encouraging the use of Thai products; one of the tenets being that "Thai people should make an effort to consume only food made from Thai products."'

Thompson, who has spent years studying Thai royal cuisine, has never heard about Rama II's admonitions of fried food either. He points to Thais using a technique called *ruan*, or cooking an ingredient that has been moistened with a little water, which existed long before the wok and frying became popular in Thailand. These dishes were cooked in or on terracotta. David explains that's how the fried mince for the first Thai salads (*larb* in Thai) was originally cooked.

'Stir-frying and deep-frying arrived with the Chinese, along with the wok. The Chinese also brought chopsticks, noodles, soy sauce and the eating of pork and duck to the Kingdom. These arrived and were digested into the Thai repertoire over hundreds of years,' says David.

Chinese traders had been travelling and settling in what was to become Thailand since the thirteenth century, but a real boom in migration began when the victorious Thai general Taksin (himself the son of a Chinese merchant) became king in the late eighteenth century, after he helped secure Siam's liberation from Burma and established a new capital that would grow to become Bangkok. Taksin pushed for increased trade with China and openly encouraged migration between the countries. By 1825 there were 230,000 Chinese people living in Thailand. By 1910, this number had more than tripled.

So here we have two options for the birth of *pat grapao*. Could it be that the idea for this dish came from twisting the mince used for larb into a wok-fried, made-to-order street-food dish, or was it descended from a Southern Chinese dish of beef stir-fried with soybean paste, garlic and holy basil?

When you discover that most of the Chinese migrants encouraged by Taksin came from the southern part of China and that, in the years 1882 to 1917, between 13,000 and 34,000 people from this region moved to Thailand each year, my feeling is that the latter theory is the most likely.

All that was left was for Thai and migrant cooks to ramp up the heat and drop the soybean paste in favour of the funky fragrance of fish sauce. 'Thais tend to tinker and make an array of additions to the basic dish,' David explains. 'Beans creep in, along with the occasional cob of corn. Oyster sauce and even chilli jam are stirred into the mix. I eschew these additions as needless intrusions into such a straightforward dish. I prefer its simplest rendition of mince, garlic, chillies, fish sauce and holy basil. What is non-negotiable are the eggs, and a bowl of fish sauce with chopped garlic and chillies.'

I immediately make a note to add a recipe for this. I take a moment to feel happy that the beans used here won't be frowned on by Thai cooks, and also to remind myself what a lovely, knowledgeable man David Thompson is.

Pat grapao moo saap *(CONTINUED)*

2 tablespoons peanut oil
500 g pork mince (see Tips)
280 g green beans, cut into 5 cm lengths
2 red shallots, peeled and thinly sliced
3 cm knob ginger, peeled and finely grated
4 garlic cloves, crushed
2 long red chillies, halved lengthways,
    deseeded, ribs removed, thinly sliced
    crossways (see Tips)
¼ cup (55 g) white sugar
¼ cup (60 ml) fish sauce (see Tips)
2 tablespoons dark soy sauce
4 eggs
the largest bunch Thai basil you can find (or
    2 small bunches), leaves picked
steamed white rice, to serve

David Thompson's authentic chillies in fish sauce

½ cup (125 ml) fish sauce
10 birdseye chillies, thinly (and very
    carefully!) sliced
2 garlic cloves, thinly sliced
1 tablespoon lime juice
pinch of finely chopped coriander

Make the chillies in fish sauce first – ideally a day ahead, as David promises that the fiery heat will temper over time. (I'm not sure I always trust him when it comes to heat. Experience and pain are great teachers.) Combine the fish sauce, chilli and garlic in a bowl. Cover and set aside. Scrub your hands and equipment well after making. Just before serving, stir through the lime juice and coriander.

Heat 1 tablespoon of the oil in a wok or large, heavy-based frying pan over high heat. Add the pork and cook, breaking up with a wooden spoon, for 4–5 minutes or until it is golden and starting to crisp up.

Add the beans, shallot, ginger, garlic and chilli to the pork and cook, stirring, for 2 minutes or until the beans are starting to soften. Add the sugar, fish sauce and soy sauce and cook, stirring constantly, for 2 minutes or until the mince is well coated, and the sauce thickens slightly but has not evaporated.

While the pork cooks, heat the remaining oil in a frying pan over medium heat. Crack in the eggs, keeping them separate. Cover and cook for 2 minutes or until the white is just set and the yolk is still runny.

Stir the basil into the pork just before serving. You want it just to colour and not cook or lose its fragrance.

Divide the steamed rice among serving plates. Spoon over the pork mixture and top each one with an egg. Serve with the chillies in fish sauce on the side.

TIPS

If possible, ask your butcher for a slightly coarser grind of pork mince than usual – ideally about 5 mm.

I'm a wimp with chilli but you can swap out the long red chillies in the pork for as many birdseye chillies as you can bear, if you want it as fiery as you'd have it in the Thai night markets.

NB: I'd call David's chillies in fish sauce a 'go careful' sauce, as it is very hot!

Use the best fish sauce you can find. Three Crabs or Red Boat are great brands available here, and it's really worth the trip to a Thai or Asian grocery to stock up. If you can only find a cheap, aggressively salty fish sauce, only use 2 tablespoons in the pork.

Potjie – one pot stew with damper

SERVES 6 **PREP** 40 minutes **COOK** 5 hours 35 minutes

Myth
When it comes to cooking pots, there is no myth – only truth, backed up by archaeology and painstaking historical research.

My Truth
After roasting, stewing is probably the second oldest form of cookery in human history. There needn't even have been a pot, as there is evidence of First Nations cultures around the world making stews in everything from cleaned animal stomachs to upturned turtle shells.

Life became much easier with the invention of the first pots, and for this we have the people of Ancient China to thank. Archaeologists have uncovered Chinese sand pots called *keng*, which were used for making stew, that date back 19,000 years, to an era of prehistoric hunters and gatherers, for whom that pot would likely have been a most valuable possession. Those early sand pots morphed into clay pots 5000 years ago, and then into bronze and other metal cauldrons, such as the Chinese *ding*.

The significance of the cooking pot is best shown by the Nine *Ding* of the Zhou kings, which were a symbol of the ruler's authority over the nine provinces of China during the Shang and Zhou dynasties around 2500 years ago.

Outside China, too, the cauldron or cooking pot has long been associated with magic and power. Cast-iron cauldrons date from the late Bronze Age and in Celtic mythology are associated with everything from the ability to resurrect the dead to being as bottomless as the Magic Pudding, such as the magical Cauldron of Dagda.

All this leads us to the *potjie* of South Africa. This three-legged cooking vessel has become synonymous with the dish that is cooked in it. The pot is descended from the Dutch oven that Dutch settlers carried to South Africa in 1652 when they landed on the Cape of Good Hope. It was also with them in their wagons as they made the Great Trek north from the Cape to escape British oppression and find somewhere to live in freedom. These *potjie* would be refilled with game hunted along the way and re-boiled every night along the journey. It has become almost as much a part of Afrikaner identity as the *braai*, their form of barbecue.

In South Africa, stews are not just significant for Afrikaners. Nelson Mandela recalled that, when he was working as a lawyer fighting against the excesses of the apartheid regime in the courts, there were only four restaurants in Johannesburg where he and other black South Africans were allowed to eat: Moretsele, Blue Lagoon, Kapitan's and Azad's. He loved fancy Kapitan's for their curried mince with ginger pickle, but at Moretsele his pick was the stew and pap (a type of maize porridge). Most of the time when Mandela and his associates were on the road defending cases they would have to eat fish and chips in their car or a sandwich on the beach, due to the harsh restrictions that were placed on the rest and movement of black South Africans, so you can see why these meals had such value.

There is one major difference between a stew and the *potjie*, and it is that a stew is stirred, while with *potjie* the ingredients are layered for cooking and not disturbed until you dig in your serving spoon and get a bit of everything, including the meat at the bottom of the pot. This would be served with pap or with a South African style of damper.

We are serving our *potjie* with Australian damper as a way of linking the common bush experiences of South Africans and Australians. South Africans have their own bush breads, including their own damper, which is often richer than the Australian equivalent as butter and eggs can be beaten into the dough.

The history of Australian damper starts with First Nations peoples, from whom it was adopted by white settlers. The earliest recipes were a dough of winnowed seeds such as native millet, spinifex or wattleseed, nuts such as those of the bunya pine, and roots, ground into a dough and cooked in the embers of a fire. As millstones used by First Nations Australians have been found dating back 30,000 years, it is likely that damper has a history equally as long, making it arguably the oldest recipe in this book. Here, however, we are using the most common of all ground grass seeds: wheat flour.

I prefer my damper cooked wrapped around sticks held over the embers rather than cooked in the ashes, which was not only the Indigenous way but also the method used by William Bond, Sydney's first baker of European origin. Bond travelled to Australia as a convict with the First Fleet, and apparently was known to be on good terms with the local Gadigal people, which might explain where he got the idea for this damper from. Contact with First Nations people may also explain how swagmen and drovers knew that white wood ash or some alkaline artesian bore water would help the bread rise in the absence of baking powder.

A 1946 article in the *Sydney Morning Herald* quoted historian James Bonwick's claim that the name 'damper' came from Bond's technique of 'damping the ashes of his oven', although there is a competing suggestion that the name came from an old Lancastrian saying that bread 'damps the appetite'.

Potjie – one pot stew with damper (CONTINUED)

¼ cup (60 ml) extra virgin olive oil
2 kg springbok shoulder and neck, cut into
    4 cm chunks (you can use pork shoulder if
    you can't find springbok or warthog)
sea salt and freshly ground black pepper
25 g unsalted butter
6 each of baby onions, small carrots and
    small turnips, scrubbed
1 bunch flat-leaf parsley, leaves picked,
    stems chopped
4 garlic cloves, sliced
2 bay leaves
1 whole star anise
1 cinnamon stick
1 tablespoon finely chopped rosemary
1 tablespoon finely chopped sage
1 teaspoon fennel seeds, crushed
1 teaspoon coriander seeds, crushed
¼ cup (70 g) tomato paste (puree)
2 cups (500 ml) chicken stock
1½ cups (375 ml) dry red wine (such as pinot
    or merlot)
3 ripe plums, halved, stones removed
1 orange, juiced
1 tablespoon caster sugar

Damper

3 cups (450 g) self-raising flour
sea salt
60 g chilled butter, cubed
1 cup (250 ml) milk, plus extra for brushing

Preheat the oven to 150°C (130°C fan-forced).

Heat 1 tablespoon of the oil in a *potjie* (or your largest flameproof casserole dish) over medium–high heat. Season the meat with salt and pepper. Cook, in batches, for 4–5 minutes or until lightly browned all over. Transfer to a plate and set aside.

Reduce the heat to medium. Add the butter, onions, carrots, turnips and parsley stems and cook, stirring, for 3–4 minutes or until browned slightly. Add the garlic, bay leaves, star anise, cinnamon, rosemary, sage, fennel and coriander seeds and cook, stirring, for 2 minutes, until aromatic.

Add the tomato paste and cook for 1 minute, then add the stock and wine. Return the meat and any resting juices to the pan. Stir to combine, then season, cover and bring just to the boil. If you are using a traditional tall and narrow *potjie*, you can remove the veg from the pot and layer the ingredients with the meat on the bottom. No stirring then! Transfer to the oven and bake for 3½–4 hours or until the meat is very tender.

To make the damper, place the flour in a bowl and season with a good pinch of salt. Add the butter and use your fingertips to rub into the flour until fine crumbs form. Make a well in the centre and fill with the milk. Cut the flour into the milk with the back of a knife until a dough starts to form, then gather into a ball.

Turn the dough out onto a lightly floured surface and knead for 5 minutes. Form into a loaf and score lines across the top. Transfer to a baking tray lined with baking paper and set aside.

Once the meat is tender, remove the *potjie* from the oven and set aside, covered to keep warm. Increase the oven temperature to 200°C (180°C fan-forced). Put the damper in the oven on the bottom rack, reduce the temperature to 170°C (150°C fan-forced) and bake for 25–30 minutes.

Line another baking tray with baking paper. Toss the plums in the orange juice and sugar. Place on the prepared tray and bake on the top rack, above the damper, for 20 minutes or until softened and caramelised.

Serve the *potjie* with the caramelised plums and a sprinkling of parsley leaves on top, with the damper on the side.

TIP

Last time culinary muse Warren Mendes and I were in South Africa, we wanted to cook a *potjie* with warthog for a big lunch, but swine flu put an end to that idea. We used springbok instead, but if you aren't using game meat, then lamb neck or chunks of pork shoulder are equally good. The main thing is to cook your *potjie* low and slow. Above all, says South African cook Jason Bonello, you are looking for the '*potjie* pot whisper' of the dish quietly cooking.

Juicy pork belly with red braise sauce

SERVES 6 **PREP** 10 minutes (plus overnight chilling) **COOK** 3 hours 15 minutes

Myth

Rubbery braised pork skin is as big a delicacy in Australia as it is in China.

My Truth

Pork belly is one of the best cuts of any meat: cheap, tasty and, when braised, a textural sensation – melty, jellied fat and chewy flesh.

The greatest of all pork belly braises are those known as red braised pork. The Hunan dish of red pork was reportedly Mao Zedong's favourite meal; it was said that he ate bowls of it every day to stay intellectually sharp.

Most famous of all of China's red braises, and the one with the best origin story, is *dong po rou*. Song-dynasty poet and statesman Su Shi is one of China's most famous gastronomes and a true polymath. His writing demonstrates his stoicism and the sometimes cheeky humour that saw him banished to Huangzhou from 1080 to 1086, during which time he lived on a farm called Eastern Slope (*Dong Po*), from which he took his nickname, Su Dong Po. It was here that the red braised pork recipe bearing his nickname was born. The story goes that he forgot his pork belly stew on the stove when a friend dropped by unexpectedly, but on discovering his mistake he was pleasantly surprised that the braised pork belly, made with yellow wine from Jiangnan, was delicious.

It's a lovely story, but it ignores two things. First, Su Shi was an enforced vegetarian (or at least pescetarian) during his exile, upon the advice of his doctors. He'd picked up a nasty eye complaint; thus clams, not pork belly, were his weakness while there. Second, while he wrote that few in China knew how to cook pork properly, he prided himself on his skill at doing so. He even wrote a poem praising Huangzhou's good pork for being 'as cheap as dung' (and thus massively undervalued by the rich). In the poem, he discusses the best way to cook pork to make it 'beautiful' in the sort of wistful terms a man deprived might use to write of the one he loves. So let's not diminish his brilliant creation with the old 'forgetful cook' myth.

Now, while red braised pork is one of China's greatest dishes, and I love the way the fat becomes almost jellied, I'm not a massive fan of the chewy stewed skin. This is undoubtedly a mark of my shallow love of pork crackling. So, we set out to see if we could try to get the best of both worlds with this recipe. Surely the prospect of more bronzed crackling can justify tinkering with a classic? (For those who like their classic *dong po rou*, just make sure the recipe you choose to cook minimises the addition of water. This is what Su Shi advises in that poem, along with long, slow cooking and yellow wine from Jiangnan, near Shanghai.)

1.5 kg piece boneless pork belly
2 teaspoons olive oil
1½ tablespoons sea salt
2 cups (500 ml) orange juice
1 cup (250 ml) water
4 cm knob ginger, peeled and thinly sliced
3 whole star anise
¾ cup (165 g) caster sugar
¼ cup (60 ml) light soy sauce

TIP

This partners well with white rice or mantou (steamed bread), plus steamed bok choy or choy sum.

Place the pork on a rimmed baking tray. Use a very sharp knife (or a stanley knife) to score the skin crossways, making the cuts about 5 mm apart. Pat the skin dry with paper towel. Place, uncovered, in the fridge overnight to dry out the skin.

Remove the pork from the fridge 30 minutes before cooking to bring it to room temperature.

Preheat the oven to 250°C (230°C fan-forced). Place the pork, skin-side up, in a flameproof roasting pan. Rub the oil over the skin and sprinkle with a little salt. Roast for 1 hour or until the skin is crispy.

Reduce the oven temperature to 160°C (140°C fan-forced). Carefully add the orange juice, water, ginger and star anise to the pan, making sure the liquid doesn't touch the crackled skin.

Roast, checking halfway through to see if you need to top up slightly with water, for 2 hours or until the pork is tender.

Transfer the pork to a plate and cover loosely with foil to rest. Transfer the roasting pan to the stovetop. Add the sugar and soy sauce and stir over low heat until the sugar dissolves. Increase the heat to high and bring to the boil. Boil, without stirring, for 10–15 minutes or until the mixture thickens.

Dunk the whole piece of pork into the sauce, meat side down, and paint the sauce up the sides. Do this carefully, without the sauce touching the crackling. Pour the remaining soy-orange-caramel sauce onto a serving platter. Add the pork, slice and serve, spooning sauce over the meat.

Customisable carbonara

SERVES 4　**PREP** 10 minutes　**COOK** 15 minutes

Myth

Carbonara is a traditional pasta of the charcoal burners around Rome, the *carbonaio*, and is made using *guanciale* and pecorino.

My Truth

It's one of the most-searched recipes in Australia, even eclipsing bolognese as our favourite pasta dish, but searching for the origins of carbonara has more twists, turns and red herrings than three series of a bingeable Nordic noir murder mystery. The common theory is that carbonara is hundreds of years old; a dish invented by the charcoal burners who worked outside Rome, made with eggs, pecorino and the local pork jowl bacon known as *guanciale*. Like all good myths, it is just persuasively romantic enough to sound true. It is not.

There's not enough evidence here to even open an investigation. The major stumbling block is that in the three most important books on the cuisine of Italy – Pellegrino Artusi's *La scienza in cucina e l'arte di mangiar bene* ('Science in the Kitchen and the Art of Eating Well', 1891), Ada Boni's volume of Roman cooking *La Cucina Romana* ('The Roman Kitchen', 1930) and Fernanda Momigliano's *Mangiare all'Italiana* ('Eating Italian Style', 1936) – there is nary a mention at all of carbonara.

While you could accept that one or two of these definitive works might have missed the dish, for all three to have done so seems significant. Especially as, only a few years after World War II, carbonara recipes start to appear in profusion, both in Italian cookbooks and works from overseas writers collating current Italian recipes, such as Elizabeth David's *Italian Food* (1954). This implies that it had either been recently invented or had got suddenly popular sometime in the 1940s.

Of course, there are examples of dishes similar to spaghetti carbonara prior to the 1940s. Historians and food sleuths point to Rome's *pasta alla gricia*, which is made with bacon, lard and pecorino, but no eggs. Or to *cacio e uova*, made with lard, eggs and cheese but without bacon, pancetta or *guanciale*. In his excellent paper on the history of carbonara, presented to the Oxford Symposium on Food in 2006, food historian Anthony F. Buccini points to a recipe of cheese and eggs (*cas' e ova*) in *Cucina teorico–pratica* ('Theoretical–Practical Kitchen', 1837) by Neapolitan cook Ippolito Cavalcanti as possibly being the earliest forerunner of carbonara. That claim is dismissed by some Italian writers, who point out that here the egg is cooked out and not creamy, plus there's no bacon of any form.

Interesting though this is, it doesn't explain the dish's name change or sudden appearance in postwar cookbooks. The only theory that stacks up for me is also the one that is most uncomfortable for many within and outside Italy: that the first carbonaras were made with Canadian bacon and American cheese! You see, the Allied invasion of Italy culminated in the landing at Anzio, south of Rome, in September 1943. Some months later, after fighting through Kesselring's German forces, US Army General Lucian Truscott was ordered to march into an undefended Rome. His GIs arrived in a starving city whose government had already surrendered before the mainland invasion. The GIs had backpacks brimming with K-rations and quartermasters' stores were full of bacon and cheese. Is it from this combination of ingredients that the carbonara evolved, perhaps inspired by that *pasta alla gricia* or *cacio e uova*?

As for the name, Rome's Campo de' Fiori has been a favourite nightspot for visitors since the eighteenth century, when dandies from all over Europe flocked there. There was even a street named after these *maccheroni*. During the occupation it would have undoubtedly drawn GIs too. In the square there was a restaurant that had been open since 1912, under the name *La Carbonara*. Did their version of the GIs' favourite pasta get the name here? Or, was it named after the copious use of black pepper in some *cacio e pepe* inspired versions of the dish, which saw the GIs give it the nickname 'Ash Spaghetti', as it looked like it had burnt flecks in it?

There is another theory for the name: that carbonara is named after the Carbonari, a secret society of middle-class Italian revolutionaries that was active in the early 1800s. They sought to push out the foreign kings, Austrian occupiers and papal forces who ruled over much of what would become Italy and to instead find a truly local, ideally republican, leader.

Given the nationality of the German leader during World War II (Hitler was born at Braunau am Inn in Austria) and his support from the papacy, what better name would there be to give to a newly created pasta dish made with ingredients supplied by an army from the world's greatest republic; an army that was trying to remove a different foreign yoke from around the country's neck?

Whatever the truth may be, the theory that carbonara was based on a pasta dish dressed with eggs and cheese, with additional ingredients added on top, got me thinking. What if we embraced the many frowned-upon adulterations of this dish? Over the years people have told me that carbonara *must* be made with cream, parsley, onions or even tomato – those last three coming from three Romans sitting outside a restaurant in the Campo de' Fiori when I was filming there.

And so, here we have what I'm calling 'customisable carbonara'. The idea of adding the peas and leeks comes from the fact that the recipe above Cavalcanti's *cas' e ova* features both peas and fried onions. (Or, I think it does – the eighteenth-century Neapolitan dialect he wrote in was a little tricky to decipher!)

Customisable carbonara (CONTINUED)

1 cup (120 g) frozen baby peas
1 cup (160 g) frozen corn kernels
8 rashers rindless bacon, coarsely chopped
500 g dried spaghetti
¼ cup (60 ml) olive oil
2 leeks, white part only, thinly sliced
5 eggs
1 cup (70 g) finely grated parmesan, plus
   extra to serve
freshly ground black pepper

Bring a large saucepan of water to the boil over high heat. Add plenty of salt.

Get your sides ready. Bring a small saucepan of water to the boil over high heat. Add the peas and cook for 2 minutes or until tender. Use a slotted spoon to transfer to a serving bowl. Cover to keep warm.

Add the corn to the saucepan and cook for 2 minutes or until tender. Drain and transfer to a separate warm serving bowl.

Heat a frying pan over medium–high heat. Add the bacon to the pan and cook for 3–4 minutes or until the bacon is crisp. Use a slotted spoon to transfer the bacon to a plate lined with paper towel to drain. Transfer to a warm serving bowl. Cover to keep warm. Save the fat and don't clean the pan!

Add the spaghetti to the boiling salted water and immediately add 1 cup (250 ml) cold water to the pan – this will help prevent the pasta from sticking together. Stir and return to the boil. Cook for 1 minute less than it says on the packet or until just al dente.

Add the oil to the remaining fat in the frying pan and heat over medium heat. Add the leek and cook for 3–5 minutes or until golden and crisp. Transfer to a plate lined with paper towel to drain. Transfer to a warm serving bowl.

Lightly whisk the eggs in a large jug with a fork. Stir in the parmesan and season with plenty of pepper. While the pasta is cooking get your warm side bowls to the table.

Using a heatproof jug, carefully take ½ cup (125 ml) of the pasta cooking water and set aside.

Call everyone to the table now – carbonara waits for no one.

Drain the pasta and return to the warm pan. Add the egg mixture and reserved cooking liquid to the hot pasta and toss until well combined. Return the pan to low heat and toss the pasta for 1 minute, being careful not to scramble the eggs. The liquid will thicken and give the pasta a silky coating.

Transfer the pasta to a serving bowl and season with pepper. Serve with the sides and the extra parmesan. Tell everyone to add what they fancy and avoid what they'd normally have to pick out.

Tacos al pastor

MAKES 10 tacos **PREP** 40 minutes (plus 1 hour freezing and 8 hours marinating) **COOK** 1 hour 35 minutes

Myth

Tacos al pastor was created by Lebanese cooks who brought the shawarma to Mexico.

My Truth

Tacos al pastor is one of Mexico's favourite dishes. It has become a big favourite north of the border, too. Just looking at the revolving tower of meat will make the similarities obvious between this dish and a Greek *gyros* or a Turkish shawarma, which was invented around 1870 by Mehmetoğlu İskender Efendi at his restaurant in the Turkish city of Bursa.

It's also fair to say that the explosion in popularity of *tacos al pastor* in the 1960s can be linked to the taco stands and restaurants that were opened by the children of Lebanese migrants in Mexico City. These migrants had fled the fall of the Ottoman Empire; left due to the introduction of conscription in 1919 to fight in the Turkish War of Independence; or simply sought to escape the escalating violence and poverty that accompanied these times.

Migrants from the Middle East had started to come to Mexico from the end of the nineteenth century, but they came in much larger numbers from the 1900s to the 1930s when the Ottoman Empire was crumbling. About 36,000 people arrived in Mexico from the Ottoman State between the late nineteenth and early twentieth centuries, with the majority coming from Lebanon and Syria. Today it is estimated that there are as many as 800,000 people of Lebanese descent living in Mexico.

Tacos al pastor were different from Turkish shawarma in that they were marinated in a very Mexican mix of chillies and spices, such as *achiote*, which gave the meat its red colour. Furthermore, the thinly sliced meat was cut directly into the taco, with some theatricality, rather than served on pita bread; and the additional toppings of fresh coriander and onion, with a final flourish of grilled pineapple, were all very tropical, all very Mexican.

The inclusion of pineapple is credited to El Tizoncito *taqueria*, one of Mexico City's contenders for serving the first *tacos al pastor*, when it opened in 1966. The recently widowed Concepción Cervantes y Eguiluz launched El Tizoncito to support herself and her four children. She had been inspired to open her *taqueria* because of the *tacos arabes* that were sold near her house, which her children loved.

This is all well and good, but I couldn't help but wonder why a taco filled with pork would be called 'tacos of the shepherd'. These last two snippets of information made me dig some more.

Tacos arabes was a local type of souvlaki that had been enjoyed by Mexicans for thirty years before the first *tacos al pastor*. These were made with lamb and had a more understated seasoning of herbs. Tellingly, the first *tacos arabes* places weren't opened by Lebanese migrants but by Mexican residents from one of the previous waves of migration from the Middle East. Both Ottoman oppression and the British capture of Iraq in 1917 saw a number of Iraqi families leave the country, eventually to end up in the Mexican city of Puebla. By the mid-1930s, the Iraqi form of shawarma, known as *gauss* or *kas*, had become a hit in the city at restaurants like Antigua Taqueria La Oriental and Tacos Arabes Bagdad. Both were founded in 1933 and specialised in these mild, herby, lamb-based tacos.

There are mutterings online that some Poblano (people from Puebla) weren't fans of the original lamb tacos, nor the beef versions that followed, and that they only became a hit in the city when pork was introduced. Those first tacos made with lamb would make some sense of the name *al pastor*, if this is the case.

So, while the children of Lebanese migrants had a big part to play in the development of *tacos al pastor*, it seems it was actually Iraqi migrants who first brought the shawarma, or at least their version of it, to Mexico.

What follows is not a recipe for traditional *tacos al pastor*, but I imagined you probably wouldn't have the revolving *trompo*, a vertical grill and easy access to traditional marinade ingredients like *achiote* paste and *guajillo* or *ancho* chillies that would require – even if you do have the two hundred friends that would be needed to eat it! It also doesn't layer that long skewer with a complicated equation of pork loin, leg steaks and neck to ensure that the flavour, texture and fat content is just right.

It does, however, capture some of the joy of eating *tacos al pastor* from a food truck in the suburbs of Los Angeles, or from a hole in the wall in that old part of Mexico City that the hotel concierge nervously tells you not to visit after dark, and it does so using pork neck, one of the most underrated cuts of pork, in my opinion.

The pairing of pork with homemade pineapple ketchup, a long-term favourite of mine, was suggested by a record of Concepción Cervantes saying that the marinade for her *tacos al pastor* was inspired by the vinegar and spices she put in her *pozole rojo* (pork and hominy stew). So, the pineapple ketchup is perfectly at home here.

Tacos al pastor (CONTINUED)

1.6 kg piece pork neck
350 g pineapple, peeled and cut into 2 cm
  chunks
1 small red onion, thinly sliced
4 jalapeño chillies, deseeded and finely
  chopped
⅓ cup coarsely chopped coriander
⅓ cup (80 ml) lime juice
2 tablespoons olive oil
sea salt
10 mini flour tortillas, warmed
crème fraîche, to serve

Marinade

½ 215 g can chipotle chillies in adobe sauce
½ white onion, coarsely chopped
2 garlic cloves, crushed
2 teaspoons ground cumin
2 teaspoons ground coriander
1 teaspoon smoked paprika
2 teaspoons lime juice
½ cup (125 ml) pineapple juice

Pineapple ketchup

⅓ cup (55 g) sultanas
1 brown onion, coarsely chopped
2 garlic cloves, crushed
⅓ cup (80 ml) tomato puree
¾ cup (180 ml) water
¾ cup (185 ml) apple cider vinegar
⅓ cup (75 g) brown sugar
2 teaspoons sea salt
pinch of cayenne pepper
8 canned pineapple rings
2 teaspoons coffee powder (or a double shot
  of espresso)
2 whole cloves
1 teaspoon allspice
½ teaspoon ground cinnamon
⅛ teaspoon ground nutmeg
⅓ cup (115 g) honey

Place the pork in the freezer for 1 hour or until firm but not completely frozen solid.

While the pork firms up, prepare the marinade. Combine all the marinade ingredients except the pineapple juice in a food processor and process until smooth. Transfer to a large glass or ceramic bowl and stir in the pineapple juice.

Use a sharp knife to cut the pork into 1 cm thick slices. Cut each slice in half lengthways to make wide strips. Weave the sliced meat onto ten metal or soaked bamboo skewers and brush over the marinade. Cover with plastic wrap and place in the fridge to marinate for at least 8 hours or overnight (or even up to 2 days for the best results). If you are going to use bamboo skewers rather than metal, soak them in cold water for about an hour before threading the pork, to prevent them burning on the barbecue.

To make the pineapple ketchup, blitz the sultanas, onion, garlic and tomato puree in a food processor until smooth.

Scrape the puree into a large, heavy-based saucepan and stir in the water, vinegar, brown sugar, salt and a big pinch of cayenne pepper. Don't wash the food processor yet – we will use it again.

Bring the mixture to the boil, reduce the heat to medium–low and then simmer gently, uncovered, for 1 hour. Stir regularly – and even more often towards the end of the cooking time.

Place the pineapple rings in the food processor and process until pureed. Add the pineapple puree, coffee, cloves, allspice, cinnamon, nutmeg and honey to the ketchup mixture. Bring to a simmer and cook for another 10 minutes or until thickened. Stir often to prevent catching on the bottom.

Press the ketchup through your finest sieve and return to a clean saucepan. Cook over low heat, stirring, for 5 minutes or until the ketchup thickens. Balance the seasoning by adding splashes of vinegar if it's too sweet or salty. Drizzle in a little more honey if it's too tart or some more coffee if it needs some added complexity.

Preheat a barbecue grill plate on high heat. Place a piece of pineapple at the end of each pork skewer, and any leftover pineapple on its own skewers.

Cook the skewers for 5–8 minutes each side or until slightly charred and cooked through. Transfer the skewers to a baking tray and cover loosely with foil for 5 minutes to rest.

While the pork rests, place the onion in a heatproof bowl. Cover with boiling water and set aside for 2 minutes to blanch. Drain and set aside to cool. Combine with the jalapeño, coriander, lime juice and oil in a bowl. Season well with salt.

Remove the pineapple and pork from the skewers. Serve in the warm tortillas topped with the crème fraîche, pineapple ketchup and coriander mixture.

TIP

For a mini *tacos al pastor* experience, leave the pork neck on the skewer, then slice down the edge of the skewer as if you are shaving a teeny *trompo*. This will give you lovely shards of pork that will fill your taco beautifully and also be easier to eat – but it won't look as good for the Instagram picture.

Roast pork for Sundays and holidays

SERVES 4 **PREP** 15 minutes **COOK** 1 hour 50 minutes

CLASSIC

Myth
You don't need apple sauce with roast pork.

My Truth
For me, some roasts are simply not complete without the right fruity accompaniment – lamb with mint jelly, duck with cherries, Christmas turkey with cranberry sauce. Most noble of all these is apple sauce with a golden haunch of crunchy, crackle-backed pork.

Apples were one of the first trees to be domesticated and crossbred by our ancient ancestors – the wild apple from the Caucasus and Xinjian meeting the crabapple of northern Europe for bigger, sweeter and juicier fruit. Originally they were most often eaten fresh, and dried or preserved for the winter. Cooking apples into a sweet or savoury sauce is very much a medieval thing. The earliest English and French cookbooks, *The Forme of Cury* ('The Method of Cooking', c. 1390) and *Le Ménagier de Paris* ('The Parisian Household Book', 1393) both have recipes for apple sauce, made with beef broth for meat days and almond and saffron for fish days. It's interesting to note that the first-century cookbook *De re coquinaria* ('On the Subject of Cooking', also known as *Apicius*) includes a recipe for a pork and apple ragù, a combination that the later cookbooks don't specify.

Even though pigs were one of the earliest animals domesticated for meat, with a history even longer than cultivated apples, it wasn't until the eighteenth century that the combination of apple sauce and roast pork became a given. This coincided with an explosion in the number of cookbooks being published, such as Hannah Glasse's *The Art of Cookery* (1747).

The logic of the pairing was undeniable. Before the industrialisation of pork production, pork was an autumn meat, with the pigs often fattened on windfall apples before being dispatched to turn into charcuterie and cuts for the long winter, so serving the prime cuts with apples seems irrefutable. Taste this recipe if you need any more convincing.

1.5 kg boned rolled pork loin
1 tablespoon olive oil
1½ tablespoons sea salt, plus extra for seasoning
2 royal gala apples, peeled and cut into wedges
12 sage leaves
1 tablespoon lemon juice

Apple sauce
6 royal gala apples
30 g butter, at room temperature
1 tablespoon brown sugar
½ teaspoon dijon mustard
1 teaspoon apple cider vinegar
large pinch of ground cloves

TIP

If you like a chunkier apple sauce, you can make this without the blender. After removing the core and skin from the apples, place the flesh in a bowl and add the butter, sugar, mustard, vinegar, pan juices and cloves. Use a fork to roughly mash and combine well. Season with salt and more vinegar, if desired.

Preheat the oven to 240°C (220°C fan-forced).

Open the pork to sit flat, rind side up. Pat the rind really dry with paper towel. Use a sharp knife or stanley knife to score the rind across the width at 1 cm intervals. Roll the pork up and secure with kitchen string at regular intervals. (If you have bought your pork already scored, rolled and tied, all you need to do is pat it dry.)

Transfer the pork, rind-side up, to a large roasting pan. Pat the rind again with paper towel to make sure it is really, really dry. Drizzle over the oil, then rub the salt into the cuts. Roast for 40–45 minutes or until the rind crackles.

For the sauce, use a small knife to score a line around the centre of each whole apple.

Reduce the oven to 180°C (160°C fan-forced). Place the whole scored apples around the pork. Roast the pork for a further 1 hour or until the pork is cooked through and the apples are tender. Transfer the pork to a platter and brush off a little excess salt. Cover loosely with foil to rest. Transfer the apples to a chopping board.

Tilt the pan on an angle and use a dessert spoon to scoop the fat layer off the pan juices in the base of the pan and transfer to a frying pan. Reserve the pan juices.

Use a knife to cut away the flesh of the apples. Discard the core. Transfer the apple flesh and skin to a blender. Add the butter, sugar, mustard, vinegar and cloves and blend until almost smooth. Add 2 tablespoons of the reserved pan juices. Blend until thick and smooth. Taste and adjust the seasoning with more vinegar if necessary.

Heat the frying pan with the pork fat over medium–high heat. Add the apple wedges and cook, tossing, for 3–4 minutes or until caramelised. Add the sage and cook, tossing, for 1–2 minutes or until lightly fried. Remove from the heat, add the lemon juice and toss until well combined.

Slice the pork and serve with the apple sauce, caramelised apple wedges and sage leaves.

Lamb

Lamb tagine - *NOT REALLY*

SERVES 6 **PREP** 20 minutes (plus resting) **COOK** 1 hour 25 minutes

Myth
Tagine is an Arabic dish.

My Truth
While tagine appears alongside stories of Aladdin, Ali Baba and Sinbad in the ninth-century story collection *One Thousand and One Nights*, it is in fact a Maghrebi (or Northwest African) dish created by the Amazigh peoples, who largely live in Morocco, Algeria, Tunisia and Libya. It is basically a ragout, and we can trace the rich and colourful history of the region through the evolution of tagine.

The dish is named after the earthenware vessel in which it is made. This two-part pot is cleverly designed to cook its contents long and slow over a small brazier in order to preserve scarce fuel. The other genius of the tagine is its conical, chimney-like lid, which allows some of the evaporated liquids to drip back into the ragout so it doesn't dry out over the many hours of cooking.

The Amazigh have had a connection with this corner of Africa since before the Holocene, but their lands and culture have been subject to periods of control and suppression by the Phoenicians, the Carthaginians, the Romans, the Byzantines and the Arabs. It was these cultures who gave the name 'Berbers' to Amazigh peoples.

If you flick through recipes for tagine you can see the influence of these cultures on the dish, whether it's the love of pairing fruit and meat that came from Persia with the Moorish expansion, the use of spices that were imported through the Arab world, the idea of mixing sweet with spicy that was a signature of Moorish food from the Arab cities around Andalusia, or a honey-heavy tagine like *mrouzia*, which was designed to help families preserve their share of the annual Eid al-Kebir sacrifice of a lamb. (And, if you see potatoes, these probably made their way over the Straits of Gibraltar from the end of the fifteenth century in the luggage of Jewish refugees fleeing the anti-Semitic violence and persecution of the Spanish Inquisition.)

The beauty of tagine is that it could welcome ingredients from wherever it was being made, whether that was lamb with caramelised onions in Marrakech or squash and honey in Fez. Even fish could be cooked in the tagine, on a trivet of bamboo to stop it sticking. The most famous iterations are perhaps tagines of lamb with dried prunes or apricots, and chicken with preserved lemon and green olives. You can find recipes for traditional tagines in my previous books, but here I have added a twist and paired classic tagine flavours with a beautiful leg of wet-roasted lamb. Is it a tagine? Not really.

---

4 garlic cloves
2 tablespoons coriander seeds
1 tablespoon cumin seeds
1 tablespoon sweet paprika
¼ teaspoon ground allspice
2 tablespoons olive oil
4 cups (1 litre) chicken stock
2 red onions, cut into thick wedges
2 cups (340 g) pitted prunes
1 cinnamon stick
2.3 kg lamb leg
sea salt and freshly ground black pepper
¾ cup (120 g) blanched almonds
¼ cup (90 g) honey
2 teaspoons orange blossom water

TIP

Buttered couscous and roast carrots and parsnips dressed with yoghurt and sumac would be great sides for this dish.

Preheat the oven to 200°C (180°C fan-forced). Place the garlic, coriander seeds, cumin seeds, paprika, allspice and 1 tablespoon of the oil in a mortar and using the pestle pound to form a paste. Add the remaining tablespoon of oil and mix to combine.

Place the stock in a flameproof roasting pan and add the onion, prunes and cinnamon stick. Place a wire rack or trivet in the pan.

Use the tip of a small sharp knife to score across the top of the lamb fat. Place on the rack or trivet. Rub the top with the spice paste and season with salt and pepper.

Roast the lamb for 1 hour–1 hour and 10 minutes for medium. Transfer the lamb to a plate and cover loosely with foil to keep warm. Set aside to rest.

Before you turn the oven off, put the almonds on a baking tray. Roast for 5–8 minutes or until toasted and a lovely deep golden colour. Remove any that get there first so they all get an even tan!

While the lamb rests, use a spoon to scoop 2 tablespoons of the fat from the top of the roasting pan (it is easy to see, as it is bright red) and transfer to a frying pan.

Heat the frying pan of lamb fat over medium heat. Use a slotted spoon to transfer half the prunes from the roasting pan to the frying pan and cook, turning very gently with an egg lifter, for 3–5 minutes or until slightly caramelised.

Place the roasting pan with the juices over medium–high heat. Add the almonds and honey, and simmer for 5 minutes or until the liquid reduces by two-thirds and thickens slightly. Stir in the orange blossom water. Return the caramelised prunes to the onion sauce. Serve the onion sauce with the lamb.

Rogan josh

SERVES 4 **PREP** 30 minutes **COOK** 2 hours 15 minutes

Myth
Rogan josh was a Persian dish before it was a Kashmiri dish, introduced to India by the Mughals.

My Truth
Rogan josh is often credited to the Mughals because its name can be translated to something like 'fat hot' in Persian, reflecting perhaps the burrowing heat that a proper rogan josh gets from loads of red Kashmiri chilli powder, or the process of frying the lamb and spices in ghee before braising.

However, there are no mentions of rogan josh in the two great works that reference early Mughal cooking. In *Ain-i-Akbari* (c. 1590), it is recorded that Akbar, the third Mughal emperor, ate *haleem*, *sambosah* (probably what we know as samosas) and biryani, while in the epic poem *Padmavat* (1540), samosas, *keema* and kebabs all cop a mention, but no rogan josh.

While there are undoubtedly some Persian and Mughal influences in rogan josh, my sense is that it originated in Kashmir. The Kashmiri words for red (*roghan*) and juice (*gosht*) give us something very close to rogan josh, and, looking at early recipes for the dish, the main quest seems to have been to try to get the sauce as red as possible.

Although slightly different versions of rogan josh are made by the Muslim and Hindu communities in Kashmir, both use local ingredients in addition to the Kashmiri chilli powder to achieve the optimal red colour – most commonly *mawal*, a crimson cockscomb flower, in the Muslim version, and *ratan jot*, the root of a flowering herb known as alkanet, in the Hindu version. The Muslim version also uses *praan*, a local wild shallot. (The Hindu version uses no garlic or onion, substituting fried asafoetida powder for that flavour.)

This leads me to the conclusion that rogan josh is and always was a Kashmiri dish that celebrated local produce; a dish that has become part of the proud heritage of both Muslim and Hindu communities in Kashmir. It is one of only seven unchanging dishes in the 36-course royal *wazwan*, a traditional feast that is the pinnacle of Kashmiri culinary culture.

The success of this curry overseas came with its adoption onto British curry-house menus in the 1960s and then the explosion of Indian cookbooks published in the UK and US in the 1980s. Leading this charge in the UK was Madhur Jaffrey. She has recipes for both styles of rogan josh in her books, and it featured on her TV show *Madhur Jaffrey's Indian Cookery*, which received a primetime slot on the BBC in 1982, and on Network 28 in Australia back in 1984. (That's the channel that eventually became SBS.)

---

2 tablespoons ghee or vegetable oil
20 whole cloves
6 cardamom pods, bruised (see Tips)
3 Indian bay leaves (see Tips)
2 teaspoons fennel seeds
1 cinnamon stick
1 large brown onion, finely chopped
4 cm knob ginger, peeled and finely grated
4 garlic cloves, crushed
1 tablespoon sweet paprika
2 teaspoons ground coriander
2 teaspoons ground cumin
1 teaspoon cayenne pepper (see Tips)
1 teaspoon ground turmeric
½ cup (125 ml) tomato puree (see Tips)
1.2 kg boneless lamb shoulder, cut into 4 cm cubes
sea salt
2 cups (500 ml) water
large pinch of saffron threads
⅓ cup (80 ml) boiling water
½ teaspoon garam masala
coriander sprigs, to serve
steamed rice, to serve

Heat the ghee or oil in a large saucepan or stockpot over medium heat. Add the cloves, cardamom pods, Indian bay leaves, fennel seeds and cinnamon stick and cook, stirring, for 30 seconds or until aromatic. Add the onion to the pan and cook, stirring, for 8–10 minutes or until golden.

Add the ginger and garlic and cook for 30 seconds or until aromatic. Add the paprika, coriander, cumin, cayenne and turmeric and cook, stirring, for 30 seconds.

Add the tomato puree, lamb and a good pinch of salt and toss until well combined. Cook, stirring often, for 3 minutes or until the lamb is well coated and just starting to change colour. Add the water and bring to a simmer. Reduce the heat to very low. Cover and cook, stirring occasionally, for 1½ hours or until the lamb is very tender. Uncover and cook for 30 minutes or until the sauce reduces slightly.

While the curry simmers away, place the saffron in a small heatproof bowl. Pour over the boiling water and set aside until serving.

Stir the garam masala into the curry and spoon into a serving bowl. Drizzle with the saffron mixture and top with the coriander. Serve with the rice, or, for a bigger meal, add breads and a nice veg curry such as Kashmiri saag, where spinach is cooked down with mustard oil, brown cardamom and lots of garlic.

TIPS

If you can find black and green cardamom pods, use two of the former and four of the latter.

If Indian bay leaves are unavailable, leave them out – don't substitute regular bay leaves.

If you can find some bright red Kashmiri chilli powder in your adventures, please use a couple of teaspoons of this instead of the cayenne to deliver a similar heat profile.

The tomato puree is added more for the colour than the flavour, but you can leave it out if it offends you.

Middle Eastern sausage rolls

MAKES 18 **PREP** 20 minutes **COOK** 40 minutes

Myth

Sausage rolls just are so *common*. They are the food of the road trip, the kids' party or the post-surf carb load.

My Truth

A few years ago, the US media went into conniptions over sausage rolls. They'd never penetrated that nation's culinary consciousness before, so they caused the sort of stir you might associate with the cruffin or the cronut. Similar fanfare greeted Michelin-starred chef Antonin Bonnet's introduction of a *friand à la saucisse* with za'atar and thyme to one of his Paris menus in 2020.

And why not? Wrapping sausage meat in puff pastry is a staple of Australian homes because it is portable, tasty and wonderfully flexible when it comes to what you do with the filling. What's not to love?

The sausage roll first appeared in the United Kingdom during the Napoleonic Wars, its creation possibly inspired by the pithiviers and mince-filled puff pastry *friands* of France (both of which were evolutions of the fourteenth-century *pâté en croûte*) but with a suitably prosaic British twist of turning it into a street-food snack. Adverts for bakers selling sausage rolls start popping up in the UK press from 1809 onwards, and within a few decades the dish had become part of everyday life there and in Australia. In 1842, there were adverts for a Launceston baker baking them fresh every day. The first UK news reference to a sausage roll was when 17-year-old Elizabeth Thompson choked on a piece of one and 'immediately expired' (*Norfolk Chronicle*, 1832).

While pies evolved as different types of dough were developed and improved upon, the sausage roll has pretty much always been made with puff pastry. Mrs Beeton's recipes in her *Book of Household Management* (1861) and *All About Cookery* (1911), and the recipe in the eight-volume *Encyclopaedia of Practical Cookery*, edited by Theodore Francis Garrett (1891), are little different from a modern sausage roll recipe. In 1876, the *Evening Mail* in London was even praising sausage rolls made with 'Australian mincemeat'!

I should, however, acknowledge the probability that the sausage roll might be related to Lebanese cheese rolls and meat rolls known as *rekakat jibneh* and *rekakat lahme*. Although these get their crispiness from layers of butter filo rather than puff pastry, the similarity is enough for me to want to hedge my bets and give our sausage rolls a Middle Eastern twist.

---

1 tablespoon olive oil
½ red onion, finely chopped
2 garlic cloves, crushed
4 cm knob ginger, peeled and finely grated
2 teaspoons ground coriander
1 teaspoon ground cumin
500 g lamb mince
½ cup (45 g) rolled oats
⅓ cup (50 g) raisins, coarsely chopped
¼ cup (40 g) pine nuts
2 tablespoons finely chopped flat-leaf
  parsley
1½ tablespoons harissa
1 tablespoon pomegranate molasses, plus
  extra to serve
2 eggs
3 sheets butter puff pastry, just thawed
1 teaspoon cumin seeds
crème fraîche, to serve

Preheat the oven to 200°C (180°C fan-forced). Line two trays with baking paper.

Heat the oil in a small frying pan over medium heat. Add the onion and cook, stirring, for 5 minutes or until soft. Add the garlic, ginger and ground coriander and cumin. Cook, stirring, for 30 seconds or until aromatic. Set aside for 5 minutes to cool slightly.

Place the lamb mince in a large bowl. Add the onion mixture, rolled oats, raisins, pine nuts, parsley, harissa and pomegranate molasses. Season with salt and pepper. Crack in one of the eggs. Use clean hands to mix until well combined.

Whisk the remaining egg and pass through a fine sieve into a small clean bowl.

Cut the pastry sheets in half. Place a sixth of the mince mixture along the centre of each piece of pastry. Brush one long edge with whisked egg. Fold the pastry over the filling, pressing to seal. Cut each roll into three pieces.

Place, seam-side down, on the prepared trays. Brush the pastry with the egg. Use a small, sharp knife to pierce the pastry tops a few times to allow steam to escape. Sprinkle with the cumin seeds. Bake for 30 minutes or until cooked through and golden.

Place the crème fraîche in a serving bowl. Drizzle over with extra pomegranate molasses and swirl by dragging the handle of a teaspoon round in a circular motion for two revolutions through the crème fraîche. Serve with the sausage rolls.

Odd note

While Australian newspaper archives from before Federation are full of people's big noses being likened to sausage rolls, the weirdest comment I came across was from a writer in Brisbane's *Moreton Bay Courier*, who, when talking about his most embarrassing experience, likened it to 'being alone at a railway station eating a sausage roll with all the girls' eyes upon you'.

Not a souvlaki

MAKES 8 **PREP** 30 minutes (plus overnight draining) **COOK** 5 hours 50 minutes

Myth
Souvlaki is usually made with lamb.

My Truth
The world of souvlaki is so confusing. What they call souvlaki in the north of Greece – skewers of grilled meat, sometimes lamb although far more often pork, wrapped in pita – are actually called *kalamaki* down in Athens. Souvlaki is a plated dish there, rather than a wrap.

If you want to be totally across Greek meat and bread etiquette, you'll also need to get a handle on the meaning of words like *kontosouvli* (bigger chunks of meat), *tylichtó* (something wrapped), *diplopito* (double bread), *dikalamo* (double meat), *souvlaki ap'ola* (with the lot), *souvlaki me pita*, *pita kalamaki* and souvlaki sandwich. Those last three mean pretty much the same as the word souvlaki does in northern and central Greece.

Then we get into the whole world of the spit, or *souvla*, which is what slices of meat are packed on to make doner kebabs and *gyros* (the Greek equivalent of the Arab shawarma). This style of rotisserie meat may have first popped up in Bursa in the Ottoman Empire in the 1850s, or on picnics around the Crimean even earlier. (You can read more about this in the introduction to *Tacos al pastor* on p. 223, as the history of rotating meat towers is tightly intertwined.)

Perhaps the reason the Greeks have so many different words for grilled meat is that they've been doing it for so darned long. In Ancient Greece, Aristophanes, Xenophon and Aristotle all wrote about the grilling of meat. In Homer's *Iliad*, the Trojan warrior Achilles sits down to grill pieces of meat on a skewer over a charcoal fire. And this is all modern stuff when compared to the 3500-year-old notched firedogs designed to hold meat-laden skewers over a small fire that were unearthed from volcano ash during an archaeological dig on Santorini.

At the risk of introducing yet another word to the grilled meat lexicon, there was also *kandaulos*, which were grilled or fried pieces of meat served with breadcrumbs seasoned with dill and cheese that appeared in writings from the fifth century BC onwards. They were mentioned by Hegesippus, who is quoted by Athenaeus in *The Deipnosophists*. Athenaeus also reports in this fifteen-volume work on food and dining that grilled skewers of meat were sold from hole-in-the-wall cookshops called *thermopolia*, or from handcarts with mounted grills.

Kandaulos was a luxurious dish, and appears to have been named after the expensive creamy sauce that accompanied the small pieces of roast (or boiled) pork. Also referred to as *kandyli* and *kandylos*, the sauce was made with donkey's and mare's milk. As the dish evolved into a more egalitarian version, goat's cheese, yoghurt and finally tzatziki were used instead.

Perhaps the most surprising discovery I made while researching souvlaki was that a spicy yellow mustard was also traditionally served with it. A seventh-century recipe from the physician Herophilos of Alexandria shows that this was similar to the hot English mustard of today, but with a little garlic and olive oil added to the ground seeds moistened with vinegar.

While Istanbul was famous for its 'hot meat' shops back when it was known as Constantinople, and French novelist Gustave Flaubert mentioned seeing souvlaki skewers cooking when he travelled through Greece as 1850 turned into 1851, the Athenian craze for souvlaki didn't really take off until the 1950s, with the first souvlaki shop opening in Livadia in 1951 selling both *kalamaki* and rotating *gyros*. Pork, rather than lamb, was often the meat of choice.

By now, mechanical vertical spits had been invented to replace the old technique of hanging a large spike of meat into an oven or tandoor; or sometimes spinning the meat at the end of a wound-up string in the oven or over the embers. The large, mechanical rotating vertical skewers of today date back to mid- to late-nineteenth-century Turkey.

I suppose this whole souvlaki/*kalamaki* thing is not that surprising when you consider the proliferation of words that denote skewered meat around the world. In fifteenth-century India they were writing about kebabs, and then there are the *shashliks* of the steppes, the *anticucho* in Peru, *kushiyaki* in Japan, the Turkish and Bulgarian *kebaps*, the lamb *chuan* of China and the beef *suya* of Nigeria. And I could go on . . .

You could say that Australia's contribution to this esteemed tradition is more recent creations like the HSP (halal snack pack) or AB ('atomic bomb'). Like those Aussie innovations, the souvlaki I present here is not really a souvlaki – it is more of a way to get most of the pleasure of the classic dish without the tedium of skewering and endlessly turning meat.

Feel free to use skewers of cubed pork shoulder instead of lamb, if you want to get all purist.

Not a souvlaki (CONTINUED)

4 garlic cloves, crushed
1 tablespoon finely chopped rosemary
2 teaspoons dried oregano leaves
1 tablespoon finely grated lemon zest
2 tablespoons olive oil, plus extra to serve
sea salt and freshly ground black pepper
2.2 kg lamb shoulder
½ cup (125 ml) chicken stock
⅓ cup (80 ml) lemon juice
2 tablespoons mint jelly
2 Lebanese cucumbers, cut into thin batons
8 Greek pita breads
½ iceberg lettuce, shredded
1 red onion, halved and thinly sliced (on a mandolin, if you have one)
2 teaspoons English mustard

Tzatziki

3 cups (840 g) Greek-style yoghurt
2 small Lebanese cucumbers, coarsely grated and squeezed to remove excess liquid
1 large garlic clove, crushed
¼ cup finely chopped mint
2 tablespoons lemon juice

Pickled grapes

300 g seedless green grapes
⅓ cup (80 ml) apple cider vinegar
¼ cup (55 g) caster sugar
2 bay leaves
1 cinnamon stick

Start by making the tzatziki. Line a colander with muslin or a new, clean cloth and place over a bowl. Spoon the yoghurt into the muslin and fold the muslin over to cover. Set aside in the fridge overnight to drain the yoghurt so it becomes thicker. Or just use shop-bought tzatziki – I won't judge you, provided you decant it into a pretty bowl.

Preheat the oven to 140°C (120°C fan-forced). Combine the garlic, rosemary, oregano, lemon zest and oil in a small bowl. Season with salt and pepper.

Score the fat on top of the lamb in a diagonal pattern. Place the lamb in a roasting pan. Add the stock and ¼ cup (60 ml) of the lemon juice to the pan. Rub the lamb all over with the herb mixture.

Cover the top of the dish with a sheet of baking paper and then cover with foil to completely seal. Roast for 5½ hours.

Increase the oven temperature to 220°C (200°C fan-forced). Remove the foil and paper, and roast for a further 20 minutes or until the lamb is golden and crispy. Transfer the lamb to a serving platter, cover loosely with foil and set aside for 10 minutes to rest.

While the lamb finishes cooking, pickle the grapes. Place the grapes in a heatproof glass or ceramic bowl. Place the vinegar, sugar, bay leaves and cinnamon stick in a small saucepan. Stir over low heat for 5 minutes or until the sugar dissolves. Add to the grapes and toss to combine. Set aside, stirring occasionally, for 30 minutes to infuse.

To finish the tzatziki, transfer the strained yoghurt to a bowl and add the cucumber, garlic, mint and lemon juice. Season well with salt and pepper and stir until well combined.

Combine the mint jelly and remaining tablespoon of lemon juice in a microwave-safe bowl. Microwave on high for 30 seconds or until the jelly softens slightly. Stir until well combined. Set aside to cool (it will look firmer again, but it will be easier to toss). Add the cucumber batons and toss until well coated.

Heat a frying pan over medium–high heat. In batches, add the pita bread and cook for 1–2 minutes each side or until warmed through. Alternatively, heat them directly over a gas flame to get some burnished markings. Wrap in a clean tea towel to keep warm and soft as you cook the rest.

Use two forks to pull the lamb apart in big shreds. Top the pita breads with the tzatziki, lettuce, cucumber, onion, pickled grapes and lamb. Add a smear of English mustard on the bread where it will touch the lamb – or just smear it straight onto the lamb!

TIP

To give traditional Greek skewers a very local twist, use cubes of good-quality kangaroo fillet (I recommend Paroo or Macro Meats) or diced marinated camel shoulder instead of the usual pork or lamb. Both animals are prolific in the Australian outback, and we really ought to be eating them. And what could be more traditional than cooking roo over (or under, or even in) fire? This sustained many generations of First Nations peoples, though the cooking technique would differ from nation to nation. In my experience, I have observed a preference in Central Australia for cooking wrapped kangaroo tail in the embers of the fire to preserve the juices, while on a trip to the Flinders Ranges, the tails were cooked over the flames.

A truly Scottish shepherd's pie

SERVES 4 **PREP** 20 minutes **COOK** 1 hour 25 minutes

CLASSIC

Myth
Shepherd's pie is a classic dish of the British Isles.

My Truth
The medieval world of pies was fancy. Blackbirds flew out of them, and everything exotic, from peacocks to truffles, went into them. The Elizabethans loaded their mince pies with the most expensive spices – black pepper, cloves, mace and saffron. But these are not our shepherd's pie. Shepherd's pie slinks into the annals of history as a way to hide yesterday's cold slices of grey roast mutton and use the potatoes no one wanted to eat. It was a cheap recipe designed to turn the unwanted into something that looked completely different.

Recipes popped up as 'baked minced mutton' in *Mrs Beeton's Book of Household Management* (1861), and as 'a casserole of mutton' in Eliza Leslie's 1840 US cookbook. Both used cold cooked meat and instructed the pie dish be lined and topped with mashed potato.

While we know shepherd's pie is a thing of great deliciousness, names like 'baked minced mutton' hardly made it sing. It took some bright spark to identify a wistful yearning for the country, at a time of belching Dickensian workhouses, tenement-lined gin lanes and dark satanic mills, and come up with this most pastoral of names.

'Shepherd's pie' was first mentioned in print in 1870 in London's *Daily Telegraph & Courier*, on a menu of the greatest Scottish delicacies, alongside cock-a-leekie and haggis. This inclusion implies that the dish was not only developed in Scotland – or at least first called shepherd's pie there – but that this happened a good while before that dinner. (How long does it take for a dish to become a national treasure? Fifty years?) In 1874, the *Ardrossan and Saltcoats Herald* claimed that shepherd's pie was one of a dozen dishes required of a plain home cook, such was its acceptance in Scotland.

By 1879, recipes for shepherd's pie were in Australian publications like the *Leader* in Melbourne and the *Albury Banner and Wodonga Express*. Here, a tablespoon of ketchup joins the gravy, onions and finely diced mutton under a well-browned mash crust. As far as I can see, this is the first recipe that's actually called 'shepherd's pie' appearing in print anywhere in the world – but I'll happily be disabused of this notion with suitable evidence. Certainly, shepherd's pie was reported as being on the curriculum of culinary schools across the UK from the early 1870s. Maybe it was just such a common dish no one thought it necessary to write down a recipe?

While the sexier Scottish name played a part in shepherd's pie's success, another significant change helped the recipe take off in the nineteenth century: German baron Karl Drais's *fleischwolf*. Without this hand-cranked meat grinder for mincing at home, which appeared in the 1840s, shepherd's pie, burgers, spag bol and many other recipes in this book would not have been as easy to make, and thus might never have become so popular. Quite a man, Drais, he also invented an early bicycle and a typewriter.

1 tablespoon olive oil
500 g lamb mince
1 brown onion, finely chopped
4 celery stalks, finely chopped
2 tablespoons tomato paste (puree)
1 tablespoon plain flour
4 garlic cloves, crushed
2 cups (500 ml) beef stock
2 tablespoons tomato sauce (ketchup)
2 tablespoons worcestershire sauce
2 thyme sprigs
2 bay leaves
½ teaspoon Maggi seasoning liquid
sea salt and freshly ground black pepper
20 g butter, melted

Creamy mash
1 kg sebago potatoes, peeled and coarsely
  chopped
50 g butter
½ cup (125 ml) pouring cream

Preheat the oven to 200°C (180°C fan-forced).

Heat the oil in a large frying pan over medium–high heat. Add the lamb mince and cook, breaking up with a wooden spoon, for 5–8 minutes or until browned. Push the mince to one side of the pan.

Add the onion and celery to the empty side of the pan. Cook, stirring, for 5 minutes or until soft. Add the tomato paste, flour and garlic, and bring the mince and veggies together. Cook, stirring, for 1–2 minutes or until well combined.

Add the stock, tomato sauce, worcestershire sauce, thyme and bay leaves. Reduce the heat to medium. Simmer, stirring often, for 15–20 minutes or until the liquid has reduced by half. Add the Maggi seasoning and season with salt and pepper.

For the creamy mash, cook the potatoes in boiling salted water for 15 minutes or until tender. Drain and return to the pan. Place the pan over medium heat and shake for about 30 seconds or until dried out. Mash until smooth, add the butter and cream and stir to combine. Season with salt and pepper. If the mash has cooled before it's time to assemble the pie, return it to medium heat and cook, stirring, for 2–3 minutes or until heated through.

Spoon the lamb mixture into an 8 cup (2 litre) capacity ovenproof dish. Top with the mash and use a fork to rough up the surface. Mrs Beeton would say something like 'with a fork, score it in every direction'. Gently brush the top with the melted butter. Bake for 30–40 minutes or until golden.

Slow-roasted pomegranate lamb shoulder with jewelled couscous

SERVES 4–6 **PREP** 30 minutes (plus resting) **COOK** 4 hours 30 minutes

Myth

As the lamb is a biblical symbol of truth and innocence, I struggle to dismiss any myth that might be associated with it . . .

My Truth

Humans have understood the value of sheep for over 10,000 years – only dogs can lay claim to a longer history by our side. We first domesticated them in either Mesopotamia or Central Asia. These early wild sheep were hairy rather than woolly, so their main value was for milk and cheese, and of course for sacrifices and feasting. We know that lamb and mutton were part of the diet of Neolithic tribes around Marseilles in 6000 BC.

The fact that sheep were easy to keep together in flocks helped the nomadic tribes of the Central Asian steppes as much as it did those earliest settlers of the Middle and Near East, who could lay down roots with a flock on hand to support them. It is fair to say that sheep were as important to the birth of civilisation as salt. Both allowed us to settle down and spend less time searching for food. (For the story of salt, I recommend reading *Salt: A world history* by Mark Kurlansky.)

While we know sheep formed a major food source in the ancient world, there was resistance to eating them in some places given their value for milk and wool. This may explain why we tend to eat either old sheep (mutton) or young sheep (lamb) rather than those in their prime. When we look at the very earliest recipes recorded on Babylonian and Assyrian tablets from Mesopotamia, dated as early as 1730 BC, these include a recipe for a lamb soup with barley rusks, *me-e puhadi*, and one for *tuh'u*, which was mutton stewed with beetroots.

The importance and portability of sheep meant that they spread far and wide across the globe during the eras of exploration. Hernán Cortés brought Merino and Navajo-Churro sheep to his hacienda outside Mexico City in 1538, after the Spanish conquest. Captain Cook had sheep on board for his second and third voyages to Australia and New Zealand, and the First Fleet picked up 28 fat-bellied sheep in Cape Town on the way to Botany Bay in 1788. These, and later animals acquired in India, proved less suited to Australian conditions than the twenty-six Merinos from the Cape of Good Hope (which were descended from the closely guarded royal flock of Spain) that landed at Port Jackson in 1797.

Of course, for all their usefulness to European colonists, the introduction of sheep also brought negative effects. Historian, author and agriculturalist Bruce Pascoe once told me that Victoria was covered in the yellow flowers of a native yam called murnong before invasion. However, the introduced sheep developed a taste for the daisies, to the point where the murnong was eaten almost to extinction, removing a vital food source for First Nations people.

In Australia, the concept of a Sunday lamb roast is an imported legacy from England, and the idea of treating yourself with roast meat comes from a time when meat was a luxury. It was served after church on Sundays and, in the early Middle Ages, after your obligatory archery practice at the English village butts. This training was enforced by parliamentary statutes and royal ordinances first made in 1363.

Obviously, the roasting of lamb also has biblical connotations, tracing back to God asking Abraham to sacrifice his son in the Old Testament; in the end, God relented and decided he'd rather have roast lamb instead. There is also the traditional Passover sacrifice of lamb, eaten with bitter herbs and matzo, as stipulated in the Torah.

Over the past 25 years, Australia's lamb roast has subtly changed. Gently pink slices of perfectly cooked leg of lamb took over from cheaper legs of mutton in the 1950s and 1960s, and you can see this in the decreasing prominence of mutton in butchers' advertisements over that period. Then an increased love of our barbecues meant that The River Café's 1995 quicker-cooking recipe for butterflied lamb leg found a willing and immediate audience here. The popularity of lamb shoulder took off in Australia from about 2007 onwards, driven by the boom in slow-roasting and pulling meats like pork. Prior to this, shoulder was previously most often seen deboned, stuffed and rolled.

Call me a slave to fashion, but I far prefer these more recent methods of cooking lamb to the traditional roast leg or rolled shoulder, not least because they recall some of the texture and flavour of lamb cooked slowly on a spit, and when cooked this way it seems to lend itself to so many different culinary interpretations – whether Greek, Spanish, French, Uzbekistani, Indian, Mexican, or Middle Eastern, as here.

Slow-roasted lamb shoulder (CONTINUED)

1.6 kg boneless lamb shoulder
1 cup (250 ml) water
2 tablespoons pomegranate molasses
sea salt and freshly ground black pepper
6 large carrots, peeled and cut into 3–4 cm
    pieces
1 tablespoon olive oil

Jewelled couscous

1½ cups (300 g) couscous
1½ cups (375 ml) chicken stock
50 g butter
1 small red onion, finely chopped
⅓ cup (55 g) currants
¼ cup (60 ml) lemon juice
1 cup (80 g) flaked almonds, toasted
1 cup (140 g) pistachio kernels, coarsely
    chopped and tossed in a little olive oil
½ cup (115 g) fresh medjool dates, pitted and
    chopped into 1 cm pieces
1 pomegranate, seeds removed
¾ cup coarsely chopped coriander
¼ cup coarsely chopped mint

Tahini yoghurt sauce

1 cup (280 g) Greek-style yoghurt
1 tablespoon tahini
1 tablespoon lemon juice

Preheat the oven to 160°C (140°C fan-forced).

Use the tip of a small, sharp knife to score across the top of the lamb fat. Place the lamb in a roasting pan. Combine the water and half the pomegranate molasses and pour around the lamb. Rub the remaining pomegranate molasses over the top of the lamb. Season well with salt and pepper. Cover with foil to completely seal.

Place the pan on the middle shelf of the oven and roast for 1 hour.

While the lamb cooks, line a large baking tray with baking paper. Place the carrot on the tray and drizzle with the oil. Season with salt and pepper.

When the lamb has cooked for 1 hour, add the tray of carrot to the oven on the rack underneath the lamb. Roast together for 3 hours or until the carrot is tender and starting to caramelise.

Remove the carrot from the oven and set aside to cool. Remove the foil from the lamb. Increase the oven temperature to 180°C (160°C fan-forced). Roast the lamb for a further 30 minutes or until it has a golden crust.

Meanwhile, to make the jewelled couscous, place the couscous in a heatproof bowl. Place the stock in a small saucepan and bring to the boil over high heat. Pour over the couscous, cover and set aside for 5 minutes or until the liquid has been absorbed. Uncover, add the butter and use a fork to fluff the grains. Set aside for 20 minutes to cool.

Place the onion and currants in a heatproof bowl. Place the lemon juice in a small jug and microwave on high for 1–2 minutes or until warm. Pour over the onion mixture and set aside for 15 minutes or until the currants are plump and the onion is lightly pickled.

Remove the lamb from the oven. Cover loosely with foil and set aside for 15 minutes to rest.

Once the couscous has cooled, add the onion mixture, almonds, pistachios, dates, pomegranate seeds, coriander and mint. Mix gently until evenly combined – don't overhandle the couscous, or it will become gluggy.

To make the tahini yoghurt sauce, mix all the ingredients together in a bowl and season with salt and pepper.

Toss the carrot through the couscous. Serve with the lamb and tahini yoghurt sauce.

Food nerd fact

Couscous was an important part of the traditional diet of the Amazigh peoples of North Africa, alongside lentils and chickpeas. The original method of making couscous by trailing your hand wet with salt water through flour to create little balls that can then be steamed, is one of brilliance. The flour used could be from wheat berries such as semolina, millet, barley or even acorns. The name couscous may even come from the Amazigh root word for 'well rolled'.

Further brilliance comes from steaming the couscous over whatever you are cooking, such as a tagine, in a porous-bottomed *taseksut*, in order to save cooking fuel. These steamers have been found in a 2200-year-old tomb from Numidia, which was an Amazigh kingdom where Algeria and Tunisia are now.

Choc desserts

Molten spiced jaffa chocolate fondant

SERVES 4 **PREP** 20 minutes (plus 2 hours chilling) **COOK** 20 minutes

Myth

The chocolate fondant or 'lava cake' was invented by one of New York's top chefs.

My Truth

The story of who invented chocolate fondant is a clash of New York culinary titans. 'It was me,' says Jean-Georges Vongerichten, the man who the *New York Times* once said had the single biggest influence on how New Yorkers dined out, thanks to his restaurants like Vong and Jean-Georges. The Alsatian chef who moved to New York in 1987 said he was inspired to make the fondant when he took a chocolate sponge out of the oven *waaaay* too soon and he liked the way the uncooked middle oozed out. He claims to have invented it in 1987, and it appeared on the opening menu at Jean-Georges at the Trump International Tower and Hotel in March 1997.

'Liar!' might scream Jacques Torres, another chef from France, who arrived in NYC in 1988 to be the corporate pastry chef at the Ritz-Carlton Hotel, and then in 1989 took over the pastry section at New York's ultimate society lunch spot Le Cirque for eleven years. (You might know him better for his more recent role as a judge on Netflix baking show *Nailed It*.) Some have suggested that Torres invented it first – he certainly had it on the menu when he was at Le Cirque – but he disarmingly denies inventing the dish, pointing to others back in France who had already made the dish before Jean-Georges.

French wonderchef and culinary dreamer Michel Bras had come up with his *coulant au chocolat* in 1981 while he and his family were thawing out over hot chocolate after a day of cross-country skiing. His aim, when he put the dish on the menu at his pioneering 3-star restaurant Bras, was a soft chocolate cake that released a '*coulée de lave chocolatée*' or 'chocolate lava flow' when cut.

'Liar!' I can almost hear David Chang, Peter Meehan and Chris Ying, the lads behind the now-defunct iconoclastic food mag *Lucky Peach*, whisper. They claimed that a dish called the 'Tunnel of Fudge Cake' made by Louisiana-raised, Houston-based Ella Rita Helfrich (1916–2015) was first. I want to shout 'Liar!' as this sounds like a prank, but it's true – home cook Ella's gooey-centred bundt cake came second in the 17th Annual Pillsbury Busy Lady Bake-Off held in 1966, and made it onto the cover of the commemorative recipe booklet that Pillsbury produced after the competition. It is undoubtedly the first oozy-centred chocolate cake I can find, in spite of what those top chefs might like to claim.

Chocolate loves spice and orange. The sweet orange originated in Southern China and Northern India as a hybrid of the pomelo and the mandarin. These facts led us to flavour this dish with five spice and ginger.

---

125 g unsalted butter, chopped, plus extra
   for greasing
150 g dark chocolate (70% cocoa), coarsely
   chopped
2 tablespoons Cointreau, Drambuie, triple
   sec or your favourite citrus liqueur
1 teaspoon finely grated orange zest
½ teaspoon Chinese five spice
3 eggs
⅓ cup (75 g) caster sugar
¼ cup (35 g) plain flour
1 tablespoon cocoa powder
glacé or naked ginger, thinly sliced, to serve

Ginger chantilly cream
1 cup (250 ml) thickened cream
2 tablespoons ginger marmalade

Grease four 1 cup (250 ml) capacity pudding moulds and line the bases with small rounds of baking paper.

Place the butter, chocolate and liqueur in a saucepan over low heat. Cook, stirring, for 5 minutes or until melted and smooth. Stir in the orange zest and Chinese five spice. Set aside for 20 minutes to cool.

Use electric beaters to whisk the eggs and sugar in a bowl for 5–8 minutes or until the mixture is thick and pale, and a ribbon trail forms when the beaters are lifted. Fold in the chocolate mixture with a metal spoon until just combined. Sift the flour and cocoa powder over the top of the egg mixture, then fold in until just combined. Divide among the prepared moulds. Place in the fridge for 2 hours or until firm.

Preheat the oven to 200°C (180°C fan-forced). Place the puddings on a baking tray. Bake for 12 minutes or until just set but the middle still feels a little wobbly. Set aside for 5 minutes.

While the puddings are resting, get your ginger chantilly cream ready. Use electric beaters to beat the cream and marmalade in a bowl until soft peaks form.

Carefully turn out the puddings onto serving plates. Serve with the chantilly cream and top with the ginger. Pray they ooze!

Roasted white chocolate family tart

SERVES 8 **PREP** 20 minutes (plus 4 hours 20 minutes chilling and 20 minutes resting) **COOK** 1 hour 10 minutes

Twist

Myth

The success of 'Dazzler's Caramatt Tart' in my 2014 *Cook Book* prompted the current roasted white chocolate revolution in Australia.

My Truth

I started my roasted white chocolate journey nearly a decade ago, when I worked with the inspirational Melbourne pâtissier Darren Purchese to develop a roasted white chocolate tart that reminded us of the Caramac chocolate bars of our youth.

The Caramac was first made in 1959 at the Mackintosh's chocolate factory in Norwich in the UK. It was basically a combination of milk, condensed milk, butter and sugar, but I reckon the condensed milk had been caramelised slowly to give the bar its golden colour and slightly toasty, nutty flavour. Making a roasted white chocolate ganache like this one was our take on the flavour, and it's been a hit at dinners and events we've put on from Abu Dhabi to Pretoria, and from the Melbourne Cup to the Sydney Cricket Ground.

Cooking down milk so it browns is not a new technique. In sixteenth-century India, the court of Akbar the Great would order vast amounts of saltpetre and Himalayan ice to make kulfi ice cream from cooked-down milk, while forgetful nineteenth-century maids leaving pots of milk on the stove are credited with the invention of Latin American dulce de leche and Mexican *cajeta*.

Cooking condensed milk is a more recent invention. Norwegian housewives boiled cans of 'Viking Melk' to turn it brown and nutty during World War II, as did cooks in postwar Communist Bloc countries like Poland and the Ukraine. It was the popularity of banoffee pie in the 1970s that taught most Australian cooks the technique.

It wasn't until 2006, however, that 'roasted white chocolate' became a thing, when Frédéric Bau, who worked for the Valrhona chocolate company, accidentally left some white chocolate buttons in a heated bain-marie overnight. The chocolate he found the next morning was a delicate, pale brown and tasted incredibly good, which gave him the idea of browning white chocolate intentionally. Bau was a lecturer at Valrhona's culinary school and included the technique in his lecture at the World Pastry Forum in 2009. This was seen by ex-chef and blogger David Lebovitz, who wrote about it online. Suddenly roasted white chocolate became an instant sensation in the US, even making an appearance in a roasted white chocolate panna cotta in Éric Ripert's 2010 cookery book, *Avec Eric*.

Here in Australia, our version of a caramelised chocolate bar was Caramilk, which was launched long before Darren and I made our roasted white chocolate tart. It was discontinued in 1994, but returned to the market to much fanfare in 2018 when we all fell in love with roasted white chocolate as the logical successor to the early 2000s craze for salted caramel. Try this tart and you'll know why.

200 g white chocolate, coarsely chopped
300 ml thickened cream
150 g unsalted butter, chopped
pinch of sea salt flakes, plus extra to serve
shaved white chocolate (see Tip) and crème
  fraîche, to serve

Sweet shortcrust pastry

1½ cups (225 g) plain flour
150 g salted butter, chilled, chopped
2 tablespoons icing sugar mixture
1 egg yolk
1 tablespoon chilled water

TIP

For fancier chocolate curls, fill a large bowl with plenty of iced water. Pipe small amounts of melted white chocolate into the water in squiggles and watch them set. Carefully lift them out to dry on paper towel. When dry, arrange on top of the tart.

To make the pastry, process the flour, butter and icing sugar in a food processor until the mixture resembles fine breadcrumbs. Add the egg yolk and water. Process until the dough just comes together. Turn out onto a lightly floured surface, gather and shape into a disc. Cover with plastic wrap and place in the fridge for 20 minutes to rest.

Roll out the dough on a sheet of baking paper until 3 mm thick. Ease into a 2.5 cm deep, 22 cm (base measurement) fluted tart tin with a removable base. Press the pastry into the flutes. Trim the excess pastry. Place in the fridge for 20 minutes to chill.

Preheat the oven to 200°C (180°C fan-forced). Line the pastry with a large sheet of baking paper and fill with pastry weights or rice. Place the tin on a baking tray and bake for 15 minutes. Remove the paper and weights or rice. Bake for a further 10 minutes or until lightly golden and crisp. Set aside to cool.

Reduce the oven temperature to 140°C (120°C fan-forced). Place the chocolate on a rimmed baking tray. Bake, stirring the chocolate every 10 minutes with a silicone spatula to spread and melt on the tray, for 20–30 minutes or until the chocolate turns a rich caramel colour. (The chocolate may look grainy at some points, but continue to mix and it will melt and eventually become smooth.) Stir in the cream until well combined. The mixture may start off looking lumpy. Bake, stirring every 5 minutes, for a further 10–15 minutes or until smooth. Stir in the butter and salt to incorporate fully.

Pour chocolate mixture into the pastry case. Place in the fridge for 3–4 hours until set.

Decorate with a big pinch of sea salt flakes and the shaved white chocolate curls – use a sharp knife or potato peeler to make these. Serve with the crème fraîche.

The unexpected surprise chocolate mousse

SERVES 4 **PREP** 20 minutes (plus 1 hour cooling and 4 hours chilling) **COOK** 5 minutes

CLASSIC

Myth

Sometime before his death in 1901, Henri de Toulouse-Lautrec, French painter, absinthe drinker and keen cook, mixed chocolate with whipped cream and eggs to create the first 'chocolate mousse', inspired by an African dancer he had drawn pirouetting lightly in the Achille Bar in Paris in 1896.

My Truth

The first problem with this poetic tale was that the diminutive artist of France's Belle Époque decided a good name for this dish would be '*mayonnaise de chocolat*'. Eww!

The second issue is that although the word 'mousse' has French origins, there are records of chocolate mousse being eaten in New York in 1892, which rather blows this myth out of the water. It seems far more likely that the idea of combining chocolate with whipped eggs and cream popped up in France in the mid-1800s. Mousses and foams were around well before that, of course. Menon, the pseudonymous food writer who coined the term 'nouvelle cuisine', was writing about them in France in the mid-1700s.

While chocolate was introduced to Europe from Central America in 1585, it was famous for the next two hundred years only as a drink. Such was its popularity that UK sugar imports leapt from 88 tonnes in 1665 up to 10,000 tonnes by 1700, to sweeten the hot chocolates and coffees that were all the rage. However, it wasn't until new milling processes were invented in the eighteenth century that it was possible to make the first solid chocolate bars (rather than hard, bitter cakes), and these cocoa-buttery bars only reached popularity by the 1820s. Thus, the timing for the invention of chocolate mousse in the mid-1800s seems increasingly plausible.

From France, chocolate mousse spread around the world, becoming one of the dinner party sensations of the 1960s – not least because it could be made in advance and was easily customised. Julia Child suggested spiking it with rum, Bénédictine or strong coffee, while Cointreau and Kahlúa were both popular in the 1970s.

The right garnish is all-important for chocolate mousse – a pretty mint leaf, three perfect raspberries. I'm a dag, so I serve mine with shards of Peppermint Crisp on top, but you could also try smashed Crunchie or torn Cherry Ripe. The recipe that follows is a first for me – a two-chocolate mousse with a hidden surprise from that king of chocolate bars, and my personal favourite, the Snickers. Invented in 1930, the Snickers was named after one of Frank Mars' favourite horses. Not a lot of people know that.

---

200 g milk chocolate, finely chopped
100 g dark chocolate (70% cocoa), finely chopped
1½ cups (375 ml) thickened cream
3 eggs, separated
2 tablespoons caster sugar
3 × 50 g Snickers bars

TIP

If you wanted to sprinkle some crushed salted peanuts on top of this I wouldn't be offended.

Combine the milk and dark chocolates and 1 cup (250 ml) of the cream in a microwave-safe bowl. Microwave on high, stirring every minute, for 2–4 minutes or until the chocolate is melted and the mixture is smooth. Set aside for 1 hour to cool.

Add the egg yolks to the chocolate mixture and use electric beaters to beat for 1–2 minutes to aerate and thicken slightly.

Use clean electric beaters to beat the egg whites in a separate bowl until firm peaks form. Gradually add the sugar and beat until thick and glossy. Fold half the egg white mixture into the chocolate mixture with a metal spoon until almost combined (you may still see the odd streak of egg mixture – don't worry, it will be incorporated more as you go). Fold in the remaining egg white mixture.

Cut half the Snickers bars into 1 cm pieces and divide among serving glasses of your choice. Top with the chocolate mousse and place in the fridge for 3–4 hours to set.

Before serving, use electric beaters to beat the remaining cream in a bowl until soft peaks form. Spoon on top of the mousse. Cut the remaining Snickers into thin slices or chunks, and place on top to serve.

Chocolate torte with smoked butterscotch sauce

FOR THE LOVER OF RUM AND COKE, BIKIE JUICE OR EVEN KLIPPIES AND COKE

SERVES 6 **PREP** 45 minutes (plus 30 minutes cooling) **COOK** 1 hour 15 minutes

CLASSIC

Myth

All the recipes in my books are solely my own work.

My Truth

Any cookbook author who tells you the above is either a liar or a control freak. For me, a huge part of the great joy that comes from writing recipes or doing dinners overseas is devising what to cook with a team of far more talented collaborators – like Michelle Southan, who is the muse behind this book, or Phoebe Rose Wood, the brilliant food director at *delicious*.magazine.

This recipe is a case in point. It is based on a chocolate torte that uber-cook Emma Warren (she wrote *The Catalan Kitchen* and *Islas: Food of the Spanish Islands*) came up with for a previous book of mine, and it was then given a whole new lease of life when everybody's ideal culinary offsider – and very talented cook in his own right – Warren Mendes and I went to South Africa to do some dinners in 2018.

We were given dessert as our course to plan and we wanted to play on a theme of a big night out in South Africa. In Australia, big nights too often end with Jackaroo Juice (Bundy and Coke) or Bikie Juice (Bourbon and Coke). In South Africa, they have Klippies and Coke. It's cheap, it's a little coarse and it has a very special place in many South African hearts. Needless to say, this recipe does work just as well with Bundaberg rum instead of Klipdrift brandy if you'd prefer. To keep with the late-night-out theme, we gave the butterscotch sauce a hit of smoke to hint at the cigarette botted – and regretted – at the end of the night.

We've customised the recipe again for this book – making it a gift that keeps on giving.

800 ml Coca-Cola (see Tips)
¼ cup (60 ml) Klipdrift brandy (or Bundaberg rum)
300 g dark chocolate (70% cocoa), finely chopped
200 g unsalted butter, chopped
4 eggs
100 g caster sugar
¼ cup (30 g) almond meal
1 tablespoon plain flour
pinch of sea salt
vanilla ice cream or crème fraîche, to serve

Smoked butterscotch sauce

300 g brown sugar
350 ml pouring cream
100 g unsalted butter, chopped
1 teaspoon apple cider vinegar
a few drops liquid smoke, to taste

TIPS

Rather than reducing the Coke, you could buy Coke syrup, which is far easier!

The torte can be eaten warm, or chilled and sliced with a hot knife.

For the torte, place the Coke in a saucepan over medium–high heat. Bring the mixture to the boil and cook for 45 minutes or until reduced to ⅓ cup (80 ml). Remove from the heat and reserve 2 tablespoons of syrup for glazing. Cool the rest and add the brandy.

Preheat the oven to 180°C (160°C fan-forced). Grease a 20 cm (base measurement) round cake pan and line the base and side with baking paper.

Place the chocolate and butter in a microwave-safe bowl. Microwave for 2 minutes or until the butter has melted. Set aside for 2 minutes to soften the chocolate. Stir until melted and smooth, then cool to room temperature.

Add the eggs, one at a time, to the chocolate mixture, whisking after each addition. Add the Coke and brandy mixture, caster sugar, almond meal and flour. Lightly whisk to combine. Spoon into the prepared pan.

Bake for 20 minutes or until firm to a gentle touch. Set aside at room temperature for 30 minutes to cool.

For the butterscotch sauce, place all the ingredients except the liquid smoke in a saucepan over medium–high heat and stir until the butter has melted and the mixture is combined. Bring to a simmer and cook for 3 minutes or until it reduces slightly. Add a drop of liquid smoke to taste (this can be quite forward, so start with one drop and add more if you like) and a little more vinegar if you think it needs it.

To serve, place the torte on a plate. Brush the top with the remaining Coke syrup so it glistens, and pour over the smoked butterscotch sauce. Serve slices with scoops of good-quality vanilla ice cream or dollops of crème fraîche, and perhaps some milk powder crumb (p. 321) spiked with edible gold dust!

The ultimate honey joy

SERVES 4 **PREP** 15 minutes (plus 1 hour chilling) **COOK** 15 minutes

CLASSIC

Myth
Cornflakes are an aphrodisiac.

My Truth
Two of Australia's greatest culinary inventions are the chocolate crackle and the honey joy. And while we know that the first recipe for the chocolate crackle appeared in the *Australian Women's Weekly* magazine in 1937, the conception of the honey joy is rather more immaculate. You'd like to think it was earlier than that, given that the 1894 invention of cornflakes (by Will Keith Kellogg, for his brother John to serve to patients at his Battle Creek Sanitarium in Michigan) predates the first Rice Bubbles or Rice Krispies by some 34 years.

This recipe could easily have been a chocolate crackle bowl, but I'm a little wary of too much hydrogenised oil and I like the idea of using a cereal created *before* the brothers fell out over whether or not cornflakes should have sugar added to them. John was against it, but then John was also the vegetarian, early-to-bed type who saw cornflakes as ideal for controlling the rampant self-exploratory urges of young men – an anti-aphrodisiac, if you like.

If you do decide to make a chocolate crackle bowl instead – it is pretty much the same technique – serve it with red seedless grapes or raspberries, and try almonds instead of peanuts. Feel free to swap out the vanilla ice cream for chocolate too, or use dark chocolate instead of white chocolate for the sauce.

250 g green grapes, halved
4 large scoops vanilla ice cream
coarsely chopped salted roasted peanuts,
    for sprinkling
4 glacé cherries, to serve

Honey joy bowls
5½ cups (220 g) cornflakes
100 g butter
½ cup (175 g) honey
½ cup (110 g) caster sugar

White chocolate magic ice topping
100 g white chocolate, finely chopped
1 tablespoon coconut oil

To make the honey joy bowls, line four 1½ cup (375 ml) glass or ceramic bowls with plastic wrap, allowing it to overhang the sides.

Put the cornflakes in a heatproof bowl. Place the butter, honey and sugar in a small saucepan over low heat. Cook, stirring occasionally, for 4 minutes or until the sugar dissolves. Increase the heat to medium and bring to the boil, then reduce the heat to low. Simmer, without stirring, for 4–5 minutes or until the syrup reaches soft-ball stage (112°C) on a cook's thermometer. (If you don't have a thermometer, drop a little of the syrup into a glass of cold water. If it cools to a soft pliable texture when tested between your fingers, it is ready.)

Pour the syrup over the cornflakes and toss until well coated. Divide among the lined bowls. Working quickly, use the back of a dessert spoon to press in the cornflake mixture firmly, moulding up the side to form a neat bowl. Place in the fridge for 1 hour to set.

To make the white chocolate topping, combine the chocolate and coconut oil in a microwave-safe bowl. Microwave on high, stirring every minute, for 2–3 minutes or until melted and smooth.

Divide the grapes among the honey joy bowls and top each with a scoop of ice cream. Drizzle with the white chocolate topping and sprinkle quickly with the nuts before it sets. Finish with a glacé cherry on top.

TIPS

I suggest making five bowls instead of four, in case you break one! Just increase the quantities accordingly.

If your kitchen is cold and the white chocolate topping starts to set, rest the container in a bowl of warm water to soften it before serving.

Antep pistachio and white chocolate baklava

MAKES 40 pieces **PREP** 50 minutes (plus 6 hours cooling) **COOK** 35 minutes

Myth
Baklava originated in Greece.

My Truth
In this recipe we combine two ideas – one a little bit common, the other venerable. This might make some people unhappy.

I know from personal experience the cruel barbs that come your way if you profess a love of white chocolate. They say it's 'not chocolate', even though both EU regulators and the US Food and Drug Administration (since 2002) deem that it is. Maybe it's because it is still seen as the gauche new kid on the (chocolate) block.

Nestlé's company history shows that they launched a white chocolate bar under the name Galak in Switzerland in 1935, promoted as a 'sensational novelty'. Launches in Japan, South Africa and the United Kingdom followed in 1936.

This was a fertile, creative period in the world of chocolate bars. The rising cost of cocoa solids, a surplus of cocoa butter from Nestlé's new malted cocoa products like Nescao (1932) and Milo (1934), and a surplus of milk powder gave impetus to the development of new chocolate bars lengthened with cheaper ingredients like nuts, wafers or even air. Other products of this period were Rowntree's Aero (1935), Nestlé's Crunch (1938) and Rowntree's Chocolate Crisp (1935; but relaunched branded as KitKat in 1937).

The United States wasn't given the gift of white chocolate until the Merckens Chocolate Factory launched a white bar in 1945, and Nestlé introduced the Alpine White bar (which included almonds) in 1948. White chocolate wouldn't really establish a foothold in the influential US market until the 1980s. In 1979, *New York* magazine restaurant critic Gael Greene called white chocolate 'the season's new whimsy', but by 1988 the *New York Times* declared that the whole of America was 'going sweet on white chocolate', with countless white chocolate restaurant dishes, and Alpine White becoming the country's second most popular chocolate bar.

All of this makes one thing certain: when the six master chefs and more than one hundred apprentices in the Helvâhâne, the dessert and confectionery department of Istanbul's Topkapi Palace kitchen, made their famous imperial baklava in the fifteenth century, it didn't include white chocolate. The first written record of baklava being made here comes from the 1400s, when poet Kaygusuz Abdal wrote of seeing 'two hundred trays of baklava, some with almonds, some with lentils'(!?). The cooks of Sultan Mehmed II were widely famed for their sweet-filled filo pastries in the fifteenth century, although the Turkish word *yufka* was used rather than filo or *phyllo*. Baklava came to play an important role in the Ottoman court in the sixteenth century, when Sultan Suleiman the Magnificent formalised the sultan's traditional Ramadan gifts of food to the elite Janissary units of his army into one single dish. He picked baklava.

On the fifteenth day of Ramadan, hundreds of trays of baklava were baked and wrapped in cloth. The presentation of this gift was layered with ritual, as the leaders of the Janissary corps came to collect trays for their cohort. They then processed back to their barracks with the treats hanging between long poles in what was called the baklava *alayı*. It was quite a party, with the procession wending through crowds of onlookers accompanied by much singing and the pounding of drums. Returning the empty trays and cloths to the palace once the baklava was eaten was a way for the Janissary leaders to show their continued loyalty to the emperor.

Dig even deeper and you find that baklava and the pastry that encases it were central to the food history of the Turkic peoples even before they conquered the Byzantine Empire to set up the Ottoman Empire. These nomadic peoples developed layering thin sheets of pan-cooked pastry as a way to replicate the oven-baked breads from the towns they attacked. Over time the sheets became thinner and thinner – so tissue-thin that you could read through them. Other ideas were merged into this pastry, with inspiration for the first baklavas coming from *baki pakhlavasi*, an Azerbaijani dish of pasta dough layered with sweetened nuts, and from Persian pastries with fragrant nut fillings flavoured with tinctures of rosewater or pussy willow blossoms.

The love of baklava spread south and east with the expansion of the Ottoman Empire, picking up minor variations in flavour or ingredients along the way. What is even more interesting is to chart the international growth of baklava, which started to become more widely known in the 1970s when Greek migrants in Australia, and Armenian and Greek migrants in the US, began to champion their own cuisines in their restaurants, rather than running more generic 'European' places that had seemed a safer bet for new migrants keen to assimilate. Baklava was so much part of those early menus that it's not uncommon for Australians to think that baklava is solely Greek, and diners in the US to think it's actually Armenian rather than Turkish.

Personally, if I were a sultan with a Helvâhâne to command, I'd order baklava made with the famous pistachios from Antep and white chocolate, because white chocolate loves the salty, nutty hit of pistachios. I'd use cheap, bogan white chocolate because I don't mind thumbing my nose at authority! And also because it holds up well during the baking process.

Antep pistachio and white chocolate baklava *(CONTINUED)*

250 g clarified butter (ghee), melted, plus
    extra for greasing
500 g pistachio kernels (see Tip)
½ cup (110 g) caster sugar
2 tablespoons ground cinnamon
good pinch of ground cloves
1 lemon, zest finely grated
¼ cup (60 ml) orange blossom water
180 g white chocolate, chopped (not too fine,
    so you can see it in the finished baklava.
    I like Cadbury Dream for this)
2 × 375 g packets filo pastry
1 teaspoon sea salt flakes
finely chopped pistachio kernels, to decorate

Honey syrup
300 ml honey
½ cup (110 g) caster sugar
1 cup (250 ml) water
1 teaspoon lemon juice

Preheat the oven to 200°C (180°C fan-forced). Grease a 24 × 35 cm × 6 cm deep baking pan with a little of the melted butter.

Process the pistachios in a food processor until finely chopped. Transfer to a bowl. Add the sugar, cinnamon, cloves, lemon zest and orange blossom water and toss until well combined. Stir in the white chocolate.

Lay out the filo and cover with a dry tea towel then a damp tea towel, so it doesn't dry out. Brush one sheet with melted butter, then lay another sheet on top and brush with melted butter. Keep stacking and brushing 15 filo sheets. Transfer to the baking pan.

Spread the pistachio mixture over the filo and smooth it out with the back of a spoon. Sprinkle with the salt. Make another stack of filo pastry, brushing each with melted butter. This time there will be 20 sheets in the stack. Lay over the top of the pistachio filling and trim any excess pastry.

Use a small knife to score the pastry through just the top pastry layer, marking out the portions you would like to serve it in later. You can do this in diamonds or rectangles. Sprinkle a little cold water over the top to help stop the filo curling up while baking. Bake for 35 minutes or until golden brown.

While the baklava bakes, make the honey syrup. Stir the honey, sugar, water and lemon juice in a small saucepan over low heat until the sugar has dissolved.

Remove the baklava from the oven and, while it is still hot, pour the syrup over evenly. Set aside for 6 hours to soak up the syrup and cool completely before cutting. Sprinkle with the finely chopped pistachios to serve. A pot of Greek-style yoghurt on the side is nice. Or a bitter Turkish coffee.

TIP

When buying pistachios, look for young pistachio slivers or the brightest, greenest pistachios you can find. Shops specialising in Turkish or Middle Eastern groceries are the best place to find these, but pistachios sold by weight at the supermarket can be good too.

Lamingtons

MAKES 15 **PREP** 30 minutes (plus cooling, resting and setting time) **COOK** 50 minutes

CLASSIC

Myth

A lamington should never be filled.

My Truth

Not since Lady Lamington's chef, Armand Galland, improvised a tea-time treat for unexpected guests at Queensland's Government House in the very late 1800s with little more than yesterday's sponge, melted chocolate and coconut has the lamington been so lauded.

While my recipe guru Michelle and I have made a giant lamington before, in a shoddy attempt at creating a social media sensation, there is no doubt in my mind that they are better smaller. In no small part because the sponge then has a far better ratio to the chocolate and coconut. Even better, then, if you treat lamingtons like mini chocolate sponges and fill them with cream and strawberry jam, like we have done here.

We're suggesting a microwave jam here, because this technique means you could also make a small batch of plum, peach or cherry jam, depending on the season, which I feel is in the spirit of the can-do, let's-fix-this-right-now attitude of Chef Galland's creation.

While at first sight this might seem like sacrilege, I should point out that there's nothing new in filling a lamington. Read the first ever recipe for 'Lamington cakes', published on 17 December 1900 in the *Queensland Country Life*, and you'll see that the sponge was cut into small cubes then halved, filled with a layer of butter icing and then re-sandwiched before covering all six sides with the same icing mixed with cocoa, and 'cocoanut', as it is rather quaintly spelt in this original. So there!

butter, at room temperature, for greasing
165 g plain flour, plus extra for dusting
6 eggs
185 g caster sugar
½ vanilla bean, split, seeds scraped
250 g milk chocolate, finely chopped
⅔ cup (160 ml) thickened cream
¼ cup (60 ml) milk
1 cup (160 g) icing sugar mixture, sifted
2½ cups (200 g) finely shredded coconut
1½ cups (375 ml) thickened cream, extra

Microwave strawberry jam
2 × 250 g punnets strawberries
½ vanilla bean
1 cup (250 ml) water
½ lemon
330 g (1½ cups) white sugar

Preheat the oven to 170°C (150°C fan-forced). Grease a 23 cm × 33 cm × 4.5 cm deep cake pan with melted butter. Dust the pan with flour and shake off any excess.

Fill a large bowl with warm water. Set aside for 5 minutes to warm the bowl. Drain and wipe the bowl dry. Use a fork to whisk the eggs in a jug. Add the eggs and caster sugar to the warmed bowl. Use electric beaters to whisk on low speed until well combined. Increase the speed to medium. Whisk for 5 minutes or until the mixture is thick, glossy and thick slow ribbons fall when the beaters are lifted.

While your eggs are beating away, sift the flour onto a large sheet of baking paper. Beat the vanilla seeds into the egg mixture. Fold half the flour into the egg mixture until just combined. Repeat with the remaining flour. Pour into the prepared pan. Bake for 20 minutes or until the cake is golden and springs back when lightly touched. Set aside in the pan for 10 minutes to cool slightly before turning out onto a wire rack to cool completely.

Meanwhile, make the jam. Cut the tops off the strawberries, discard the hull or calyx – yes, they both mean the green leaves at the top. But *before you do*, cut off any strawberry flesh from around the leaves that you were about to discard. Phew, that was close! Finely chop this rescued flesh and place in a bowl, then put in the fridge to reserve.

Now coarsely chop the hulled strawberries and place in a very large microwave-safe bowl. Add the vanilla bean and water. Juice the lemon and add the juice to the bowl. Check the squeezed lemon half, and if there are any seeds in it, scoop them out and discard them. (The seeds are good for adding more pectin, which gels in the presence of acid, helping the jam set, but they are a pain to pick out of the finished jam!) Add the squeezed lemon half to the bowl and stir to combine. Microwave on high for 5 minutes or until the strawberries soften. Set aside.

Place a saucer in the freezer to chill. Place the sugar in a microwave-safe bowl. Microwave on high for 2 minutes or until it's warmed through slightly.

Lamingtons *(CONTINUED)*

Stir the warmed sugar into the strawberry mixture and microwave on high, stirring every 5 minutes, for 30–40 minutes or until set. To test when the jam is ready, spoon a little touch of the jam onto the chilled saucer. When you push your finger through the jam and it wrinkles, it is ready. If you are a jam pro, you can tell by the strawberry shortbread smell and the way the jam will drip more slowly off your wooden spoon. Set aside to cool.

Use a serrated bread knife to cut the sponge slab into 15 squares. Place a wire rack over a baking tray.

Place the chocolate, cream and milk in a microwave-safe bowl. Microwave on high, stirring every minute, for 3–5 minutes or until the chocolate has melted and mixture is smooth. Stir in the icing sugar until well combined. Allow to cool and thicken slightly.

Get ready to make the lamingtons: set up your production line with the cake squares, chocolate mixture, coconut on a tray or plate, and a wire rack.

Place one square of cake in the chocolate mixture. Using two forks, turn to coat, allowing the excess to drip off. Move to the coconut and toss until well coated. Place on the wire rack.

Repeat with the remaining cake squares, chocolate mixture and coconut. Leave the lamingtons for 1 hour to set.

Use electric beaters to beat the extra cream in a bowl until firm peaks form.

Use a small serrated knife to cut each lamington in half horizontally. Spread with a little of the jam and sprinkle on some of the reserved strawberry pieces (remember the extra from the hulls that you saved in the fridge?). Dollop the whipped cream over the jam and top with the remaining lamington half.

TIP

Fresh lamingtons are delicious but if you are lucky to have any left over, place them in an airtight container in the fridge. The next day, the strawberry chunks in the jam become a little chewy and are just as irresistible.

Chocolate self-saucing pudding

(THAT'S EXTRA SAUCY AND DREAMS OF CHERRY RIPES)

SERVES 4 **PREP** 15 minutes (plus 10 minutes standing) **COOK** 50 minutes

CLASSIC

Myth
The Cherry Ripe was a British invention.

My Truth
How do you measure success? Having a statue of you erected in your home town? Having a bit of Antarctica named after you? Having a school set up in your name? How about having a bridge over the Yarra in Melbourne named in your honour? All this Sir Macpherson Robertson achieved before his death in 1945 but, in my book, he should be remembered for one thing above all these: in 1924, he invented the Cherry Ripe. He is also the bloke behind Old Gold, Columbines caramels and the Freddo Frog, but with the impending one hundredth anniversary of the Cherry Ripe – which Ray Morgan research discovered in 2013 made up 10 per cent of all chocolate bars sold in Australia – let's sing a hymn of praise to this.

Robertson was born in Ballarat and started his career in confectionary as a sugar-stirrer at the Victoria Confectionary Co. In June 1880, he began making his own sweets in his mother's bathtub using an old nail tin and small furnace. Later, Robertson would also introduce fairy floss, chewing gum and the Crunchie to Australia, but those very first lollies he made were sugar mice. Always a master of self-promotion, we know this because Robertson recorded it all in a rather romanticised memoir called *A Young Man and a Nail Can*!

Robertson is also remembered for his philanthropy – he funded Mawson's Antarctic expeditions and part of the Royal Botanic Gardens in Victoria – and, unlike many of his business peers of the time, he was a keen proponent of social justice. He refused to blacklist unionists, encouraged the Female Confectioners' Union and even proudly drove the company's grey draughthorses in a march in support of the eight-hour work day. All in all, he was an amazing Australian to whom we wanted to pay homage with a dessert.

We've stayed true to Robertson's original and rather sophisticated idea for the Cherry Ripe with the very Australian combination of dark chocolate, coconut and cherries, and paired it with an old country recipe for self-saucing chocolate pudding that I've adopted and scurrilously tried to make my own over the years. (It comes from a faded copy of a 1975 community cookbook called *Over the Range*, which was a fundraiser for the Benalla Auxiliary of the Braille and Talking Book Library.)

Serve this dessert with a dollop of crème fraîche or vanilla ice cream, and do leave the pudding to rest before serving . . . we've made this one extra saucy, and resting for ten minutes allows the sauce to thicken deliciously!

---

80 g butter, melted, plus extra for brushing
670 g jar morello cherries, pitted
1 cup (150 g) self-raising flour
⅓ cup (35 g) cocoa powder, plus extra to dust
¼ cup (20 g) desiccated coconut, plus extra to serve
1 cup (220 g) brown sugar
½ cup (125 ml) coconut milk
1 egg
½ cup (125 ml) boiling water
double cream or vanilla ice cream, to serve

Preheat the oven to 180°C (160°C fan-forced). Brush an 8 cup (2 litre) capacity ovenproof dish with melted butter. Place on a baking tray lined with baking paper.

Drain the cherries through a sieve over a jug and reserve 1¼ cups (310 ml) of the syrup. If you don't have quite enough, top up with a little water to make up the amount. Place the drained morello cherries in the ovenproof dish in an even layer.

Sift the flour and 2 tablespoons of the cocoa powder into a bowl. Stir in the coconut and ½ cup (110 g) of the brown sugar.

Whisk the coconut milk, egg and butter in a jug until combined. Add to the flour mixture and use a wooden spoon to stir until smooth. Spoon into the prepared dish and use the back of a spoon to smooth the surface.

Put the remaining brown sugar and cocoa powder in a bowl and mix until evenly combined. Sprinkle evenly over the top of the pudding mixture.

Place the reserved cherry syrup in a small saucepan and heat over low heat until warmed through. Add the boiling water. Gradually pour the warmed cherry syrup mixture over the back of a spoon onto the pudding. Bake for 50 minutes or until a cake-like surface forms on top and a skewer inserted halfway into the centre comes out clean.

Remove from the oven and set aside for 10 minutes for the sauce to thicken slightly. Dust with the extra cocoa and coconut, and serve with the double cream or ice cream.

Flourless chocolate cake

SERVES 8 **PREP** 20 minutes (plus cooling) **COOK** 45 minutes

Twist

Myth

Flourless chocolate cake is a health-conscious gluten-free invention of Californian origin.

My Truth

The first English-language recipe for flourless chocolate cake was indeed published in the *Los Angeles Times* in 1940 (as a 'chocolate souffle cake', by Grace Turner), closely followed by another US recipe, the 1947 'Roulage [sic] Léontine' by Dione Lucas. This gossamer-light flourless chocolate sponge roll filled with whipped cream featured in Lucas's *The Cordon Bleu Cookbook*. Both recipes take a soufflé approach, beating the egg yolks with sugar, vanilla and melted chocolate, then folding in whipped egg whites. However, both also credit the original recipe as coming from France, so flourless chocolate cake wasn't invented in California.

We know that one of the very first mentions of chocolate cake comes from a 1779 letter from the Marquis de Sade to his wife. (He was complaining about a lack of chocolate icing on the cake she had sent to him in prison – see p. 324.) While there is a very strong connection between France and chocolate cakes in this era, we must look further south for the earliest flourless chocolate cake, and to the sister of France's last queen, Marie Antoinette – yes, the one who supposedly said, 'Let them eat cake'.

Marie Antoinette was born in Austria in 1755, and had a favourite sister, Maria Carolina, who was born in 1752. As children they were inseparable and had to be split up by their governess during lessons because they were so badly behaved together. Like Marie Antoinette, Maria Carolina was also married off to a king, specifically the king of Naples, and at sixteen she left Austria for Italy.

The Naples into which she arrived in 1768 was obsessed with chocolate ice cream – the first recipe had appeared in 1692, and by 1775 a Neapolitan doctor was claiming (in the first ever book about ice cream) that chocolate *sorbetto* was the cure for everything from gout to scurvy – but that wasn't what the homesick but headstrong Maria Carolina yearned for. She demanded that the Neapolitan cooks make her a taste of home: a cake of chocolate and almonds like the ones that were all the rage in Vienna at the court of the Holy Roman Emperor, which by this time was her brother, Joseph II, who had ascended the throne following the death of their father in 1765.

The cake she requested sounds like a precursor of the sachertorte, a dense Viennese chocolate cake supposedly invented in 1832. Another precursor recipe from around this time is found in the 1749 *Wienerisches bewährtes kochbuch* ('Tried and True Viennese Cookbook'). It's not hard to imagine that Maria Carolina may have shared the resulting taste of home with her favourite, cake-loving, little sister after Marie Antoinette arrived in Versailles in 1770, thus ensuring the recipe passed into French use.

While no copy exists of the recipe that Maria Carolina's cooks created, there is a flourless chocolate cake from the region just around the coast from Naples that is famous throughout Italy, the *torta caprese*. The legend on the isle of Capri is that this dish was '*uno dei pasticci più fortunati della storia*' (one of the luckiest mess-ups in history), when a cook at one of the local tearooms mistook almond meal for flour.

The dish's name, however, gives away a far more ancient past than this twentieth-century origin story. 'Torte' was the Austrian word for a cake or tart. In Italy it was *crostata*. Is the *torta caprese* thus descended from the creation of Neapolitan court cooks to appease their homesick Austrian queen? It seems at least as possible as the romantic 'mistaken ingredient' story that we've seen so many times before.

Discovering how flourless chocolate cake came to Australia took far less detective work, and a lot less time spent trying to decipher eighteenth-century Austrian texts written in Upper German. This we can clearly trace back to British-born Dione Lucas. Remember her, from all the way back in the first paragraph? Lucas was said to be the first woman to graduate from Le Cordon Bleu cookery school in Paris, and also claimed to have cooked for Hitler prior to World War II (and said that he wasn't a vegetarian!). But after she published *The Cordon Bleu Cookbook*, this English-born chef went on to become a superstar, and one of the first TV chefs. Her primetime show in 1948 on the US CBS network pulled double the ratings of the next highest-rating show in the same time slot – a variety show hosted by Hollywood superstar Gloria Swanson.

According to some excellent research by Australian academic Jillian Adams, in 1956, Sir Frank Packer imported Lucas to do some cooking demos in department stores around the country. These appearances were filmed and broadcast on televisions throughout the stores as a potent advertisement for the power of TV, and the desirability of one for the 'modern woman'! As the Roulade Léontine (by now she'd corrected the original misspelling) was very much her signature dish, it is likely she would have demoed it here either on this visit or subsequent trips in 1958 or 1960; if so, it would have appeared in one of the *Australian Women's Weekly* magazine lift-outs that Packer ensured were printed to publicise her visits.

On this basis, head to Geelong and to Deakin University's excellent library, where you can see a copy of one of these free lift-outs – and there is the recipe!

The flourless chocolate cake over the page is not Lucas's recipe; this one uses a little blue cheese, which is a late 1990s trick for making chocolate taste richer. You won't notice it's there, I promise.

Flourless chocolate cake *(CONTINUED)*

170 g unsalted butter, chopped, plus extra
    for greasing
350 g dark chocolate (70% cocoa), finely
    chopped
50 g soft blue cheese, crumbled, plus extra
    blue cheese to serve
⅓ cup (75 g) caster sugar
6 eggs, at room temperature, separated
sea salt
whipped cream, to serve (optional)

Balsamic roasted red grapes

400 g seedless red grapes, snipped into
    smaller clusters
1 tablespoon olive oil
2 tablespoons balsamic vinegar

Preheat the oven to 170°C (150°C fan-forced). Grease a 20 cm (base measurement) springform cake pan with butter. Line the base with baking paper.

Place the butter and chocolate in a large microwave-safe bowl. Microwave on high, stirring every minute, for 3–5 minutes or until melted and smooth. Stir in the cheese until almost melted. Stir in half the sugar and set aside to cool.

Add the egg yolks to the chocolate mixture and stir until well combined. Use electric beaters to whisk the egg whites and ¼ teaspoon of salt in a large clean, dry bowl until soft peaks form. Add the remaining sugar and whisk until the mixture holds its shape and is thick and glossy. Fold a third of the egg white mixture into the chocolate mixture with a metal spoon until just combined. Repeat in two more batches.

Pour the chocolate mixture into the prepared pan. Bake for 25 minutes or until the cake is just set. Turn the oven off and leave the cake in the oven to cool completely – this finishes the cooking process and results in the most sensational texture. Do not be tempted to skip this process, no matter how good it smells. Once the cake has cooled, remove it and set aside.

When the cake has been removed from the oven, roast the grapes. Preheat the oven to 220°C (200°C fan-forced). Line a rimmed baking tray with baking paper. Place the grapes on the tray and drizzle with the oil and vinegar. Season with salt. Roast for 15 minutes or until the grapes start to collapse a little and get a bit wrinkly.

Top the cake with the roasted grapes . . . and some extra blue cheese, if you want to be controversial. If not, a nice bowl of whipped cream would be just as good.

TIPS

If you like your cake a little less bitter, this recipe works just as well using 40% cocoa instead of 70% cocoa dark chocolate.

This cake is best served at room temperature. If you make it ahead of time, store in an airtight container in the fridge, then warm each slice in the microwave for a few seconds to serve.

For some contrast, you could roast half the grapes and then serve the rest fresh and sliced, for crunch.

Non-choc
desserts

A trifle peach Melba

SERVES 10 **PREP** 30 minutes (plus overnight chilling and cooling) **COOK** 20 minutes

Twist

Myth

The best things in life start with happy marriages.

My Truth

This is no doubt true, but even unhappy marriages can produce great joy. Take the 1554 wedding of England's first queen, Mary I, daughter of Henry VIII, to Prince Philip of Spain (later King Philip II). This young Spanish prince brought with him courtiers and their households, including their cooks, as well as more of a sense of political duty than love for his 37-year-old bride. Mary, on the other hand, was reportedly rather taken with the handsome Spaniard.

While the impact of this influx was not as great as the arrival of Catherine de' Medici's cooks at the French court 21 years earlier, and subsequently on French food, it did introduce to England the *bizcocho borracho* or 'drunken cake' of the Iberian peninsula. This is itself the wonderful progeny of a marriage between two of Spain's great culinary inventions, sponge cake and fortified wine.

While this combo became popular in England (and was far more successful than Mary's loveless marriage; Philip could write only that he felt 'reasonable regret' on hearing the news of her death), it is not until almost one hundred years later that it pops up in another great union, as the foundation of a classic trifle. Previously the word trifle had been used interchangeably with 'fool' for any thick cream loaded with sugar and flavourings such as fruit, ginger or rosewater. Jelly appears to be an eighteenth-century addition, and the hundreds and thousands were originally sugar-coated caraway seeds. Each of these marriages of techniques enhanced the reputation of trifle such that it is now lionised across the globe in forms such as the *zuppa inglese* of Italy and the 'tipsy cake' of the American South.

Here, food guru Michelle and I have done something we've loved to do over six years of writing recipes together – colliding two classics in hopefully a more harmonious marriage than Mary and Philip's.

The flavours of peach and raspberry go as well together in a trifle as they did in 1892 when Auguste Escoffier paired them in an ice cream dessert to honour Dame Nellie Melba's success as principal soprano of The Royal Opera. This dinner, at The Savoy in London, was thrown by Melba's lover, Prince Philippe, Duke of Orléans, who would later be cited in Melba's divorce proceedings. He fled to Africa for two years after the scandal, never to be reunited with Melba again.

Born Helen Porter Mitchell in the Melbourne suburb of Richmond, Melba's rise to fame was initially full of setbacks – including that short and rather unfortunate marriage in Queensland that she fled to Europe to avoid – before she found happiness and great acclaim as one of the world's leading sopranos and one of the most famous people of her era. I think she would have liked this trifle, even if it's not presented in an ice sculpture of a swan, as Escoffier's *pêche Melba* was. And if there is anything to learn from this, it is that the course of true love never runs as smoothly as dessert.

A trifle peach Melba (CONTINUED)

600 ml thickened cream
180 g white chocolate, finely chopped
2 × 85 g packets raspberry jelly crystals
2½ cups (625 ml) boiling water
375 g raspberries
460 g bought round double unfilled vanilla
    sponge cake
¼ cup (60 ml) peach schnapps
700 g can (or tub) peaches in syrup, drained
2 fresh peaches, cut into thick wedges, grilled
honey, to drizzle

Custard

1½ cups (375 ml) milk
1 vanilla bean, split lengthways, seeds
    scraped
3 egg yolks
½ cup (110 g) caster sugar
¼ cup (35 g) plain flour

Sugared flaked almonds

½ cup (40 g) flaked almonds
2 tablespoons caster sugar
1 teaspoon sea salt

Start by making a white chocolate cream. Place the cream and chocolate in a microwave-safe bowl. Microwave on high, stirring every minute, for 2–4 minutes or until the chocolate has melted and the mixture is smooth. Set aside for 1 hour to cool slightly, then cover and place in the fridge for 6 hours or overnight to thicken and chill.

Place the jelly crystals in a heatproof bowl. Add the boiling water and stir until the crystals dissolve. Set aside for 1 hour to cool. Pour into a 23 cm (15 cup/3.75 litre capacity) straight-sided trifle bowl. Add 250 g of the raspberries. Place in the fridge for 4 hours to set.

To make the custard, combine the milk, vanilla bean and seeds in a saucepan. Cook, stirring, for 5 minutes over medium heat or until the mixture almost comes to a simmer. Remove from the heat, cover and set aside for 5 minutes to infuse. Discard the vanilla bean.

Whisk the egg yolks and sugar in a bowl until pale and creamy, then whisk in the flour until well combined. Gradually whisk in the milk mixture. Place the mixture in a clean saucepan over medium heat. Cook, stirring, for 4–5 minutes or until the mixture boils and thickens. Pour into a heatproof bowl, cover the surface with plastic wrap and place in the fridge for 2 hours to cool completely.

While the custard cools, make the sugared almonds. Line a baking tray with baking paper. Place the almonds in a frying pan. Cook over medium heat for 2–3 minutes or until they start to toast. Sprinkle the almonds with the sugar and cook, stirring, for 1–2 minutes or until the sugar dissolves and coats the almonds. Transfer to the lined tray and sprinkle with salt. Set aside to cool and harden.

Trim the top and bottom of the sponges to remove the brown crust. Cut one sponge in half to make two semicircles. Place on top of the jelly and pull apart to fit snugly against the wall of the bowl. Cut a wedge from the remaining sponge to neatly fit into the gap left over so you have an even layer. Drizzle the sponge with the peach schnapps and top with the canned peaches. Drizzle with the cooled custard.

Use electric beaters to beat the chilled white chocolate cream until firm peaks form. Spoon on top of the trifle. Top with the grilled peaches and the remaining raspberries. Drizzle with honey and sprinkle with the sugared almonds.

TIPS

You could poach your own peaches for this trifle, if peaches are in season, and if you can be bothered.

For a quick variation, try changing up the jelly. I find port wine jelly makes a nice change.

If you are looking for an alternative trifle, check out my recipe for orange and chocolate trifle with homemade jelly online.

Baked cheesecake

SERVES 10 **PREP** 20 minutes (plus chilling and cooling) **COOK** 1 hour 15 minutes

CLASSIC

Myth

There are 100 recipes in this cookbook.

My Truth

Actually, there are around 105 recipes in this book. You can put this down to 1) my generosity; 2) my inability to make hard decisions about what to cut; 4) my inability to count; or 4) my guilt at including a recipe I have made many times before, as is the case here. I suppose I could have put some spurious spin on cheesecake, like marbling it with matcha, but it would be akin to putting sunnies on the Mona Lisa, as the original recipe that cake whisperer Kate Quincerot developed for me is flawless. Not to mention that to dump cheesecake would be to deprive you of its 2800 year history.

For as long as humans have been making cheese, we've been making cheesecakes. The Ancient Greeks loved them; a version called *plakountas* was even served to athletes during the very first Olympic games in 776 BC. The island of Samos and the city of Athens both claim the dish was invented there. Either way, their ideas were similar – to whip cheese with honey and eggs, and bake it in a pastry crust. The Ancient Greek physician Aegimus authored an entire book on the art of making cheesecake in the fifth century BC, but this is now lost. We do have Cato the Elder's Ancient Roman recipe for *placenta*, from around three hundred years later, where layers of crisp pastry are interspersed with sheep's cheese mixed with honey.

It was in the Middle Ages that cakes made with cheese really hit their straps. Henry VIII loved 'maids of honour' tarts, which more discreet royal biographers of the day suggested was how Anne Boleyn wooed the randy king. Anne had been appointed maid of honour to Henry's first wife, Catherine of Aragon, in 1522. These tarts had jam hidden under the orange and nutmeg flavoured cheese, much like the Argentinian tradition of spreading marmalade or jam on the base of cheesecakes before baking. (Anne married Henry in 1533; the marriage was far less of a success than the cheesecake.)

Recipes for cheesecake have dotted cookbooks ever since those days of doublets and hose, but the invention of commercial cream cheese in 1872 and the arrival of the handheld domestic mechanical whisk at almost exactly the same time made them cheaper and far easier to cook. In recent years, cheesecake has been one of the leading candidates for dessert deconstruction. While I'm more than happy for you to smash crumbs and scoop pillows of whipped cream, cheese and sugar onto a plate, it'll never match the thrill of the first slice of this fully constructed version.

250 g granita or digestive biscuits
60 g caster sugar
75 g butter, melted

Filling
750 g cream cheese, at room temperature, chopped
1 cup (220 g) caster sugar
4 eggs
2½ tablespoons lemon juice
1 teaspoon vanilla extract
¼ teaspoon sea salt
300 ml double cream

Preheat the oven to 175°C (155°C fan-forced). Line the base and side of a 23 cm (base measurement) springform cake pan with baking paper. Double wrap the outside of the pan with extra-wide, strong foil to create a waterproof seal. Before you start, find a roasting pan which is large enough to fit your cake pan comfortably.

Process the biscuits in a food processor until finely crushed. Transfer the biscuit crumbs to a bowl and stir in the sugar. Add the melted butter and mix until well combined. Spoon into the lined pan and use the back of a spoon to press firmly and evenly over the base. Bake for 10 minutes. Set aside while you prepare the filling.

Place the roasting pan in the oven to heat up, and boil a kettle of water. Use electric beaters to beat the cream cheese on medium speed until smooth and creamy. Add the sugar and beat until the sugar has dissolved. (Check by rubbing a small amount of the cream cheese between two fingers to see if it is still grainy. If so, beat on!) Add the eggs one at a time, beating well after each one. Reduce the speed to low. Add the lemon juice, vanilla and salt, and beat until well combined. Lastly, beat in the cream.

Re-boil the kettle. Pour the cream cheese mixture over the biscuit base. Remove the roasting pan from the oven and carefully place the cheesecake in the pan. Place the pan with the cheesecake back into the oven. Pour boiling water into the roasting pan to a depth of about 2 cm. Bake for 1 hour 5 minutes. After this time has finished, do not open the oven door, just turn the oven off and leave the cheesecake in the oven for at least another hour before removing. This is very important to allow the cheesecake to finish cooking and also stops it cracking.

Set the cheesecake aside and allow it to cool completely in the springform pan before releasing. Cut into wedges and serve with berries, cream or an orange salad.

Pineapple and black pepper tarte tatin

SERVES 6 **PREP** 15 minutes (plus 25 minutes cooling) **COOK** 45 minutes

Twist

Myth

The creation of *tarte tatin* was a happy accident when one of the Tatin sisters – it could have been Stéphanie, it might have been Caroline – dropped that day's apple tart upside down but served it nonetheless.

My Truth

The truth is that this caramelly upside-down tart was already a longstanding classic in the Sologne region in France where the Tatin sisters ran their little hotel dining room in Lamotte-Beuvron in the late nineteenth century. Tarte tatin historians like Henri Delétang present evidence that the sisters' upside-down apple tart was cooked in the countryside around Lamotte-Beuvron from the 1880s onwards. This 'tarte solognote' took its name from the Sologne region. The sisters' restaurant didn't open until 1894. By 1903, when a group of rail enthusiasts visited their dining room, 'Fanny' (Stéphanie) Tatin's apple tart was 'famous all over Sologne', they recorded. They even referred to it as a 'tarte Tatin'.

The popularity of this myth demonstrates the power of great marketing. The story of the two sisters overcoming adversity was so famous and so alluring that, years after their death, they and the dish became internationally feted when it made the menu of Paris's coolest celeb hangout, the restaurant Maxim's, in the 1950s with the sisters' name attached to it.

I'd usually make this with an Aussie apple like granny smith or, better yet, pink lady, but I've done that so many times before. The acidic robustness of pineapple and the spicy heat of black pepper is a fitting occasional diversion from the norm. It looks pretty, too, and the liquid gold that leaches out of the pineapple makes a delicious pineapple caramel.

1 large (wide) pineapple
⅓ cup (75 g) caster sugar
20 g butter, chopped
freshly ground black pepper
1 large sheet (375 g) frozen butter puff pastry
   (we used Carême brand), just thawed
1 tablespoon finely chopped coriander stems

Preheat the oven to 200°C (180°C fan-forced). Cut the ends off the pineapple. Stand upright, then cut downwards to remove the skin and little 'eyes'. Cut crossways into 7–10 mm slices. You'll need 7 or 8 slices, depending on how wide your pineapple is. Use a small round cutter to core the slices.

Sprinkle the sugar into a 22 cm ovenproof non-stick frying pan. Place over medium heat and allow the sugar to melt, swirling the pan gently. When it is almost all dissolved, remove from the heat and add the butter. Swirl gently but don't stir.

Add half the pineapple slices and return to the heat. Cook for 2–3 minutes each side or until lightly golden and the juice starts to release. Transfer to a plate and repeat with the remaining pineapple.

Return the pan to medium heat. There will be quite a bit of juice from the pineapple left in the pan. Bring to the boil and cook for 3 minutes or until reduced and syrupy (you'll need to remove from the heat so the bubbles can subside and you can check how thick it is getting). Set the pan to one side to cool for 10 minutes.

Grind the pepper into a sieve and use only the coarser grains and none of the dust, to get a fruitier peppery taste with less heat. Season the syrup liberally with the pepper. Place a pineapple slice in the centre of the pan, then arrange the others around, overlapping to fit. Cut a 26 cm round from the pastry and ease over the pineapple – careful, that caramel is hot. Use the handle of a wooden spoon to push the pastry down the side slightly. Cut a few slits in the pastry to let steam out as it cooks.

Bake for 30 minutes or until the pastry is deep golden and the pineapple mixture is bubbling. Set aside in the pan for 15 minutes to cool slightly.

Using a tea towel, carefully place your hand on the pastry and pretend you are mixing sweet tunes on your decks. Rotate the tart a little bit this way, a little bit that to help free it from the pan. You might need to run a knife around the edge.

Place a large serving plate over the pan. Carefully turn over so the tart lands on the plate. Sprinkle with the coriander stems and serve warm or at room temperature.

Knickerbocker glory

SERVES 6 **PREP** 20 minutes (plus 3 hours chilling) **COOK** 5 minutes

CLASSIC

Myth
The Knickerbocker glory is as New York as hot pretzels, Central Park carriage rides and King Kong atop the Empire State Building.

My Truth
The Knickerbocker glory might sound like the most American of desserts, but while the name of this marvellous tall glass of layered ice cream, jelly, fruit and whipped cream with a cherry on top was stolen from a little-known sundae invented in the United States, it was made famous, and transformed into the dessert we know today, in the United Kingdom in the 1920s.

While ice cream and sorbets have a venerable history stretching back 2500 years, and they were favourites of European, Persian and Indian royalty from the time of Nero through to the late Renaissance, Americans were among the first to bring this frozen treat to the masses. It was also loved by the country's founding fathers. During the summer of 1790, George Washington spent the princely sum of $200 on 'iced cream' from a confectioner on Chatham Street in New York. He already owned his own ice cream machine at Mount Vernon, which he purchased for 'one pound, thirteen shillings and three pence' in 1784. Thomas Jefferson had an eighteen-step recipe for making the ice cream he served to guests at Monticello, and James Madison served it at his presidential inauguration.

The first ice cream parlour opened in New York in 1776, and New Yorker Nancy Johnson invented the first small-scale ice cream churner in the 1840s. (Agnes Marshall also came up with the idea at about the same time in the UK.) The US's seemingly insatiable desire for the cold stuff also saw the creation of the ice cream soda in 1874 by Robert M. Green in Philadelphia. However, the introduction of laws in some cities forbidding the trading of drinks on the Sabbath also unofficially outlawed drinking sodas. In soda's place arose the ice cream sundae, initially served only on these Sundays.

The first sundaes were no more than ice cream and the fruit syrups that were used in sodas, but soon everyone was in on the sundae and upping the game. By 1909, the *Ice Cream Trade Journal* listed countless variations, including the French sundae, Black Hawk sundae, Cherry Dip sundae, Knickerbocker sundae, Bismarck sundae and George Washington sundae.

It is the Knickerbocker sundae that interests us here. It had previously been mentioned in the June 1903 edition of *Practical Druggist* with the same elements as described in the *Ice Cream Trade Journal*: ice cream, chocolate syrup, fresh raspberries, glacé cherries and the rather fancy addition of rose essence.

The seemingly unrelated name makes more sense when you consider that the word 'Knickerbocker' had become synonymous with New York City swankiness. The term traces its origins to the Dutch settlers who came to New York in the 1600s; 'knickerbocker' became slang for the style of trousers the poshest of these settlers wore, and the word eventually came to represent the top end of town and the city itself, especially Manhattan. (In fact, one side of my family is descended from these knickerbockers. Perhaps this is where my love of outlandish pants comes from? But I digress . . .)

In 1809, Washington Irving chose the pen name 'Diedrich Knickerbocker' for his book *A History of New York*, a satirical work that greatly popularised the use of the term to refer to all things New York. An elite society hangout, the Knickerbocker Club, was formed in 1871. New York had a local 'Knickerbocker Beer', and an uber-fancy sixteen-storey Knickerbocker Hotel that opened in 1906 (and closed during Prohibition). When the NBA granted a charter franchise to New York in 1946, along came the New York Knickerbockers, more commonly known as the Knicks. New York's first baseball team also had the same name one hundred years earlier!

So, if you understand the word 'knickerbocker' to be an expression of NYC civic pride, then the name Knickerbocker sundae seems like a pretty smart marketing move. It wouldn't become a Knickerbocker glory, however, until it migrated across the Atlantic in the 1920s, along with flapper haircuts and the Charleston.

The UK had been crazy for ice cream ever since Swiss entrepreneur Carlo Gatti had introduced it in the 1860s, and 'penny licks' sold from street carts in reusable glass dishes had become a favourite treat of the working class. The Brits adopted the Knickerbocker glory in a similarly obsessive fashion to how they had previously taken ownership of Boston's humble baked beans. It was here that meringues and fruit jelly started to be added to the dish, along with whipped cream and nuts. Adding the word 'glory' was perhaps a refence to the glorious, layered height of the sundae in the glass.

The Knickerbocker glory was made famous across the UK by the J. Lyons & Co. restaurant chain, as part of a promotion for their 'Corner House' cafes. Unfortunately, the promo was built around ice-cream sundaes named after pieces of clothing – thus linking the name Knickerbocker with the trousers rather than the slang name for New York. They also had the Plus Fours sundae and the Charlie Chaplin Waistcoat(?!). The deliciousness of the Knickerbocker glory made it the standout hit of the promo, however, and it became a constant on the menu of what was the Maccas of its day in the UK. From there, it was embraced across the country, while the hot fudge sundae and the banana split became the sundaes of choice in the US.

Knickerbocker glory *(CONTINUED)*

85 g packet strawberry jelly crystals
1 cup (250 ml) boiling water
300 g strawberries, hulled and finely chopped
12 scoops vanilla ice cream
18 mini meringue kisses
1½ cups (375 ml) thickened cream, whipped
½ cup (65 g) flaked almonds, toasted
maraschino cherries, to serve

Chocolate fudge sauce

100 g dark chocolate, finely chopped
¾ cup (185 ml) pouring cream
¼ cup (55 g) brown sugar
1 tablespoon glucose syrup
1 teaspoon vanilla extract

Berry coulis

250 g punnet strawberries, hulled and finely chopped
125 g punnet raspberries
1 tablespoon icing sugar mixture

Start by making the jelly. Place the jelly crystals in a heatproof bowl and add the boiling water. Stir to dissolve the crystals, then pour into a 12 cm × 17 cm glass or plastic container. Place in the fridge for 3 hours to set. Cut into 2 cm cubes.

Next, make the fudge sauce. Place the chocolate in a heatproof bowl. Combine the cream, sugar, glucose and vanilla in a small saucepan and cook, stirring, over low heat until the sugar dissolves and the mixture is smooth. Increase the heat to medium and bring almost to the boil. Pour over the chocolate and set aside for 5 minutes for the chocolate to soften, then stir with a metal spoon until melted and smooth. Set aside to cool.

To make the berry coulis, process the strawberries, raspberries and icing sugar in a food processor until smooth. Strain through a fine sieve into a jug. Discard the solids, which will basically just be seeds that will only get stuck in your teeth – so don't skip this step!

Divide half the chopped strawberries among six tall 1½ cup (375 ml) sundae glasses. Top each glass with a scoop of ice cream. Drizzle with a tablespoon of the berry coulis. Top with the remaining chopped strawberries. Crush 2 meringues into each glass. Top with another scoop of ice cream and another tablespoon of coulis. Top with the jelly cubes and whipped cream. Drizzle with a little fudge sauce. Crush over the remaining meringue and sprinkle with the almonds. Top with the maraschino cherries. Or, other than the final cherry flourish, feel free to serve up this dish however you want. This is a dish of pure joy, not of rules!

Leftover hot fudge sauce will keep in an airtight container in the fridge for up to 2 weeks. Serve on ice cream, drizzled over the brownies on p. 329 or with the crepes on p. 289.

Leftover berry coulis will keep in an airtight container in the fridge for up to 1 week. Serve folded through the cream used to fill the sponge on p. 324, drizzle over the cheesecake on p. 278, or top the pavlova on p. 299 with fresh berries and drizzle with the coulis.

Food nerd fact

As well as the early Knickerbocker sundaes, there are also records of a Knickerbocker shake made with cream, egg whites and orange syrup in 1919, coinciding with the zenith of the Temperance movement and the imminent introduction of Prohibition, which boosted interest in non-alcoholic liquid entertainment.

INSTEAD OF PEANUTS, TRY COARSELY CHOPPED PEPITAS OR WALNUTS, WHICH ARE JUST AS CLASSIC.

Hotteok pancakes with peanuts and brown sugar

MAKES 12 **PREP** 20 minutes (plus 1 hour proving) **COOK** 15 minutes

Myth

As *hotteok* are little known in Australia, no myths have arisen around them here.

My Truth

This might be one of the least recognised dishes in this book, but in my opinion no visit to Seoul is complete without sampling these slightly chewy, caramel-filled rice flour pancakes. They're a popular street food that brings together cheap ingredients to make a sweet, warming treat for cold winter days. The phrase 'the *hotteok* stall is burning' is also a common way to describe any noisy situation.

The name *hotteok*, which loosely translates as 'barbarian rice cake', is a clue to the dish's origin. In 1882, Chinese soldiers and merchants travelled to Korea to help restore order after the Imo Mutiny, an uprising against the king and against increasing Japanese influence on the government. These merchants brought with them glutinous rice cakes and dumplings made using flour from the indigenous rice that had been cultivated in China for 2000 years. (This rice flour is also the main ingredient of Japanese *mochi*, which first appeared in the eighth century BC.)

Some of these merchants remained in Korea, selling rice cakes at market stalls, and over time traditional fillings like pork or red bean paste were replaced with ingredients like honey, rice syrup and brown sugar, which were more popular with Korean customers. Peanuts were added later as a way of stopping the caramel that formed inside the rice cake during frying from dripping onto people's chins, which could leave painful scarring! You'll still find peanuts popping up, and doing the same job, in *hotteok* today.

The fact that there was a concentration of *hotteok* street stalls around the Chinese Embassy in Seoul, plus the fact that when Japan annexed Korea in 1910 they renamed *hotteok* 'Jina bread' (meaning 'Chinese bread'), both support this provenance story. However, if I were taking the usual myth-busting approach, I would now point out that Koreans were enjoying sweet glutinous rice cakes before the arrival of those Chinese merchants.

According to an 1849 entry in the *Dongguk Sesigi*, a record of seasonal customs, Koreans would take to the fields during spring to admire the wildflowers and would snack on pan-fried glutinous rice flour cakes called *hwajeon*. The recipe in the *Dongguk Sesigi* says these were sweetened with honey or caramel, and fancier versions were decorated with petals from the azaleas that were in bloom.

Whatever their provenance, these *hotteok* are a treat worth discovering in Seoul or in your own kitchen. Just remember to grease your hands when shaping them, and to beware of that potentially scalding filling when biting in!

1½ tablespoons vegetable oil
250 g sour cream
2 tablespoons pure icing sugar, sifted
125 g frozen cherries
maple syrup, to serve

Dough

¾ cup (185 ml) milk, warmed
2 teaspons (7 g sachet) dried yeast
2 tablespoons caster sugar
1¼ cups (185 g) plain flour
½ cup (100 g) rice flour

Filling

½ cup (110 g) brown sugar
¼ cup (35 g) roasted unsalted peanuts, coarsely chopped
1 teaspoon ground cinnamon

Start by making the dough. Combine the milk, yeast and sugar in a bowl and set aside for 5 minutes, until frothy. Combine the plain flour and rice flour in a bowl. Gradually add the yeast mixture and stir until combined. Turn out onto a lightly floured surface and knead until smooth. Place in a large lightly greased bowl, cover with plastic wrap and rest in a warm place for 1 hour or until doubled in size.

While your dough proves, make the filling by combining the ingredients in a bowl.

Knock back the dough and roll into a thick log. Divide into 12 even pieces. Roll a piece of dough into a ball, then flatten out on a lightly floured surface to an 8 cm disc. (Greasing your hands with a little oil can help here if things get sticky.) Add 3 teaspoons of the peanut mixture to the centre, then gather in the side and pinch to enclose the filling. Flatten back into an 8 cm disc. Repeat with the remaining dough and filling.

Heat 2 teaspoons of the oil in a large non-stick frying pan over medium heat. Add four pancakes and cook for 2 minutes each side or until well browned and slightly puffed, using a spatula to press down to ensure the pancakes remain flat. Repeat with the remaining oil and pancakes.

Combine the sour cream and icing sugar in a bowl. Serve the pancakes topped with the sour cream mixture. Working quickly, coarsely chop the frozen cherries and scatter over the top. Serve with the maple syrup.

Crepes suzette

SERVES 4 **PREP** 10 minutes (plus 30 minutes chilling) **COOK** 45 minutes

CLASSIC

Myth

Sometimes the truth is better than the story.

My Truth

Humans have been eating out for millennia, whether because our houses didn't have kitchens (due to the prohibitive cost or the risk of fire they presented), because we were travelling, or because we were having a night on the town. This could be at a hole-in-the-wall cookshop in Pompeii, a set price, set menu *table d'hôte* in some French backwater tavern before the Revolution, or in a rumbustious saloon in the Chinese city of Kaifeng back in the twelfth century, when it was the biggest city in the world. However, the restaurant as a glamorous destination is a much more recent development.

Back in the mid-eighteenth century, it was fashionable among the well-to-do of Paris to be a little fey and weak, in those strange days of 'consumptive chic'. Grand dining rooms of mirrors and gilt were set up with menus that would restore the fashionable invalid feigning the ravages of tuberculosis. Hence the French word *restaurer*, meaning 'restore', in 'restaurant'. These places also allowed the emerging bourgeoisie in the years before the French Revolution to sample the lifestyle of the aristocrats they would soon depose.

The Revolution and Madame Guillotine ensured that in a few years there were many top chefs from grand houses looking for employment. This perhaps helps to explain why by 1804 there were five hundred restaurants in Paris. While there were celebrity chefs during the nineteenth and twentieth centuries, like Carême and Escoffier, in these times much of the power resided with the maître d's of the grand dining rooms, rather than with the chef.

It was the waiters who plated up the food for guests and, as a direct step up in theatrics, nearing the end of the nineteenth century the waiters even started to cook dishes for customers at the table using a chafing dish. This trend gave us steak diane (see p. 172) and Sydney socialites tossing their own spag bol in the middle of the twentieth century (see p. 195), but the most famous of all these dishes is crepes suzette. The story goes that in 1895, Henri Charpentier, a fifteen-year-old assistant waiter at the Café de Paris in Monte Carlo, was making crepes tableside for Edward, the Prince of Wales, and his glamorous female companion after they had whiled away a few hours at the casino next door. The future Edward VII of England was a famous playboy and womaniser, which helps this story seem extra believable. It was very late at night, and young Henri was one of the last waiters still on duty.

Freaked out at being confronted with the prince, his female companion and sixteen of Edward's closest friends, Henri managed to singe the crepes when the booze used to finish the dish caught fire. Edward was rather impressed not just by the flames but also by the flavour that the char gave the dish. He instructed Charpentier to name the dish not after him, but after his companion – Suzette. Charpentier recalled that he was rewarded by the prince for this act with the gift of a panama hat, a cane and a jewelled ring.

Fifty years later, Charpentier also revealed that the crepes suzette recipe was the result of experimenting with a crepe dish that his foster mother used to make for him, and adding a splash of booze, which was what all the smart dining rooms in Paris were doing at the time, so he copied them! Charpentier would go on to work at Maxim's and La Tour d'Argent in Paris, as well as the Café Royal and the Savoy in London. Apparently, he ended up as chef to business magnate John D. Rockefeller in the United States, where he popularised crepes suzette on that side of the Atlantic.

Through all this time Charpentier kept to his version of the story in spite of detractors throwing shade, including the *Larousse Gastronomique* (he was too young to have been allowed to serve such an illustrious guest, they said), and the owner of Paris's Restaurant Marivaux, a Monsieur Joseph. He claimed the dish was his, created after he supplied the crepes for an actress nicknamed Suzette to cook on stage in an 1897 Comédie-Française production. He suggested she flambé them for a more impressive visual effect, and Paris's top restaurants took the idea from there.

Yes, I also prefer the story of the bumbling fifteen-year-old. And, in fact, I don't think it's such a big leap for the crepes suzette that I ate at La Tour d'Argent one long hot summer's night in Paris, overlooking the illuminated Notre-Dame hunched on the banks of the Seine, to have descended from the recipe Charpentier brought to Paris when he worked there, rather than something that happened in a play 30 minutes' walk across town. At La Tour d'Argent, their version was as simple as the recipe here.

Crepes suzette (CONTINUED)

1 cup (250 ml) freshly squeezed orange juice
½ cup (110 g) caster sugar
30 g butter, chopped
½ cup (125 ml) Drambuie or Cointreau

Crepes
1 cup (150 g) plain flour
1½ cups (375 ml) milk
2 eggs
20 g butter, melted, plus extra 30 g cold
butter, for greasing

To make the crepes, sift the flour into a large bowl and make a well in the centre. Lightly beat the milk and eggs in a jug, then gradually add to the flour, whisking gently to combine. Whisk in the melted butter. Place in the fridge for 30 minutes to rest.

While the batter rests, make the sauce. Combine the orange juice and sugar in a large frying pan over low heat. Cook, stirring, for 2 minutes or until the sugar dissolves. Increase the heat to medium. Add the butter and cook for 5 minutes or until the mixture reduces and becomes slightly syrupy. Pour half the sauce into a bowl and set aside.

Place the extra cold butter in the centre of a sheet of paper towel. Pull the sides up around the butter to make a bundle and enclose. Use the flat base of the butter in the paper towel to wipe over a 20 cm (base measurement) crepe pan or frying pan over medium heat. Place the wrapped butter to one side on a plate while the crepe is cooking, and re-use for each new crepe.

Pour 2½ tablespoons of the batter into the pan and immediately swirl to cover the base. Cook for 2 minutes or until crisp around the edges and golden underneath. Flip the crepe over and cook for 1 minute. Transfer to a plate. Cover with a clean tea towel to keep warm. Repeat with the remaining batter, greasing the pan between each crepe to make 12 crepes.

Place the large frying pan with the half the sauce left in it back over low heat and cook, stirring, for 1–2 minutes or until warmed through. Fold half the crepes into quarters and place in the frying pan. Turn to coat in the sauce. Stir in half the Drambuie or Cointreau. Remove from the heat and place the pan somewhere clear (so no curtains flapping about). Carefully use a long match or lighter to ignite the sauce. When the flames subside, divide the crepes among serving plates. Repeat with the remaining sauce (reserved in the bowl), liqueur and crepes.

TIPS

If you have two large frying pans, divide the sauce among the pans and warm and flame straightaway, one after the other.

If you are going to flambé your crepes, you could try the method shown in the picture on the opposite page. Warm your chosen booze in a small saucepan, then carefully ignite and pour the flaming liquid over the crepes.

Rhubarb crumble with custard

SERVES 6 **PREP** 20 minutes **COOK** 50 minutes

Twist

Myth
Crumble is British.

My Truth

The origin of the crumble as we know it in Australia is always traced back to the ration-ravaged wartime years in the United Kingdom. This was a time when the ingredients for classic pies were hard to find and shortcut recipes abounded, such as topping sweet and savoury pie-fillings with a crumble of flour, lard and sugar (or cheese, if the filling was savoury). Here, say the books, crumble was born.

Certainly, recipes for crumble only start to pop up in British cookbooks after World War II, and a cursory scan of cookbooks from the preceding century, like *Mrs Beeton's Book of Household Management* (1861), *The Encyclopaedia of Practical Cookery* (1891) and Escoffier's *Le guide culinaire* (1903), reveals recipes for apple snow, apple hedgehog, apple dumplings, apple fool, apple cheesecake, apple charlotte, suet apple pudding and apple amber (like an apple version of a lemon meringue pie), but nothing with a baked topping other than apple pie (which dates back to the fourteenth century). There is no apple crumble anywhere.

The earliest UK recipe I can find for apple crumble is from a Northern Irish newspaper called the *Northern Whig* in 1942. That recipe actually suggests that it is not a suitable wartime recipe because it uses so much butter. Interestingly, this reference (and comments from a reader and the recipe columnist) implies that the recipe predates World War II, and came from the idea of topping apples with the rubbed-together ingredients of shortbread before the dough was pulled together. Hot apple shortbread recipes date from 1903, but these were originally topped with a fully formed slab of dough rather than a crumble of the ingredients.

While the UK claims the crumble as their own, they are actually being a bit naughty and the teensiest bit jingoistic. In Australia, apples baked with a bread-crumb or cake-crumb topping are found from the start of the twentieth century, but the first mention of apple crumble in the Australian media is from a 1935 edition of the Melbourne *Argus*, pipping the UK by some years. In a letter, 'Helpful' from Toorak suggests topping apples stewed with cloves and sugar with an at least one-centimetre thick layer of self-raising flour, sugar and butter. This is then sprinkled with coconut and baked, which also makes it the first example I can find of a crumble topping that's customised with a fourth ingredient. Needless to say, this also predates the accepted wisdom that crumble was a wartime British invention by a good few years.

However, the crumble has even deeper roots in the United States. 'The apples grown in the vicinity of New York are universally admitted to be the finest of any', wrote English cookery guru Mrs Beeton in 1861. If we take her at her word, it is unsurprising that apple recipes were extremely popular in American cookbooks of the time. There was no hesitation about baking spiced stewed apples in the home oven or the camp oven, and topping them with everything from dough (for apple cobbler, or the delightfully named apple slump), breadcrumbs (for brown betty or pandowdy) or even stale, milk-soaked rusks (for swiss pudding) or cracker crumbs (for Boston's mock apple pie).

It was from these antecedents that arose the apple crisp – apples baked under a crisp topping of sugar, flour and butter. This starts to appear during the hard years of World War I and the subsequent depression: in a 1916 edition of the *Freeport Journal-Standard*; a 1921 edition of the *Essex County Herald*; and in regional cookbooks like 1924's *Everybody's Cook Book* and the *Modern Priscilla Cook Book*. I have found an earlier recipe for apple crisp dating to 1915 (in the Clarksburg *Daily Telegram*), but here the crisp is a flour, sugar and butter base bound with egg, rather than a true crumble topping.

Read through these recipes, and it isn't just the ingredients that are the same: every one includes the word 'crumbly' in the method when describing the desired consistency for the topping after the ingredients have been worked together. Surely, you would think, this is where the 'crumble' comes from. But the story might not end there. Early apple crisp recipes are sometimes attributed to German or Amish settlers, so there is a suspicion that the idea for this topping might actually be based on a German or Austrian 'streusel', a cake topping that uses the same three ingredients but with more sugar and less flour. For me, this is case closed.

While I love classic apple crumble, there is something slightly more magical about the rosy glow of a crumble that has the tart acidity of rhubarb to gussy up the filling. Orange juice adds further pep, and the ginger plays to both fruits' love of spicing. It is, of course, served with custard, but I've also included a little custard powder in the filling to both sweeten and thicken. This is a nod to streusel, those first desserts of apples baked with cake crumbs, which were sometimes bound with a little crème anglaise.

Rhubarb crumble with custard *(CONTINUED)*

melted butter, for greasing
1 bunch rhubarb, trimmed and cut into 4 cm pieces
2 large granny smith apples, peeled and cut into 1 cm wedges
2 tablespoons caster sugar
½ cup (125 ml) freshly squeezed orange juice
25 g butter, finely chopped
2 teaspoons custard powder
2 tablespoons finely chopped glacé or naked ginger

Crumble topping

1¼ cups (185 g) plain flour
150 g chilled butter, chopped
½ cup (110 g) brown sugar
½ cup (70 g) macadamias, coarsely chopped
⅓ cup (30 g) rolled oats

Vanilla custard

1½ cups (375 ml) milk
1 vanilla bean, split lengthways
4 egg yolks
¼ cup (55 g) caster sugar

Preheat the oven to 180°C (160°C fan-forced). Generously grease an 8 cup (2 litre) capacity ovenproof dish with melted butter. Combine the rhubarb, apple, caster sugar and orange juice in the dish. Dollop with the chopped butter. Cover with foil and bake, stirring once, for 20 minutes or until the fruit is just starting to soften.

While the fruit bakes, make the crumble topping. Place the flour in a large bowl. Add the butter and use your fingertips to gently rub in the butter until it is the consistency of coarse, chunky breadcrumbs. Add the brown sugar, macadamias and oats, and toss until well combined.

Remove the fruit from the oven. Sprinkle with the custard powder and ginger. Top with the crumble topping. Bake, uncovered, for 30 minutes or until golden.

While the crumble bakes, make the custard. Place the milk in a saucepan. Use a small, sharp knife to scrape the seeds from the vanilla bean into the milk, and add the vanilla bean pod as well. Bring just to the boil over medium heat – watch this, as it is a short moment between simmering and boiled-over.

Strain through a fine sieve into a heatproof jug. Discard the vanilla bean unless you want to rinse it, dry it and use it to flavour a little pot of caster sugar.

Whisk the egg yolks and sugar in a bowl until thick and pale. Gradually whisk the hot milk into the egg mixture. Return to the pan over medium–low heat. Cook, stirring constantly with a wooden spoon, for 5 minutes or until the custard thickens and coats the back of the spoon. Pour into a heatproof serving jug. If not using straight away, cover the surface with plastic wrap to stop a skin forming.

Serve the crumble drizzled with the custard, or with the custard in a jug on the side.

TIP

To save some time and effort, you could buy a good supermarket custard and scrape the seeds of a vanilla bean into it. You'll fool most people and it will still be delicious with the crumble. (Is that a terrible thing to say?!)

Lemongrass and lime leaf meringue pie

SERVES 8 **PREP** 40 minutes (plus cooling and chilling) **COOK** 1 hour 5 minutes

Twist

Myth

Sometimes you can't see the wood for the trees.

My Truth

While this isn't as silly as saying you can't judge a book by its cover (because you pretty much always can these days), a more apt contemporary saying might be that you can't tell the truth from all the myths that bury it. Nowhere is this more true in my opinion than food history on the internet, where hypotheses get repeated as truth until they become almost set in stone, without even a pebble of truth to have ever backed them up. The humble lemon meringue pie is no exception.

For example, two oft-repeated but under-supported claims are that the first lemon meringue pie was made by Alexander Frehse of Switzerland in the early nineteenth century, or that Dorset botanist Emile Campbell-Browne had his cook make one for the Seventh Earl of Shaftesbury at the Wimborne St Giles Hunt Ball in 1875. Even if there were a menu to prove this, this claim comes later than others that are better supported.

The most interesting example of repetition leading to the perception of truth concerns Mrs Elizabeth Coane Goodfellow, who ran Philadelphia's hippest cake shop for fifty years from 1801 onwards, and later started one of the first cooking schools in the United States. The Goodfellow claim seems to have been less rigorously refuted than the Frehse or Campbell-Browne stories, in part because, although she didn't write down any of her recipes, she was very famous for her coconut cream pie and lemon puddings. When her students, such as Eliza Leslie, recapped her lessons in their own cookbooks, long bows were drawn and, as if by magic, the proposition that Goodfellow invented the lemon meringue pie was made. However, as Patricia Bixler Reber points out on her excellent blog, Researching Food History, Goodfellow's recipe in Leslie's *Seventy-five Receipts, for Pastry, Cakes, and Sweetmeats* (1828) was not only for a lemon pudding rather than a lemon meringue pie, but it also uses whole eggs in the set custard filling. The whole point of a lemon meringue pie is that the curd or custard is made with egg yolks only, so that the leftover whites can be used to make a frosting or meringue topping.

There were other recipes around at that time that looked much more like a lemon meringue pie than Goodfellow's. An English dish called chester pudding was the first of these to make it to print, in J. H. Walsh's *The English Cookery Book* (1859), but Nancy Breedlove's lemon cream pie was probably earlier. Breedlove ran an Illinois hotel that Abraham Lincoln frequented between 1831 and 1856, when he was practising law in the state. He loved Breedlove's pie so much that he asked her for the recipe, and it is said to have been frequently on the menu at the White House after he became president.

Breedlove's recipe wasn't published until 1913 (when she was 80, and the Gettysburg Address was celebrating its fiftieth anniversary), but it is startlingly similar to chester pudding, other than that hers was thickened with corn starch rather than pounded almonds. Both are lemon meringue pies in all but name.

Of course, there had been meringue-topped fruit desserts prior to these. In *A Proper Newe Booke of Cokerye* (1545), there is the delightfully named 'dyschefull of Snowe', while pseudonymous French cookery writer Menon had '*pommes meringuées*' in his 1739 cookbook. However, it does seem certain that the idea of topping a lemon curd or lemon custard pie with meringue and calling it a 'lemon meringue pie' was solidly American.

The world's first published recipe for lemon meringue pie was in the US periodical *American Agriculturalist* in 1869. It's pretty much indistinguishable from a modern recipe. Within ten years, lemon meringue pie was all over the US. I counted nineteen recipes published between 1876 and 1878 in newspapers across the country, and one in a recipe pamphlet from the Maizena corn starch company in 1870.

And we know that the name is even older than this. When commenting on New York's scandalous lemon meringue pie poisonings of 1878, a steward of the Fifth Avenue Hotel told the *New York Herald* that they had been making lemon meringue pies for 'thirty years' without mishap. (For those of you with a CSI bent, the theory of the day was that the pies from Schinkel's Bakery of 40th Street and 8th Avenue had become poisonous when the acid from the lemon juice reacted with the verdigris of poorly cleaned copper pans.)

The first mentions of lemon meringue pie in the press in the UK and Australia come from reports about these deadly poisonings. Mentions of chester pudding, however, appear decades earlier. We know that *The Australasian* newspaper ran a recipe for one in 1866, although the recipe itself no longer exists. Chester pudding is also mentioned as the dessert served at a Wrexham mayoral dinner in 1875.

The bitter truth is that a dish becoming famous is as much about the right name as the right recipe. Would chocolate mousse be the hit it is today if it were called chocolate mayonnaise? Would quiche Lorraine have the same cachet if it were still called *quiche au lard*? And would we get as excited about a lemon meringue pie if it were instead called a chester pudding or a lemon custard pie?

How about if we gave it a South-East Asian twist, with the flavours of lemongrass and makrut lime leaf – what impact would that have on the fame of the dish?

Lemongrass and lime leaf meringue pie *(CONTINUED)*

1 cup (250 ml) pouring cream
4 makrut lime leaves, crushed in your hands
   to break the leaves
2 lemongrass stalks, halved lengthways and
   bruised with a rolling pin
6 eggs
¾ cup (165 g) caster sugar
⅓ cup (80 ml) lime juice
⅓ cup (80 ml) lemon juice

Shortcrust pastry

1½ cups (225 g) plain flour
125 g butter, chopped and chilled
2 tablespoons icing sugar mixture
1 egg yolk
2 tablespoons chilled water

Meringue

4 egg whites
pinch of cream of tartar
1 cup (220 g) caster sugar

Place the cream, lime leaves and lemongrass in a small saucepan over low heat and bring almost to the boil. Remove from the heat and set aside for 30 minutes to infuse and cool.

Whisk the eggs in a jug. Add the cream mixture, sugar, lime juice and lemon juice and whisk until well combined. Cover and place in the fridge for 1 hour to develop the flavours further.

To make the pastry, process the flour, butter and icing sugar in a food processor until the mixture resembles fine breadcrumbs. Add the egg yolk and water, and pulse until the pastry just starts to come together. Wrap in plastic wrap. Place in the fridge for 30 minutes to rest.

Roll the dough out on a lightly floured surface to 4 mm thick. Ease into a 3.5 cm deep, 23 cm (base measurement) fluted tart tin with a removable base. Trim the excess pastry. Stand the tin on a baking tray and place in the fridge for 30 minutes to chill.

Preheat the oven to 200°C (180°C fan-forced). Line the pastry with a large sheet of baking paper and fill with pastry weights or rice. Place the tin on a baking tray and bake for 15 minutes. Remove the paper and weights or rice. Bake for a further 10 minutes or until lightly golden and crisp. Cool slightly.

Reduce the oven to 160°C (140°C fan-forced). Strain the cream mixture into the tart case. Discard the solids. Bake for 30 minutes or until just set. The centre may seem a little wobbly still when tapped. Set aside in the tin for 30 minutes to cool slightly and firm up a little, before transferring to the fridge for 2 hours to chill. Leave in the tin.

Reheat the oven to 200°C (180°C fan-forced). Use electric beaters to whisk the egg whites and cream of tartar in a large clean, dry bowl until stiff peaks form. Gradually add the sugar, 1 tablespoon at a time, beating constantly until the sugar dissolves and the mixture is thick and glossy.

Spoon the meringue over tart. Bake for 5 minutes or until the meringue is golden.

TIP

Once you've mastered this pie, try it with other bolder flavour combinations, such as lime, lemon and strained passionfruit.

Pavlova

SERVES 10 **PREP** 20 minutes (plus cooling) **COOK** 1 hour 30 minutes

Myth
Pavlova is from New Zealand.

My Truth

It has become a source of some national shame that Australia's signature dessert might actually be the creation of our trans-Tasman rivals. Well, I am here to tell you not to worry. We've got this, Australia!

Russian prima ballerina Anna Pavlova toured Australia and New Zealand in 1926, and Australia again in 1929. Both tours were the biggest cultural events in those years. Many New Zealanders will tell you that pavlova was created in 1926 by an unnamed Wellington chef who decorated the dessert with kiwifruit in order to replicate the green roses on Anna Pavlova's tutu. This is based on an unattributed story in a biography of Anna Pavlova written in the 1980s. Emeritus Professor Helen Leach of the University of Otago dismisses this version of events in her book *The Pavlova Story: A slice of New Zealand's culinary history*, as she could find no evidence to support the claim.

Leach's research did, however, find three desserts from this period named after Anna Pavlova. First, a 1926 layered jelly that features neither cream nor meringue, in an NZ recipe pamphlet from the Davis Gelatine Corporation. Then there's the Dunedin version of pavlova, small coffee and walnut meringue kisses, which also sounds nothing like our pav. The closest thing is a 1929 Kiwi recipe for 'pavlova *cake*', where the meringue is split and filled with cream and preserved fruit, like a meringue version of a Victoria sponge.

It was a recipe for one of these meringue cakes published in the *Australian Woman's Mirror* magazine in 1935 that Western Australian chef Bert Sachse was seeking to improve upon when he created his cream and fruit topped dessert and called it simply 'pavlova'. Sachse was head chef at Perth's Esplanade Hotel, where Anna Pavlova had stayed in 1929, and it was his version of the pavlova that went on to become a worldwide hit. Kiwi claims of pavlova ownership hinge upon the fact that the meringue cake in the magazine was credited to an NZ reader, which fails to acknowledge that Bert's creation was a distinct improvement on and development of the recipe.

It's also something of a moot point, because we can show Australia had meringue cakes before they appeared in New Zealand. The recipe most commonly cited as NZ's earliest filled meringue cake was in the 1926 edition of Emily Futter's *Home Cookery for New Zealand*. However, in 1922, a very similar recipe for meringue with cream filling had appeared in *Australian Home Cookery*. That's unsurprising, because Miss Emily Futter was the author of that tome as well! So surely this means the dessert Sachse was inspired by was originally Australian?

I'd also suggest that what makes a pavlova a true pav is that the meringue is *topped* with cream and fruit rather than *filled* with it. That's what made Sachse's pavlova special, and what we love about pavlova today. Here, too, Australia has the first claim, in the 1928 recipe for a 'meringue cream gateau' in NSW's *Molong Express*, which is a pavlova by another name. The meringue is even made with vinegar, like some modern pavs, and then topped with whipped cream and preserved fruit.

So now we have an overwhelming weight of evidence that the first meringue dish simply called 'pavlova' came from Australia; that the first recipe that reads like a modern cream and fruit pavlova came from Australia; and that recipe on which New Zealand's pavlova claims are based seems to have originated in Australia too.

To close the case, I refer to the excellent research of New Zealander Dr Andrew Paul Wood and Australian Annabelle Utrecht, who have made it their quest to shed light on pavlova's origins. Utrecht dismisses the idea that New Zealanders were the first to name a dessert after Anna Pavlova, pointing to a US ice cream bombe called 'strawberries Pavlova' that appears at the turn of the century.

Wood and Utrecht also argue that the meringue cake on which the NZ claim is based is actually a simplified descendant of the layered meringue cakes of the Austrian Habsburg Empire, such as the late-eighteenth-century *spanische windtorte*, or 'Spanish soufflé cake'. This is a nest of crisp meringue filled with fruit, cream and currants or grated chocolate, which is then topped or closed with a sheet of meringue. There's no pillowy marshmallow centre, however, and no use of vinegar or cornflour.

In the nineteenth century, descendants of that Austrian layered soufflé cake – like Germany's *schaum torte* (aka foam cake) and *baiser torte* (aka kiss cake) – spread around the world with migration. German migrants who moved to the American Midwest in the mid-1800s took the *schaum* cake with them, and mentions pop up in German-language US newspapers of the time, like in *Die Freie Presse für Texas* ('The free press for Texas') in 1884.

Is now the time to note that the parents of Bernard Herbert Francis (aka Bert) Sachse emigrated from Tschausdorf, Prussia, around 1855? The first recipe for *schaum torte* in Australia appears in the Adelaide *Mail* in 1935, the same year that Bert created his pavlova in Perth. It instructs for the upper crust of the meringue to be broken off before the void inside is filled with fruit, and *then* the cream, with the broken crust used as garnish.

Pavlova *(CONTINUED)*

Now, I'd love to say that this filling of the meringue and adding the fruit first is enough to class the *shaum torte* as mere inspiration for our Molong meringue cream gateau, and I would, had I not discovered a recipe for 'German Dessert' in a May 1913 edition of the *Ogden Standard* from the US state of Utah. This is a large meringue made with vinegar and topped with crushed fruit and cream. So, it seems that we'll have to share the pavlova honours with the United States – especially as the first recipes for adding cornflour to meringues also came from the US, in corn starch manufacturers' recipe booklets of the 1860s.

Barring the discovery of new evidence that would lead to this case being reopened, I'm happy to stand behind the claim that the first true pavlova was made by Bert Sachse, even if it was based on a culinary idea that originally came from Germany or the US.

6 egg whites, at room temperature
½ teaspoon cream of tartar
1½ cups (330 g) caster sugar
1 teaspoon vanilla extract
1½ cups (375 ml) thickened cream
5 kiwifruit, peeled, sliced (see Tip)

Preheat the oven to 150°C (130°C fan-forced). Draw a 22 cm circle on a piece of baking paper. Turn the paper pencil-side down onto a large baking tray.

Use electric beaters (preferably a stand mixer so it's easy to add the sugar) to whisk the egg whites and cream of tartar in a large clean, dry bowl until firm peaks form. Gradually add the sugar, 1 tablespoon at a time, beating constantly, until the sugar dissolves and the mixture is thick and glossy. When the meringue is glossy and you can rub a little between your fingers without feeling the grain of the sugar, beat in the vanilla.

Spoon the meringue mixture onto the paper, using the drawn circle as a guide to make a neat round. Use a flat-bladed knife to shape the sides of the meringue to make furrows by sweeping upwards.

Bake for 10 minutes, then reduce the oven temperature to 110°C (90°C fan-forced). Bake for a further 1 hour 20 minutes or until the meringue is crisp and dry. Turn the oven off. Leave the pavlova in the oven, with the door closed, to cool completely.

Use electric beaters to whisk the cream in a bowl until firm peaks form. Top the pavlova with the cream and heaps of kiwifruit. We can't take everything from our Kiwi friends.

Yes, you can top the pav with strawberries, raspberries, pitted cherries, pith-free orange segments spritzed with rosewater, and so on – or, use three mangoes and two passionfruit, if you want to be parochially Aussie. You could even use Chinese gooseberries – which is what kiwifruit used to be called in English before New Zealanders hijacked them too!

Food nerd fact

As its archaic name suggests, the Chinese gooseberry finds its root in China. Its original name in Chinese, *mihoutao* – meaning 'macaque fruit' – refers to the monkeys' love for it, according to the *Compendium of Materia Medica*, a sixteenth-century Chinese medical encyclopedia by Li Shizhen. The earliest mention of the fruit dates back to the Song dynasty in the twelfth century.

Pisang goreng

SERVES 6 **PREP** 20 minutes (plus overnight freezing) **COOK** 15 minutes

Myth

Sugar bananas are the best bananas to use for *pisang goreng*.

My Truth

I will gladly be the first to acknowledge that sugar bananas are one of the traditional varieties to use for this classic Indonesian dessert. They are straighter than the Cavendish bananas we usually see in Australian supermarkets these days, which might give them an aesthetic edge and make them easier to fit in the fryer, but I actually prefer the flavour of the bog-standard ones for this dish.

And so, if we are doing an Aussie version of this dish, which is a favourite for a mid-morning snack or afternoon smoko in its homeland of Indonesia, then let's keep it nice and down to earth.

After all, if we wanted to get *really* purist we'd be tracking down soft, fragrant and gently acidic Indonesian *pisang raja* bananas for this dish, but that would make it time-consuming and rather more pricey for what is traditionally a cheap street snack!

It isn't just fried bananas that Indonesians love – they are keen on all their fritters and crackers – but it might be a surprise to learn that it was the Portuguese who introduced fried snacks to the region after they colonised Malacca in 1511. With the forts and trading posts that they set up in the sixteenth century came the Portuguese love of fried foods. These were reinterpreted with local ingredients but inspired by the fried treats that would be prepared after the fasting and penance of Ember Days of the Catholic Church, which marked the changing of the four seasons, or the *quatuor tempora*. Perhaps unsurprisingly, these seasonal observances were initially timed to match closely with the old pagan solstice feasts.

(Interestingly, in Japan, where Portuguese missionaries and traders first started visiting in 1543 and also established trading posts in the late sixteenth century, this holy-day frying not only inspired the Japanese dish of tempura but also gives it its name.)

I think these bananas need ice cream, and while shop-bought vanilla or chocolate will certainly do, I heartily suggest making a batch of your own cheat's coconut soft-serve ice cream the day before. This is based on an old country Australian hack of freezing condensed milk and cream and then whipping them together.

1 cup (200 g) rice flour
½ cup (75 g) plain flour
2 tablespoons custard powder
1 teaspoon baking powder
½ teaspoon sea salt
1⅓ cups (330 ml) ice-cold water
8 firm lady finger, sugar or regular bananas,
   peeled and halved lengthways
peanut or vegetable oil, for frying
shredded coconut, toasted, to serve
golden syrup, to serve

Soft serve coconut ice cream

600 ml thickened cream
395 g can condensed milk
¾ cup (185 ml) coconut cream, chilled well

To make the ice cream, use electric beaters to beat the thickened cream in a bowl until soft peaks form. Add the condensed milk and coconut cream and beat until the mixture thickens and starts to hold its shape. Place in an airtight container and freeze for at least 8 hours or overnight.

To make the batter, combine the rice flour, plain flour, custard powder, baking powder and salt in a large bowl. Make a well in the centre. Add the water and use a balloon whisk or fork to whisk until well combined.

Add enough oil to a saucepan to come halfway up the side. Heat over medium–high heat until the oil reaches 190°C on a cook's thermometer (or until a cube of bread turns golden in 10 seconds after being added to the oil).

Working in batches, dip the banana in the batter and then carefully lower into the oil. Cook, turning once during cooking, for 2–3 minutes or until golden brown. Transfer to a tray lined with paper towel to drain.

Serve the banana fritters with scoops of the ice cream. Sprinkle with the coconut and drizzle over the golden syrup.

Tiramisu

SERVES 6 **PREP** 20 minutes (plus overnight chilling) **COOK** 20 minutes

Myth

Tiramisu is just a coffee-flavoured version of an English trifle.

My Truth

While we know that the idea of soaked sponge cake was introduced to England from Spain in the fifteenth century (see p. 275 and p. 324), the English like to point to their own Gervase Markham and his recipe for 'bisket-bread' as proof that they were making the sponge fingers so essential for a tiramisu back in the seventeenth century.

The recipe in his 1615 book *The English Huswife* lays claim to being the first sponge cake recipe written in English, but to me it reads more like sponge fingers or savoiardi. My research showed that Markham probably copied his biscuit bread recipe anyway. While debunking another false sponge-creation claim – that of Giobatta, a pastry chef who was part of a Genovese delegation to the court of Ferdinand VI in Madrid in 1749 – I discovered a very similar (if slightly lower and slower cooked) recipe for the ladyfinger, or savoiardi, biscuits that were the signature treat of the Duchy of Savoy in what is now Milan. Savoy was on Genoa's northern border, and these biscuits had been made since the late fifteenth century, so Giobatta would have known all about them in the eighteenth century. Markham too!

What's interesting is that, with the savoiardi biscuits on hand and the technique of whipping eggs with sugar over a bain-marie to make a zabaione (which is the other essential component of tiramisu) available since the fifteenth century, by the sixteenth century, everything was in place to make a tiramisu except the flavourings, but tiramisu didn't become popular until the 1980s.

While we don't have any tiramisu recipes or mentions before the twentieth century, we do have a number of trifle-like desserts popping up, including one that was created for Cosimo de' Medici in Siena in the seventeenth century, and Pellegrino Artusi's recipe for *dolce Torino* in his seminal cookbook *La scienza in cucina e l'arte di mangiar bene* ('Science in the Kitchen and the Art of Eating Well', 1891). This is a lurid cake-like trifle of sponge fingers soaked in a crimson spiced liqueur called *alkermes* and layered with a chocolate butter cream. His *sformato di savoiardi con lo zabaione* was closer to being a true precursor of tiramisu, but here the biscuits were dunked in marsala fortified wine, covered in an uncooked custard and baked in a mould, rather than set in the fridge with a warm, cooked zabaione. (This is in part because refrigerators for the home were not invented until 1913, and only became common in the 1920s and 1930s.)

It is perhaps worth noting here that savoiardi are traditionally served with a glass of warm zabaione. In the Veneto, they use the local dialect word *sbatudin* for these egg yolks beaten over heat with sugar. This was served as a pick-me-up to sick children and new mothers, as well as a fortifying pre-wedding night treat for newlyweds. Interestingly, in the twentieth century, the trend of adding a shot of coffee to your *sbatudin* emerged, but by this time the idea that zabaione and *sbatudin* were '*tirami su*' – Italian for 'pull me up' – was already firmly established.

It was in the north-east of Italy that the true tiramisu was born. In fact, the first recipe for tiramisu appears in Giovanni Capnist's *I Dolci del Veneto* ('The Desserts of Veneto') in 1983, although Capnist admits that this rather wonderful combination of whipped zabaione, mascarpone and coffee was on restaurant menus in Treviso well before the book's publication.

A plethora of chefs and bakers from Treviso claim to have invented tiramisu in the 1960s, but one claim stands out to me as the most interesting. In the early 1960s, a woman known locally by some as the 'true mother of tiramisu', Speranza Garatti, had a dessert of savoiardi set in a glass with mascarpone cream on her menu. It was called *coppette imperiale*, and in 1973 the venerable Italian magazine *La Cucina Italiana* credited Garatti with the creation of tiramisu, even if the flavourings and the name weren't yet in place.

Garatti claimed to have taught Ado Campeol, owner of Le Beccherie, how to make it. It was Ado who changed the name to tiramisu, possibly after the restorative shot of *sbatudin* that was served to patrons at Treviso's local brothels, or inspired by a dessert from the Friulian town of San Canzian d'Isonzo, 100 kilometres to the east, near Trieste.

Here we find the missing link between Artusi's savoiardi desserts and the tiramisu from Treviso that's a worldwide hit today. In the 1930s, chef Mario Cosolo had a glass of marsala-soaked sponge, chocolate *crémeux* and a marsala zabaione on the menu at his Trattoria al Vetturino. This *coppa vetturino* was free of both mascarpone and coffee – and the presence of any marsala would also be frowned upon in Treviso – but in a 1950 poster depicting Mario and his dessert creation, it is referred to as '*tirime su*', as the local dialect has it. His daughter says the name changed to this around 1945.

Ado Campeol's wife, Alba, disputed Speranza Garatti's story, saying that she invented the dish, inspired by the *sbatudin* her mother-in-law gave her after the birth of one of her children. She spiked the foam with coffee and then developed this into a dish with Le Beccherie chef Roberto Linguanotto. This is a tale that Linguanotto also confirmed, and it leaves me feeling that they all contributed to the creation of a true Italian dessert that's an awfully long way from English trifle and that garish Italian reinvention, *zuppa inglese*.

Tiramisu (CONTINUED)

¾ cup (185 ml) freshly brewed espresso
   coffee, cooled
1 cup (250 ml) Frangelico
3 egg yolks
⅓ cup (75 g) caster sugar
250 g mascarpone
½ cup (125 ml) thickened cream
400 ml double cream
200 g packet thin savoiardi biscuits (24
   biscuits minimum)
1 tablespoon dark cocoa powder, sifted

Hazelnut praline dust

¾ cup (105 g) hazelnut kernels
½ cup (110 g) caster sugar
¼ cup (60 ml) water

Line an 11 cm × 21 cm × 6 cm deep loaf pan with baking paper, allowing the two long sides to overhang.

Combine the espresso and Frangelico in a bowl.

Use a balloon whisk to whisk together the egg yolks and sugar in a heatproof bowl over a saucepan of simmering water (making sure the bowl doesn't touch the water). Whisk continuously for 3–4 minutes or until the mixture is thick and pale. Remove from the heat and keep whisking for a further 1–2 minutes or until the mixture cools.

Add the mascarpone to the egg mixture and whisk until well combined and the mixture starts to thicken and hold its shape.

Use electric beaters to beat the thickened cream and ½ cup (125 ml) of the double cream in a bowl until firm peaks form. Gently fold the whipped cream into the mascarpone mixture. Set aside.

Dip 8 biscuits in the coffee mixture and place lengthways in the prepared pan in two rows of four. Top with half the mascarpone mixture. Dust with 1 teaspoon of the cocoa powder. Dip half the remaining biscuits in the remaining coffee mixture and place on top. Top with the remaining mascarpone mixture and another teaspoon of cocoa powder. Dip the remaining biscuits in the remaining coffee and place on top. Cover with plastic wrap and place in the fridge for at least 6 hours or overnight to set.

To start on the praline, preheat the oven to 180°C (160°C fan-forced). Line a baking tray with baking paper. Place the hazelnuts on the tray. Bake for 8 minutes or until roasted and the skins are starting to crackle off. Place the hazelnuts in a clean tea towel and rub to remove the skins. Place the skinned hazelnuts back on the tray.

Combine the sugar and water in a small saucepan and stir over low heat until the sugar dissolves. Increase the heat to medium and bring to the boil. Simmer for 5–8 minutes or until the syrup becomes a rich golden colour. Pour over the hazelnuts on the tray and leave to set.

Break up half the praline, then place in a food processor and process until coarse crumbs form. Break the remaining praline into shards.

Use a balloon whisk to whisk the remaining double cream in a bowl until soft peaks form (do not overbeat). Use the paper to lift the tiramisu from the pan onto a serving plate. Sprinkle with the remaining cocoa powder. Top with the whipped cream, sprinkle with the crushed praline and serve with the praline shards.

Pouding chômeur

SERVES 6 **PREP** 20 minutes (plus 10 minutes cooling) **COOK** 35 minutes

CLASSIC

Myth

The greatest dish to come out of Canada is poutine.

My Truth

Now, while I do love that grandfather of every plate of loaded fries you've ever enjoyed, the cuisine of Canada is much more than just poutine. What about delicious butter tarts and the Nanaimo bar, for starters? Canadian cuisine knows how to transform simple components into something special, and how to champion the best ingredients raised, grown or harvested locally. For my money, it is *pouding chômeur* that is exemplary of this cuisine that loves being as flavourful as it is frugal.

During the Great Depression, unemployment in Canada hit 30 per cent and everyone needed something cheap and delicious to cheer them up. Thank heavens then for the Quebec production line workers who, in 1929, first made this 'unemployed pudding' (as the name translates). Originally it was made with stale bread and a brown sugar butterscotch, but by 1939 economic conditions had improved and bakers were using a dollop of buttery cake batter and locally harvested maple syrup instead. Quebec is, after all, at the centre of Canada's maple syrup industry.

The Slow Food Foundation has suggested the recipe for *pouding chômeur* was based on a dessert created by Georgianna Falardeau to brighten the dark days after the crash. She was married to the notoriously unpredictable conservative mayor of Montreal, who opposed conscription and built public washrooms for the unemployed during the Depression. Quite how the recipe became so closely associated with Quebec is not explained.

Similarly unsupported claims are made about *pouding chômeur* being based on *cachettes aux petits fruits*, a sponge-topped French Canadian stewed berry dessert, but with brown sugar or maple syrup replacing the berries in winter. I should note, however, that pudding recipes had taken up numerous pages in Canadian cookbooks of the late nineteenth and early twentieth centuries, and even featured in the long extended title of the first cookbook written and published in Quebec, *La cuisinière Canadienne* ('The Canadian Cook', 1840).

Perhaps ironically, given its name, over the years *pouding chômeur* has become a symbol of Canadian working-class unity, sometimes even being served at political demonstrations as a potent and tasty symbol of the worker as much as the unemployed. So, if you like, think of baking these tasty puddings as a little act of sedition.

---

melted butter, for greasing
1½ cups (225 g) plain flour
1 teaspoon baking powder
½ teaspoon sea salt
125 g butter, chopped, at room temperature
⅔ cup (150 g) caster sugar
1 egg
⅔ cup (125 ml) milk
pecans, toasted and coarsely chopped,
    to serve
thickened cream, to serve

Caramel syrup

50 g butter
1 cup (220 g) dark brown sugar
1 cup (250 ml) maple syrup, plus extra to
    serve (optional)
½ cup (125 ml) warm water
1 vanilla bean, split lengthways

Preheat the oven to 180°C (160°C fan-forced). Grease the base and sides of six 200 ml dariole moulds or a Texas 6-cup muffin pan. Line the bases with little rounds of baking paper.

To make the caramel syrup, combine the butter, brown sugar and maple syrup in a small saucepan. Cook, stirring, over medium heat until the sugar dissolves. Add the water. Use a small sharp knife to scrape the seeds from the vanilla bean into the pan, and add the vanilla bean as well. Bring to the boil and cook for 3–4 minutes or until it reduces slightly. Don't overcook or else you risk ending up with maple taffy! Remove the vanilla bean from the syrup.

Spoon 2 tablespoons of the caramel syrup into each mould. Stand the moulds on a baking tray and place in the fridge for 10 minutes to chill.

While the caramel chills, sift the flour, baking powder and salt into a bowl. Set aside. In a separate bowl, use electric beaters to beat the butter and caster sugar until pale and creamy. Add the egg and beat well. Gradually fold in a little of the flour mixture, then stir in a little milk. Repeat this process until all the flour mixture and milk is added and a smooth batter forms.

Divide the batter among the moulds. Bake for 25 minutes or until golden and a skewer inserted in the centre of one comes out clean. Set aside for 5 minutes to cool slightly before inverting onto serving plates.

Serve the puddings warm, sprinkled with the pecans and drizzled with the remaining caramel and cream. If you *really* love maple syrup, add a drizzle of that too.

Coconut sticky rice with mango

SERVES 4 **PREP** 10 minutes (plus overnight soaking) **COOK** 35 minutes

Myth
This dish is delicious anytime.

My Truth
This dessert is truly a Thai obsession, no doubt thanks to the fact that the mango has a spiritual dimension to match its supreme tastiness. The fruit made it to Thailand and Malaysia with Buddhist monks in the fourth century BC after first being domesticated about 1500 years earlier in an area covering eastern India, Bangladesh and Myanmar. Mangoes had a special significance to those monks because Gautama Buddha's spiritual awakening was prompted by a mango tree.

Mangoes became so ensconced in Thailand that the first known example of written Thai script, which was carved on a stone stele in 1292, recorded how the king at the time, Ramkhamhaeng (1279–1298), had planted mango trees across his capital and in the temples.

By 1884 there were one hundred types of mango growing in the kingdom. This has grown to two hundred cultivars today, with names like the monitor lizard egg mango, the lady's eyebrow mango and the husband parting from wife mango. Buddhism has also thrived. It is still practised by 94 per cent of the population in Thailand.

The growth in the popularity of mango sticky rice to reach national dish status is harder to trace, but it seems to have taken place as the love of the country's perennial favourite, the forest mango (which was sucked rather than cut), waned in favour of more fleshy, cuttable mangoes. In the 1940s there was a burst of mango sticky rice shops popping up in Bangkok. Some, like Boonsap Desserts and Kor Panich, which opened in 1947, are still operating today, such is the popularity of the dish.

Do try this dish with a little chilli, toasted sesame seeds, crispy yellow mung beans or with the rice flavoured with jasmine blossoms, but remember this dish is at its most delicious when your choice of mango is in season.

1¼ cups (250 g) glutinous rice
400 ml can coconut milk
2 pandan leaves, twisted and tied in a knot
½ cup (110 g) caster sugar
½ teaspoon sea salt
2 teaspoons rice flour
3 mangoes, cheeks removed, peeled and thinly sliced (see Tip)
black sesame seeds, for sprinkling

TIP

Use the ripest, best tree-ripened mangoes you can find. This may be worth an adventure out to your local Asian markets or farmers' market.

Place the rice in a sieve and hold under cold running water until the water runs clear. Transfer to a large bowl and cover with plenty of cold water. Cover the bowl with a tea towel. Set aside at room temperature for at least 6 hours or overnight to soak.

Line a steamer with muslin or cheesecloth (if your steamer has small holes which the rice won't go through, you can skip lining it). Drain the rice and transfer to the steamer. Spread out evenly over the muslin or cheesecloth. Place the steamer over a saucepan of simmering water. Cover and steam for 30 minutes or until the rice is just tender but still firm to the bite.

While the rice steams, place the coconut milk, pandan leaves, sugar and salt in a saucepan over medium heat. Cook, stirring, for 3–4 minutes or until the sugar dissolves and the coconut milk is almost to the boil (but do not, please, boil).

Transfer the rice to a large bowl. Remove the pandan leaves from the milk mixture. Pour ½ cup (125 ml) of the milk mixture into a bowl and reserve. Add the remaining milk mixture to the rice and stir to combine. Cover with the tea towel again and set aside, without stirring, for 10 minutes or until the liquid is absorbed.

While the rice is set aside, add the rice flour to the reserved milk mixture. Stir until well combined. Microwave on high, stirring every 30 seconds, for 2 minutes or until the mixture thickens.

Use a small bowl or ramekin to spoon the rice into mounds on serving plates. Top with the sliced mango. Drizzle with the thickened milk mixture and sprinkle with the sesame seeds.

Baking

Pastéis de nata

MAKES 18 **PREP** 30 minutes (plus 15 minutes chilling) **COOK** 30 minutes

Myth
Wherever Portuguese missionaries went they introduced chillies, cashews and Portuguese custard tarts.

My Truth
The first two of these great gifts may be true, and while you'll certainly find versions of Portuguese custard tarts in Jakarta, Macau and Brazil, all places that the missionaries went, these came well after the chilli and the cashews had been introduced by monks and merchants in the sixteenth century.

The eventual arrival of *pastéis de nata* was a later part of Portugal's colonial and trading expansion, for, while the recipe for these crispy, creamy custard delights was based on venerable principles, they only really appear in their own right in the eighteenth century.

Pastries and baking are a religion in Portugal, and the country's reputation as a great baking nation is also based on religion. This Catholic country had loads of convents and rich churches, and all of these required nuns' white wimples and other liturgical vestments to be starched regularly. The best way to do this without staining was to use egg whites – lots and lots of egg whites. Even more egg whites were required to stick gold leaf to religious statues and gild the halos of saints in paintings, as well as to clarify the wine used for communion. This left the nunneries and monasteries with the problem of what to do with all the remaining egg yolks in such a warm climate. The answer was to bake, and a whole tradition of baked specialities from religious houses ensued.

There is a dizzying variety of egg-yolk-based pastries around Portugal, but it is the little tarts baked by Hieronymite monks at the very grand Mosteiro dos Jerónimos that have taken centre stage. These were so well regarded that affluent citizens of Lisbon would take a riverboat down the Tagus to the monastery in the parish of Saint Mary of Bethlehem (aka Belém) for their fix.

I'm indebted to my friend, Portuguese baking goddess Mafalda Carvalho Agante, who taught me all this as well as the recipe for these *pastéis de nata*. On a trip to Lisbon, she indulged me in such sugar-dusted pastry nerdery as introducing me to many of those other sweet egg-yolk baked delights, known locally as *doces conventuais* ('convent sweets'), like seventeenth-century *pão de ló de Alfeizerão* or *pão de Ovar* (a stickier, creamier version, and an intentionally undercooked version of the older sixteenth-century sponge-like *pão de ló*), *ovos moles* and *pastéis de Tentúgal*.

We also visited the Mosteiro dos Jerónimos bakery and shop in Belém. After a period of religious oppression in post-Napoleonic times (around 1820), the monks sold the recipe to the sugarcane refinery that used to supply them. So, since 1837, the custard tarts were no longer baked by monks. I also watched *pastéis de nata* come straight from the oven at major tart rivals Manteigaria in the city. It was here that I picked up the thumb-pressure trick employed in this recipe, which encourages the frilly layers of toasty edge required for a perfect Portuguese custard tart.

The last question is whether to enjoy the tarts you bake at room temperature or still a little warm from the oven. I'll tell you my feelings on this at the end of the recipe that follows!

Pastéis de nata (CONTINUED)

melted butter, for greasing
1 large sheet (375 g) frozen butter puff pastry
  (we used Carême brand), just thawed
2 cups (500 ml) milk
1 lemon, zest peeled into strips
1 cinnamon stick
¼ cup (35 g) plain flour
7 egg yolks
1 cup (220 g) caster sugar
100 ml water
icing sugar, to dust
ground cinnamon, to dust (optional)

Grease a large baking tray and line with baking paper. Grease the bases and sides of eighteen ⅓ cup (80 ml) capacity muffin holes with melted butter.

With the long edge facing you, roll up the pastry sheet lengthways into a tight log. If the pastry gets too soft, place on a tray and chill until firm enough to handle.

Cut eighteen 2 cm thick slices from the pastry roll and place on the lined tray. Place in the fridge for 10–15 minutes or until firm.

Working with 1 pastry slice at a time, dip your fingers in water to prevent sticking and press the dough out on a clean surface to a rough 8 cm disc. Ease the disc into a hole on the muffin pan. Now it is all about your thumbs. Place them in the centre of the disc and gently press the pastry over the base, using quick tapping movements. Slowly working outwards, press the pastry from the centre of the base up the side, coming about 5 mm above the edge of the pan (the pastry will be very thin at the base, which is fine – just make sure there are no holes). You want the base to be thin and the edge of the pastry disc to be facing upwards at the edge around the top of the tart shell. This is how you get those crispy, frilly edges on a great *pastéi de nata*. Place in the fridge until needed.

Preheat the oven to 240°C (220°C fan-forced). Place a large baking tray on the top shelf of the oven.

Combine the milk, lemon zest and cinnamon stick in a large saucepan over medium–high heat and bring to the boil. Remove the lemon zest and cinnamon stick, and discard.

Transfer one-third of the hot milk mixture to a bowl and gradually add the flour, whisking until smooth and combined. Set aside.

Whisk the egg yolks in a heatproof bowl. Gradually add the remaining hot milk, whisking until well combined. Whisk in the flour mixture. Strain through a fine sieve into a jug and set aside.

Combine the sugar and water in a very clean heavy-based saucepan over medium heat. Swirl the pan gently to dissolve the sugar. Once dissolved, bring the mixture to 108°C on a sugar thermometer. Gradually whisk the syrup into the egg mixture.

Pour the egg mixture among the pastry cases. You want them to be about three-quarters full. Bake for 20–25 minutes or until just set and blackened in patches. The filling will swell and rise a lot during cooking, but then deflate again.

Remove from the oven and cool slightly. Use a flat-bladed knife to gently prise the tarts from the pan and transfer to a wire rack to cool. Dust with icing sugar and cinnamon, if desired. I like to eat these when they are still a little warm and, somewhat controversially, without any cinnamon sugar.

Carrot cake

SERVES 8 **PREP** 30 minutes (plus cooling) **COOK** 55 minutes

Myth
Carrot cake is a product of the 1970s.

My Truth
While using vegetables like carrot, zucchini and beetroot in cakes is seen as a 1970s thing, or perhaps something attached to the ration-book years of World War II, the roots of veg-based desserts go back much further.

There is a recipe for sweet carrot pudding in the earliest known Arabic cookbook, *Kitab al-Tabikh* (the full title of which translates to 'The Book of Cookery Preparing Salubrious Foods and Delectable Dishes Extracted from Medical Books and Told by Proficient Cooks and the Wise'). Abu Muhammad al-Muthaffar ibn Nasr ibn Sayyār al-Warrāq, who wrote this tome in Baghdad around 950 AD, recommends slicing tender carrots and cooking them down with honey and pistachio oil into what sounds like an early version of carrot halva, the Punjab's famous sweet, which arrived in India with the influx of chefs from Persia in the fifteenth and sixteenth centuries.

It should be noted that it was in the tenth century that less-woody purple and red carrots first arrived in Europe from Afghanistan. Prior to that, carrots were gnarly roots grown largely for seeds or leaves, and were a long, long way from the orange carrots of today, which were raised by Dutch horticulturalists in the seventeenth century.

Carrot puddings made it back to England after the Crusades. John Brand, cook to England's much-maligned King John in the thirteenth century, was famous for adding eggs to his carrot puddings, and these morphed into sweet carrot custard tarts. The only recipe I can find for these 'carrett puddings' is made with pumpkin, but after pumpkin made it over the Atlantic in the sixteenth century, it was often substituted into traditional carrot recipes. (If you have an original sixteenth-century recipe or earlier that uses carrot, please DM me!)

In the seventeenth century we edge towards the creation of carrot cake with a frittata-like carrot pudding from Giles Rose (in 1682), chef to Charles II of England, and a carrot custard thickened with bread, cream and eggs from plant-based-eating pioneer John Evelyn in his *Acetaria: A Discourse of Sallets (1699)*. A similar custard appears in a puff pastry tart in Hannah Glasse's *The Art of Cookery* (1747).

It's in the emerging nation of the United States that carrot cake as we would recognise it finally appears. The first recorded mention is actually from an account of George Washington's farewell meal with his officers from the Continental Army at the Queen's Head Tavern (now called Fraunces Tavern) in lower Manhattan in December 1783. The carrot tea cake served that day was not as moist and fluffy as modern versions, but it was definitely a cake. It used eggs, butter, sugar, cinnamon, nutmeg, mashed cooked carrots and flour, which made for a dense, un-iced cake that needed lots of whipped cream. No record was made of Washington's reaction to the cake, but the tavern's owner, Samuel Fraunces, would subsequently be invited to be steward of his presidential household, so it can't have been terrible.

After that first mention in New York, carrot cake pops up sporadically, in *L'Art du Cuisinier* (1814) as a *gateau de carrottes*, in a French cookbook published in England in 1827 and as a *rübelitorte* in an 1892 manual from a housekeeping school in Kaiseraugst, Switzerland. Recipes from the US are found in *The 20th Century Bride's Cook Book* (1929) and the *Chicago Daily News Cook Book* (1930). Judging by a slew of responses to a request for carrot cake recipes in a 1932 edition of the *Maryborough Chronicle*, using carrot in cakes, often fruit cakes, was already well established in Queensland.

All of these carrot cakes are without any cream cheese icing, which was added around the same time that carrot cakes hit the mainstream in the United States, in the 1960s – the first mention of this icing I can find is in a reader's letter to the *Washington Post* in 1964.

If there's any major advance in the carrot cake presented here, it is to increase the amount of icing and adding the toffee pecans. Otherwise, one bite should spark mental images of 1970s bell-bottoms, gold lamé tights and crimplene pants suits in a nice shade of taupe. Or, knowing the history of the dish, maybe now it will be more likely to inspire images from *Hamilton*.

Carrot cake (CONTINUED)

melted butter, to grease
¾ cup (105 g) raisins, coarsely chopped
½ cup (125 ml) hot black tea
1¼ cups (185 g) self-raising flour
1 cup (150 g) plain flour
1 teaspoon ground cinnamon
1 teaspoon mixed spice
½ teaspoon bicarbonate of soda
1 cup (220 g) brown sugar
2½ cups (600 g) coarsely grated carrot
¾ cup (90 g) pecans, coarsely chopped
½ cup (125 ml) vegetable oil
4 eggs, lightly whisked

Maple pecans

½ cup (60 g) pecans
2 tablespoons maple syrup
1 teaspoon sea salt

Cream cheese frosting

500 g cream cheese, chopped, at room
   temperature
200 g butter, chopped, at room temperature
3½ cups (560 g) icing sugar mixture
2 teaspoons vanilla extract

Preheat the oven to 180°C (160°C fan-forced). Grease two 20 cm (base measurement) round cake pans with melted butter. Line the bases with baking paper.

Place the raisins in a heatproof bowl and pour over the hot tea. Set aside for 15 minutes to soak and cool.

Sift the flours, cinnamon, mixed spice and bicarbonate of soda in a large bowl and stir in the sugar. Add the carrot and pecans and stir until combined. Make a well in the centre. Add the oil and eggs to the flour mixture and stir to combine. Add the raisins and tea liquid, and mix until well combined. Pour evenly among the prepared pans.

Bake for 30–40 minutes or until a skewer inserted into the centre of the cakes comes out clean. Set aside in the pans for 5 minutes to cool slightly before transferring to a wire rack to cool completely.

For the maple pecans, increase the oven temperature to 200°C (180°C fan-forced). Line a baking tray with baking paper. Place the pecans on the tray in a single layer and drizzle with the maple syrup. Toss a little, then lay them all flat with a little bit of space between them (this allows maple syrup shards to form and attach to the pecans). Bake for 15 minutes or until toasted and caramelised. Remove from the oven and while hot, sprinkle with salt. Set aside for 15 minutes to cool completely.

To make the frosting, use electric beaters to beat the cream cheese and butter in a bowl until well combined. Add the icing sugar and vanilla and beat until pale and creamy. (Note that you won't need all of the cream cheese frosting to ice the cake – there is extra to serve on the side!)

Place one carrot cake on a serving platter. Top with a good layer of frosting. Top with the remaining cake and another good layer of frosting. Carefully lift the pecans off the tray with the maple shards attached and decorate the cake.

Banana bread with bananas foster, butterscotch sauce and roasted skim milk powder crumbs

SERVES 6 (with banana bread left over) **PREP** 30 minutes (plus cooling) **COOK** 1 hour 10 minutes

Myth

Banana bread is one of those magnificent recipes like minestrone, *pain perdu* or shepherd's pie that was invented solely as a way to use up leftovers.

My Truth

In Australia, there were two big food trends associated with the year 2020: a sudden boom in sourdough baking, and banana bread being the year's most-searched recipe. With the economy on a downswing and money tight, it seems cooks were looking for a way to use the proportion of the 16 kilograms per person of bananas Aussie shoppers buy each year that was going brown.

It has been suggested by some historians that the first banana bread was similarly invented in the face of the hard times of the Great Depression. This sounds like it makes sense, but the truth is that the increased availability of baking powder and pushes by both banana importers and baking companies to maintain sales in the face of the recession had more of an impact than any no-waste ethos.

Chemical leavening agents like baking powder were more widely available in the 1930s, but it had also been around much earlier. Pearl-ash, as alkaline baking soda was originally called, had been discovered in the United States and patented by Samuel Hopkins in 1790 (the first patent in US history), and it featured in baking recipes in the first printed American cookbook, Amelia Simmons's *American Cookery* (1796). There were no banana bread recipes in the book, however, because the first record of bananas making it to the US was in 1870, when Captain Lorenzo Baker arrived in Jersey harbour with a load he'd purchased in Jamaica. Baker would go on to establish the Boston Fruit Company in 1885, just as Minor Cooper Keith's Costa Rica plantations started exporting bananas to the US. Baker and Keith would then go on to form the United Fruit Company in 1899.

By the start of the twentieth century, figures show that banana sales were booming, and Baker and Keith controlled almost 75 per cent of the market. Banana prices had already dropped to a level that allowed them to become an everyday, everyone food. Banana recipes had also started to proliferate. There is a cake studded with banana and tamarind in Sarah Tyson Rorer's 1902 cookbook, a banana pudding recipe in Mary Harris Frazer's *Kentucky Receipt Book* (1903), and the banana split was invented in 1904 to cash in on the trends of soda shops and ice cream.

The first true banana bread recipe appeared in *My New Better Homes and Gardens Cook Book* (1930), but this is quickly followed by other recipes using baking powder and mashed banana to make a cake or loaf, including in *The New Banana* from the United Fruit Company (1931) and *Balanced Recipes* (1933) from the Pillsbury Flour Mills Company.

The United Fruit Company's presence on this list is worth noting because, by 1929, this mega banana importer and prototype multinational corporation (think the Amazon or Apple of its day) had both a home economics department, writing recipes to help push banana sales, and an education department, helping drive banana demand through pro-banana school programs.

The United Fruit Company is further worth noting because, as the UK's *Financial Times* put it in 2007, 'United Fruit gave the world not just bananas, but also "banana republics".' The company was implicated in deforestation, a coup in Honduras, the deposing of a Guatemalan president who was hostile to the company and pushing agrarian reforms, and the 1928 shooting of Colombian workers who were striking for better conditions by a Colombian army regiment. When they were arrested for the shooting, some of the soldiers had fistfuls of US dollars in their pockets, which had allegedly come from United Fruit's agents. Ships from United Fruit's fleet of refrigerated transport vessels were even involved in the Bay of Pigs Invasion in Cuba in 1961!

The base banana bread recipe here differs little from these 1930s originals, but we've turned it into a drizzle cake by using banana's best friend, rum. We've also added some rum-flambéed bananas in the style of the 1951 recipe for bananas foster. Incidentally, this is another recipe developed specifically to sell bananas, by Brennan's Restaurant in New Orleans. Owner Owen Brennan asked his chef to come up with a hit dessert using bananas, as Brennan's brother's fruit and veg import business, Brennan's Processed Potato Company, had a surplus of bananas it needed to shift. The recipe helped.

Banana bread with bananas foster (CONTINUED)

80 g butter, melted, plus extra for greasing
2 cups (300 g) self-raising flour
1 teaspoon ground cinnamon
⅔ cup (150 g) brown sugar
80 g butter, melted
½ cup (125 ml) milk
2 eggs, lightly beaten
1 cup (240 g) mashed banana (you will need
    2–3 overripe bananas)
vanilla ice cream, to serve
gold leaf, to decorate (optional)

Roasted skim milk powder crumbs

1 cup (125 g) skim milk powder
50 g butter, melted
1 tablespoon caster sugar

Butterscotch sauce

60 g butter
1 cup (220 g) brown sugar
½ cup (125 ml) thickened cream
¼ cup (60 ml) golden syrup

Bananas foster (aka flambé rum bananas)

80 g butter
3 firm bananas, peeled, cut in half crossways
    then lengthways
⅓ cup (75 g) brown sugar
¼ cup (60 ml) dark rum

Preheat the oven to 180°C (160°C fan-forced). Grease an 11 cm × 21 cm × 6 cm deep loaf pan with melted butter. Line the base and two long sides with baking paper, allowing it to overhang.

Sift the combined flour and cinnamon into a large bowl. Stir in the sugar and make a well in the centre. Add the butter, milk and eggs and stir until well combined. Add the banana and stir until just combined. Spoon the mixture into the prepared pan and smooth the surface.

Bake for 45–50 minutes or until a skewer inserted in the centre comes out clean. Remove from the oven and set aside in the pan for 5 minutes. Turn out onto a wire rack to cool completely.

While the banana bread cools, make the skim milk powder crumbs. Line a baking tray with baking paper. Combine the skim milk powder and butter in a bowl. Roughly spread the mixture in a thin layer on the prepared tray and sprinkle with the sugar. Bake, rotating the tray halfway through for even toasting, for 8 minutes or until lightly golden. Remove from the oven, toss, and set aside to let the crumbs cool in the pan. You could also add lots of edible gold powder to the crumbs before cooling if you like.

For the butterscotch sauce, place all the ingredients in a saucepan and stir over low heat until the sugar dissolves. Increase the heat to medium and bring to the boil. Remove from the heat and set aside.

To make the bananas foster, place the butter in a large frying pan over medium heat. Add the banana, cut side down, and cook for 2 minutes or until golden. Turn the banana over and cook for 1 minute. Carefully transfer to a plate. Add the sugar to the pan and cook, stirring, for 2–3 minutes or until the sugar starts to dissolve. Return the banana to the pan.

Remove from the heat and place the pan somewhere clear (i.e. with no curtains or nylon batwing sleeves flapping about) and add the rum. Being careful (and if you are game), ignite the rum using a long match or lighter. When the flames subside the bananas are ready to serve. Handle them carefully as they will be tender and can fall apart easily, depending on how ripe they were originally.

To serve, cut slices of banana bread and place on serving plates. Add the bananas foster. Top with the ice cream and drizzle with the butterscotch sauce. Sprinkle with the roasted skim milk powder crumbs and decorate with the gold leaf, if using.

Food nerd fact

Bananas have their own story here in Australia, where banana plants first arrived from Fiji in the 1850s. Originally they were seen as ornamental plants, with 'nanas for eating continuing to be imported from Fiji. This changed with the establishment of plantations later in the nineteenth century at places like Carnarvon in Western Australia and in Far North Queensland. Here, the arrival of sugarcane cutters from Fiji who were also skilled with banana farming helped the local industry, as did Chinese workers leaving the goldfields of Palmer River in the late 1870s, who helped establish plantations around Cooktown, Cairns and Tully. The plantations near Coffs Harbour in New South Wales were established in 1891 by Herman Reich. Issues of disease and monoculture farming saw other growing areas drop away in the twentieth century, leaving Queensland firmly as our largest banana producer.

Sponge cake

SERVES 6–10 **PREP** 20 minutes (plus cooling) **COOK** 25 minutes

Myth
Sponge cake is not a scintillating topic of conversation.

My Truth
'You know how interesting the purchase of a sponge-cake is to me,' wrote Jane Austen to her sister Cassandra in 1808. No one is quite sure if she was genuinely excited by the subject or passing sarcastic comment on the dreariness of discussing shopping for baked goods.

Now, I would hold that 'spunge-cake', as it was known for at least fifty years prior to Jane's letter, could not ever be called boring. After all, here is a cake that so fixated Donatien Alphonse François, better known as the Marquis de Sade, that in 1779 he wrote a long letter complaining not about conditions in his prison but about a chocolate sponge that his wife had sent to him.

The famous sexual adventurer who lent his name to 'sadism' was miffed because he wanted the cake iced on the top *and* the bottom, and it wasn't. Furthermore, he demanded a better chocolate filling so the cake smelled intensely of chocolate when he opened it.

He would have been more miffed if he'd been a Viking. Not only did they not have chocolate back then, but the first cakes – the word comes from the Old Norse word *kaka*, for 'cooked thing' – wouldn't have had the porous texture that comes from chemical leavening or from keeping bubbles suspended in an egg foam by heating until the bubbles expand and the egg's proteins set to capture the impression of the space created. In fact, the earliest cake recipes are really dumplings, puddings, custards, biscuits or breads. Or they were, until the creation of the first egg-foam sponges and the magical innovation of hand-beating. Whisking, it seems, was a Renaissance skill, with recipes from that time calling for between one and a half to three hours of beating!

Sponges are almost undoubtedly Spanish in origin, signalled by the fact that in Italy sponge cakes are called '*pan di Spagna*', such as the one that appears on the menu for a party at the Castel Sant'Angelo in Rome at the end of the 1500s.

Spanish Jews fleeing the Inquisition took the recipe for sponge with them, calling it *pan de España* (Spanish bread). The first credit of sponge to Spain comes from the 1554 wedding of Queen Mary I of England to Spain's Prince Philip. Philip brought Spanish cooks to England for the event and one of the dishes served was *bizcocho borracho*, sponge soaked in fortified wine. Besides being the foundational idea behind English trifles (p. 275) and tiramisu (p. 305), here is proof that sponge cake started as an Iberian thing.

---

melted butter, for greasing
1¼ cups (185 g) plain flour, plus extra for dusting
6 eggs, at room temperature
¾ cup (165 g) caster sugar
1 teaspoon vanilla extract
¾ cup (185 ml) thickened cream
200 g crème fraîche
1 cup (320 g) raspberry jam
1 teaspoon finely grated lemon zest
icing sugar, to dust

TIP

Using an electric hand beater rather than a fancy stand mixer allows for more air incorporation. Beating at medium speed also helps.

Preheat the oven to 170°C (150°C fan-forced). Grease two 20 cm (base measurement) round cake pans with melted butter. Dust the pans with the extra flour and shake off any excess.

Fill a large bowl with warm water. Set aside for 5 minutes to warm the bowl, which makes for a fluffier and more stable foam. Discard the water and wipe the bowl dry.

Use a fork to whisk the eggs in a jug. Add the eggs and sugar to the warmed bowl. Use electric beaters to whisk on low speed until well combined. Increase the speed to medium. Beat for 7 minutes or until the mixture is thick and glossy, and slow ribbons fall when the beaters are lifted. Beat the vanilla into the egg mixture.

While the eggs are beating away, sift the flour onto a large sheet of baking paper.

Fold half the flour into the egg mixture until just combined. Do this sparsely and quietly, as if you were tucking in a recalcitrant toddler who has only just nodded off to sleep. Repeat with the remaining flour just as calmly.

Divide the mixture evenly between the prepared pans. Bake for 20–25 minutes or until the cakes are golden and spring back when lightly touched. Set aside in the pan for 10 minutes to cool slightly before transferring to a wire rack to cool completely.

Use electric beaters to whisk the cream and crème fraîche in a bowl until firm peaks form. This mixture needs to be firm as it will be supporting the weight of the top sponge and will need to do so without it all squidging out the sides.

Once cool, spread one sponge with jam and scatter with lemon zest. Dollop with the whipped cream and top with the remaining sponge. Dust with icing sugar to serve.

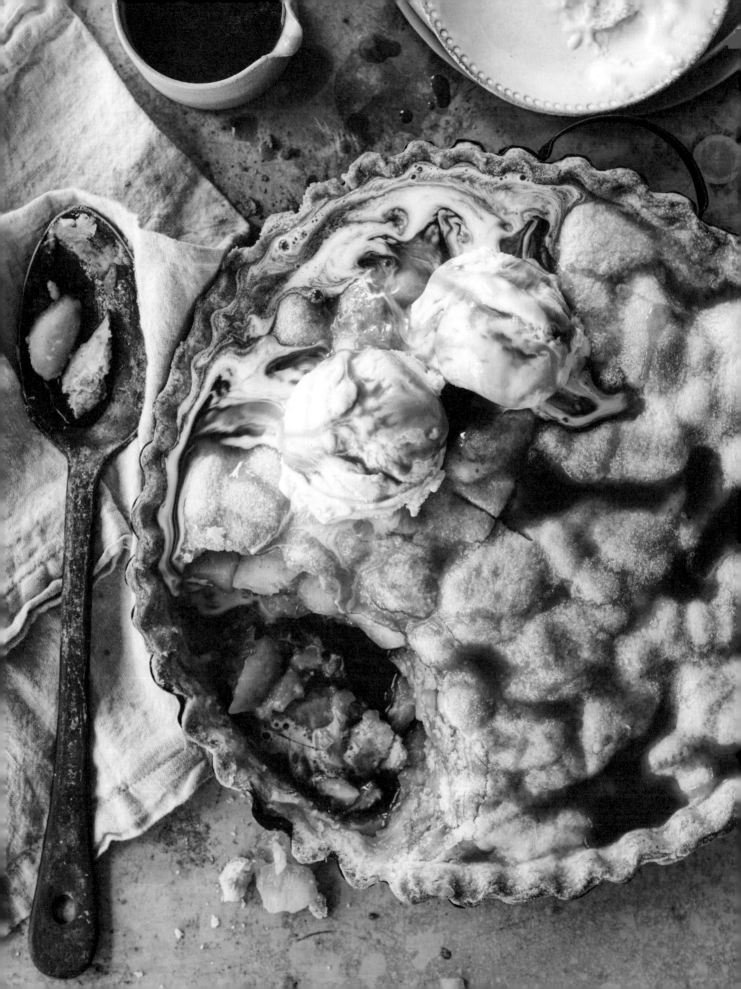

Apple pie served à la mode
(WITH ICE CREAM)

SERVES 8 **PREP** 30 minutes (plus resting and cooling) **COOK** Cooking time 1 hour 15 minutes

Myth
Apple pie is American.

My Truth
Well, obviously apple pie is American. 'As American as apple pie' is literally the benchmark for Americanness!

John Chapman is credited with clearing land and planting apple orchards across the American Midwest in the late eighteenth century, thereby earning himself the nickname 'Johnny Appleseed', filling the pie dishes of the emerging nation and ensuring the country's rich trove of apple-centric sayings, such as 'upset the applecart'.

However, the first recorded apple pie can be traced back far, far further. The Dutch cookbook *Een notabel boecxken van cokeryen* ('A Notable Book of Cooking', c. 1514) included a recipe for a lattice-topped apple pie. There's even a recipe for one in the first English-language cookbook, *The Forme of Cury* ('The Method of Cooking', c. 1390), although the filling contains pears and figs as well as 'applys', and it was cooked in a 'coffyn' of inedible pastry. Early medieval pastry was made with flour and water, and wasn't meant to be eaten – it was just there to contain the contents of the pie and protect them from the flames. So, apple pie is also Dutch and English.

Wherever the Dutch and the British colonised, apple pie followed. It became commonplace in the United States, but only after the introduction of European bees in 1622, because without them, the trees planted by Johnny Appleseed would have struggled to pollinate.

While the history of the apple pie is longer than that of the US, it was here that a freshly baked apple pie cooling on the windowsill became the symbol of a perfect home life. So much so that during World War II, when journalists asked American GIs what they were fighting for, the soldiers would reply, 'For Mom and apple pie'.

The term à la mode, which in France refers to something being fashionable (or, alternatively, to beef braised with red wine), has a very different meaning in the US when attached to pie. While a hotel in Duluth, Minnesota called La Perl, which was helmed by a Swiss-born former personal chef to Presidents Pierce and Buchanan, is said to have served blueberry pie and vanilla ice cream and called it 'pie à la mode' back in 1885 on its launch menu this was not how the name became popular. Perhaps in part because some Duluthians knew it as 'pylie mode'.

The fame of the phrase comes down to a concert pianist named Professor Charles Watson Townsend dining at New York's premier restaurant, the extremely swank and fashionable Delmonico's, in 1896. Townsend had ordered apple pie à la mode, but the waiter had never heard of it. Townsend feigned astonishment that the famous Delmonico's, which had a hand in inventing everything from the wedge salad and eggs benedict to baked alaska and lobster newberg, was so out of the loop.

He asked for the maître d' and pointed out that even a small restaurant upstate was serving the dish, so Delmonico's must be slipping behind the trends. He demanded the maître d' ring that small restaurant to corroborate his story. The maître d' was astonished to discover that apple pie à la mode was on the menu up in unfashionable Cambridge, and in his shock he promised that the dish would from then on always be available at Delmonico's.

Needless to say, Townsend had invented the name for this combination at the Cambridge Tavern the previous week, ordering his apple pie 'à la mode' every night, and the name had stuck there.

The conversation was overheard by a journalist from New York's *The Sun* newspaper, and the story that appeared in the paper the next day spread across the nation, ensuring that apple pie à la mode was suddenly on many more menus than just those at Delmonico's and the Cambridge Tavern.

Apple pie served à la mode *(CONTINUED)*

20 g butter, plus extra melted butter for greasing
2 kg pink lady apples, peeled, cored, quartered, cut into 2 cm thick slices
2 strips lemon zest (about 2 cm wide and 6 cm long)
¼ cup (60 ml) lemon juice
½ cup (110 g) caster sugar, plus extra 2 tablespoons
½ teaspoon ground cinnamon
1 egg, lightly whisked
vanilla ice cream, to serve

Sweet shortcrust pastry

3 cups (450 g) plain flour
200 g butter, chopped and chilled
2 tablespoons icing sugar mixture
2 egg yolks
⅓ cup (80 ml) chilled milk

Salted apple caramel sauce

1 cup (220 g) caster sugar
40 g butter
½ cup (125 ml) pouring cream
1 teaspoon sea salt
100 ml apple cooking juices (see Tip)

TIP

You'll need 100 ml of juices from draining the cooked apples. If you don't have enough, make up the difference with apple juice or water.

Start by cooking the apples. Melt the butter in a large, deep frying pan over medium heat. Add the apple, lemon zest and juice, and ¼ cup (55 g) of the sugar. Cover and cook, stirring occasionally, for 10–15 minutes or until the apple slices are tender but still hold their shape. Uncover and cook, stirring often, for a further 5 minutes or until the liquid from the apples has evaporated. Transfer to a large colander set over a large bowl to catch the juice (you will need this to make the caramel). Set aside for 1 hour to allow the liquid to drain off and the apples to cool completely. Remove the lemon zest.

Grease a 5 cm deep, 24 cm (inside lip top measurement) round pie dish with butter.

While the apples cool, get the pastry ready. Process the flour and butter in a food processor until the mixture resembles fine breadcrumbs. Add the icing sugar and process until just combined. Add the egg yolks and milk. Process until the dough just comes together. Turn out onto the benchtop and bring the dough together to form a smooth ball.

Roll two-thirds of the pastry out on a sheet of baking paper to about 4 mm thick and large enough to fit the pie dish. Line the dish with the pastry. Press the remaining pastry into a disc about 2 cm thick and wrap in plastic wrap. Place both the pie dish and the wrapped pastry in the fridge for 30 minutes to rest.

Preheat the oven to 200°C (180°C fan-forced). Place a baking tray in the oven to heat.

Transfer the cooled and drained apples to a bowl. Add the cinnamon and the remaining sugar and toss until well combined.

Brush the pastry case with some whisked egg, and spoon in the apple mixture. Roll out the remaining pastry on a sheet of baking paper until large enough to fit the top of the pie. Place over the apple mixture. Press the edges to seal, then trim the excess. Brush the top with the whisked egg and sprinkle with the extra sugar. Cut a small cross in the top to allow steam to escape. Place the pie on the hot tray and bake for 20 minutes.

Reduce the oven to 180°C (160°C fan-forced) and bake for 30 minutes or until the pastry is crispy and golden.

While the pie bakes, make the caramel sauce. Place the sugar in a saucepan over low heat. Stir until the sugar starts to dissolve and turns a rich golden colour (if you have a few lumps of sugar, don't worry, they will dissolve). Remove from the heat and allow the bubbles to subside. Carefully add the butter, cream, salt and reserved apple cooking juices. Stir to combine. Return to medium heat and cook, stirring, for 2 minutes or until the mixture is smooth and thickens slightly.

Set aside the pie for 10 minutes before serving with the ice cream and apple caramel sauce.

Food nerd fact

As well as blueberry pie and apple pie 'à la mode', newspapers from the end of the eighteenth and the start of the nineteenth century praise peach pie à la mode and pumpkin pie à la mode. Take this as inspiration!

Milk choc chunk brownies with roasted apricots

MAKES 8 **PREP** 15 minutes (plus cooling) **COOK** 1 hour 25 minutes

Myth

Brownies have always been chocolate flavoured.

My Truth

If you've ever heard the phrase 'chocolate brownie', that should rather give this myth away. The presence of the prefix implies that there were previous brownies that weren't chocolate.

In the 1896 edition of the influential *Boston Cooking-School Cook Book*, there is a recipe for brownies made with molasses. Ten years later, in the 1906 edition, that recipe is gone, replaced by a brownie that uses chocolate and no molasses. Interestingly, it is remarkably similar to a recipe for chocolate cookies from the 1896 edition, just with less flour.

While molasses and chocolate have their colour in common, the sale of 'brownies' in the 1897 Sears Roebuck mail order catalogue may give clues that the name does not come from the colour. The Sears catalogue supplied isolated farming families across the US with everything from sacks of flour, tinned caviar and children's sailor suits to ploughs and even laudanum. In that 1897 catalogue there are also a number of 'brownie' products seeking to cash in on the massive success of Palmer Cox's magazine cartoon strip *The Brownies*.

These mischievous sprites were a sensation among children of the day, and their name and image were merchandised on all manner of products. There were Brownie dolls, Brownie songs, Brownie card games and Brownie sodas. Even the famous Box Brownie camera took its name from Cox's characters. It seems that Brownies you can eat were just another merchandising stream.

There is much conjecture and even some outright lies told about that Sears catalogue, such as that it featured a recipe for chocolate brownies, or that the brownies were actually made with molasses. The truth is that there is nothing in the original to support either claim; just the words 'Brownies, in 1-lb papers [wrapping]', priced at $1.50 for a dozen or 14 cents each.

It seems likely that Sears wasn't alone in naming a sweet snack after the fairy sprites. While no one is credited with being the sole creator of the brownie, one well-documented origin story comes from Chicago's lavish Palmer House Hotel. The hotel's chef made a chocolate 'bar cookie' – which is American baking speak for our 'slice' – glazed with apricot jam to place in the lunch boxes of the wealthy guests who descended on the city for the massive 1893 Chicago World's Fair.

The World's Columbian Exposition, as the fair was formally known, was a smash hit, attracting more than 27 million visitors during the six months it was open. This is even more impressive when you consider that the total population of the US at the time was only just over 66 million.

The idea for the brownie came from Bertha Palmer, Chicago's most prominent socialite, whose husband happened to own the Palmer House Hotel. The brownie she envisioned had to be quite something – a light dessert that was still decadent, could be eaten with the fingers and would reflect well on the hotel's reputation as one of America's finest dining rooms. And judging by her forceful character, no doubt Bertha, in her role as one of the organisers of the Expo, would have championed the brownie at every turn. After all, this was a woman who, as well as being a famous beauty, was a noted philanthropist who set up a free network of kindergartens in Chicago, and even secured the largest bank loan ever (at the time) to rebuild the Palmer House Hotel on an even grander scale after the first building burnt down in the Great Chicago Fire of 1871. What Bertha wanted, Bertha got done!

The recipe for the Palmer House brownies wasn't published at the time, but later the hotel revealed it was built around 1 lb of butter and 1 lb of chocolate with only 8 oz of flour and 12 oz of sugar, and walnuts were included in the batter.

Given the massive success of the Expo and the status of Palmer House, it seems possible that Sears, also based in Chicago, might have found a supplier to bake similar chocolate brownies for their catalogue published four years later. It's also possible that the Sears brownies were the molasses variety, and that as they grew in popularity, the Palmer House brownies were called 'chocolate brownies' to differentiate them. Whatever the case, the chocolate brownie obviously pervaded the United States' culinary popular culture, as the next chocolate brownie recipes appeared in 1904 in two cheaply produced community cookbooks. Eleanor Quimby's brownies in the New Hampshire Congregational Church of Laconia's cookbook had vanilla and salt in them. The Service Club of Chicago's cookbook had a recipe for a 'Bangor Brownie' – seemingly named after Bangor, Maine – which, like the Palmer House brownies, used walnuts.

I can tell you that by 1912, the image of the brownie as a sort of chocolate cake made with a lot less flour and much more butter was set in stone, but the history remains whenever the qualifier 'chocolate brownie' is used today. The brownies in this recipe are decadent, to match Bertha Palmer's vision for the dish, and we have paired them with roasted apricots as a nod to apricot jam that glazed the Palmer House original.

Milk choc chunk brownies *(CONTINUED)*

200 g dark chocolate (70% cocoa), coarsely
    chopped
185 g butter, chopped
1 cup (210 g) brown sugar
3 eggs
1 egg yolk
¾ cup (110 g) plain flour
⅓ cup (35 g) cocoa powder
350 g Cadbury milk chocolate, broken into
    squares
double cream, to serve

Vanilla roasted apricots

12 apricots, halved, stones removed
1½ tablespoons caster sugar
1 vanilla bean, split lengthways, seeds
    scraped (bean reserved)
¼ teaspoon ground cardamom

Preheat the oven to 160°C (140°C fan-forced). Line a 16 cm × 26 cm slice pan with baking paper, allowing the two long sides to overhang.

Place the dark chocolate and butter in a large microwave-safe bowl. Microwave on high, stirring every minute, for 2–3 minutes or until melted and smooth. Set aside for 5 minutes to cool slightly.

Use a balloon whisk to whisk in the sugar, eggs and egg yolk until well combined. Add the flour and cocoa powder and whisk until well combined. Stir in the milk chocolate squares. Spoon into the prepared pan and bake for 45 minutes or until just set in the centre. Set aside in the pan to cool.

Increase the oven temperature to 180°C (160°C fan-forced). Line a baking tray with baking paper. Place the apricots cut-side up on the prepared tray. Use your fingertips to rub the sugar, vanilla seeds and cardamom together in a small bowl. Sprinkle over the apricots. Add the split vanilla bean to the apricots. Roast for 30–35 minutes or until tender and lightly caramelised.

Cut the brownie into squares and serve with the double cream and roasted apricots.

VARIATIONS

Adding a spice like cardamom, nutmeg, allspice or cinnamon would work well in these brownies. You could put a spin on the milk chocolate chunks and replace them with 350 g white chocolate or macadamia nuts. Or, take a tip from Nigella: dump the chocolate chunks, and pour half of the brownie mix into your lined tin. Layer with thin slices of chilled cream cheese (about 200 g will do it). Top with the rest of the brownie mix and bake at 180°C for about 30 minutes, until the brownie layers are cooked but the cheese is still soft.

Instead of the roasted apricots, you could try grilled figs, strawberries roasted with vanilla syrup or black pepper, or caramelised bananas with a sour cream butterscotch.

Food nerd fact

The inimitable Bertha Palmer even persuaded Auguste Rodin to lend his sculpture *The Kiss* to the Chicago World's Fair, despite opposition from puritanical members of the organising committee, who insisted the sculpture could only be displayed behind a velvet curtain, lest the nudity and sensual subject matter shock unsuspecting patrons!

The world's best biscuit

Myth

This is the world's best biscuit.

My Truth

It is!!!

Now, as a founding secretary of ABAS – the Australian Biscuit Appreciation Society – and a former Bangladeshi Biscuit Baron – yes, I had my own range of biscuits in that country! – I know a bit about biscuits. And while Sweden's *dinkel-cookies*, Chinese almond cookies, Tim Tams, Romany Creams (the more PC name for what were once known as Gypsy Creams, but with a chocolate cream filling), handmade Monte Carlos, caramel-filled Argentine *alfajores*, crisp Dutch *speculaas*, German cinnamon *zimtsterne*, Greek *kourabiethes* and *melomakarona*, Scottish shortbread, Mexican ginger pig-shaped *marranitos* and Britain's Chocolate Hobnob all hold important positions in the Biscuit Hall of Fame, it was a biscuit developed at the end of 2019 that has taken my crown for the best biscuit in the world.

It is based on a chocolate chip cookie, so this obviously gives it a head start, but by upping the ratio of chocolate and adding nuts and fruit we take the CCC to another level.

Here, it's less about the cookie dough and all about the chewy dried cranberries and golden toasted macadamias, but it still has just enough biscuit crumbs to make it a pleasure to hoover them up after. And the only way you can disprove this claim to the best biscuit crown is to bake it and find out for yourself. If you don't agree, please send me the recipe for your contender for the crown!

4 × 180 g packets white chocolate (I use Cadbury Dream because the chunks keep their shape best)

2 cups (300 g) plain flour, sifted

1 teaspoon sea salt

1 teaspoon baking powder

250 g butter, chopped, at room temperature

⅔ cup (150 g) light brown sugar

¼ cup (55 g) dark brown sugar

½ cup (110 g) caster sugar

2 tablespoons water

1 teaspoon vanilla extract

1 egg, lightly whisked

500 g macadamias, coarsely chopped, leaving them as chunky as you can

500 g dried cranberries

Preheat the oven to 180°C (160°C fan-forced). Line two large baking trays with baking paper. Break the white chocolate into squares.

Sift the flour, salt and baking powder into a bowl. Use electric beaters to beat the butter, brown sugars and caster sugar in a bowl until pale and creamy. Add the water, vanilla and egg and beat until well combined. Beat in the flour mixture until just combined. Transfer to a very large bowl.

Stir in the chocolate squares, macadamia chunks and dried cranberries until well combined. With this amount of chunks it will be very thick and heavy – think of the dough merely as mortar to bind them. The mixture should come away from the sides of the bowl and form a ball. If the mixture is sticky, add a little more flour.

Drop heaped dessertspoonful-sized balls of the mixture, well spaced, onto the lined trays until you have enough balls for the number of biscuits you want (see Tip). Bake for 10–12 minutes or until just golden. Set aside on the tray to cool slightly before transferring to a wire rack to cool completely. Reserve some and enjoy the rest right now!

I like to split this batch of dough into a couple of bakes. Scrape any excess dough together and form into a thick (5 cm or so) sausage. Wrap in baking paper, twist the ends and pop into a labelled freezer bag. Store in the freezer until needed. When you want to cook them, slice the dough sausage into 1–2 cm thick slices using a serrated or bread knife and place on a lined baking tray, well spaced. Bake for 10–15 minutes or until golden. Rest on a wire rack to cool before serving. It's best to only bake as many biscuits as you need at once – these CCC will siren-call to you from the biscuit tin in the middle of the night if you bake extra!

THE AUSTRALIAN BISCUIT APPRECIATION SOCIETY WORLD BISCUIT TOP 30

1. Chocolate chip cookies

2. Sweden's *dinkel-cookies* – you can see through these spelt and sunflower-seed cookies, so you expect the crunch but not the chew

3. The Tim Tam – Original or Double Coat only; sublime when used in the Tim Tam suck

4. Crisp Dutch *speculaas* – it's the bite of ginger and crisp thinness of the biscuit that make these stand out. For many, the ginger snap or ginger nut might sit here – but this is not their list

5. Fig Newtons or fig rolls – it's the chew from the wodge of fig-jam filling for me, but the slightly cakey exterior is another surprise

6. Britain's Chocolate Hobnob – oaty, crisp and chocolatey. A logical improvement on the chocolate digestive, like moving from Arnie to the T-1000

7. Kingstons or Romany Creams – these are superior versions of more prosaic cream-filled biscuits like the bourbon cream or custard cream

8. Mint Slice – as much a dessert as a biscuit

9. Chinese almond cookies – so crumbly

10. Senegalese *cinq centimes* – peanut butter biscuits plus

11. Danish *vaniljekranse* – so crispy, buttery and sweet with vanilla

12. Anzacs – the perfect dunker

13. Oreos – I'm a twister

14. Homemade monte carlos – worth the effort

15. Filipino *silvanas* – this cream-filled sandwich of cashew biscuits is seldom seen but never forgotten

16. Greek *melomakarona* – what's not to love about honey and walnuts in a biscuit?

17. Scottish shortbread – cold fingers and a warm heart are the secrets to crisp but buttery shortbread. The best I've eaten are made by my mother-in-law – or by one of her friends, but I'd never admit that in print!

18. Argentine *alfajores* filled with caramelly dulce de leche – the perfect gift from Buenos Aires

19. Iranian *nan-e berenji*, which are an essential part of any New Year (*Nowruz*) in that part of the world. Flavoured with cardamom, rosewater and poppy seeds, think of them as a rice-flour, butter-free shortbread

20. Greek *kourabiethes* – impossibly light and tender crescents with much problematic icing sugar

21. Mexican ginger *marranitos* shaped like little piggies

22. Ginger nuts – tooth-crackingly crunchy, making them great for dunking and for stacking in a sandwich filled with whipped cream

23. German cinnamon *zimtsterne* – the reason Germany invented Christmas

24. India's Parle-G – the bestselling biscuit in the world is a taste everyone should try at least once. They are wonderful with a cup of tea

25. Norwegian *sirupsnipper* – all buttery and loaded with white pepper, cinnamon and aniseed

26. The Afghan – cornflakes make these chocolate cream-sandwich biscuits extra crispy and crunchy

27. Oatmeal creme pies – whether soft and chewy oatmeal cookies filled with a thick seam of vanilla buttercream or something else familiarly creamy

28. The Yo-Yo – these often have too much custard powder, but at their best, a formidably friable biscuit

29. Jaffa Cakes – a little too spongy for me, but I don't mind peeling off the orange gel and dark chocolate topping and throwing away the sponge base

30. Ginger and turmeric sourdough biscuits – you're having a laugh, aren't you? Swedish *hallongrotta* are a far better inclusion in the ABAS Top 30.

This book is dedicated to my mother, Jennifer. Thank you for everything you've given me, given up for me and taught me. Love you, Ma!

The origins of this book began almost a decade ago when I was asked to write a monthly column uncovering the unlikely heritage of the world's greatest dishes. For all that time tilting at windmills, formidable food guru Michelle Southan was my Sancho Panza. She's a woman who, like Sancho, is obsessed with reality, not fantasy – in this case, the reality of making sure that any dish you cook will be the best it can be; the recipe as guaranteed to be failsafe as it can be.

I am so delighted that Michelle is a part of this book as my partner in crime. She helped me to develop and test the recipes, based on the historical detail I uncovered, her encyclopaedic recipe knowledge and our shared obsession with flavour. Whether taking a recipe back to its roots or off in a completely new direction, she's one of the best in the world. Expect a few reactionary squeals of pain and howls of rage – as some of the stuff in this book doesn't make for easy reading – however, when you try a massaman curry with the original ingredients of orange juice and sultanas (p. 190) reinstated, you will wonder why we ever let those ingredients go.

Our editor, Kathryn Knight, has done a sterling job pulling me back from the precipice of obsessive, 3000-word intros and pushed me to justify my claims with facts. In the process she has sculpted this book into one of which I'm very proud, and one that's far, far more readable! Tracy Rutherford took a similar approach as recipe editor. Thank you both.

When it came to actually making this book happen, I am hugely indebted to my publisher, Izzy Yates, for her calm vision and steely belief in this project that has seen me commit to Penguin Random House as the new home for my books. It was wonderful to have her so present during all stages of this book, including the shoot. PRH publishing director Justin Ractliffe has also provided wise counsel along the way. Huge thanks to them both.

Of course, the third reason for my excitement at joining Penguin Random House is to reunite with the ridiculously talented publisher Alison Urquhart on my next project – more news on that to come! I am sure gun publicist Laura Nimmo will let you know about it via the media when the time comes, or you will find out from Rebekah Chereshsky, who looks after the marketing, or the fantastic team behind their social media channels. I'm grateful for all they've also contributed to this book.

I am doubly #blessed to be supported in this book by rock solid foundations in Warren Mendes and Emma Warren, who are both incredibly knowledgeable and as potty about flavour as me. These two highly valued long-term collaborators have generously allowed their experience to amplify mine. They helped with the recipes, ramping up the flavour and also cooking everything you see photographed in the book. It was an epic task driven by Mr Mendes' prodigious organisational skills.

After being a long-term admirer of their beautiful work, this was my first time working with stylist Hannah Meppem and photographer William Meppem. The photographs here speak to their combined talent and also to their commitment to this project. I'm a little in awe, and extremely grateful. They've both brought a realness to the food that I hope you'll appreciate, and that I love. This is food for eating.

Designer Kirby Armstrong put up with my endless tinkering and developed a fantastic design that has given this book both structure and some welcome breeziness. My thanks to her, and to Mei Yen Chua, who complied the index (which is a job that frazzles my nerve endings just thinking about it).

So much of what I say and write is informed by working with the team at *delicious.*magazine, taste.com.au and *delicious. on Sunday* in *Stellar. delicious.* is a family I've been part of for two decades, and the team, led by the inspirational Kerrie McCallum, Samantha Jones, Phoebe Rose Wood and Fiona Nilsson, brings so much joy and pleasure into my life at work or play! I could never thank any of them enough for anything and everything.

Likewise, my thanks to Brodee Myers-Cooke and her team at taste.com.au, where that original column ran all those years ago and for whom I still have the honour and pleasure of writing each month.

Big thanks to Sarrah Le Marquand, Bree Player, Nadine Tuback and Katie Hendry at *Stellar* – writing my *delicious. on Sunday* column there for the Sunday newspapers has been as fun as it is rewarding.

Thanks also to my manager and good friend Henrie Stride, who has steered my career for the past twelve years and who made this book happen; lawyers David Vodicka and Yasmin Naghavi, who have handled the legals with equal aplomb; and Aaron Hurle, who has been keeping me solvent and honest for many years now. Charlotte James has looked after my socials for as long, and taught me so much in that time. It is still a delight to work with all these people after so many years.

Thank you also to my amazing sisters, Eleanor and Katie, for all they have done for me, and for my mum, while we've been separated by the pandemic. Above and beyond . . .

And finally to Emma, Jonathan, Will and Sadie. You are the reason for all of this. Sorry for all of the trial recipes you had to taste, and thanks for the honest feedback you gave! Take comfort that this book is all the better for it.

I also am indebted to all the amateur and professional food historians whose obsession has been a bounty to harvest. I've tried to credit them throughout the book, but special props to the wonderful Food Timeline website, founded in the United States by Lynne Oliver and run by Virginia Tech University, the Australian Food Timeline, created by Jan O'Connell, Patricia Bixler Reber's 'Researching Food History' blog, and all who contribute to the slightly obsessive academic papers and journals out there, such as the *Journal of Ethnic Foods*, who have tried to unpick each tapestry of lies to find the one shimmering silver thread of truth running through it. I am in awe of so much of this proper academic research, and I acknowledge that I stand cool in the shadow of their wings.

Massive props are also due to libraries and those educational institutions that have digitised so many folios and ancient recipe books so we can see for ourselves whether a much talked about Indian dish was actually mentioned among the sixteenth-century court papers of Akbar the Great, or not. Many commenters online say it is, but too often when you actually look in the book, it isn't. That was so much harder to do ten years ago than it is today. The National Library of Australia, the Library of Congress in the US and the British Library have also done some sterling work in digitising hundreds of years' worth of newspapers and magazines, which were invaluable in rewriting so much food history to more closely approximate the truth.

Finally, thank you for buying this book. Do keep in touch with me on Facebook, Twitter and Instagram at @mattscravat, or on TikTok at @mattpreston. And please send me pics of the dishes you cook from this book. I'd love that!

INDEX A–Z

Note: Page numbers in italics denote Tips and Food nerd facts

MORE VALUABLE INDEX BY THEMES

Leftovers: dishes that will keep on giving the next day

Authentic puttanesca 32
Sweet potato and ancient grain salad 71
Pumpkin soup 73
Potato salad 78
Caramelised onion, Gruyere and feta quiche 96
Sri Lankan cashew curry 103
Roast chicken with chicken-fat rice 113
Teriyaki chicken 125
Kung pao chicken 136
Working-class chicken korma 145
Quicker butter chicken 150
Old-school chilli con carne 158
Beef goulash 179
Beef rendang 180
Beef lasagne 183
Massaman curry 190
Spaghetti bolognese 195
Sweet and sour pork and prawn meatballs 201
Potjie with damper 213
Lamb tagine 230
Lamb rogan josh 232
A truly Scottish shepherd's pie 240
Slow-roasted pomegranate lamb shoulder 243

Left-afters: desserts that will keep on giving the next day

Roasted white chocolate tart 250
Chocolate torte with smoked butterscotch 254
Antep pistachio and white chocolate baklava 258
Lamingtons 263
Flourless chocolate cake 269
A trifle peach Melba 275
Baked cheesecake 278
Rhubarb crumble 293
Lemongrass and lime leaf meringue pie 295
Tiramisu 305
Pastéis de nata 315
Carrot cake 319
Banana bread with bananas foster 321
Apple pie 327
Milk choc chunk brownies 329

Feed a crowd

Easy paella 16
Poke buffet 25
Aussie prawn and fish pie 43
Gravlax 57
Bogan nachos 68
Sweet potato and ancient grain salad 71
Potato salad 78
Caramelised onion, Gruyere and feta quiche 96

Spinach and ricotta filo toasties 107
Working-class chicken korma 145
Old-school chilli con carne 158
Beef lasagne 183
Massaman curry 190
Spaghetti bolognese 195
Potjie with damper 213
Customisable carbonara 219
Lamb tagine 230
Middle Eastern sausage rolls 234
Not a souvlaki 237
Slow-roasted pomegranate lamb shoulder 243

Desserts to feed a crowd, or bring-a-plate winners

Roasted white chocolate tart 250
Chocolate torte with smoked butterscotch 254
Antep pistachio and white chocolate baklava 258
Lamingtons 263
Flourless chocolate cake 269
A trifle peach Melba 275
Baked cheesecake 278
Pineapple tarte tatin 280
Knickerbocker glory 283
Hotteok pancakes 287
Rhubarb crumble 293
Lemongrass and lime leaf meringue pie 295
Pavlova 299
Tiramisu 305
Pastéis de nata 315
Carrot cake 319
Banana bread with bananas foster 321
Sponge cake 324
Apple pie 327
Milk choc chunk brownies 329
The world's best biscuit 333

Minimal washing up

Easy paella 16
California rolls 23
Oysters with finger lime 30
Authentic puttanesca 32
Moulesabaise 51
Ceviche/Sebiche/Kokoda 52
Pumpkin soup 73
Risotto 108
Sri Lankan cashew curry 103
Six-minute chicken satay 128
Jerked chicken 133
Working-class chicken korma 145
Apricot chicken tray bake 148
Old-school chilli con carne 158
Massaman curry 190
Potjie with damper 213
Red braise pork belly 217

Lamb rogan josh 232
Pineapple tarte tatin 280
Milk choc chunk brownies 329

Fire me up: cook on the barbecue

Poke buffet 25
Six-minute chicken satay 128
Jerked chicken 133
Quicker butter chicken 150
Barbecue ribs, kalbi style 161
The ultimate burger 163
Beef fajitas 169
Tacos al pastor 223

Super savers! Dishes that won't break the budget

Authentic puttanesca 32
Tuna mornay bake 38
Arroz de camarão 47
Falafel plate 63
Pumpkin soup 73
Potato salad 78
Creamy spinach and ricotta gnocchi 81
Almost Neapolitan-style pizza 84
Zucca zucchini frittata 91
Vegan coleslaw 93
Chicken kiev 122
Six-minute chicken satay 128
Jerked chicken 133
Working-class chicken korma 145
Old-school chilli con carne 158
Barbecue ribs, kalbi style 161
Beef fajitas 169
Beef stroganoff 176
Cheat's ramen 199
Pork potstickers 207
Customisable carbonara 219
A truly Scottish shepherd's pie 240
The ultimate honey joy 256
Crepes suzette 289
Pavlova 299
Pouding chômeur 308
Sponge cake 324

Make ahead and freeze for ease

Prep and put your feet up: dishes that require minimal attention

Prep ahead/start the day before

Sidekicks: versatile side dishes

Sauces, dressings and more: multipurpose condiments

Lantern

UK | USA | Canada | Ireland | Australia
India | New Zealand | South Africa | China

Lantern is part of the Penguin Random House group of companies whose
addresses can be found at global.penguinrandomhouse.com

First published by Lantern in 2021

Cover design, internal design and typesetting by Kirby Armstrong
Cover and internal photography by William Meppem
Prop and food styling by Hannah Meppem and Emmaly Stewart
Food preparation by Warren Mendes, Emma Warren and Jaimee Foley
Hair and makeup by Terri Farmer
Recipe editing by Tracy Rutherford
Recipe development by Michelle Southan
Index A–Z by Mei Yen Chua, Swallow Books

Printed and bound in China by 1010 Printing International Limited

 A catalogue record for this
book is available from the
National Library of Australia

ISBN 978 1 76104 444 1

penguin.com.au